Ancient Greece

Using Evidence

Ancient Greece

Using Evidence

Pamela Bradley

Edited by David Patterson

Edward Arnold
A division of Hodder & Stoughton
MELBOURNE LONDON NEW YORK AUCKLAND

Edward Arnold (Australia) Pty Ltd
A division of Hodder & Stoughton
80 Waverley Road
Caulfield East Victoria 3145

First published by
Edward Arnold (Australia) Pty Ltd in 1988
Reprinted 1989, 1990, 1991, 1992

Copyright © Pamela Bradley 1988

National Library of Australia
Cataloguing-in-publication data

Bradley, Pamela.
    Ancient Greece: using evidence.

    Bibliography.
    Includes index.
    ISBN 0 7131 8327 6.

    1. History, Ancient — Methodology, 2. Greece —
    History — To 146 B.C. I. Title.
938

Text design by R. T. J. Klinkhamer
Cover design by R. T. J. Klinkhamer
Illustrations by Alan Smith
Typeset in Goudy Old Style by SRM Production
Printed by Macarthur Press Pty Ltd

Front cover: A Hellenistic Greek onyx cameo of the third century BC, thought
to represent Alexander and Olympias. (Kunsthistorisches Museum, Vienna.)

Contents

CONTENTS

List of maps

List of illustrations

Prologue

EVERYTHING WE KNOW ABOUT ancient civilisation depends on evidence of various kinds. Such evidence will of course vary in nature, quality and extent, and it is the task of the historian of ancient times to weigh up all the available evidence on a particular issue so that reasonable conclusions may be drawn from it. Sometimes there is very little evidence at all, so that statements based on it must be cautious and tentative. In other cases there is a vast array of evidence which will enable historians to make confident judgments and draw firm conclusions.

Our evidence for ancient history can be summarised in four categories: archaeology, literature, numismatics and epigraphy.

Archaeological evidence

This type of evidence is especially fascinating because it consists of the material remains of the past; that is, it includes the buildings, monuments, temples, artefacts and so on that have survived. For example, the excavations at Knossos in Crete and at Mycenae on the mainland of Greece provide evidence about life and society of early Greek times. Similarly, the ruins at Olympia, the remains of the Athenian agora and the buildings on the Acropolis at Athens help us to build a more complete picture of life in ancient Greece at later periods in its development.

The remains of the Temple of Athena, called the Parthenon

A perfectly preserved fourth-century lamp scratched with the names of six men, all of whom had something to do with the navy and the dockyards. Why they scratched their names on the lamp is unknown

Fragment of a saucer on which is scratched an inventory of household objects — casserole, pitcher, oil vase and drinking cup

Pottery, both broken and unbroken, provides historians with one of the most valuable forms of archaeological evidence. Pottery had an infinite range of uses, such as for transporting oil, grain and wine, and as household utensils, roofing tiles, water pipes, lamps, and standards of weights and measures.

Scenes painted on pottery illustrate aspects of mythology and show ordinary people at work and at play.

In archaeological excavations, pottery can be used to date the site and to indicate trading activities there.

Waste pipe from a fountain in the Athenian agora — made of terra cotta and carefully jointed

Literary evidence

Only a fraction of the writings of ancient peoples has survived into modern times; nevertheless, we possess a great deal of literary material that tells us about the personalities, society and events of the ancient world. For example, we can marvel at the epic poems, *The Iliad* and *The Odyssey*, the work of the great Greek poet, Homer; we can read the dramas of Greek playwrights like Sophocles; we can enjoy the comedies of the Athenian writer Aristophanes; we have many of the speeches of the

A painted amphora showing Dionysus, god of fertility and wine, being presented with a fawn by two of his maenads (priestesses of Dionysus)

A demareteion of Syracuse, c.479, struck after the Syracusan victory over Carthage. Greek cities chose particular symbols for their coins, which reflected their independence — a local deity or god, a hero, a plant or an animal, or a mythological group. The inscriptions on the coins were usually in abbreviated form and included information such as the name of the city of issue and sometimes of the official responsible, or the particular event being celebrated

Athenian statesman, Demosthenes; and more important still, we can closely examine the work of historians who lived and wrote in ancient times — people like Herodotus, Thucydides and Xenophon.

Suggested titles for further study of literary evidence are given at the end of each chapter in this book, and the bibliography lists details of all work cited.

Numismatic evidence

The study of coinage is called numismatics. Ancient coins fit into both of the first two categories of evidence, because they are a form of archaeological evidence which usually provides some form of written material as well — sometimes a name, symbol, or legend (the inscription on a coin) may appear. From coins, the historian can learn about the leaders and events they commemorated, what those who issued the coins wished to have remembered about themselves (coins can often be a form of propaganda), and many other technical details. Numismatic evidence is plentiful in Greek and Roman history — so much so that anyone seriously interested in the study of ancient coins can build up a good, interesting collection without too much expense. Most coin stores carry ancient Greek and Roman coins that can be purchased readily and fairly inexpensively.

Epigraphic evidence

The study of inscriptions is called epigraphy and is of great importance in ancient history. Inscriptions appear on monuments, public buildings and tombstones, and on clay and stone tablets. Some inscriptions record laws, tribute (tax) lists for conquered peoples and treaties, while others commemorate the deeds of great leaders or list the names of those who fell in battle. As well as giving us information about aspects of religious life such as oracles, cult rites, thanksgivings and prayers, inscriptions also provide details of private and social life such as the sale of private property, loans, wills and dowries.

Like coins, inscriptions are partly archaeological evidence, partly written evidence. One of the most famous epigraphic discoveries was that of the Rosetta stone, found almost 200 years ago in Egypt. This stone contained the key to the decipherment of the ancient Egyptian hieroglyphics. More recently, in 1953, the Linear B tablets — found in Crete — were deciphered, which helped to advance our knowledge of early Greek civilisation.

Left: This inscription is an example of a decree by which cities honoured foreign citizens (a proxeny decree). The text, dated about 415 B.C., mentions the Athenian archon Charias. The man honoured in the decree was probably an Ionian (because of the use of Ionic letters)

Above right: Fragment from a list of Athenian archons (magistrates) — the Athenians used the names of the archons to identify particular years. On this fragment can be recognised the names of Hippias (526–525), Cleisthenes (525–524), Miltiades (524–523) and Calliades (523–522)

Below right: Part of a list of winners in the great dramatic contest held in Athens — the city Dionysia. It records the victory of the famous tragic poet, Sophocles, in 448–447

Introduction

The geography of Greece

The Greek polis

Features which unified the Greeks

The geography of Greece — its political, economic and social influence

A NY STUDY of ancient Greek society must begin with an appreciation of the physical characteristics of Greece. Landform and climate do not explain the vast and varied achievements of the ancient Hellenes, but they have determined and influenced many of the political, economic and social developments that occurred.

Landform

Characteristics

Greece is a land of rugged limestone mountains. To the north the high Pindus chain, running north to south, divides the Peninsula. In the west the ranges border the sea and in the east they cut laterally, dividing the plains of Thessaly, Boeotia and Attica from each other. In the Peloponnese they again run north to south, extending out into its capes and promontories — but they do not stop there, for their peaks and ridges form the islands of the Aegean. Narrow valleys and long gulfs separate the high ridges.

Rugged limestone mountains

There are many small fertile plains but only a few large ones, which were of great significance in the economy of ancient Greece. Some are coastal, like the elongated plain of Achaea which extends along the southern coastline of the Corinthian Gulf, while others — like the plain

Few large plains

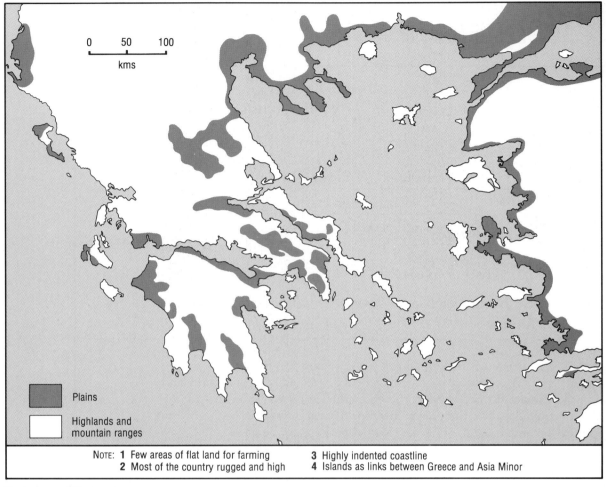

NOTE: 1 Few areas of flat land for farming   3 Highly indented coastline
2 Most of the country rugged and high   4 Islands as links between Greece and Asia Minor

Physical map of Greece

of Laconia — are cut off from the sea by a ring of mountains.

Effects of landform

Defence

The mountain barriers and the high and infrequent passes made communication and transporation difficult, so that movement of people and goods was usually by sea. Although armies on occasion crossed these barriers, the mountains did provide some defence for city-states, and the narrow passes were important in that they allowed small forces to contain larger armies — for example, during the Persian invasion of 480 B.C. the pass at Thermopylae was held by a small number of Greeks, until they were betrayed.

Although the mountainous nature of Greece is not wholly responsible for the character of Greek political development, the isolation of city-

states from their neighbours did give rise to strong feelings of independence and autonomy, love of freedom, and great civic pride. City-states (*poleis*) developed their own forms of government, institutions and community life. The corporate life of a polis — in which town and country were bound together — was enjoyed by all citizens, and the physical conditions enabled them to realise what they called *autarkeia* (self-sufficiency).

Strong feelings of independence and autonomy

The separateness of Greek poleis also contributed to jealousies, point-less and destructive quarrels and a reluctance to unite. Without geographi-cal barriers, it would have been easier to amalgamate into a single political unit.

Interstate jealousies and quarrels

With limited amounts of arable land and poor, thin soil over much of the uplands, an increase in population and subsequent food shortages led to a search for new lands. During this extensive colonising movement in the eighth and seventh centuries B.C., the Greeks established settlements as far afield as the Black Sea, North Africa and Spain.

Colonisation

The mountains provided summer pastures for animals, timber for fuel and building, and cypress and cedar for ship construction, and the crystalline and limestone rocks were a source of marble and limited minerals.

Resources

Influence of the sea

Characteristics

Greece has a deeply indented coastline; the sea penetrates far inland, a condition which keeps most districts in close contact with it. There are

Highly indented coastline

3

Typical indented coastline of Greece

many safe harbours and anchorages, especially along the east coast.

Aegean Basin — islands

The Aegean Basin is a definite geographical unit, shut in by the outer line of islands — Cythera, Crete, Carpathos and Rhodes. The inner islands are like stepping stones between Greece and Asia Minor.

The Isthmus of Corinth

The Gulf of Corinth almost cuts mainland Greece into two parts: central Greece and the Peloponnese. The narrow isthmus between the Corinthian and Saronic Gulfs played a vital role in Greek development.

Effects

Sailors and traders

Since the chief form of travel for most Greeks was by sea, they became expert sailors and navigators as well as enterprising traders. There were already Greek sailors in Neolithic times, and traders sailed the Mediterranean before the colonising movement gained strength.

Contact with the older civilisations of the east

Despite the many dangers of winter sailing and the lack of accurate navigational devices (such as the modern compass), the Greeks were inevitably led out into the Aegean Sea, whose waters were favourable in the summer, when steady winds blew along its coasts. Between Attica and Asia Minor the sailor need never have been out of sight of land or without a safe anchorage for the night. These conditions encouraged the Greeks to go eastward, and the Aegean became the focal point in the exchange of goods and ideas between Europe, Asia and Egypt.

Development of an inquisitive spirit

Where harbours were lacking — for example, in the west and in Thessaly — there was little economic and political development. It has been suggested that states like Athens, which took easily to the sea, developed a more inquisitive spirit and a wider outlook. Athens reached her peak — culturally as well as politically and economically — in the heyday of her naval supremacy. Herodotus (sometimes called 'The Father of History') travelled throughout the Mediterranean, and Solon, the sixth-century Athenian reformer, also spent much of his life travelling the Aegean. The Ionian traders of the Asiatic coastline led the way in formulating new philosophies about the world and man's place in it.

The colonisation movement was seaborne, and its success depended on the seamanship of the Greeks and the development in the construction of warships — an example of these being the penteconter, which was a galley with fifty oars.

Colonisation by sea

The Isthmus produced by the indentations of the Corinthian and Saronic Gulfs was important in the defence of the Peloponnese. It cut off the basically Dorian Peloponnesians from the rest of Greece and it could be easily defended by walls built across its narrowest section (a distance of approximately 7 kilometres). The cities of the Isthmus, such as Corinth and Megara, had access to the trade of both western and eastern seas and controlled traffic passing along the main north-south route to central and northern Greece. Light ships were often dragged on carts along a stone-paved way (*diolkos*) built across the Isthmus to save the long haul around the Peloponnese.

Importance of the Isthmus of Corinth

Climate

Characteristics

In the mountains the winters are severe, and the inland plains suffer extremely hot, enervating summers. However, the climate of the south and east is generally sunny and moderate. The summers are hot, and rain is virtually unknown in the summer months.

Sunny and moderate in the south and east

Effects

For most of the year the Greeks spent a large part of their lives outdoors. They congregated in open spaces such as the marketplace, or *agora*, where they met friends and discussed politics and other topical issues — usually seeking the shade of the colonnades which adorned public places. (These porches, or *stoa*, later gave the Stoic philosophers their name.) In the marketplaces there was a mingling of classes and people; their assemblies were held in the open and their theatres also were open to the sky. The Greeks lived a very public life.

Outdoor life

Most sailors and traders restricted their voyages to the summer months because of the stormy winters and dangerous seas.

Travel

Armies usually stopped fighting during winter, either settling into winter quarters or returning home, to begin the campaigning season in the following spring or summer.

Mapping exercise

On an outline map of Greece and Asia Minor,
mark the following features:

Cities
Athens ⎤
Sparta ⎥
Corinth ⎥
Megara ⎬ Mainland
Argos ⎥
Thebes ⎦
Chalcis ⎤
Eretria ⎦ Euboea
Mytilene ⎤
Miletus ⎥
Ephesus ⎬ Asia Minor
Halicarnassus ⎦

Important sites
Olympia
Delphi
Mt Olympus

Seas and waterways
Ionian Sea
Aegean Sea
The Hellespont
The Bosphorus
The Black Sea (Pontus Euxinus)

Islands
Euboea
Thasos
Lesbos
Samos
Chios
Naxos
Delos
Rhodes
Corcyra

The Dark Ages (approximately 1100–800 B.C.)

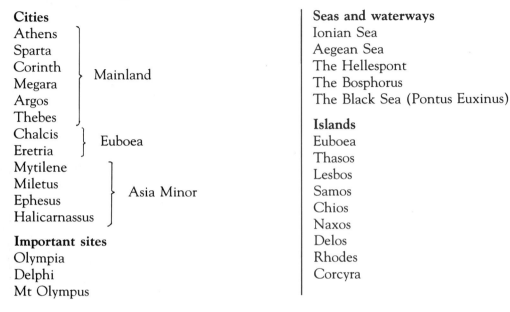

Opposite: Map showing
direction of Greek migrations
after the Dorian invasions of
approximately 1200 to 1000
B.C.

The Dark Age of Greece refers to that period between the decline of
Mycenaean society and the great colonising movement of the eighth
century B.C. The Mycenaean centres declined and then were destroyed;
archaeological evidence suggests that both internal strife and attacks from
outside were responsible.

Between approximately 1200 and 1100 B.C. the Dorians, a branch of
the Indo-Europeans from the Danube area, began invading northern and
north-western Greece; at a later date they occupied the more fertile areas
of the east and the south, including the Peloponnese.

Associated with the Dorian invasion was a great migration of the pre-
Dorian population to the islands of the Aegean and the coasts of Asia
Minor. Among the migrants were the Ionians, who were to play a major
part in the development of Greek civilisation. These Ionians were of the
same race as the people of Athens, who had provided a haven for refugees
fleeing the Peloponnese.

6

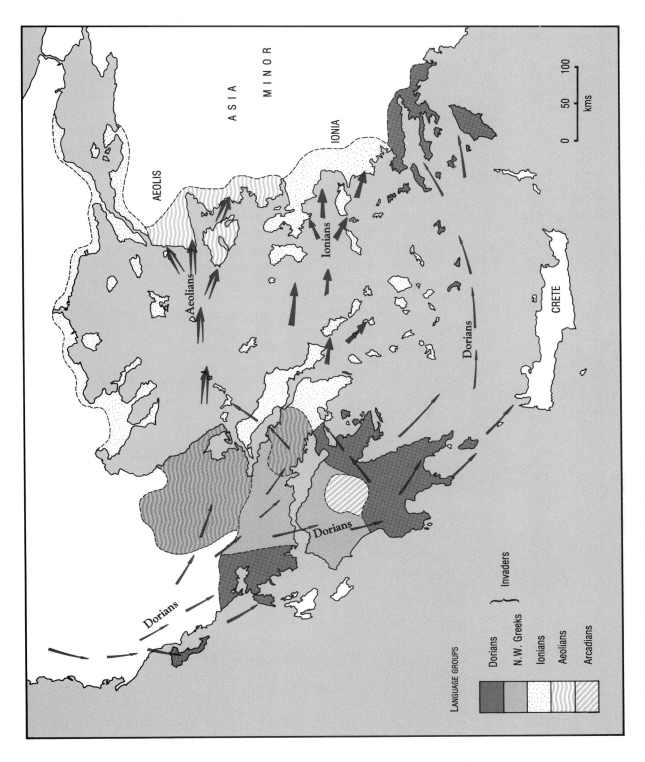

ASIA

MINOR

AEOLIS

IONIA

CRETE

Aeolians

Ionians

Dorians

Dorians

Dorians

LANGUAGE GROUPS

Dorians

N.W. Greeks

Ionians

Aeolians

Arcadians

Invaders

0   50   100

kms

The Greek polis

A history of separate city-states

After the so-called Dark Ages, the country was divided into a large number of independent units — the poleis (singular: *polis*). Greece did not exist as a country in the modern sense; therefore it is inaccurate to speak of a 'history of ancient Greece', for there was no such thing — it was rather the history of a group of small political units, with first one predominating for a time and then another. The Greeks occasionally referred to themselves as Hellenes, but more particularly as Athenians, Corinthians, Spartans, Thebans and so on.

Need to understand meaning of 'polis'

It is impossible to understand their achievements and the workings of their minds without a clear understanding of what was meant by the word 'polis'. There is no equivalent word in English; it is often translated as 'city-state', but the Greek polis was really neither a city nor a state in the modern sense of those words — the closest we can come to its real meaning is 'community of people'. A polis was a self-governing (autonomous) community which included

Features of the polis

- the acropolis — stronghold of the community and centre of public life;
- the town or city built around the acropolis;
- the villages and the countryside;
- the people of the city and the countryside;
- the political, cultural, religious and economic way of life.

The Acropolis at Athens

Origin of the polis

There are no records to help us understand the origin of this unique concept, although historical, geographical and economic reasons can be suggested.

In times of unsettled conditions the inhabitants of a plain or a valley may have had to defend themselves, and so fortified a high, rocky outcrop that could be easily defended. Here the ruler would live, and it probably became a meeting place and religious centre. The acropolis — the word means 'high town' — became the stronghold of the community, around which the people lived.

The acropolis

A central market in which the farmers could sell their produce would have been necessary, and the Greek habit of preferring to live in the town and walk to their fields may have led to the market being converted into a market town beneath the acropolis.

Market town at base of acropolis

In time, a number of towns and villages may have amalgamated into one political unit. This process was called *synoecism*.

Synoecism

Because of the variety of landforms within a single area (a strip of fertile plain, of upland pasture, of forested mountain and slopes and of barren mountain summits), quite small areas were able to become reasonably self-sufficient.

Self-sufficiency

The ancient Greek wanted to play a part in running the affairs of the community and to participate in the many and varied activities enjoyed through the polis. He could do this more effectively in a small unit.

Need to participate in a community

Features of the polis

Size

The ideal size, in terms of population, was considered by Plato in his *Republic* to be 5000 citizens, while Aristotle's *Politics* suggests that the citizens should know each other by sight. The polis had to be large enough to be self-sufficient, but not too large to govern itself. Hippodamus, who designed the Piraeus, said the ideal size was 10 000 citizens, but this, if women, children, foreign (but resident) craftsmen and slaves were included, implied a population of approximately 100 000. Only three poleis had in excess of 20 000 citizens: Athens and, in Sicily, Acragas and Syracuse.

Ideal number of citizens

Variation in size

The Spartans, after conquering Messenia, had one of the largest poleis (approximately 5120 square kilometres), while the large commercial centre of Corinth occupied a polis of approximately 528 square kilometres. Some islands were divided into several poleis; for example, the island of Ceos had four of them.

Variations in area

9

Diagram showing the structure of population in Athens, mid-fifth century

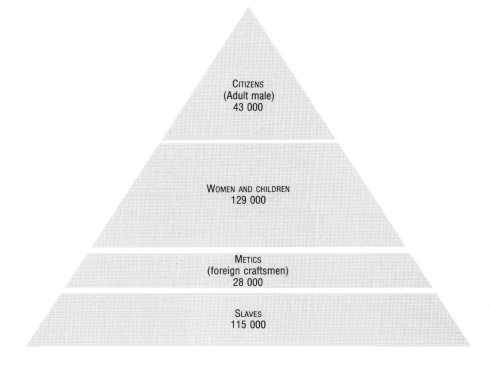

CITIZENS
(Adult male)
43 000

WOMEN AND CHILDREN
129 000

METICS
(foreign craftsmen)
28 000

SLAVES
115 000

Citizenship

Citizenship restricted

Citizenship was restricted to adult males, but the definition of 'adult' varied from city to city; for example, in Athens a boy was regarded as a citizen at eighteen, while in Sparta a citizen had to be thirty years of age. Usually both parents had to have been born in the city, but sometimes it was necessary for only one to have been born there.

Obligations and responsibilities

Political responsibility

Every citizen was expected to take his political responsibility seriously, and everyone took pride in the affairs of the polis. They had strong feelings of patriotism; even when it was necessary for their survival, they found it difficult to join with their fellow Hellenes in a common defence.

Athenian participation

The state's authority was total and affected every aspect of their lives; a citizen in Athens found loitering in the agora (marketplace) when the ecclesia (assembly) was being held, was branded with red paint and rounded up to attend the assembly. The red marks showed people that he had been avoiding his responsibilities. When the annual religious/dramatic festival was held, most would attend; the entrance fee was small, but those who could not afford this payment were given it out of public funds.

10

In Sparta, where the state dominated the lives of the Spartans from birth to death, men were expected to marry at twenty years of age and to live in barracks until they were thirty. Anyone who violated the code of honour by which Spartan peers lived was reduced to the status of 'inferior', stripped of citizenship rights, and ridiculed.

Spartan's life dominated by state

Forms of government

There was great variation in the forms of government existing in the city-states, as each developed the form which suited it best.

Variety in forms of government
Monarchs and tyrants

Originally city-states were governed by a king (monarchy) who was often replaced by a group of nobles (aristocracy) or a group who owed their political power and position to wealth (timocracy). Sometimes these oligarchies (government by the few) were overthrown and a tyrant seized power for a short time, bringing benefits to his state before being in turn overthrown and replaced by another form of government, such as a liberal oligarchy or a democracy (where all citizens had the right to vote, to make laws and to be elected to official positions). Sparta was an example of a 'mixed constitution'; that is, she retained her kings and adopted some democratic features, but favoured oligarchic rule. Athens experimented with democracy.

Oligarchy and democracy

Within each city-state there was often strife — party and class struggles, factional jealousies and political intrigue.

Party and class strife

Disunity

Owing to their need to be free and independent — and to some extent, to their geographical isolation — the Greeks united in a political sense only twice: in the Trojan Wars (c.1190 B.C.) and the Persian Wars (490–479 B.C.). Their relationships were marked by commercial jealousies and rivalries, shifting alliances and interstate wars.

Lack of unity

Links or connections between poleis

Guest friendship (*proxenia*) existed between individuals and between different city-states, despite wars and political rivalries. It was often extended to the political sphere as well, when a state's envoy or adviser in commercial matters resided in another city.

Proxenia

An agreement whereby the citizens of one city could be given citizenship in another was known as *isopoliteia*. Agreement on legal aid to be granted to a citizen in the territory of another was called *symbola*.

Isopoliteia
Symbola and colonial ties

Although colonies became independent politically, there remained sentimental and religious ties with the mother city.

The major states of Greece

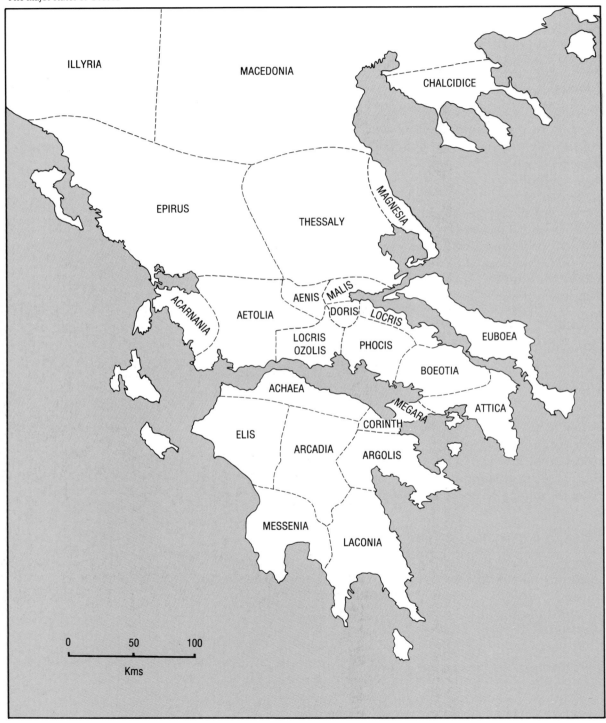

ILLYRIA

MACEDONIA

CHALCIDICE

EPIRUS

THESSALY

MAGNESIA

ACARNANIA

AETOLIA

AENIS MALIS

DORIS LOCRIS

LOCRIS OZOLIS

PHOCIS

LOCRIS

EUBOEA

BOEOTIA

ACHAEA

MEGARA

ATTICA

CORINTH

ELIS

ARCADIA

ARGOLIS

MESSENIA

LACONIA

0   50   100

Kms

Features which unified the Greeks

There were three major sources of unity among the Greeks:
- language — although there were different dialects;
- literature — for example, the epic poems of Homer: *The Iliad* and *The Odyssey*;
- religion — they worshipped the same pantheon of gods, although each city had its patron deity.

Religion

Two important aspects of their religion were (a) oracles and (b) religious festivals.

Oracles

The Greeks sought to learn the will of the gods for practical guidance about specific matters in everyday life, and the most popular way of obtaining this was through the consultation of oracles. H. W. Parke tells us that an oracle was 'a formal statement from a god usually given in answer to an enquiry or else the place where such an enquiry could be made'.[1]

There were many oracles in the Greek world, but the most renowned was the oracle of Apollo at Delphi (central Greece). It played a highly important role in the life of the ancient world.

Religious festivals

Hellenic religion expressed itself in several great Panhellenic festivals, the most significant of which were the Games. These were among the chief bonds of unity in a divided Greece. The most important of the Games were those held at Olympia in honour of the god Zeus, which continued in existence for over 1000 years. However, this was only one of four festivals (sometimes called the Crown Games, as winners were awarded crowns or wreaths). The Pythian Games were held in honour of Apollo at Delphi every four years. The Isthmian Games, held at Corinth in honour of Poseidon, God of the Sea, took place every two years, as did the Nemean Games, in honour of Zeus, at Nemea.

Assignment: The Delphic oracle and the Olympic Games

In attempting the following assignment, students should make use of the plentiful source material—both archaeological and written—that is available on both topics.

The Delphic oracle

Research carefully and make notes on each of the following points:

1 The origin of the cult of Apollo at Delphi.
  (a) Was there a cult earlier than that of the Earth Goddess at Delphi?
  (b) What was the legend concerning the introduction of the worship of Apollo?
2 The site of Delphi.
  (a) What made this site so impressive?
3 The sanctuary and its buildings.
  (a) Describe the plan of the sanctuary.
  (b) What were the Omphalos Stone and the Castalian Spring?
  (c) Describe the Temple of Apollo, the Treasuries, the Tholos, Theatre and Stadium.
  (d) Describe some of the dedications made to Apollo.
4 Procedure in consulting the oracle.
  (a) Who was the Pythia? How was she selected? What duties did she have?
  (b) What were the methods of inducing inspiration? (There is some dispute about this.)
  (c) What were the main features in the ceremony of consultation?
  (d) How were replies given to the enquirer?
5 The influence of the oracle.
  In what way did the oracle influence
  (a) colonisation;
  (b) tyranny and foreign kings;
  (c) appeasement of Persians during the Persian Wars;
  (d) power politics between Athens and Sparta.

6 Other examples of oracular prophecies.
  Note some of the nonpolitical questions for which they gave answers.
7 The importance of the oracle as a unifying force.
  The oracle was important as a meeting place—and a place for the exchange of information—and for its association with
  (a) the Pythian Games;
  (b) the Amphictyony.

This sphinx, about 2–3 metres high, originally stood on top of an Ionic column. It was dedicated to Delphi from the people of Naxos, c.550. It shows the type of elaborate sculpture dedicated by the tyrants

The site of Delphi

This bronze figure of a
charioteer was dedicated by
the brother of Hieron, tyrant
of Syracuse, to commemorate
a victory in a chariot race

The temple at Delphi

Source material

1 Evidence found in excavations at Delphi,
   and material now housed in the Delphi
   Museum.
2 The Homeric *Hymn of Apollo*.

This hymn ends by describing how

Phoebus Apollo then took it in mind whom he
would bring of men as his worshippers who would
serve him in rocky Pytho. Then while pondering
he was aware of a swift ship on the wine-dark sea
and in it were good men and many—Cretans
from Minoan Knossos who offer sacrifices to the
lord Apollo and announce the oracles of Phoebus
Apollo of the golden sword whatever he speaks in
prophecy from the laurel-tree beneath the gorges
of Parnassus.[2]

3 Hymn to Apollo written in the late eighth or early seventh century, probably by Cynaechus of Chios.

There is a place beneath the snowy crest
Of high Parnassus, where towards the west,
A foothill lies. Behind, a great cliff towers
And under it a deep glade darkly lowers
Then paused Apollo and made known his will:
Here shall my temple rise, fashioned with skill
On all sides, filled with beauty: it shall be
An oracle, and men shall come to me
At Delphi for true counsel — men of Greece
And of the wave-washed isles that fleck the
    seas.[3]

4 Herodotus: *The Histories*. This includes many references to Delphi and the advice given.

I:51–8, 93	Consultations of King Croesus of Lydia, son of King Alyattes.
I:66	Advice on Lycurgus' system of government and Spartan expansion.
IV:152, 156–7	Colonisation of Cyrene.
V:66, 91–2	Tyranny in Corinth and Sicyon; corruption of the Oracle.
VI:35, 133–7	Miltiades in the Chersonese; Miltiades at Paros.
VII:140–3	Athens' fate during the Persian Wars.
VII:148	Argos, concerning the Persian Wars.
VII:167–71	Crete, concerning the Persian Wars.
VII:220	Sparta's fate during the Persian Wars.

5 H. W. Parke: *Greek Oracles* (secondary source).

The Olympic Games

Research carefully and make notes on each of the following points:

1 The origin of the Games at Olympia. Consider

(a) early legends concerning the origins of the Games;

(b) the traditional date for the founding of the Festival (776 B.C.);

(c) that the importance of the games began with the leadership of Sparta in the Peloponnese.

2 The site of Olympia.

3 The sanctuary and buildings.

(a) What was the Altis? What buildings were found there?

(b) For what purposes were the Hippodrome, Stadium, Gymnasium and Palaestra used?

(c) What other buildings were found at Olympia?

4 Rules and regulations.

(a) Who was permitted to compete?

(b) What were the rules regarding preparation and training?

(c) Explain the job of the heralds (*spondaphores*) in regard to the Sacred Truce. Why was a truce necessary?

(d) How were the judges (*hellenodikai*) chosen? What preparations were made?

5 The schedule of events.

(a) Over what period of time did the Games extend? Was this always the case?

(b) Events were added gradually. What were the main sports contested at Olympia?

(c) Explain how some of these were conducted.

(d) What ritual and sacrifice accompanied each stage of the proceedings?

6 Rewards for victory.

(a) What was the only prize presented to the victors?

(b) What honours awaited the victor on his return to his native city?

(c) What event particularly attracted the wealthy?

7 The political importance of Olympia.

How important were the Games for the scattered Greek colonies? What benefits were gained by individuals and city-states from these Panhellenic festivals?

Source material

1 Archaeological evidence.

Much of the information on ancient Games comes from excavations of stadiums; also from sculptures, such as Myron's Discobolus (discus thrower), Polyclitus' Doryphorus (spear thrower) and 'The Apoxyomenus' (athlete engaged in scraping oil off with a strigil), and from vase paintings which depict such events as chariot races, javelin and discus throwing, long jumping, athletes practising to music, training, and the triumphant return of the athletes.

Olympia

The starting line in the stadium at Olympia

Halteres: hand-held lead weights, used as balancers in the long jump

A Roman copy in marble of
the famous *Discobolus* (discus
thrower) by Myron. The
original was in bronze, c. 460

A small bronze of wrestlers

Runners (From a vase
painting)

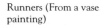

2 Written evidence.
  (a) Lists of victors are found in many sources.
  (b) Pausanias was a Greek from Asia Minor who travelled throughout Greece in about A.D. 174. He left a very detailed account of everything he saw in his *A Description of Greece*.
  (c) Pindar, a poet from Thebes, wrote splendid odes for the winners of the Greek athletic festivals. An example of these is given below.

  Olympia, mother of gold-crowned games,
  Mother of Verity, where prophets seek
  the favour of Zeus, search to know his
    pleasure
  by making offerings in sacred flames;

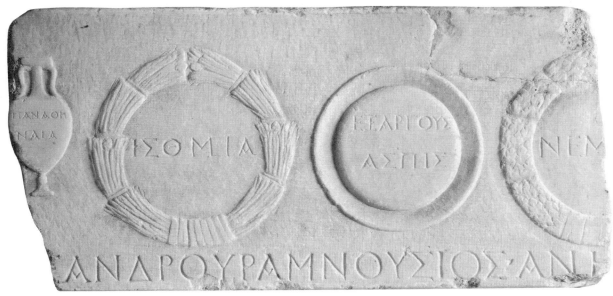

A relief from the base of a statue shows the prizes that a successful athlete could win at the Games. The relief represents a pitcher from Athens, a wreath from Corinth, a shield from Argos and a wreath from Nemea (Courtesy of the Metropolitan Museum of Art, New York)

ask what hope he has for those
Straining for the victor's crown
After wearying training performed;
Zeus' will is found through pious prayer.
O, Pisan grove with feathery trees
receive our festival hymn with flowers.
Glorious is the fame henceforth
of him on whom your favour falls.
Many roads there are to sweet success
If the gods will bless his mortal
Timosthenes, fate has given you and
Your brother to Zeus — He gave you victory
at Nemean games; then on Alcimedon's
brow

he placed the wreath of champion
at Olympia, too.
Graceful and virile to see, matching action
to beauty he was victorious at wrestling,
Thereby adding glory to his homeland
  Aegina,
fair island where above all they honour
Themis, friend of Zeus the hospitable.[4]

Pindar — 8th Olympian ode

Further reading

Andrewes, A. *Greek Society.*
Finley, M. I. *Early Greece — the Bronze and Archaic Age.*
Hammond, N. G. L. *A History of Greece to 322 B.C.*
Kitto, H. D. F. *The Greeks.*
Muir's Atlas of Ancient and Classical History.

2

Greek colonial expansion, 800–500 B.C.

Reasons for colonisation
Developments contributing to the success of Greek colonisation
Procedure for establishing a colony
Effects of colonisation

BETWEEN 800 AND 500 B.C. the Greeks embarked on a widespread colonising movement; by the sixth century, Greek settlements were scattered throughout the Mediterranean and Black Sea areas. It was through this movement that Greek culture reached Asia, Africa and southern Europe, and it changed the economic and cultural history of Greece itself and of the whole Mediterranean basin.

Sources for this period

Archaeological evidence

Most of the source material for this period comes from archaeological remains, particularly from decorated pottery. Emigrating families took with them their domestic utensils for use until local kilns could be built, although some were taken because they were art objects. Once colonies were established, pots and jars were used for both storage and trade. Unlike iron (which corroded) and bronze and precious metals (which were often melted down), broken pottery (potsherds) has survived. Building remains—particularly of temples—and weights, measures and coins are also of special interest to the archaeologist.

Literary evidence

There are no historical records of this period, except for some fragments of poetry and a few inscriptions from non-Greek sources. Hecataeus of

Miletus, who had a great interest in geography, recorded *A Journey Round the World*, but it remains only in fragments. The best literary evidence is the work of Herodotus, who in his *Histories* gives us details not only of the Greek world, but of the affairs of places outside Greece.

Most ancient sources tend to emphasise the mythical elements and the part played by individuals, rather than the more general economic and social aspects. The geographer Strabo, living 700 years after the events he describes, repeats the accepted story of the foundation of Syracuse in Sicily; this reveals the traditional type of account.

Traditional accounts unreliable

> Archias, sailing from Corinth, founded Syracuse about the same time that Naxos and Megara (also in Sicily) were established. They say that when Myscellus and Archias went to Delphi to consult the oracle, the god asked whether they preferred wealth or health. Archias chose wealth and Myscellus health, and the oracle then assigned Syracuse to the former to found, and Croton (in southern Italy) to the latter... On his way to Sicily, Archias left a part of the expedition to settle the island now called Corcyra (modern Corfu)...[1]

Reasons for colonisation

Most colonial ventures were due to general rather than particular causes, although there were special reasons which applied to some states.

According to Finley, the aspect most mother cities had in common was 'a condition of crisis severe enough to induce the mobilisation of the resources required for so difficult a venture as an overseas transplantation—', and in this movement the element of compulsion was basic.[2]

Conditions of crisis

Land shortage

The colonial movement was a response to population and agrarian difficulties; most colonies were agricultural settlements, established by men in search of land.

There was a shortage of land for a number of reasons:

1 Greece was a land of limited fertility and the small number of areas suitable for farming could not support the growing population. Hesiod, the Boeotian farmer and poet, in his *Works and Days*, advised that 'there should be an only son to feed his father's house, for so wealth will increase in the home; but if you leave a second son you should die old'.[3]

Few flat areas; population pressure

The Achaeans, who were dominant in the colonisation of southern Italy, lived in an area restricted between the mountains of the northern Peloponnese and the Corinthian Gulf.

Examples: Achaea, Megara and Thera

Megara, an active coloniser in the Hellespont and Propontis area, was very limited in territory; as Isocrates said, the Megarians 'farmed rocks'.

Thera was a relatively barren, small island and could not support a large population; when drought became severe, farmers were forced to seek a new home overseas, at Cyrene in Libya.

Exceptions: Athens and Sparta

The fact that Athens did not colonise during this period indicates that the plain of Attica was large enough to support her growing population. Sparta, on the other hand, found an alternative to colonisation for her land hunger. She conquered the neighbouring state of Messenia, which was more fertile than Laconia.

Best land held by nobles

2 A monopoly of the land was held by a few influential families, and this trend accelerated. Hesiod, in his typically gloomy tone, describes how the noble lords of the district held tracts of the best land and robbed the peasants even of their poor land holdings.

Land tenure

3 The form of land tenure practised in Greece contributed to the shortage of land. Primogeniture, by which the eldest son inherited the family farm, left younger sons landless. Even if a farm was divided equally among sons, the holdings eventually were of insufficient size to farm efficiently.

Persian Empire limits expansion of Ionians

4 The cities of Asia Minor were unable to expand inland, under the pressure of population, owing to the proximity of the Persian Empire. Miletus and Rhodes could not expand due to the strength of Caria and Lycia, and so looked elsewhere. Miletus established approximately ninety colonies around the fertile Black Sea region, where land and resources were plentiful.

Trade

Early contact of Greek traders with east and west

Commercial factors were not so important in the establishment of early colonies, although Greek traders had been in contact with both eastern and western countries and would have known of suitable sites and the possibility of resources. Greek products had reached Sicily and Etruria sometime before the colonists arrived in Italy, and Al Mina, in northern Syria, was the earliest of the Greek trading settlements in the east.

Trading settlements: Massilia, Emporion and Naucratis

There were a few genuine trading posts, particularly in the west, such as Pithecusae, on the island of Ischia (to tap the iron and copper trade from northern Italy); Massilia, at the mouth of the Rhône River (on the tin route), and Emporion (Ampurias) — a Greek name meaning 'market' — on the northern coast of Spain. Naucratis, in Egypt, was also a trading centre. These settlements were not proper poleis, but rather meeting points between the Greek world and the non-Greek world.

Some colonies were founded on sites which guarded trade routes or were suitable for the imposition of tolls on passing trade, and for piracy. Thucydides tells us that piracy became a common profession among Hellenes, and far from being regarded as disgraceful, was in fact considered to be quite honourable.

Imposition of tolls, and piracy

The island colony of Pithecusae founded the settlement of Cumae on the adjacent coast of Italy, and it was well placed to raid or tax trading vessels from Etruria. The settlement of Zancle (later called Messana), on the Sicilian side of the Straits of Messana, had little land and was originally occupied by pirates. When Zancle promoted the foundation of Rhegium on the Italian coast, these two Chalcidian colonies exercised control of the passage through the Straits.

Zancle and Rhegium

Exploitation of trade was not the primary reason for colonisation, but trade considerations became more important as the movement gained impetus.

Trade not an early consideration

Political and social discontent

Political strife was a common feature of life in most Greek cities at this time, when administration was generally in the hands of aristocracies such as the Bacchiads of Corinth and the Penthilids of Mytilene. There was competition for leadership among the noble families and this often led to a disaffected noble taking the initiative and leading a group of colonists to a new settlement.

Nobles promoted colonisation to remove opposition

At first these aristocratic rulers governed quite well, but more frequently they began to govern in their own interests, often resorting to violence against the lower classes. Aristotle wrote, in his *Constitution of the Athenians*, that there was civil strife between the nobles and the people for a long time.

The aristocrats realised the need to promote colonial ventures to remove citizens who were discontented with their rule.

Special reasons

Naucratis in Egypt

The settlement in Naucratis was mainly an eastern Greek venture. Greek traders had been making at least casual visits to Egypt from the middle of the seventh century.

'Bronze men' from Ionia

According to Herodotus, Psammetichus, King of Egypt, was driven from his throne. He planned revenge and sought advice from an oracle, whose answer was that he would be helped by 'bronze men from the sea'. When sea raiders from Ionia and Caria, wearing bronze armour, landed on his coast, he befriended them with 'promises of rich rewards'. They

Land granted at mouth of Nile

entered his service and helped him defeat his enemies; in return, he gave them 'two pieces of land, opposite one another on either side of the Nile'.

A later Egyptian ruler, Amasis, brought them to Memphis to protect himself. 'They were the first foreigners to live in Egypt.' Later, they were given Naucratis as a commercial headquarters for any Greeks who wanted to settle in Egypt. Land was also granted to those who simply wanted to trade, on which they could build temples and altars.

A settlement of many Greek trading states

Naucratis was nothing like the colonies of Italy and Sicily. It owed its existence to the continued good favour of the Egyptian king, and the various Greek states trading there (Miletus, Chios, Samos, Aegina, Corinth and Athens) saw that their interests were protected. From the merchant class were appointed the *prostatai*, officers in charge of the port, who acted as magistrates for the town. The life of this rich Greek community, admitted to a country which had long mistrusted foreigners, must have been unusual.[4]

Plan of the city of Naucratis; note the number of Greek states involved.

Naucratis, located 80 km from the sea on the east bank of the Canopic branch of the Nile, was excavated between 1884 and 1903 by a number of archaeological teams. It was an unusual Greek settlement because of the manner in which it was founded and the number of Greek states involved.

Most of the finds in Naucratis have been of finely decorated votive offerings. Pottery from the eastern Mediterranean, from Corinth, Athens and Sparta has been found.

Temple of Apollo
Temple of Hera
Hellenion
Temple of Aphrodite
Scarab factory
Fort

Temple of Apollo (Milesian)
The Temple of Apollo was built by the Milesians in the early days of the settlement.
Temple of Hera (Samian)
The Temple of Hera was established by the Samians, according to scraps of inscribed sixth-century pottery.
Temple of Aphrodite (Chian)
An early, simple temple to Aphrodite contained pottery from Chios.
Temple of Zeus (Aeginetan)
The Temple of Zeus, built by the Aeginetans and mentioned in Herodotus, was not found.
Hellenion (sanctuary — joint venture of several eastern Greek states)
These remains may have been of the large sanctuary, Hellenion, mentioned in Herodotus and founded jointly by the Eastern Greek states. Inscriptions on vases name several Greek gods, but the most common inscription refers to 'the gods of the Greeks'.
Scarab factory
A factory for making faience scarab seals, certainly intended for Greek markets.

Using evidence — Greeks in Egypt in the sixth century

Herodotus provides literary evidence for the use of Greek mercenaries in Egypt in the seventh century (resulting in the Greek settlement at Naucratis). There is also archaeological and epigraphic evidence that Greek mercenaries continued to be used in Egypt in the sixth century.

The following inscription was scratched by Greek soldiers on the left leg of the huge, rock-cut statue of Rameses II at Abu Simbel, over 1000 kilometres up the Nile. (These statues have since been moved beyond the reach of the waters of the Aswan Dam.) The inscription reads:

> When King Psammetichus came to Elephantine, those who sailed with Psammetichus the son of Theocles wrote this; and they came above Kerkis as far as the river allowed; and Potasimto led those of foreign speech and Amasis the Egyptians; and Archon the son of Amoebichus wrote us and Pelequos the son of Eudamus.

Psammetichus II led an expedition in about 591 B.C. against the Nubian kingdom, and Greek soldiers held important positions in the army.

The inscription is followed by graffiti of the type defacing many walls and monuments, but it does reveal the origins of the mercenaries.

> Helesibus the son of Ieus
> Telephus the son of Ialusio . . . wrote me
> Pytho the son of Hamoebich[us]
> Pabis of Colophon together with Psammata

The statue of Rameses II at Abu Simbel

25

Agesermo[s]
Pasiphon the son of Hippos
Krithis wrote this
Homogusob(?) [the King] first led the army in company with Psammetichos

The translation is by M. N. Tod, in *A Selection of
Greek Historical Inscriptions*.

Taras in southern Italy

*Spartan offspring
found Taras*

The Spartans themselves did not colonise; instead they conquered their
neighbours, the Messenians. With most husbands away from home during
this long military campaign, Sparta found it necessary to take emergency
measures to maintain the population; many illegitimate children were
born. However, when they grew up and matters returned to normal,
citizenship restrictions were imposed on them. Resenting their lack of
rights, they began to stir up revolt but were forced to emigrate, and so
founded the colony of Taras (Tarentum) in Italy.

Taras (Tarentum) was built
on a fine peninsula,
embracing a large lagoon. It
had the best harbour in
southern Italy (just as it has
today) and was surrounded by
good cornlands

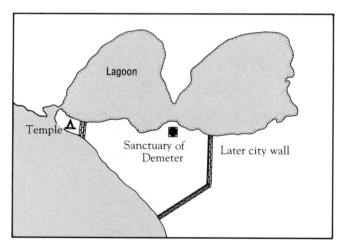

Developments that contributed to the success of Greek colonisation

Since the colonising movement was seaborne, and at some time the
colonists might expect to fight the local inhabitants, their success depended
on their skill in seamanship and warfare.

*Warships, hoplites and
organising skills*

The earliest type of warship was replaced in the seventh and sixth
centuries B.C. by the triaconter (thirty oars) and the penteconter (fifty
oars). (This development is believed to have been the work of a Corinthian

A triaconter (thirty-oared boat) taken from a Black Figure vase, c.570

This clay plaque found at Sunium shows part of a ship with soldiers on board. The steersman can be seen, but the rowers have to be imagined (c.700)

The earliest known Greek hoplite armour, c.720. The breast-plate (cuirass) and helmet were made of bronze

shipbuilder.) Ramming now replaced boarding as the usual battle tactic.

The improvement in armour and weapons—such as the bronze helmet, corselet, greaves, shield, thrusting spear and short sword—helped in dealing with hostile native populations. Herodotus mentions the 'men of bronze' from Ionia who were used as mercenaries by the Pharaoh of Egypt.

The Greeks, unlike many of the people with whom they came in contact, had the resources, energy and organising skills needed to spread so far afield.

Colonists always faced the danger of shipwreck, as shown in this section from an eighth-century geometric vase from the colony of Pithecusae

Procedure for establishing a colony

Apoikia — contrast with earlier and later colonies

A Greek colony was called an *apoikia* (settlement far from home) and differed from later colonies, such as Athenian cleruchies and Roman colonies, in being politically independent of the mother city. The earlier Phoenician colonies were not intended as permanent settlements, but were trading posts for the collection and distribution of goods and the maintenance of their ships.

A public enterprise

The oikistes

The founding of a colony was a public enterprise directed by the mother city, which provided the founder, or *oikistes*. The oikistes became the traditional hero of the new colony, and cults in his honour were faithfully observed. He was usually chosen from among the noble families of the city, and when a colony wished in turn to establish a settlement of its own, it usually invited an oikistes from the original mother city. The oikistes organised the settlers and if there were insufficient numbers from the founding city wishing to join, he would enlist people from other poleis. There were many such joint enterprises.

Religious approval

Before settlers left the mother city, their venture was expected to be sanctified by religion. This involved consulting one of the oracles, usually the oracle of the god Apollo at Delphi or at Didyma (in Asia Minor). The oracle was appealed to for a favourable prophecy and for information about the best locations. The god was regarded as the divine leader (*archegates*), and worshipped in the new settlement. Sacred envoys, called *theoroi*, were charged with maintaining contact with the oracle.

Hammond reports that the leader of the Parian colony at Thasos was told by the oracle: 'Announce to the Parians O' Telesicles that I bid you found a conspicuous city in the island of Eeria'.[5] He adds that the leaders of Gela were instructed: 'Entimus and cunning son of famous Croton, go you both to Sicily and inhabit that fair land, when you have built a town of Cretans and Rhodians together beside the mouth of the holy river Gela and the same name as the river'.[6]

Oracular instructions

The sites chosen for new settlements included small offshore islands, with later extension to the adjacent mainland (Ischia–Cumae, Platea–Cyrene); peninsulas (Sinope, Mesembria, Tarentum); sheltered harbours (Odessus, Syracuse); estuaries (Tyras, Olbia); and straits (Zancle, Rhegium). A chosen site could also be a place where there was a high acropolis. Large, exposed sites could only be settled by powerful states.

Most common sites selected

Since the settlement was to be independent and self-sufficient, a variety of people were needed from the outset. Settlers included soldiers, who accompanied the first wave of colonists if opposition was expected from the native inhabitants.

Soldiers

The oikistes took with him the sacred fire from the hearth of the mother city, and earth to be scattered at the new site. He also established political institutions similar to those of the mother city; for example, Heraclea, a colony of Taras which was itself a colony of disaffected Spartans, had a college of ephors and a gerousia similar to that of Sparta.

Sacred fire and earth

Priests introduced into the new colony the religious institutions, festivals and city cults which were to be replicas of those of the mother city. Temples were some of the first buildings to be constructed.

Priests

Surveyors made a plan of the settlement and divided the land into plots called *kleroi*, which the farmers obtained by drawing lots, thus establishing private tenure from the start. A variety of craftsmen were included and traders might be attracted later if the colony was located at a strategic site, or if the hinterland was rich in resources.

Surveyors and craftsmen

Colonists did not have an automatic right to return to their native city. In fact, if the reason for the settlement was to relieve overpopulation at home, the founder may have been responsible for taking steps to make sure the colonists stayed there. There are examples of returning colonists being driven off with slings at Eretria. In other cases return might be permitted provided that each returning colonist left behind an adult male of his family, to protect the future welfare of the colony.

No automatic right to return home

Sentimental ties with the mother city were exceptionally strong, but the colony remained politically independent. There were, however, a few exceptions to this rule, as in the case of Corinth, which liked to keep some control over its colonies. Thucydides records a speech of the Corinthians: 'Though they [Corcyraeans] are colonists of ours, they have

Ties with mother city

29

never been loyal to us . . . we did not found colonies in order to be insulted by them, but rather to retain our leadership and to be treated with proper respect'.[7]

Mapping exercise

On the map opposite are shown the 'mother cities' which led the way in colonisation.

1 Draw individual maps of (a) the Propontis–Black Sea region, (b) the north-west Aegean and (c) the western Mediterranean, showing Italy, Sicily and the coastline of Spain.
Mark in the colonies listed below and beside each one place the symbol of its mother city. (Look up the names of the mother cities in the list of major texts — e.g. Bury — and reference books in order to find out which were their main colonies. You will need to allow for some variation in the spelling of place names.)

2 Which mother cities seem to have founded the most colonies
   (a) in the Black Sea region?
   (b) in the western Mediterranean?
   (c) overall?
3 Which colony was founded furthest from its mother city?
4 Which two areas appear to have been most favoured for founding settlements? Can you suggest reasons for this?
5 Where was 'Magna Graecia'? Why was it so called?
6 Why was 'Neapolis' chosen as the name for several Greek colonies?

Propontis–Black Sea	N. W. Aegean	Western Mediterranean		Africa
1 Chalcedon	1 Mende	1 Corcyra	13 Leontini	1 Naucratis
2 Byzantium	2 Scione	2 Cumae	14 Naxos	2 Cyrene
3 Heraclea	3 Torone	3 Neapolis	15 Gela	
4 Abydos	4 Methone	4 Rhegium	16 Selinus	
5 Cyzicus	5 Potidaea	5 Sybaris	17 Massilia	
6 Sigeum	6 Pydna	6 Croton	18 Emporion	
7 Sinope	7 Thasos	7 Posidonia		
8 Trapezus	8 Neapolis	8 Taras		
9 Apollonia		9 Syracuse		
10 Istros		10 Acragas		
11 Olbia		11 Zancle		
12 Lampsacus		12 Catana		

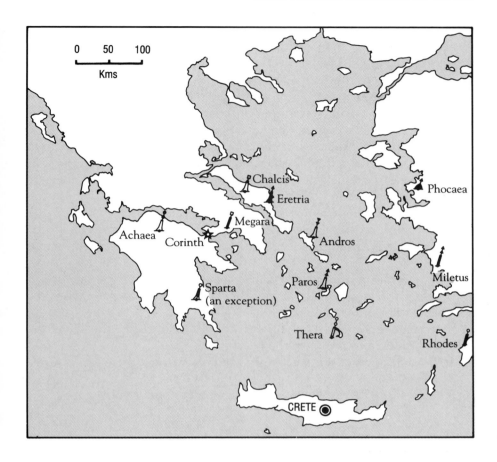

Use of source material

The foundation of Cyrene

Refer to Herodotus, IV:152–3.

Sources

Herodotus gives two versions of the foundation of Cyrene on the coast of North Africa in about 630 B.C. Although some of the facts are dramatised, it is the best account — with the help of a fourth-century inscription — of any early colony.

The colonists came from the island of Thera, and the story begins with the Delphic oracle's order to colonise Libya. The Theraeans did nothing about the oracle's instructions and the island suffered seven years of severe drought, during which 'every tree withered and died'. After a second visit to the oracle, they decided to send out a party representing the seven

Reason for colony

villages in Thera 'and brothers were to draw lots to determine which should join it'. Two fifty-oared galleys transported the colonists, under the leadership of Battus. They settled at first on the offshore island of Plataea, but later moved to the site of Cyrene.

Site

Compulsion

The fourth-century inscription adds that those who refused to go were punished by death and confiscation of property and that those who went were not permitted to return home for five years.

Later prosperity

The community prospered, and in the sixth century new colonists from the Peloponnese and from Dorian lands joined the settlement. By 500 B.C. Cyrene was well equipped with major temples and could compete with mainland cities in buildings and in wealth.

Features of Herodotus' account

Note the following features of Herodotus' account:

1 The Delphic oracle played a part in the decision to colonise.
2 There were difficulties in feeding the population on this small, barren island.
3 The removal of one son per family may indicate that the practice of dividing the land equally among sons had already produced farms too small to support an individual.
4 The number of original colonists was small, indicated by the size of the two ships used to transport them.
5 It was a decision of the state to send the colony, and there was a degree of compulsion.
6 The men probably took wives from among the native inhabitants.

Silver coin from Barca, daughter colony of Cyrene; this face shows a silphium plant, of which the sap was prized as a medicine

A scene from a Spartan vase or cup, called the Arcesilaus vase. King Arcesilaus II of Cyrene (c.569–568) is shown seated. It appears that he is watching the weighing, packing and storing of either wool or silphium, for which Cyrene was famous. The Spartans were linked with Cyrene, since Dorians had colonised Thera, the mother city of Cyrene

The colonisation of Sicily

Refer to Thucydides, VI:2–5.

Thucydides' account of the Sicilian campaign during the Peloponnesian War includes an introductory passage on the colonisation of Italy and Sicily, which began about 750 B. C.

Thucydides on Sicily

Note the following features of Thucydides' account:

1 The God Apollo, consulted at Delphi, was regarded as the divine leader (*archegates*) of the colony — 'there they erected an altar in honour of Apollo the Founder'.

2 Colonists often had to fight for possession of the land — 'the Chalcidians went forth from Naxos [a town in Sicily] and driving out the Sicels by force of arms, founded first Leontini, then Catana'.

Manner of founding colonies

3 The original city nominated a founder for a new venture — 'and 100 years after their own foundation they sent out Pamillus and founded Selinus; he had come from Megara, their own mother state'.

4 Sometimes cities combined to send out colonists — 'Antiphemus of Rhodes and Entimus of Crete came with their followers and together built Gela'.

Map showing the extent of Greek settlement at the end of the colonising period (approximately 6th century)

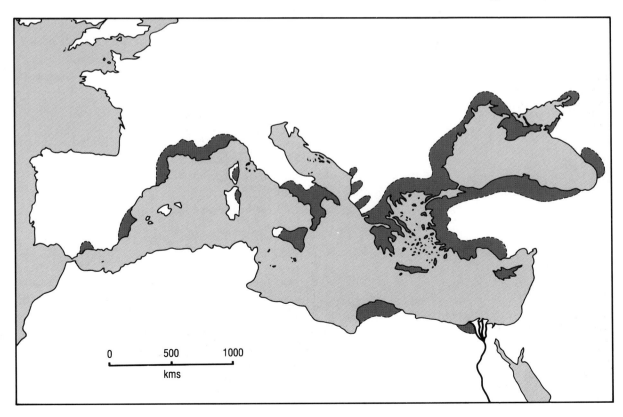

Character of colonies

5 The new state became a replica of the old, introducing the institutions of the original city—'the inhabitants of Gela founded Agrigentum . . . and gave to it their own institutions'.

6 Colonies in turn founded their own colonies, as in the case of Gela, above.

The effects of colonisation

The results of the colonial movement cannot be overestimated, but they must not be seen in the light of a modern economic revolution. The transformation from a primitive agricultural economy to one based on trade, industry and money took three centuries. Even in the fifth century Greece was still largely agricultural.

Economic and social effects

Agriculture

Import of grain

Large expanses of fertile land were found around the shores of the Black Sea, at Cyrene in North Africa, in southern Italy and in Sicily. This encouraged the growth of grain products such as corn and wheat, which were needed to feed the growing population of mainland Greece.

Population pressure eased

Population pressure on the limited land available at home was eased also by the exodus of colonists for these fertile areas.

Breakdown of family tenure

There was a breakdown in the system of family ownership of land. Individuals had their own farms in the colonies and this helped to undermine the custom in Greece of hereditary tenure, which had been partly responsible for the shortage of land.

Large estates of the wealthy

The upper classes, who had involved themselves in trade and industry, invested their growing wealth in more land, building up huge private estates. This monopoly of the best land was often acquired at the expense of the small farmers.

Trade and industry

Control of waterways

Trade grew rapidly as the Greeks gained control of all the important waterways such as the Hellespont and the Bosphorus, which respectively controlled the entrance to the Propontis and the Black Sea. The centres of exchange along the main lines of communication—such as Byzantium, Chalcedon, Potidaea, the Isthmian cities, Corcyra and Syracuse—benefited most.

Raw materials

Products from the forests, lands and mines of the colonies, such as gold, silver and iron, timber, wool, hides, wheat and dried fish, were exchanged

These pictures illustrate stages in the development of pottery

Left: A protogeometric vase, c. tenth century

Right: A geometric funeral krater of the eighth century (Courtesy of the Metropolitan Museum of Art, New York)

Left: An oinochoe from Rhodes (late seventh century)

Right: An Attic amphora, with chariots depicted (c.620)

for finished articles from the homeland. This in turn stimulated the pottery, metalwork and textile industries. The pottery industry (dominated by Corinth, Athens and Aegina) boomed, as containers were needed for oil, wine and grain and there was an increasing market for the finer vases of Corinth and Athens. Bronze armour and metal utensils from Corinth, swords from Chalcis and jewellery from Ionia were in demand, as were the fine woollen textiles from Miletus. In addition, shipbuilding kept pace with trade.

Industry: pottery, metalwork, textiles

35

Slavery

Free labour

There had already been a limited type of slavery of the domestic type in Greece, but now the need for cheap labour—in industry, in the mines and on the large properties of the rich—resulted in a highly profitable slave trade. The slaves came from among those captured or subjugated by the colonists in their conflicts with the native populations. The use of slaves worsened the position of the free peasant farmers, as they could not compete with slave labour, and it encouraged the growth of luxury among the upper classes, so widening the gap between the two groups. The lower the poor freeman sank, the more he was at the mercy of the greedy landlord class.

Free farmers further disadvantaged

Coinage

First coins from Lydia

The usual method of exchange until the seventh century B. C. was barter, usually in the form of metal bars. With the increase in trade between the kingdom of Lydia in Asia Minor and the Ionian cities along the coast, a more satisfactory means of exchange was needed. Coins made of electrum (a natural compound of gold and silver) were stamped, guaranteeing their quality and weight.

Aeginetan and Euboic standards

The use of coinage spread throughout the regions bordering the Aegean Sea, where two standards of silver currency came into use: that of Aegina and Euboea. Although the Aeginetan coinage was the first to appear, the Euboic standard had the wider circulation.

An early coin from seventh-century Corinth: A silver stater (4 drachmas), showing Pegasus and the swastika

Coins from Magna Graecia (Sicily and southern Italy): (a) coin from Taras (2-drachma piece) shows the interest of the colony in the sea and fishing—on one side the patron god of the city rides a dolphin, while the other side features a sea horse and a shell; (b) a freshwater crab from Acragas; (c) a cockerel from Himera; (d) a four-horse chariot, with winged goddess, from Syracuse

One of the earliest coins from Lydia in Asia Minor, made of electrum (a natural alloy of gold and silver)

Coinage facilitated trade and industry, but widened the gap between rich and poor. Money was easier to accumulate than goods, and the wealthy classes began hoarding the relatively scarce coins and profiteering at the expense of the poor classes. The rich would buy up large amounts of corn when there was a glut, hold on to it until there was a shortage, and then sell it at a profit. The use of credit grew, and the wealthy charged very high rates of interest (18–30 per cent). The small farmer became hopelessly in debt to the wealthy, and because the law of debt was extremely harsh the wretched peasant, in a bad year, could be forced to part with his land and his household goods; he might perhaps even barter away his freedom and become enslaved.

Trade made easier

Hoarding and speculation by rich

Harsh debt laws

Changes in social classes

Economic development caused a change in the whole social system from one in which there were two classes, the nobility and peasants, to one in which a third class emerged. The nobility was undermined by the emergence of the 'new rich'. Wealthy traders invested in land and intermarried with impoverished noble families, creating a system in which wealth in general counted more than birth. As Theognis, the sixth-century Megarian poet, complained: 'wealth mixes the classes'.

Emergence of the 'new rich'

Commercial rivalry

Fierce competition and strife between city-states forced cities to make alliances in accordance with their trade interests, and sometimes economic rivalry broke into open warfare. The Lelantine War of the seventh century began as a minor land dispute between Eretria and Chalcis and developed into a general war involving much of Greece.

Economic alliances and disputes

Cultural and political effects

Hellenic culture spread throughout the Mediterranean. The Greeks took with them their institutions, religion, art, alphabet, philosophy and poetry, and much of this culture was assimilated by the people of the Black Sea regions, North Africa, Italy and Spain. As the Greeks made contact with these so-called barbarians, they realised and appreciated the bonds that united them as Hellenes. Yet there was some enrichment of Hellenic culture from contact with the people of the colonial areas; for example, art and literature became bolder in expression.

Awareness of Greek nationality

Exchange of ideas and culture

The stage was set for political and social revolution, as class conflicts became inevitable. Where reform did not occur, or where it was unsuccessful, the aristocratic governments were overthrown, in some cases by tyrants.

Class conflicts and tyrants

This Athenian oinochoe, made about 520, reveals the contact between the Greeks and the people of Africa (Courtesy of Museum of Fine Arts, Boston)

The temple at Paestum (Posidonia) in southern Italy

Essay topics

1 Choose three colonies, each one from a different part of the Mediterranean, and explain why they were founded and by which city; give some details of their character and development. Include some information taken directly from ancient source material.

2 In what ways did the cities of Greece benefit from colonisation? Did all groups share equally in the growing prosperity which resulted from the colonial movement? Explain.

Further reading

Primary sources

Herodotus. *The Histories*, II:154, 178; IV:150–9, 162–7, 200–5.
Thucydides. *The Peloponnesian War*, VI:2–5, I:24–7, 36.

Secondary sources

Boardman, J. *The Greeks Overseas.*
Burn, A. R. *The Lyric Age of Greece.*
Bury, J. B. & Meiggs, R. *A History of Greece.*
Finley, M. I. *Early Greece – the Bronze and Archaic Ages.*
Graham, A. J. *Colony and Mother City in Ancient Greece.*
Hammond, N. G. L. *A History of Greece to 322 B. C.*, pp. 109–24.
Kitto, H. D. F. *The Greeks*, pp. 79–90.

Greek tyrants of the seventh and sixth centuries B.C.

3

The nature of tyranny

Character of tyrannies varied from 7th to 4th centuries

TYRANNY, in the Greek world, was a recurring form of government, but it did not always have the same character. The first tyrants of the seventh and sixth centuries, with which we are concerned in this chapter, were welcomed as leaders of revolt against aristocratic governments, while the later tyrants of Asia Minor and Sicily conformed more to the modern meaning of the term.

Later prejudice against tyranny

Tyrants have received unfavourable treatment from their biographers, who were either aristocratic in sympathy or exhibited the prejudice of later democracies, when it had become normal practice to hate tyrants.

Source material limited

Source material for this period is limited, and there are no contemporary historians or documents. Poets (who were more concerned with their personal feelings) and artists are our chief sources for the seventh and

40

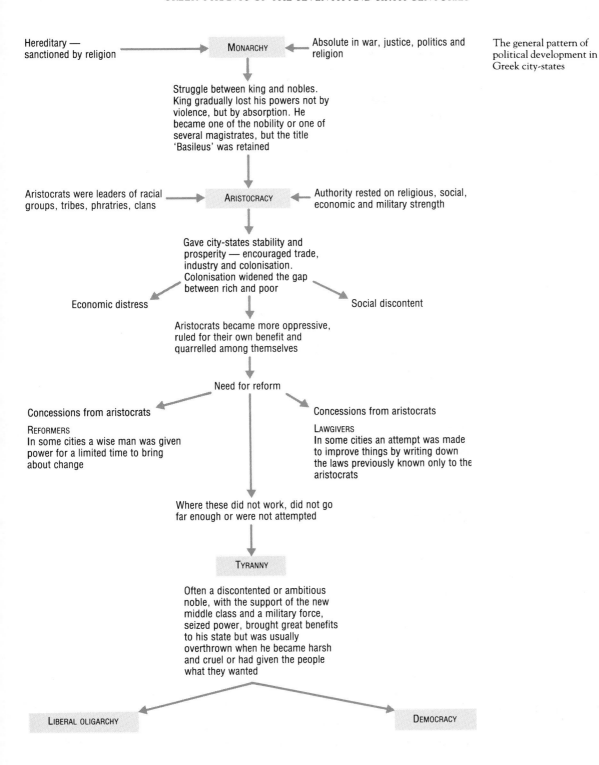

Hereditary — sanctioned by religion → **MONARCHY** ← Absolute in war, justice, politics and religion

The general pattern of political development in Greek city-states

Struggle between king and nobles. King gradually lost his powers not by violence, but by absorption. He became one of the nobility or one of several magistrates, but the title 'Basileus' was retained

Aristocrats were leaders of racial groups, tribes, phratries, clans → **ARISTOCRACY** ← Authority rested on religious, social, economic and military strength

Gave city-states stability and prosperity — encouraged trade, industry and colonisation. Colonisation widened the gap between rich and poor

Economic distress

Social discontent

Aristocrats became more oppressive, ruled for their own benefit and quarrelled among themselves

Need for reform

Concessions from aristocrats

REFORMERS
In some cities a wise man was given power for a limited time to bring about change

Concessions from aristocrats

LAWGIVERS
In some cities an attempt was made to improve things by writing down the laws previously known only to the aristocrats

Where these did not work, did not go far enough or were not attempted

TYRANNY

Often a discontented or ambitious noble, with the support of the new middle class and a military force, seized power, brought great benefits to his state but was usually overthrown when he became harsh and cruel or had given the people what they wanted

LIBERAL OLIGARCHY

DEMOCRACY

41

sixth centuries. Herodotus gives a relatively clear picture of sixth-century tyrants such as Pisistratus, but his account of earlier examples, like Cypselus, is confused with legend and folklore. Thucydides is brief and selective, while the fourth-century philosophers, Plato and Aristotle, see tyranny in terms of their own day.

Definition of 'tyrannos'

Tyrannos — nonhereditary sole rule

The word *tyrannos* was originally a neutral one, which was used as a synonym for 'king', but it described a ruler who had no hereditary right to the power he seized. The term did not imply any judgment about the tyrant as a person or the quality of his rule. This concept probably changed with the second generation of tyrants.

Features of a tyrant

The following points can be used to describe a tyrant:

- He was generally a usurper.
- He seized power with popular support and some military force.
- He had no lawful authority to rule.
- He was an autocrat.
- He provided strong and more effective government.
- He was not necessarily an oppressor or a wicked ruler.

Note that although Pisistratus of Athens conforms in many ways to the general pattern of tyrants described here, he will be dealt with in the chapter on Athens.

Table 3.1 Early tyrants

Mainland Greece

The Isthmus			Athens
Corinth	*Sicyon*	*Megara*	
Cypselus Periander Psammetichus	Orthagoras Myron Cleisthenes	Theagenes	Pisistratus Hipparchus Hippias

Asiatic Greece

Asia Minor	
Samos	*Miletus*
Polycrates	Thrasybulus

Reasons tyrants came to power

Aristocratic rule

The cities of Greece were ruled by aristocrats, whose claim to the authority to govern was based on their quality as the *aristoi* (best men), their monopoly of the political machine, their control of the law and religion and their military strength. They also provided the cavalry, and were a class of privileged experts.

However, the colonial movement brought about great economic changes which the aristocrats were unable to control, and as the old order broke down they were faced with an internal crisis. Thucydides says that in general tyrannies were established in city-states as revenues were increasing, when Greece was becoming more powerful and progressing in the acquisition of wealth; it was in the Isthmian cities of Corinth, Megara and Sicyon, on the main trade routes to the east and west, that commercial expansion was greatest and new developments most acutely felt.

Economic changes broke down the old order

Economic changes

Many traders grew very rich, but were outside the circle of the aristocracy. They felt their wealth entitled them to political privileges. They became ambitious, and were impatient of the aristocratic monopoly of political power, especially the control of the leadership positions in the city-states.

New 'middle' class make demands

The new prosperity was reflected in a change in warfare. The method of hand-to-hand fighting used by the aristocracy was replaced by that of the new massed phalanx of heavily armed hoplites. The new 'middle' class could now afford the hoplite armour and weapons, and the phalanx tactics depended on discipline and effective cooperation. This new development was bound to lessen the importance of the nobles and gave the 'middle'

New form of warfare — hoplites

Hoplites in phalanx formation — detail from a Corinthian oinochoe referred to as the Chigi vase (c.650–625)

class the means by which to claim a share of power in the state. It can be no coincidence that tyrannies first came into being a generation or so after the introduction of hoplites.

Position of poorer classes deteriorated

The poorer class — the mass of the working farmers — found their position had worsened with the general increase in wealth. The nobles became greedier at their expense and the law of debt reduced many to serfdom. Under such laws, a person who could not repay his debts could forfeit his freedom.

Oppression by aristocrats

As the aristocracies were challenged, their reaction to criticism was to use their power arbitrarily, for their own advantage, and greater harshness and oppression occurred. Their government became increasingly remote and incompetent.

There was considerable infighting among the aristocrats for power and honour. This lack of unity provided the opportunity for seizure of power by a tyrant.

Methods by which tyrants seized and maintained power

The Cypselids of Corinth

A herm of Periander, bearing the inscription 'Periander of Corinth, son of Cypselus: practice is everything'

Cypselus of Corinth is believed to have been a commander of the army, or 'polemarch', and because of the fairness of his decisions, he became popular. He killed the leader of the ruling clan, the Bacchiads, and exiled the remainder of the clan, who took refuge in Corcyra. According to Aristotle, he did not need a bodyguard during his thirty-year reign.

His son Periander ruled for forty-four years, but was more militant and kept a bodyguard 300 strong. Periander's government was not automatically welcomed as his father's had been and he grew suspicious, and jealous of opposition. This is seen in his reaction to the advice of his friend and ally, Thrasybulus of Miletus, concerning the cutting down of the stalks of wheat that were taller than the rest. (Refer to Herodotus, V:92.) However, a bodyguard of 300 would not have been enough to protect him if he had not had the goodwill of the majority of the people.

Little is known of Orthagoras of Sicyon, but it is believed he gained power after a career in the army during which he distinguished himself in a frontier war with Pellene in Achaea, an achievement for which he was made general. He then overthrew the Heraclid aristocracy. His rule was moderate and peaceful, and he kept all the laws.

Cleisthenes, the third of the tyrants of Sicyon, seized power from his brother and gained popular support. The Orthagorids tried to give a constitutional appearance to their rule, according to Aristotle, and they roused the national spirit of their people.

Theagenes of Megara

The main reference we have to Theagenes of Megara (c.640 B.C.) is that he obtained a bodyguard and slaughtered the cattle of the rich. His daughter married Cylon, an Athenian who tried with the help of Megarian troops to seize control of Athens about 632 B.C.

In 535 Polycrates, tyrant of Samos, seized the citadel with fifteen hoplites and, as Herodotus says, 'at the outset had divided his realm into three and gone shares with his brothers, Pantagnotus and Sylosan; later, however, he killed the former and banished the latter (the younger of the two) and held the whole island himself'.[1]

Polycrates of Samos

Contributions of tyrants to their cities

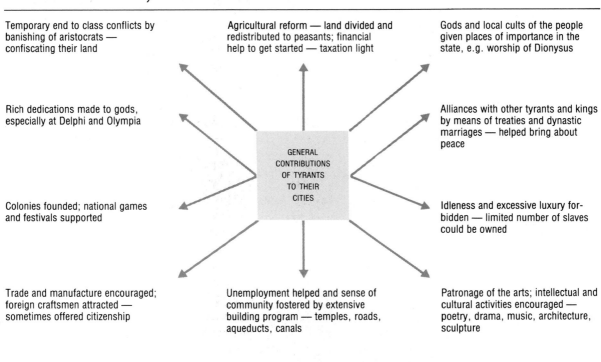

Temporary end to class conflicts by banishing of aristocrats — confiscating their land

Agricultural reform — land divided and redistributed to peasants; financial help to get started — taxation light

Gods and local cults of the people given places of importance in the state, e.g. worship of Dionysus

Rich dedications made to gods, especially at Delphi and Olympia

Alliances with other tyrants and kings by means of treaties and dynastic marriages — helped bring about peace

GENERAL CONTRIBUTIONS OF TYRANTS TO THEIR CITIES

Colonies founded; national games and festivals supported

Idleness and excessive luxury forbidden — limited number of slaves could be owned

Trade and manufacture encouraged; foreign craftsmen attracted — sometimes offered citizenship

Unemployment helped and sense of community fostered by extensive building program — temples, roads, aqueducts, canals

Patronage of the arts; intellectual and cultural activities encouraged — poetry, drama, music, architecture, sculpture

NOTE: Not every tyrant carried out all of the above. Our knowledge of many tyrannies is limited, but most of these points would have been a feature of the Cypselid and Pisistratid tyrannies.

Dedications to the gods, and national festivals

Both Cypselus and Periander made rich dedications at Delphi and Olympia to win the approval of the gods for their rule, and Periander instituted the worship of Dionysus, and organised the Isthmian Games.

Orthagoras sacrificed on behalf of the state in his capacity as chief priest, dedicated at Olympia, and supported Delphi in a sacred war with

Regimes sanctified by dedications

A hammered bowl found at Olympia and engraved with the words 'The sons of Kyselos [Cypselus] dedicated this bowl from Herakleia'; it was probably offered to the gods in thanks for a successful expedition (Courtesy of Museum of Fine Arts, Boston)

the port of Crisa, through which pilgrims going to Delphi passed. Cleisthenes brought this war to a successful conclusion, and then celebrated the Pythian Games at Delphi.

According to Thucydides, Polycrates 'conquered a number of the islands, among which was Rhenea, which he dedicated to the Delian Apollo'.[2]

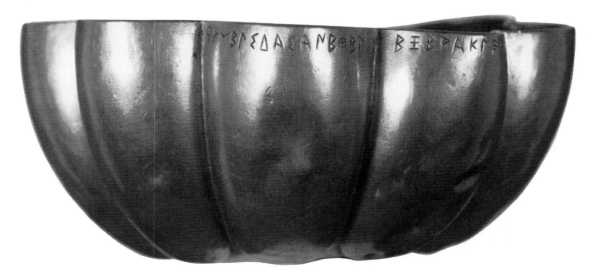

Agriculture, trade and industry

Land distribution and moderate taxation

Little is known of Cypselus' domestic policy, but he distributed land among his supporters, was moderate in his taxation, and introduced a new standard of currency based on the form used by Samos rather than that used by Aegina.

The pottery industry

Periander raised revenue from tolls on traffic passing through Corinth; also, the pottery industry flourished at this time. Corinthian potters could not keep up with demand. Roof tiles were invented and terracotta slabs for decoration of brick and timber temples were exported, prefabricated, from Corinth.

Buildings

Temples, roads, tunnels, harbours

Under Cypselus the first stone temples were built, and Periander laid a roadway, the *diolkos*, for hauling ships across the Isthmus.

Cleisthenes of Sicyon constructed a colonnade, while Polycrates of Samos has been described as 'the most magnificent of tyrants' because of his ambitious building program. This included the construction of a tunnel, by Eupalinus of Megara, to bring water to the city. The architect,

46

An example of the type of
Black Figure pottery
produced under Cypselus and
Periander, for export
(c.615–600)

The diolkos built across the
Isthmus for dragging cargo
ships from the Saronic Gulf
to the Corinthian Gulf

Rhoikos, was also employed by Polycrates to build a magnificent temple to Hera and a huge breakwater provided Samos with an adequate harbour. Theagenes of Megara built a tunnelled water-supply system and a pillared fountain.

The arts

Lavish court life

Periander maintained an elaborate court, where he entertained artists such as the poet and musician, Arion of Methymna. According to Herodotus, Arion was 'the most distinguished musician of that date, and the man who first, so far as we know, composed and named the dithyramb and trained choirs to perform it in Corinth'.[3] The dithyramb was a choral chant to Dionysus and influenced the birth of tragedy. The Doric and Ionic styles of architecture were also promoted.

Origin of tragedy in Corinth

School of sculpture in Sicyon

Artists attracted to the court of Cleisthenes included Dipoenus and Scyllus of Crete, who founded a leading school of sculpture in marble. Cleisthenes spent lavishly when he entertained. Thirteen suitors — from all parts of the Mediterranean — entered a competition for his daughter's hand in marriage, and he supposedly entertained them for one year. One negative aspect of Cleisthenes' attitude to the arts was related to his hatred of Argos. He forbade the recital of the Homeric Cycle because it depicted Argive princes as heroes.

Poets in Samos

Ibycus, a poet from Rhegium in Italy, and Anacreon from Teos in Ionia settled at Polycrates' court. Gem cutting also was an art practised in Samos and Herodotus tells us the story of the engraved ring which Polycrates valued above all else.

Foreign policy

Cypselus keeps peace

Cypselus maintained peace both at home and abroad, but he kept a check on the exiled Bacchiads on the island of Corcyra by founding the three colonies of Leucas, Ambracia and Anactorium, under the governorships of his three illegitimate sons. These colonies also safeguarded the trade route to Italy and Sicily. He made an alliance with Thrasybulus of Miletus and married his (Cypselus') son Periander to the daughter of the tyrant of Epidaurus, Procles.

Marriage alliance

Colonies

Periander was more warlike and maintained a fleet of warships in both the Adriatic and Aegean Seas, as well as adding to Corinth's colonial empire — Apollonia and Illyrica in the west and Potidaea in the northern Aegean. These colonies controlled the trade route to the east from the Adriatic, across northern Greece and Thrace. He conquered Corcyra and there installed his son Lycophon. Despite his marriage alliance with Procles of Epidaurus, Periander later dispossessed him. His close friendship with Thrasybulus of Miletus assisted Corinthian traders in Egypt and the Black Sea. He maintained relations with non-Greek rulers such as Alyattes

Good relations with other rulers

of Lydia, and when the Lydians wanted to dedicate at Delphi, they used the Corinthian treasury.

Cleisthenes made allies by offering military aid and was probably the first to develop a navy in Sicyon. His chief efforts in foreign policy were towards north and south, rather than east and west. He was warlike, and noted for his vigorous opposition to Argos. It has been suggested that his was a tyranny of racial prejudice. In his hatred of Argos he went so far as to remove the remains of an Argive hero from a shrine in the market place of Sicyon and to change the names of all the tribes of Sicyon which were the same as those of Argos. *Cleisthenes' opposition to Argos*

Polycrates, according to Herodotus, had a fleet of 100 fifty-oared galleys with a force of one thousand bowmen; he captured many islands and a number of towns on the mainland as well. He was the leader of those resisting their rulers, and gave hope of protection to all his neighbours! 'He concluded a pact of friendship with Amasis, king of Egypt, sealing it with a mutual exchange of presents.'[4] Amasis sent 'to the goddess Hera in Samos, two likenesses of himself in wood . . .'.[5] *Naval conquests by Polycrates*

Overthrow of the tyrannies

Periander, towards the end of his reign, revealed the brutality and oppressiveness typical of tyrants as we understand them. He murdered his wife in a fit of rage; one of his sons died in raising a revolution against him and his youngest son died at the hands of the people of Corcyra. He took his revenge, killing fifty of the ringleaders and sending 300 youths to become eunuchs at the court of Alyattes of Lydia. His successor was his nephew Psammetichus, who was assassinated (582) only a few years after becoming tyrant of Corinth. The houses of the Cypselids were razed to the ground until not a vestige of the hated tyranny was left. The priests at Delphi issued a statement that the oracle had warned that disaster would come from the offspring of Labda and Aetion.[6] *Periander's brutality*

Last of Cypselids assassinated

By 555 the successors and family of Cleisthenes were driven from Sicyon and Delphi again denounced the tyranny. *Orthagorids driven out*

Theagenes of Megara did not establish a dynasty. He married his daughter to Cylon of Athens who, with the help of Theagenes, attempted to seize power in Athens. When he failed, the Megarians threw out Theagenes. An aristocratic oligarchy took over, but shortly afterwards was replaced by a democratic regime. *Theagenes overthrown*

Polycrates was murdered—not by his subjects but by Oroetes, the Persian governor of Sardis, incited by another Persian governor. Herodotus says that Polycrates' ambition—he 'was the first Greek we know of to plan the dominion of the sea'—caused him to be lured to his death.[7] *Polycrates murdered*

The weaknesses of tyranny

Tyrannies shortlived; rarely survived second generation

1 The existence of tyranny depended on the personal qualities of the tyrant.
2 The tyrant was not the only ambitious and capable person in his state, but there was no place for others in this form of government.
3 The only form political rivalry could take was that of conspiracy and assassination.
4 Tyranny involved, at some point, restrictions on freedom; once it had gained for the people what they wanted, they would not tolerate it. Usually in the second generation — at the latest in the third — the tyrant was assassinated or overthrown, or he abdicated. The form of government that followed varied from state to state.

Writing assignment

Write no more than half a page on each of the following:
1 Explain how a rapid influx of wealth helped the rise of tyrants to power, particularly in the cities of the Isthmus.
2 Explain in detail what changes occurred in weapons, armour and style of fighting in the seventh century. To what extent was this related to the rise of tyrants in this period?
3 Why were there very few dynasties established by tyrants?

Essay topic

With reference to at least *two* tyrants, outline the contributions each made to his city.

Further reading

Primary sources

Herodotus. *The Histories*, V:66–70, 90–6; III:39–43, 119–22; VI:127–33.
Thucydides. *The Peloponnesian War*, 1:12–16.

Secondary sources

Andrewes, A. *The Greek Tyrants*.
Burn, A. R. *The Lyric Age of Greece*.
Bury, J. B. & Meiggs, R. *A History of Greece*.
Hammond, N. G. L. *A History of Greece to 322 B.C.*
Kitto, H. D. F. *The Greeks*.
Ure, P. N. *Origin of Tyranny*.

4 Sparta

The land of Sparta
Spartan development to the sixth century B.C.
Spartan society
The Spartan education system
The Spartan army
Spartan government
The Peloponnesian League

Spartan system intrigued ancient Greeks

THE SPARTANS have intrigued and mystified both ancient and modern scholars. Their secretiveness, tough discipline and un-questioning obedience to the state astonished their contemporaries. Their courage and military achievements were admired and their well-balanced constitution received approval even from Aristotle, who had some severe things to say about Sparta. Those who disapproved of democracy were loud in their praises for the Spartan form of government, although it was never imitated. Spartan women were unique in their training, appearance and influence, but were often criticised for their unruly conduct and self-indulgence, while many Spartan customs were misunderstood and shocked the rest of Greece. The Spartan system was interpreted in a variety of ways and brought reactions which ranged from enthusiastic commendation to severe disapproval.

Misunderstandings about them

It is important to remember that although the Spartan system was rigid, it did undergo changes: in the organisation and composition of the army, in land tenure, in the position of women and in the economy. These changes occurred predominantly in the fifth and fourth centuries and must be taken into account when comparing Sparta with Athens in the fifth century. The position of women in Spartan society is a good example of this.

Some changes occurred from the 6th to the 4th century

52

Sources

Despite the reasonable amount of source material available, there is very little that can be said about Sparta with complete certainty, and in fact many questions about Sparta's economic, social and political way of life can only be answered with probabilities.

There is little information about Sparta in the eighth and seventh centuries except that drawn from archaeological evidence and from legendary material related by Pausanias (Books 3 and 4) and the latter's record is questionable. The closest contemporary source was the poet Tyrtaeus, who lived at the time of the second Messenian war in the seventh century, but of his patriotic poems only fragments survive. Two other poets, Alcman from Lydia and Terpander from Lesbos, are helpful for this period.

From the seventh to the early fifth century, no author's works about Sparta have survived. In the fifth century Herodotus and Thucydides recorded valuable information about Sparta in the time of the Persian and Peloponnesian Wars, but much of it deals with foreign relations.

Of the fourth century sources Xenophon, Plato and Aristotle are the most noteworthy. Plato and Aristotle discuss the Spartan system with reference to their own political philosophies. Plato idealised the Spartan constitution and it is mainly due to him that the myth of Sparta arose.

Plutarch, who lived from A.D. 46 to 120, wrote *The Life of Lycurgus*, which is essential reading for anyone interested in Sparta. However, when writing about Lycurgus he was greatly influenced by the careers of two later Spartan kings of the third century, and it is believed that his history transfers third-century conditions to the early days of Sparta's history.

None of these authors knew very much about early Sparta; indeed, they knew very little about the way the Spartan system worked in their own times.

Lycurgus

According to Plutarch and other ancient sources, the Spartan system (social code, military and land system and political constitution) was the work of a lawgiver called Lycurgus, about whom little was known.

Plutarch begins his account of the life of Lycurgus with the words:

> There is so much uncertainty in the accounts which historians have left us of Lycurgus, the lawgiver of Sparta, that scarcely anything is asserted by one of them which is not called into question or contradicted by the rest.[1]

H. Michel believes it is safe to say that not a single statement in Plutarch's work 'can be accepted with certainty and that even the very existence of Lycurgus is strongly open to doubt'.[2] A. Andrewes says that 'if there was a real Lycurgus we know nothing of him'.[3] Perhaps he was

Sources few and unreliable

Little information for the 8th and 7th centuries

Herodotus and Thucydides in the 5th century

Xenophon, Plato and Aristotle in the 4th century

Plutarch important, but with much erroneous information

Lycurgus the lawgiver

His existence is open to doubt

just a name to the Spartans and when a crisis occurred in the seventh century, 'the reformers represented their reforms as the restoration of the neglected laws of this Lycurgus'.[4]

Ancient origin of many aspects of Spartan life

If he did exist, we still cannot take seriously the view that the whole way of life of Sparta, and its constitution, were the work of Lycurgus, since many of its features can be traced to earlier times. Segregation of the sexes, separation of boys and young men into age groups, communal meals and education under strict supervision were all customs inherited from an earlier period. The structure of the government — except for the dual kingship — developed from the type of government that was very common in ninth and eighth century Greece.

The land of Sparta

The descriptive maps on pages 55 and 56 clearly illustrate the advantages of Sparta's position in the Peloponnese.

Spartan development to the sixth century — an overview

Before 900

The Dorian presence was evident in Laconia at the end of the eleventh century. Four adjacent villages were founded on the west bank of the Eurotas River.

900

Synoecism ('amalgamation' or 'joining together') saw these villages united as a single city — Sparta.

The system of dual kingship evolved.

800

The Spartan attempt to control Laconia was slow — a fifth village was incorporated into the city of Sparta.

750

Sparta became master of all Laconia; survivors from pre-Dorian times were reduced to the status of serfs (helots), and other Dorian settlements were made politically subordinate to Sparta (perioeci).

Sparta conquered Messenia — an alternative to colonisation. Messenians were also reduced to the status of serfs.

A constitutional crisis occurred between kings and aristocracy, and the council, or gerousia, was formed. Plutarch says:

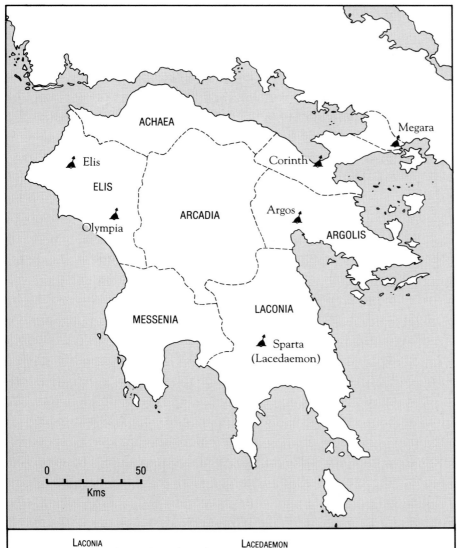

Map of the Peloponnese

LACONIA
- name given to the territory of Sparta
- over 4000 sq.km
- greater part is mountainous
- fertile Eurotas valley

MESSENIA
- milder and moister climate than Laconia
- larger and more fertile plain

LACEDAEMON
- Dorians of Laconia and of the towns of the *perioeci* were together referred to in ancient times as Lacedaemonians
- in common usage, Lacedaemon/ Lacedaemonians came to mean the same as Sparta/Spartans

Sparta's position in the
Peloponnese

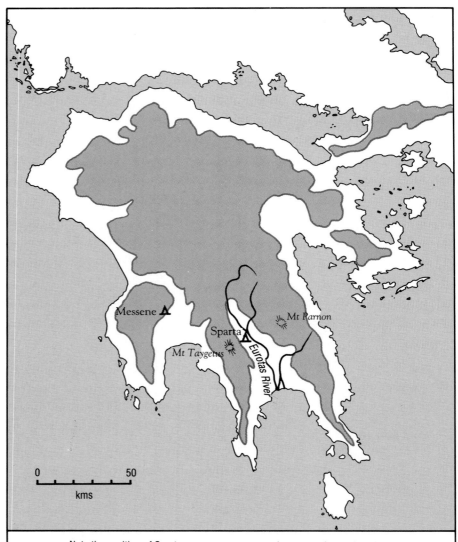

Note the position of Sparta:
- in the fertile Eurotas valley
- surrounded by steep, high and
  continuous mountain ranges —
  Taygetus (west), Parnon (east),
  Arcadian Mts (north)
- rugged sea coast in south and
  east
- all principal passes into Laconia
  leading to Sparta; the strength of
  its frontiers shows their
  advantages for defence without
  need of a city wall

Amongst the many changes and alterations which Lycurgus made, the first and of greatest importance was the establishment of the Council which having power equal to the kings in matters of great consequence... gave steadiness and safety to the Commonwealth.[5]

Taras, in Southern Italy, was founded by Sparta in about 707.

700

This was a period of great prosperity in Sparta — ceramics, sculpture, architecture, music and poetry flourished, and trade with the east was widespread.

650

Now occurred the second Messenian war — the Messenians revolted, with the support of other Peloponnesian states. During the seventeen-year-long conflict Tyrtaeus, a poet from Ionia, inspired the Spartans with his martial poems and songs.

> Rise ye sons of heroic Sparta, ye sons of warrior fathers
> With your shield on the left protect you
> And with your right your spear hurl boldly
> Spare not in the least your lifeblood
> For this is not like to Spartans![6]

Sparta defeated the Messenians, and with this she reached the limit of her territorial expansion. The Spartiate population now made up less than one-twentieth of the total. The population of Messenia was enslaved and the land divided into *kleroi*, or allotments for Spartans.

A second constitutional crisis arose between nobles and commons, to bring about 'democratic changes'. Tyrtaeus speaks of the proper ordering of the state:

> They heard the voice of Phoebus and brought hence from Pytho, oracles of the God... The beginnings of counsel shall belong to the god honoured kings... and to the men of elder birth; after them shall the Commons answering them back with forthright ordinances, both say things honourable and do all that is right... so shall the common people have victory and might.[7]

600

Changes appeared in the Spartan way of life — the practice of austerity, devotion to duty, and iron discipline. Foreign imports practically ceased. There were signs of decay in Laconian art. To quote Plutarch once again: 'In the next place, he [Lycurgus] declared an outlawry of all needless and superfluous arts'.[8]

550

Sparta won military successes against Tegea and Argos; her defeat of Argos placed her at the head of a loose confederacy of all Peloponnesian states except Achaea and Argos.

Sparta's policy changed — to political domination by alliances rather than by gaining new territory.

Ephors became supreme (a democratic institution). They fought against tyranny, and were a check on the kings.

Spartan society

The figures which follow demonstrate, in diagrammatic form, aspects of Spartan society — its structure, rights of citizenship, conditions pertaining to the various classes, and the place in society of Spartan women.

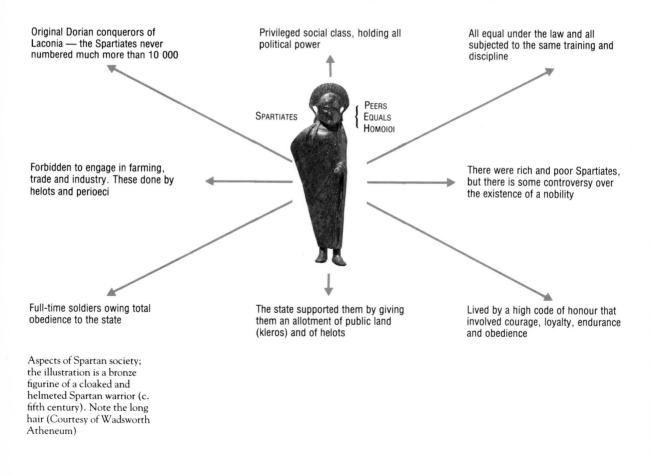

Original Dorian conquerors of Laconia — the Spartiates never numbered much more than 10 000

Privileged social class, holding all political power

All equal under the law and all subjected to the same training and discipline

SPARTIATES

PEERS
EQUALS
HOMOIOI

Forbidden to engage in farming, trade and industry. These done by helots and perioeci

There were rich and poor Spartiates, but there is some controversy over the existence of a nobility

Full-time soldiers owing total obedience to the state

The state supported them by giving them an allotment of public land (kleros) and of helots

Lived by a high code of honour that involved courage, loyalty, endurance and obedience

Aspects of Spartan society; the illustration is a bronze figurine of a cloaked and helmeted Spartan warrior (c. fifth century). Note the long hair (Courtesy of Wadsworth Atheneum)

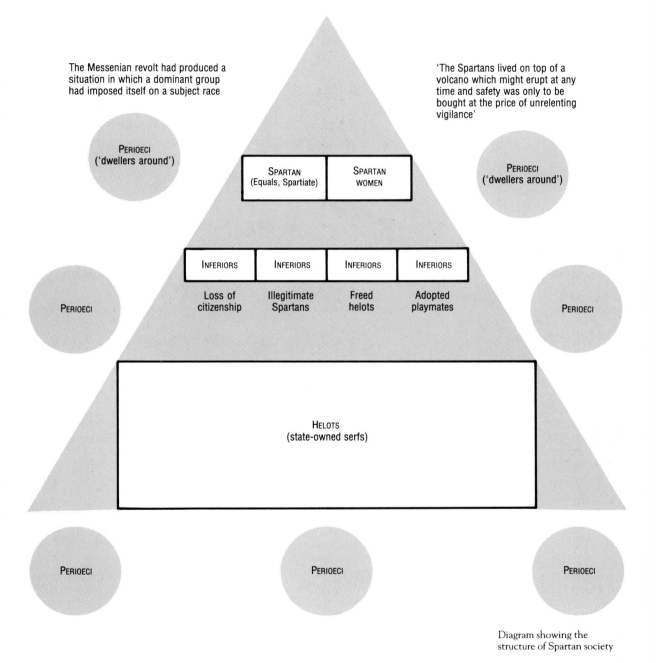

The Messenian revolt had produced a situation in which a dominant group had imposed itself on a subject race

'The Spartans lived on top of a volcano which might erupt at any time and safety was only to be bought at the price of unrelenting vigilance'

PERIOECI ('dwellers around')

PERIOECI ('dwellers around')

SPARTAN (Equals, Spartiate)

SPARTAN WOMEN

PERIOECI

PERIOECI

INFERIORS

INFERIORS

INFERIORS

INFERIORS

Loss of citizenship

Illegitimate Spartans

Freed helots

Adopted playmates

HELOTS (state-owned serfs)

PERIOECI

PERIOECI

PERIOECI

Diagram showing the structure of Spartan society

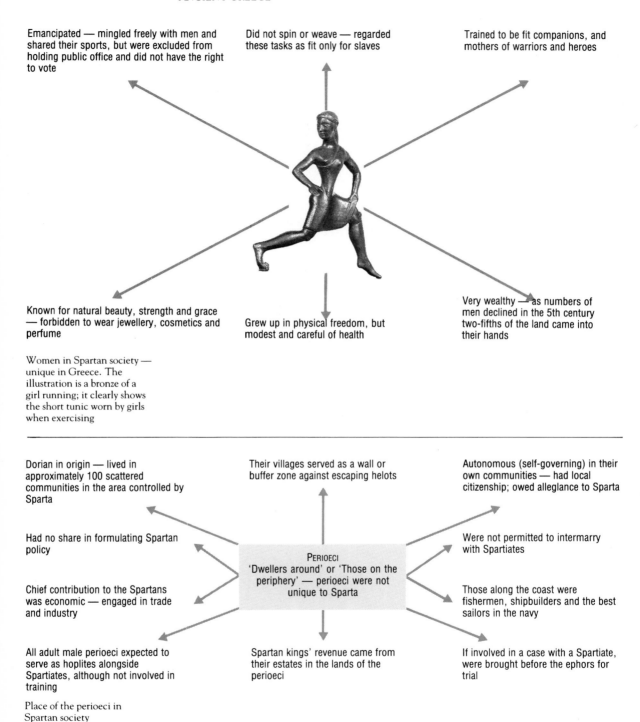

Emancipated — mingled freely with men and shared their sports, but were excluded from holding public office and did not have the right to vote

Did not spin or weave — regarded these tasks as fit only for slaves

Trained to be fit companions, and mothers of warriors and heroes

Known for natural beauty, strength and grace — forbidden to wear jewellery, cosmetics and perfume

Grew up in physical freedom, but modest and careful of health

Very wealthy — as numbers of men declined in the 5th century two-fifths of the land came into their hands

Women in Spartan society — unique in Greece. The illustration is a bronze of a girl running; it clearly shows the short tunic worn by girls when exercising

Dorian in origin — lived in approximately 100 scattered communities in the area controlled by Sparta

Their villages served as a wall or buffer zone against escaping helots

Autonomous (self-governing) in their own communities — had local citizenship; owed allegiance to Sparta

Had no share in formulating Spartan policy

PERIOECI
'Dwellers around' or 'Those on the periphery' — perioeci were not unique to Sparta

Were not permitted to intermarry with Spartiates

Chief contribution to the Spartans was economic — engaged in trade and industry

Those along the coast were fishermen, shipbuilders and the best sailors in the navy

All adult male perioeci expected to serve as hoplites alongside Spartiates, although not involved in training

Spartan kings' revenue came from their estates in the lands of the perioeci

If involved in a case with a Spartiate, were brought before the ephors for trial

Place of the perioeci in Spartan society

60

Write one paragraph in answer to each of the following questions.

1 Explain how the perioeci contributed to Sparta's economy.

2 In what way did they become more important to the Spartans in the fifth century?

3 Why did the perioeci never rebel?

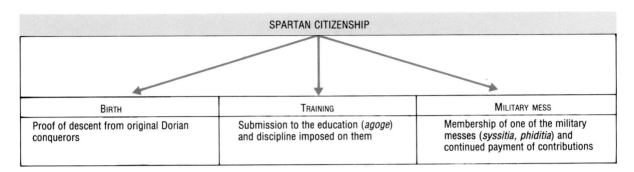

SPARTAN CITIZENSHIP

BIRTH	TRAINING	MILITARY MESS
Proof of descent from original Dorian conquerors	Submission to the education (*agoge*) and discipline imposed on them	Membership of one of the military messes (*syssitia, phiditia*) and continued payment of contributions

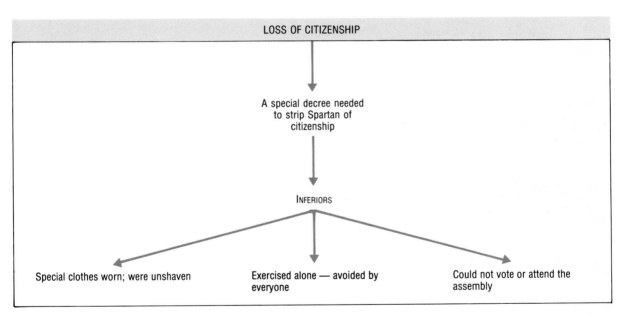

LOSS OF CITIZENSHIP

A special decree needed to strip Spartan of citizenship

INFERIORS

Special clothes worn; were unshaven

Exercised alone — avoided by everyone

Could not vote or attend the assembly

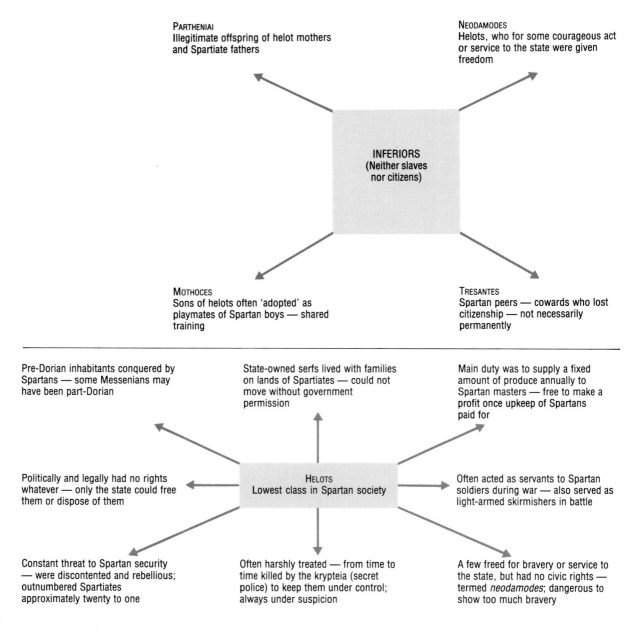

PARTHENIAI
Illegitimate offspring of helot mothers and Spartiate fathers

NEODAMODES
Helots, who for some courageous act or service to the state were given freedom

INFERIORS
(Neither slaves nor citizens)

MOTHOCES
Sons of helots often 'adopted' as playmates of Spartan boys — shared training

TRESANTES
Spartan peers — cowards who lost citizenship — not necessarily permanently

Pre-Dorian inhabitants conquered by Spartans — some Messenians may have been part-Dorian

State-owned serfs lived with families on lands of Spartiates — could not move without government permission

Main duty was to supply a fixed amount of produce annually to Spartan masters — free to make a profit once upkeep of Spartans paid for

Politically and legally had no rights whatever — only the state could free them or dispose of them

HELOTS
Lowest class in Spartan society

Often acted as servants to Spartan soldiers during war — also served as light-armed skirmishers in battle

Constant threat to Spartan security — were discontented and rebellious; outnumbered Spartiates approximately twenty to one

Often harshly treated — from time to time killed by the krypteia (secret police) to keep them under control; always under suspicion

A few freed for bravery or service to the state, but had no civic rights — termed *neodamodes*; dangerous to show too much bravery

Write one paragraph in answer to each of the following questions.

1 Read Plutarch's reference to the *krypteia* and the helots in his *Lycurgus*; explain why this and other accounts of the deeds of the krypteia may have been exaggerated.

2 What does Plutarch say was the annual fixed amount of produce supplied by the helots to their Spartiate masters?

The influence of the helots on Spartan foreign policy

- The Spartans did not encourage foreign contacts or visits.
- They hesitated to undertake military campaigns far from home in case of a helot revolt during the army's absence.
- They supported oligarchies — governments which were controlled by a privileged few — because they feared democracy and its impact on the helots.

The Spartan education system

According to Plutarch, the aim of the Spartan education system was to produce prompt obedience to authority, the ability to endure pain and hardship, and courage and victory in battle. The Spartan poet Tyrtaeus said that the only quality in a man worth admiring was courage.

Aim of Spartan education

Age groups

Spartan boys and youths were divided into age groups, through which the state gradually increased the severity of the training and discipline.

The first six years of a boy's life were spent at home, where discipline was imposed by the mother with the help of a nurse. (Read Plutarch's account in *Lycurgus* of the treatment of newborn babies and the early care given to young children.)

From birth to six at home

In their seventh year the boys were introduced to Spartan discipline when they left home to live in barracks with others of the same age. From this time until they completed their education, they were under the control of a public guardian or supervisor of education, called a *paidonomos*. This post was filled only by Spartans of great repute. A body of youths (about nineteen to twenty years old) with whips assisted him to chastise students for misbehaviour. At no time were the boys without supervision, as any citizen had the right to discipline them if the guardian was absent.

Boys left home in 7th year

Public guardian

In this first period of their education, from six to twelve years, they were gradually introduced to physical skills and hardships. By the age of ten they were taking part in public competitions.

From the end of their twelfth year to the end of their eighteenth year, they were ready to face the rigours of intensive training as a type of cadet soldier, and could be tried out in the army for noncombatant service. Both Plutarch and Xenophon (the latter in his *Constitution of the Lacedae-monians*) describe the discipline imposed on the boys. They were trained to go barefoot at all times in order to run faster, scale heights more easily and clamber down cliffs. The one garment issued to them served all year through, no matter what the weather. They exercised naked, did their

Rigorous training began at thirteen

Harsh conditions imposed to develop skills for war

own housekeeping in the barracks and plucked reeds by hand to make a bed. Small amounts of food were served, as this was intended to make them more able, if necessary, to go without it on a campaign. Stealing food to supplement their diet was acceptable at times, as long as they were not caught. This custom was intended, according to Xenophon, 'to make the boys craftier and more inventive in getting in supplies, while at the same time it cultivated their war-like instincts'.[9]

They developed the ability to depend on themselves, to track, spy and scout. However, if a boy was caught stealing he was punished severely 'as being a sorry bungler in the art'.[10]

Adolescents kept occupied

Xenophon continues by saying that at adolescence, 'when the froth of insolence rises to the surface; when, too, the most violent appetites for Pleasure invade the mind', that was precisely the moment when the state imposed constant labours on the growing youth and devised for him 'a subtle system of absorbing occupations'.[11]

The boys were trained in modesty by being required to observe special rules relating to behaviour in public, such as keeping silent and gazing down at all times when walking through the streets.

Class of eirens permitted to marry

In their nineteenth year, the Spartans entered the class of *eirens*. They were now combatants, but not yet front-line soldiers. From eighteen to twenty they were drilled in a huge school — modelled on the army — and were captained by other youths who had passed their twentieth year but had not yet reached full manhood: this would be attained at thirty. They were permitted to marry at twenty, but still lived full time in the barracks, had no private life and only visited their wives occasionally, in secrecy.

Xenophon explained that the Spartans 'showed a still greater anxiety in dealing with those who had reached the prime of opening manhood'.[12]

Front line combatants from twenty-four years of age

From twenty-four to thirty they were front-line combatants, but not much is known about this class except that it is possible that a picked corps of knights (300) was selected from among them. Three citizens in the prime of life each selected 100 youths, giving reasons for their choice. This was a great honour, but it forced those who were rejected to keep a constant eye on those chosen, to note some slip in the code of honour, and it forced them all to compete and attempt to outdo each other.

Full citizens at thirty years of age

At the end of their thirtieth year, the Spartans became full citizens and had the right to participate in the assembly. They lived no longer in the barracks but at home with their wives and families, although they were expected to dine every night in the public mess. They were now allowed to let their hair grow, as this denoted physical vigour. According to Plutarch, 'they took a great deal of care of their hair', as it made them appear taller, and 'added beauty to a good face, and terror to an ugly one'.[13] Herodotus recounts how, on the eve of the battle of Thermopylae, Leonidas and his 300 Spartans spent time curling and adorning their hair;

Grew hair long when reached manhood

Spartans hunting boars (from a Black Figure Spartan cup, c.550) (Courtesy of Musée du Louvre)

as Xerxes, the Persian king, was informed: 'it is the common practice of the Spartans to pay careful attention to their hair when they are about to risk their lives'.[14] From thirty until sixty years of age the Spartan citizen continued to be liable for military service.

Education of girls

From Plutarch we hear that the education of girls was aimed at producing healthy bodies, so that 'the fruit they conceived might take firmer root and find better growth and that they, with this greater vigour, might be the more able to undergo the pains of childbearing'.[15]

Vigorous physical training for child-bearing

Although girls lived at home, they may have been organised into bands, as were the boys. At times they exercised with the boys, and they participated in most sports: running, wrestling, throwing the javelin and discus, and ball games. One of the most strenuous exercises they performed was called *bibasis* and involved jumping up and down, each time touching their buttocks with their heels. In Aristophanes' play *Lysistrata*, the Spartan women are caricatured in the person of Lampito.

> *Lysistrata*: Welcome Lampito my dear. How are things in Sparta? Darling, you look simply beautiful. Such colour, such resilience! Why, I bet you could throttle a bull.
> *Lampito*: So could you my dear, if you were in training. Don't you know I practise rump jumps every day?
> *Lysistrata*: And such marvellous breasts, too.[16]

Aristophanes' caricature of Spartan women

In the choral and dancing competitions there was just as much rivalry among the girls as among the boys, but it is not certain whether they

Competitions similar to those of the boys

65

danced naked at certain feasts to harden their bodies. According to Plato, the girls of Sparta did not live a trivial life involved with 'wool work', but shared in the gymnastics and music of the boys.

Disadvantages of Spartan education

Spartan training did not produce resilience

The Spartans were taught a way of life. The system of training (*agoge*) was successful in that it achieved a stable city-state and produced courageous and loyal citizens, but it did not encourage resilience to cope with change. During the fourth century it became obvious that the Spartans were unable to adapt satisfactorily to changing conditions.

Public competitions

Enjoyed music

The Spartans enjoyed music. Dancing to the flute or the lyre was done by both boys and girls; however, most of these dances represented battles, military drill or wrestling, or simulated wild animal hunts. Religious dances were also common. Their songs, says Plutarch, 'had a life and spirit in them that enflamed and possessed men's minds with an enthusiasm and ardour for action'.[17]

Singing and dancing competitions

Choral and dancing competitions were held annually. At the Festival of the Gymnopaediae, at which all Spartan males competed, whole battalions of soldiers both old and young sang of their prowess and courage, and of deeds yet to be performed.

Flogging contest

One endurance contest which was notorious was the flogging of the youths at the altar of Artemis Orthia. Frequently boys died during this ceremony, but a statue of honour was erected to the boy who endured the longest. It may have been tied in with initiation and the shedding of blood as a bond between man and god.

Organised games and fights

Once a year two teams of youths, representing Lycurgus and Heracles, were chosen to face each other in combat. They met on an island in a river, having first sacrificed a pup and watched a fight between two boars. The aim of the fight was to drive the opposing team into the river. There were no rules, and kicking, biting and eye-gouging were allowed. The purpose of this is not known, but all fighting in Sparta was organised.

An annual ball game in which there were teams of fifteen seemed to have as its sole object possession of the ball at the end of the game; this could be achieved by any method.

The public messes

These public meals have been called by a variety of names — among them *syssitia* (singular: *syssition*) and *phiditia* (singular: *phidition*).

Plutarch said that these common meals were devised by Lycurgus to strike a blow at luxury, since both rich and poor shared the same meal.

Origin of public messes (syssitia)

Xenophon maintained that Lycurgus invented them in order, by bringing the people out into the open, to prevent poor behaviour and failure to obey orders. These views are erroneous, however, as such meals were not unique to Sparta and were of ancient origin. They were basically military messes of approximately fifteen members, or half a company; later, they lost their military character.

Membership of a mess was a prerequisite for Spartan citizenship; Plutarch gives a detailed account of the election to a syssition. The voting had to be unanimous. It was conducted by each member placing a ball of bread in a basin called a *caddichus*. If a candidate was acceptable, the ball of bread was round and soft; if a member wished to reject a candidate, the ball of bread was flattened. It only required one negative vote to disqualify a young man.

Citizenship depended on membership

The meals were held (possibly in tents) in a large, open space by the side of the Hyacinthine Way, and attendance every day was compulsory among Spartan peers. The evening meal was always eaten there. The only acceptable excuses for nonattendance were sickness, hunting expeditions or public sacrifices.

Compulsory attendance daily

Each peer was bound to make a monthly contribution of grain, fruit and wine from the produce of his *kleros*.

Monthly contributions

The messes also enabled young Spartans to listen to the conversations of their elders, learning of the honourable deeds performed by Spartans for their state. Furthermore, the public nature of these meals put a restraint on indecent language, bad conduct and drunkenness.

The Spartan army

The Spartan army went through a series of changes — both in organisation and in numbers — during the sixth and fifth centuries. These corresponded to crisis periods in Sparta's history.

Highly skilled and formidable soldiers

The individual Spartan soldier was highly skilled and courageous; fighting as a member of a disciplined and closely coordinated army, he was a formidable enemy. The whole education system and way of life was designed to produce this result.

Hoplites in battle — a scene from a Corinthian krater (6th century) (Courtesy of Musée du Louvre)

The body of a Spartan warrior being carried by his comrades from the field of battle — painted on a kylix by a Laconian artist (c. 550–540)

Assignment: The Spartan army

1 Describe the appearance of a Spartan hoplite. How did hoplites prepare for battle?
2 What was a phalanx? How important was it in procuring a Spartan victory?
3 Who in Sparta was liable for military service?
4 What part did the inferiors, perioeci and helots play in the army?
5 How important was religion to the army?
6 Explain the duties in battle of the kings, ephors and polemarchs.
7 What other people accompanied the army into battle?

8 What information does Plutarch's *Lycurgus* give about the army?
9 What do the passages in Herodotus VII: 103–7 and 208–9 reveal about the Spartan hoplite?
10 Choose an outstanding Spartan commander and a famous battle in which the Spartan army, under his command, was seen at its best. Give a brief account of the commander's tactics against the enemy in this battle.

Spartan government

Despite what the rest of Greece thought about some aspects of Spartan life, most philosophers and observers praised the Spartan form of government. However, they disagreed about what to call it, as it comprised four distinct parts, some of which were oligarchic and some democratic. Unlike most other states in Greece, Sparta also retained her hereditary kings.

Generally praised by ancients

Plato could not decide if it was a democracy or a tyranny, since it had blended the best features of each and avoided their worst aspects. Aristotle described it as a happy mixture of democracy and oligarchy, while the Roman statesman Cicero called it 'a mixed constitution'.

Difficulty of classification

There is no doubt that it was an oligarchy, as the number of enfranchised (able to vote and stand for office) Spartans was very small and this privileged body of Spartan peers ruled a huge population of perioeci and helots who had no say in government. Sparta always favoured oligarchic rule, particularly in allied states. There were, however, democratic aspects within the oligarchy, such as the assembly and the institution of the ephorate (see page 73). In other words, Sparta was a fairly democratic state if you happened to be a Spartiate! If you were not a full citizen, then you had practically no democratic rights at all. As we have seen, 95 per cent of Sparta's population belonged to this latter group.

Oligarchic form of government

Nevertheless, for the Spartiates, the Spartan constitution was a fairly well-balanced one which avoided some of the weaknesses of the radical form of democracy found in Athens.

Dual kingship

Origin

The Agiad and Eurypontid royal families

It is believed that there was a coalition of two distinct tribes, each with its own chief or king, sometime in the ninth century. One tribe lived around Sparta, its kings belonging to the clan of the Agiads, while the second tribe was probably from southern Laconia where the Eurypontids were the ruling clan. When the two houses agreed to join politically, the kings were given equal powers under the constitution. Over a period of time the kings' powers were restricted.

Functions

Only one king on campaigns

Military   The kings were the supreme commanders of the army. Only one of them was selected to lead a campaign, while the other remained in Sparta. According to Herodotus this law originated about 507 B.C., when Cleomenes and Demaratus were joint commanders of an expedition against Athens. There was a difference of opinion between the two commanders, and 'this divergence of policy gave rise to a new law in Sparta. Previously both kings had gone out with the army but this was now made illegal and it was further provided that one had to remain in the capital'.[18] The kings normally had the right to declare war — but never did so — and in the field they had the absolute right of deciding life or death.

Attended and checked by ephors

Two ephors accompanied the king and kept close supervision on his leadership during the war; he could be recalled and heavily punished if the campaign failed. The king was also accompanied by a bodyguard of 100 picked men, and inclusion in this guard was the greatest honour.

Approval by gods necessary

Religious   The kings were regarded as intermediaries between the gods and men, and held their office as long as the gods were pleased. If things went wrong, the king was to blame. Every ninth year the ephors looked in the skies for a sign of the gods' approval or disapproval.

Priests

The kings were priests of Zeus Lacedaemonios and Zeus Uranios, the gods of their respective families. Every month they offered solemn sacrifices to Apollo for the city. 'On the first and seventh days of every month each king is given a full grown animal to offer in sacrifice in the temple of Apollo, also a bushel of barley meal and a Laconian quart of wine'.[19]

Sacrificed prior to battle

Before leaving on a campaign the king sacrificed to Zeus, and if the omens were favourable the army could proceed to the frontier, where more sacrifices were performed for Zeus and Athena. Fire from these sacrifices was carried with them throughout the entire campaign.

The kings appointed two *pythioi* to consult the Oracle at Delphi and to present them with the Pythia's directions. They were responsible for the safe keeping of all the oracles.

Judicial   The kings had only limited judicial duties. They decided on the marriages of orphaned heiresses, and had control of all matters concerning highways and the adoption of children.

Minor judicial duties

Limitations of power

- The dual nature of the kingship ensured that each could keep a check on the other.
- A monthly oath was taken jointly, by the kings and ephors, whereby the kings' office was guaranteed as long as they acted constitutionally.
- The kings were reported upon by the ephors during campaigns.
- The kings could be — and at times were — deposed by the people.

Kings kept in check

Special honours and marks of distinction

- The kings were supported at the expense of the state, and when on military service were 'allowed for their own use as many cattle as they wish'.[20]
- They were given the skins of all sacrificed animals, and received part of the spoils of war.
- At the syssition they were served their meal first, and were given double portions.
- At religious festivals they were given seats of honour and when they entered the assembly, all those present — except the ephors — rose to their feet.
- On their death special ceremonies were observed. A man and a woman from each household had to wear a sign of mourning. People from all over Laconia attended the funeral, declaring that the late king was the best they had ever had, and no public meetings or elections could be held for the ten days of official mourning.

Treated with honour in life and in death

Succession

The king was succeeded by his eldest son, but a son born prior to his father's accession to the throne had to give way to the first son born after his father became king. The nearest male relative became the regent for a child, or himself became king if there were no children.

Son born after father's accession took precedence

Gerousia (council)

The gerousia was the oligarchic element in the constitution.

Origin

According to Plutarch, it came about as part of Lycurgus' attempt to safeguard the state by 'allaying and qualifying the fiery genius of the royal office'.[21] It was more likely the result of a conflict between the kings and nobles about the time of the first Messenian War.

Membership

Body of elders

There were twenty-eight members plus the two kings. Membership was restricted to Spartans over sixty years of age who were therefore no longer liable for military service. Thus it was a body of elders, who held their office for life, and it was regarded as a reward for merit. Members were elected by the Spartiates in the assembly, but it is not certain whether the candidates were from noble families or whether 'the best families' mentioned by Aristotle meant those of wealth and renown. However, membership of the council was a highly honourable and much sought-after office. Plutarch said that they had to be 'the best and most deserving men past sixty years old'.[22]

Highly honoured position

Selection

Candidates chosen by acclamation

Selection was by acclamation (shouting and clapping), and Plutarch describes in some detail the procedures for this.

The candidates were brought in one by one, their order of appearance being decided by lot, and in an adjoining room selected people listened to the loudness of the shouting for each candidate. The results were recorded in order. Once the successful candidate was declared, he was taken in triumphant procession around the city to all the temples, he attended a special banquet, and he was honoured in verse and song. Aristotle disapproved of this method as 'childish'.

Functions

Prepared bills

The gerousia was a *probouleutic* body. This meant that it prepared and deliberated on bills to be presented to the assembly for voting. If it was not happy with the assembly's vote on an issue it could decline to accept it, by adjourning — in which case the bill would not be passed.

Criminal court

The gerontes (members of the gerousia), kings and ephors acted as a court of justice for criminal cases. They tried cases of murder and treason, and imposed penalties ranging from death to banishment and fines. This select body of elders exerted a great influence in political affairs.

Ephorate

The ephorate was a board of five ephors, who were the chief magistrates and administrative officials in Sparta. The word 'ephor' means 'overseer'.

Origin unknown

Origin

The origin of this office is unknown and controversy on the subject has continued among historians, who have put forward several theories:
- The ephors were originally priests and astrologers.
- The ephors were created by the kings to carry on government while they were away at war.
- The ephors were originally connected with the five villages and may have been chiefs who became advisers to the kings. This is the most commonly held theory.

By the 7th century were very powerful

It was not until the seventh century that the ephors won their great political power, which slowly increased until they had taken over the main powers of the kings. They had formidable powers as representatives of the people.

Most democratic aspect of constitution

Election

Any Spartan peer over thirty could stand for the office of ephor. They were elected by the assembly annually, and each month they exchanged oaths with the kings. They took office at the full moon after the autumnal equinox and issued a proclamation to all citizens to shave their moustaches and obey the laws.

Functions

1 As representatives of the people they were expected to keep a check on the kings both at home and abroad, and they could summon the kings before them for misdemeanours.

Checked on kings and received foreign envoys

2 They dealt with foreign embassies. According to Xenophon, before foreign representatives could enter Sparta they had to halt at the border and wait for permission from the ephors. Once in Sparta, envoys made their proposals or demands to the ephors, who then decided if they should go before the assembly.
3 If war was declared, the ephors decided which age classes should go and issued orders mobilising the army; they gave instructions to the generals, and recalled them if they failed.
4 Their power over lesser magistrates was great. At the end of a magistrate's year of office he gave an account of himself to the ephors, who decided if any punishment was in order.

Controlled magistrates

5 They were in total control of the training and discipline of the young. Any misconduct was reported to them and Spartan youths were given a

Supervised training

Gave orders to krypteia

regular physical examination. The ephors also chose the three captains of the elite corps of the Spartan army.

6 The krypteia (secret police organisation) was under orders from the ephors. It has been portrayed as a tyrannical and vicious weapon, used to murder helots indiscriminately. Plutarch said of it:

> The magistrates despatched privately some of the ablest of the young men into the country from time to time armed only with their daggers . . . . In the daytime they hid in out-of-the-way places and there lay close, but in the night issued out into the highways, and killed all the helots they could light upon'.[23]

Helot control

The ephors, according to Aristotle, upon entering office used to declare war on the helots so that they could be massacred without offending the gods; in other words, declaring them public enemies allowed them to be killed with impunity. The krypteia was more probably a body of eighteen to twenty-year-old youths at the disposal of the ephors for special service, such as in times of helot restlessness. Membership formed part of the training of the youths — they served for two years — and provided a useful method for removing undesirables, specifically helots, who had to be constantly kept in check.

7 The ephors summoned and presided over sessions of the gerousia and the assembly, and initiated legislation.

Judicial functions

8 With the gerousia, they acted as a court of criminal justice and carried out punishments; they were criminal judges in cases involving perioeci, and they constituted the supreme civil court.

Limitations

Answerable to the people

Despite the ephors' great powers, they were subject to certain restrictions. They were elected for one year only, and when they became private citizens once again they could be called to account for their actions.

Assembly (ecclesia, or apella)

There is no real evidence that the word 'apella' was used in ancient times to describe the assembly at Sparta, although some modern historians (for example, V. Ehrenberg) use it consistently. Others prefer the common term, 'ecclesia'.

Membership

All citizens over 30

All Spartiates over thirty were eligible to sit in the assembly. Those who had lost their citizenship rights could not attend.

Functions

The assembly met once a month at the full moon, in the open air, under the chairmanship of the ephor, who also introduced proposed legislation. It could not discuss or amend proposals, but simply vote for or against them.

Passed or rejected legislation

Questions of war or peace, the signing of treaties, the appointment of generals, the election of the gerousia and ephors, issues of disputed succession to the throne, and the freeing of helots were the main functions of the assembly.

Limitations

If the ephors disapproved of a motion passed by the assembly they could refuse to proclaim it, thereby causing it to lapse. This was one undemocratic feature of the Spartan constitution.

Undemocratic aspect

The Peloponnesian League, or 'The Lacedaemonians and their allies'

The Spartans referred to themselves as Lacedaemonians.

Origin and growth

Originally Argos had been the most powerful city in the Peloponnese, but by the end of the sixth century B.C. Sparta had emerged as the political and military *hegemon* (leader) and Argos began to decline.

The aim of Sparta's foreign policy during the sixth century was protection against Argos and freedom from tyranny.

Sparta had already acquired two powerful allies in Corinth and Elis, by deposing the last Corinthian tyrant (c.580) and by helping Elis to gain control of the Olympic Games (c.570).

Freed cities from tyranny

When Sparta defeated Tegea in a frontier war, rather than annex the territory she offered the Tegeans a permanent defensive alliance. This was a turning point in her foreign policy.

Alliances rather than annexation

After 555, Sicyon, Megara, Aegina, Troezen, Epidaurus and other states in the central and northern Peloponnese joined the League, each one signing a separate defensive alliance with Sparta.

Spartan superiority was not guaranteed, however, until she had defeated Argos in battle, which occurred in 546.

Features of the League

The League, which included all Peloponnesian states except Argos and Achaea, was restricted in purpose to questions of war; recognised the

Mutual protection

autonomy and territorial integrity of its members; created a strong military cordon in the Peloponnese, providing insulation for Sparta and security for her neighbours; opposed tyrannies and favoured oligarchies.

Organisation

Bi-cameral council to discuss war and peace

A Council of Allies met when questions of war arose. The Council comprised two equal and independent bodies:

1 The Assembly of Spartiates, representing the Lacedaemonian state as head of the alliance.
2 The Congress of Allies, in which each state had one vote and a majority vote was binding on all members.

If both these bodies voted alike on matters of policy, then the whole alliance was committed to the policy.

No tribute except in war
Allies' interests considered

No tribute was levied except in times of war, when two-thirds of the allies' military forces were required for a certain number of months.

Sparta had to take account of the sentiments and interests of her allies — particularly Corinth, which could and did sometimes sway the majority of the congress against her. The allies did not always agree with everything Sparta did but they were generally loyal, and the League was a very stable organisation. It formed the nucleus of the Hellenic League's defence of Greece against the Persians in 480 B.C.; Sparta's leadership was accepted by all Greeks at the beginning of the fifth century.

Generally a stable and solid league

Essay topics

1 What were the political and military obligations of a Spartan citizen to his state?
2 How important were each of the following in the Spartan system?
  (a) helots
  (b) perioeci
  (c) ephors
  (d) kings

3 Discuss Aristotle's view that the Spartan constitution was 'a happy mixture of democracy and oligarchy'.

Class discussion
'Education should teach a total way of living.' Do you agree or disagree with this statement? Give your reasons.

Further reading

Primary sources

Aristophanes. *Lysistrata.*
Aristotle. *The Politics.*
Herodotus. *The Histories.*
Pausanias. *A Description of Greece,* vol. III.
Plutarch. *The Lives of the Noble Greeks (Lycurgus).*
Xenophon. *The Constitution of the Lacedaemonians.*

Secondary sources

Andrewes, A. *The Greek Tyrants.*
Barrow, R. *Greek and Roman Education.*
——— . *Sparta.*
Bury, J. B. & Meiggs, R. *A History of Greece.*
Ehrenberg, V. *From Solon to Socrates.*
Hammond, N. G. L. *A History of Greece to 322 B.C.*
Michel, H. *Sparta.*

The development of Athens in the sixth century

5

Social and political organisation in Attica at the beginning of the century

Economic conditions at the beginning of the century

Solon the reformer, 594–593

The Pisistratid tyranny 546–510

The reforms of Cleisthenes, 508

Basis of democracy laid in 6th century

A THENS in the sixth century was transformed from a second-rate polis, dominated by aristocrats and plagued by economic and political problems, into a prosperous city with a sense of unity, optimism and increasing confidence. This was achieved through the work of men such as Solon, Pisistratus and Cleisthenes. They led Athens towards a democracy and they laid the foundations of a sound economy and a rich and expanding culture. Athens' greatness in the fifth century was, in part, a reflection of the work of these men.

Sources

Solon

Herodotus

Thucydides

As in the case of Sparta, the early history of Athens is obscure because of the lack of contemporary written sources. Historians have had to rely solely on fragments of poetry (such as the poems of Solon); pottery and other archaeological remains; a few laws, which may have been altered at a later date, and lists of magistrates such as the eponymous archons, after whom the years were named. Herodotus gives some details of the period from Solon to Cleisthenes, while Thucydides makes some references to early Athens, such as the traditional account of the synoecism ('joining-together') of Attica under Theseus and the assassination (514 B.C.) of Hipparchus, brother of Hippias the tyrant.

Aristotle's *Athenian Constitution*, written in 330 and preserved on papyrus, is very useful, but it needs to be remembered that Aristotle interpreted the Athenian institutions of the early period according to his philosophical ideas of the fourth century.

Aristotle

Plutarch's *Life of Solon* is one of our few detailed sources and was probably based on a wide range of authorities available to him at the time; he may also have had at his disposal the complete poems of Solon.

Plutarch

However, much of the information available can be questioned and many texts vary somewhat in their account of this period.

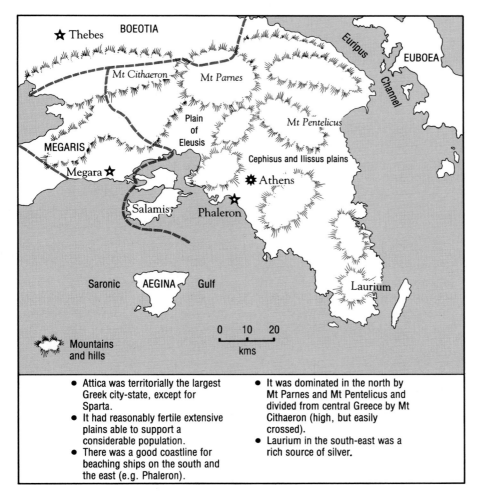

- Attica was territorially the largest Greek city-state, except for Sparta.
- It had reasonably fertile extensive plains able to support a considerable population.
- There was a good coastline for beaching ships on the south and the east (e.g. Phaleron).

- It was dominated in the north by Mt Parnes and Mt Pentelicus and divided from central Greece by Mt Cithaeron (high, but easily crossed).
- Laurium in the south-east was a rich source of silver.

Attica

Unification of Attica (synoecism)

Attica was a geographical unit, and as such the conditions were favourable for it also to be a political unit. Originally Attica was divided into a number of independent poleis, but at some early date a gradual and peaceful unification (synoecism) under the rule of Athens developed. There was no transfer of population and no subjugation of one group by another, as was the case in Sparta. All free men in Attica became Athenians.

Prelude to the sixth century

Greece was inhabited during the Bronze Age — this period is referred to as that of the Mycenaean civilisation.

1200

The Dorian invasions occurred approximately between 1200 and 1000 B.C. Athens, however, was bypassed; she became for a time the chief city on the mainland.

1100

Many people fleeing from the Dorians sought refuge in Attica, but there were too many of them and, as a result, there began a series of Ionian migrations to Asia Minor and the islands of the Aegean. In the words of Thucydides:

> For when people were driven from other parts of Greece by war or by disturbances, the most powerful of them took refuge in Athens, as being a stable society; then they became citizens and soon made the city even more populous than it had been before, with the result that later Attica became too small for her inhabitants and colonies were sent out to Ionia.[1]

1000

The 'dark ages' spanned approximately the years 1100 to 800; this period witnessed the protogeometric and geometric phases of pottery — Athenian pottery was the most abundant and artistic in the Greek world.

800

Athens lost the lead in Greece, as she did not participate in the colonising movement — she had no immediate land hunger.

The power of the king declined; the nobles elected two magistrates — archon (ruler) and polemarch (leader in war) — to assume some of the king's authority.

700

Kingship ceased to be hereditary and became an annual magistracy—*archon basileus*, or 'king-archon'. Government was now firmly in the hands of the aristocrats (*eupatridae*).

Athens was not yet affected by the economic problems which resulted in the tyrannies of Corinth, Megara and Sicyon, but some signs of discontent with noble rule was reflected in the appointment of six judges (*thesmothetae*) associated with the other three archons. Plutarch comments:

> The minds of the leaders of the people are lawless
> Nor do they abide by the holy ordinance of Justice.[2]

632

An attempt to create a tyranny was made by Cylon (an Athenian noble), backed by his father-in-law Theagenes, tyrant of Megara. This attempt failed, owing to lack of popular support. Athenians were not yet sufficiently discontented to try revolutionary methods.

621

Laws were codified by Draco. Up to this time, Athenian laws were not written down, and could be interpreted by the nobles in an arbitrary fashion. Not much is known of Draco's code, except for his law concerning homicide. The law of debt was extremely severe and many suffered under it.

The written laws did not end the discontent, and conditions deteriorated rapidly.

Social and political organisation of Attica at the beginning of the sixth century

Tribes (phylae)

There were four Ionian tribes, to one of which each person belonged.
Each tribe was divided into a number of phratries (perhaps three).

'Brotherhoods' (phratriae)

Phratries were neighbourhood organisations whose members worshipped the same cult figure. They were the basis of citizenship. On maturity, an Athenian was registered on the list of his phratry.

Originally only the members of clans (nobles, the elite) belonged, but gradually others—such as small landowners, craftsmen and other non-nobles—formed themselves into cult organisations and were admitted to the phratries.

Clans (gene)

Clans were composed of related noble families who could claim descendancy from a common ancestor.

Not all noble families within a clan (*genos*) were as well-to-do as others, and there was usually a leading family within each clan. They were often in conflict with each other and they dominated the social, political and economic life of Attica.

Table 5.1   Social classes

Eupatridae	Georgoi	Demiourgoi	Thetes
'High-born' nobles and large land-owners — a minority, who occupied the fertile plain. Held all high offices (archons, judges, priests); sat in the Council of the Areopagus	Small farmers — could sit in the assembly and could vote	Craftsmen — able to sit in the assembly and to vote	Free (but landless) labouring class; had no political rights at all

Table 5.2   Aristocratic government

Magistrates	Council of Areopagus	Assembly (Ecclesia)
Nine magistrates (archons) elected annually from nobles • Eponymous archon (chief magistrate) gave his name to the year • Polemarch — military commander • Archon basileus (king-archon) — religious duties • Six thesmothetae (judges) — recorders of law	Council of nobles (eupatridae) elected for life — ex-archons controlled the administration of the state; supervised the magistrates, safeguarded the constitution, inflicted penalties without the right of appeal	Elected magistrates and decided on some matters of state, but had limited powers

Economic conditions in Attica at the beginning of the century

The law of debt

There was a very deep and widespread distress among the lower classes. Andrewes states that 'the immediate and urgent problem arose from the hardship caused to the small landowners by the current law of debt'.[3] According to Plutarch, 'All the common people were weighed down with the debts they owed to a few rich men',[4] while Aristotle believed that 'the harshest and bitterest aspect of the constitution for the masses was the fact of their enslavement'.[5]

Harsh law of debt

By the law of debt a loan was secured on the personal freedom of the borrower; those who failed to repay could become a slave at home or be sold overseas.

According to Plutarch there was an ever-increasing number of small farmers—called *hektemoroi*, or 'sixth parters'—who were virtual serfs, working the land of the rich estate owners. They had contracted to hand over one-sixth of the produce of the land they tilled, and this land was marked with stone pillars (*horoi*) which indicated that there was a pledge or obligation of the hektemoroi to the creditors. If they failed to pay the one-sixth, they and their families became his slaves.

Hektemoroi

Hammond believes that much of the land of Attica could not be sold, as it belonged to the family and not the individual. In these cases, when a farmer fell into debt he could not pledge his land, but only the produce of it.

Poorer families and the landless could pledge only themselves to raise money 'and could be seized by their creditors, some of them being enslaved at home and others being sold to foreigners abroad. Many parents were even forced to sell their own children (for there was no law to prevent this), or to go into exile because of the harshness of their creditors'.[6]

In one of his poems, Solon expresses his distress:

I observe, and within my heart there is sadness and deep distress,
As I see the most ancient land in all the Ionian sphere undermined.[7]

The greed of the upper class

Economic competition, which resulted from colonisation, affected the Athenian markets. The large landowner could easily exchange produce of oil and wine for imported grain, but the smaller farmer could not

The poor exploited by the rich

compete. When he tried to get help from a wealthy neighbour he was ruthlessly exploited.

Speculation — high rates of interest

The use of coinage was not yet widespread in Attica, but the richer classes found it easier to buy luxury goods from overseas with silver coins than by barter. They also exported corn in return for silver, creating famine conditions for the poor classes. They were able to more easily hoard their wealth, using it to speculate and to lend at great rates of interest. The gap between the rich and poor widened.

War with Megara

Disruption of trade by war

Athens was at war with Megara for possession of the island of Salamis, just off the Attic coast. This disrupted Athenian trade.

Economically Athens was in a deplorable state at the beginning of the sixth century, but the exploited poor could not have improved their situation without the help of other social elements in Athens who were also dissatisfied — for example, the class of new wealthy who had no political rights.

Solon the reformer, 594–593

The need for a mediator/reformer

Conditions ripe for tyranny

The nobles realised that the danger of revolt and subsequently of possible tyranny was great for several reasons.
1 Tyrannies had been set up in neighbouring states.
2 There had been a previous attempt at tyranny by Cylon.
3 Those in debt were increasing and were demanding a complete redistribution of land.
4 A new discontented class, with wealth but no political rights, had emerged.
5 Political quarrels between clans and leading families began to disrupt Athens.

Compromise needed by nobles

To avoid losing everything in a revolution, the more moderate nobles showed political wisdom. They saw the need for a new order of things, and were prepared to accept intervention and some compromise.

Plutarch records that the most level-headed of the Athenians began to look towards Solon. They saw that he, more than anyone else, stood apart from the injustices of the time and was involved neither in the extortions of the rich nor the privations of the poor.

A sculpture thought to be of Solon, but not reliably identified

His background and qualifications for the position

- He was of noble birth but of only moderate means. Perhaps he was a second son who did not inherit the family estate.
- He had become a trader, and was better able to understand economic affairs. He travelled widely and may have been associated with the intellectual movement in Ionia.
- He was well known and highly respected before his appointment to the archonship.

Understood the problems of both sides

He expressed his views in public recitals of his poetry in the agora. In these poems he sympathised with the grievances of the poor and criticised the nobles for their greed and selfish indifference to the wellbeing of Athens.

> You who have soared to the surfeit of riches
> Quieten your heart that swells up with ambition
> Humble the mind that is proud, for not all will
> Go to your liking, nor we for ever obey.[8]

He made it clear, however, that he did not support revolutionary methods and was against the grasping nature of the one party and the arrogance of the other.

He also built a reputation for himself in the war with Megara over Salamis, and wrote strongly about the need to fight for the island instead of betraying it.

He was chosen archon in 594, 'for the rich were ready to accept him as a man of wealth and the poor as a man of principle'.[9]

His aims

Aimed at eunomia — reign of good order

His main objective was the welfare of the total community before that of any one particular class. To achieve this, he aimed at 'the reign of good order' (*eunomia*), under which each class would have its proper place in the state. To create a balanced and fair situation, he had first to remove the grievances of the poor.

His economic reforms

Initial reform — seisachtheia

Seisachtheia meant 'the shaking off of burdens', and included

Freedom from debt and slavery

1 the cancellation of outstanding debts which involved giving as security the personal freedom of the peasant (this was made retrospective, so that all those who had become slaves were freed);
2 a law forbidding loans to be secured in this way in the future;
3 the removal of all *horoi* (pledge-markers), eliminating the class of hektemoroi;
4 the return of those who had been sold abroad: how this was achieved is unknown — they must have been repurchased and then set free, while those in exile were free to return home.

Solon described his initial achievement in the following way:

The people I assembled with these aims:
Did I abandon any unfulfilled?
You, my best witness in the court of Time,
You mighty mother of Olympian gods,
Black Earth — testify! For from your breast
I tore the pillars planted everywhere
And set you free, who then had been a slave.
How many men to Athens I restored
(Their native city, founded by the gods),
Who had been sold for just or unjust cause;
And others, exiled by the pressing need
That follows debtors, who no longer spoke
The Attic tongue – so wide their wanderings.
Those here at home in shameful slavery
Who trembled at their masters' every mood,
I gave their freedom.[10]

Results

1 Once again Attica became a land of free peasants, but Solon did nothing about the conditions which had led to borrowing in the first place, and did not provide the peasants with land with which to start their new lives. They were left disappointed and dissatisfied, as they had expected him to redistribute some of the land of the wealthy.

Reforms did not go far enough for peasants

2 The wealthy lost control over large areas of land that the hektemoroi worked for them; they also lost the interest on loans. However, their own estates remained intact and they continued as great landowners, although Solon did limit the amount of land which could be owned by a single person, so as to prevent the growth of dangerously large estates.

Plutarch says:

Did not really satisfy either group

> At first his policy did not please either party. The rich were angry at being deprived of their securities, and the poor even more so, because Solon did not carry out a redistribution of the land as they had expected or impose a strictly equal and uniform style of living upon everybody.[11]

3 In order to relieve the problem resulting from an increased number of landless peasants, Solon placed a temporary ban on the export of agricultural products (except olive oil, of which there was a surplus) to prevent famine prices. Previously, speculation by the wealthy had meant that poorer Athenians could not afford to pay the high prices being demanded for the basic necessities of life.

Prevented speculation in essential products

4 Because he realised that the country was for the most part poor and unproductive, Solon encouraged many of the landless to turn to learning a craft.

Crafts encouraged

Encouragement of growth in trade and industry

Citizenship offered to foreign craftsmen

Athenian citizenship was promised to foreign craftsmen who settled with their families permanently in Attica. Master potters from Corinth and Aegina moved to Athens and there contributed to the rapid growth of the Athenian pottery industry. Solon encouraged specialisation.

New standard of coinage, weights and measures

Athens had previously moved in the area of trade dominated by Aegina, but Solon wished to extend her trade to Asia Minor and Thrace in the east, and westward to Sicily. The carrying trade of these areas was in the hands of Euboea and Corinth, so Solon introduced a new standard of weights, measures and coinage based on those used by those states. The silver mines at Laurium were now developed more fully.

It was against the law to be idle, and if a man expected to be looked after in his old age he had to teach his son a trade.

Effectiveness of his economic reforms

Alleviated distress and improved economic prosperity

He took the first step towards making Attica a nation of free citizen landholders, but he did not go far enough. He simply alleviated distress instead of solving the problems causing it. These were the seeds of future discontent.

His encouragement of trade and industry laid the basis for the greater prosperity of all classes.

Solon encouraged tradesman such as potters, who produced fine pieces of Black Figure pottery (c.550) (Courtesy of Musée du Louvre)

Other legislation

Solon devised a code of law, a large part of which dealt with family matters such as dowries, wills, adultery and marriages of heiresses. Others dealt with aspects of agriculture, such as water regulations. Plutarch gives details of these in his *Life of Solon*, Chapters 20 to 25. These laws were to remain in force for one hundred years and were inscribed on revolving wooden tablets, called *axones*, placed for all to see.

Code of laws devised

Political reforms

Solon has often been described as the 'Father of Democracy', but this was not a commonly held belief in the fifth century, when that title was generally given to Cleisthenes. Solon himself would not have understood the word *demokratia* and would never have tried to implement such a revolutionary system. He believed in moving slowly and his aim was to leave all the positions of power as he found them, in the hands of the top class, but at the same time to give the people a share in the other processes of government, which they had never before possessed. He took some steps which were of fundamental importance to the development of the later democracy.

Did not introduce democracy to Athens

Timocratic government

A timocracy is a form of government in which the political rights of the citizens — and in particular the qualifications for high office — are determined by degrees of wealth. In the case of Athens, there were four classes based on property.

Timocracy

Four census classes   At some time before Solon's archonship, the three earlier classes (*eupatridae, georgoi, demiourgoi*) were partially replaced by three classes defined according to the military role they had to play: the *hippeis* (cavalry) *zeugitae* (hoplites) and *thetes* (without military duties). According to Plutarch, Solon took a census to assess every citizen's property and created another class from the wealthiest of the hippeis. This class he called the *pentacosiomedimni* (the men of 500 bushels).

Classification according to wealth

> I gave to the people as much esteem as is sufficient for them,
> Not detracting from their honour or reaching out to take it
> And to those who had power and were admired for their wealth,
> I declared that they should have nothing unseemly.
> I stood holding my mighty shield against both,
> And did not allow either to win an unjust victory.[12]

Table 5.3	Assessment of wealth		
Pentacosiomedimni	*Hippeis*	*Zeugitae*	*Thetes*
Those whose estates or property could produce 500 bushels per year of wet or dry goods, or their equivalent	Those producing 300 bushels (or its equivalent) a year and with enough wealth to equip themselves for the cavalry	Those producing 200 bushels a year or its equivalent, and able to outfit themselves as hoplites	Those with less than 200 bushels a year or its equivalent; they served as light-armed troops, and rowers

Table 5.4	Political rights associated with wealth		
Pentacosiomedimni	*Hippeis*	*Zeugitae*	*Thetes*
Eligible for all top positions, i.e. • nine archons and treasurers Members of • Council of Areopagus as ex-archons Eligible for • new Council of 400 • Assembly	Eligible for • lower offices of state • new Council of 400 • Assembly	Eligible for • lower offices of state • new Council of 400 • Assembly	Could not hold office Eligible for • Assembly

The effects of this new economic basis of government

Broke absolute political monopoly of nobles

Archons By admitting men to the highest offices of state provided their income was appropriate, Solon broke the monopoly of the nobles.

Council of Areopagus This former aristocratic council was recruited from ex-archons, and so now included many wealthy non-nobles. It was still a body with great prestige, as it was made up of the top class only, but Solon could not leave it with so much power over the assembly. He therefore changed its functions. It no longer had any direct part in legislation, but became the protector of the constitution, guardian of the laws and chief court for cases of homicide.

Council of 400 (Boule) If Solon did create a new Council of 400 (some doubt this), it was recruited from the top three classes and its main duty was to prepare the agenda for the assembly; this was previously the main function of the Areopagus.

Assembly (ecclesia)   Solon opened this to all classes of citizens. This meant that the thetes were now able to get some experience in government, which was a step towards a more democratic system. *Lower classes given greater political responsibility*

All citizens, regardless of class, could nominate and vote for magistrates; indirectly vote for the Areopagus; have the final decision on legislation, war and peace, and have the right to call magistrates to account after their year of office.

Heliaea (people's court)   This was the name given to the ecclesia when it sat as a court. As all citizens (including thetes) were included in this, it was probably the greatest step towards democracy.

Aristotle said that when the people have control of the judicial system, they have control of the state. The Heliaea was the final court of appeal against the decisions of archons; it tried magistrates accused of mismanagement while in office, and any citizen could raise a charge when anybody was wronged by an unlawful action. *The Heliaea was the most democratic institution*

According to Aristotle, the three most democratic reforms of Solon were:

> First and most important, the ban on loans on the security of the person; next, permission for anyone who wished to seek retribution for those who were wronged; and third, the one which is said to have contributed to the power of the masses, the right of appeal to the jury-court.[13]

Although Solon wanted to found a state based on justice, personal freedom for individuals and increased political responsibility, he never imagined a democracy. He paved the way for others to improve and build on his work. *Paved the way for others to follow*

Solon's departure from Athens

Solon left Athens for ten years to continue his travels, leaving his system on trial. He departed because too many people wanted to question and 'cross-examine him on points of detail' and he was 'anxious to disengage himself from these complications'. He had failed to satisfy either side; as he himself remarked: 'in great affairs you cannot please all parties'.[14] *A system on trial*

Assignment: The Pisistratid tyranny at Athens

This assignment is an essential part of the study of the chapter. Its completion is a prerequisite for understanding the work that follows.

The years preceding Pisistratus' seizure of power

1 Aristotle says that after Solon's departure from Athens, 'the city continued in a state of turmoil' and that it was the office of archon 'over which strife always arose'.[15]

   Explain this by referring to
   (a) the years of *anarchia*;
   (b) the irregular archonship of Damasias.

2 According to Plutarch, 'the people of Athens once more broke up into contending parties'... 'None of these parties thought of an equitable settlement, but each counted upon improving its position and overwhelming its opponents'.[16]
   (a) Name the three factions and their aristocratic leaders.
   (b) What groups of people comprised these factions and what political aims does Aristotle assign to each group? Is it likely to have been as clear cut as this?
   (c) What improved Pisistratus' reputation with the people prior to his seizure of power?

Pisistratus' attempts to establish a tyranny

1 'In the first phase of his dictatorship he lost his power before it had really taken root' (Herodotus).[17]
   (a) In what year did he seize power for the first time?
   (b) What method did he use?
   (c) What was Solon's attitude to this tyranny?
   (d) Why was it so shortlived?

2 'To bring about his return to power they devised between them what seems to me the silliest trick which history has to record' (Herodotus).[18]
   (a) To whom is Herodotus referring when he says 'they devised between them'?
   (b) What was this 'silliest of tricks'?

3 'He became afraid of the parties and withdrew.' (Aristotle).[19]
   (a) Why was Pisistratus forced to leave Athens a second time?
   (b) Where did he spend his exile? How important to his future career was this ten-year period?

4 'It was only in the 11th year (536–535) that he tried to recover his rule by force, with the support of many others' (Aristotle).[20]

   Who were the 'many others' from whom he gained support for his final attempt to establish a tyranny?

Means by which Pisistratus maintained his power

Write a few lines on each of the following:
   foreign mercenaries and wealth;
   some opponents in exile;
   hostages — sons of leading families;
   reconciliation of some nobles by being a 'constitutional tyrant';
   influence in the appointment of archons;
   benefits given to the people;
   weakening of the judicial influence of nobles in local regions by institution of a system employing rural judges.

Features of his rule, 536–527 B.C.

'Pisistratus administered the city's affairs moderately, and more like a citizen than a tyrant' (Aristotle).[21]

1 Pisistratus was interested in the welfare of the farmers. In what ways did he make life easier for the small farmer, and strengthen Athenian farming generally?

2 Trade and industry were promoted by his extensive connections and alliances, particularly in the Hellespont.

(a) How did he gain control of Sigeum and the Thracian Chersonese?

(b) What was the significance of these gains around the Hellespont?

(c) What particular industry benefited from the expansion of markets?

(d) What were the Athenian 'Owls', which carried Athenian trade and prestige everywhere?

3 His building program served two purposes: it created employment for craftsmen and the city poor and glorified his regime.

Give some details of the public works and the building of temples undertaken in his reign.

A silver 4-drachma coin produced by Pisistratus, c.540. It features Athena on one side and the owl and olive branch on the other. These coins were referred to as 'Attic owls' and symbolised the unity of Attica. They later represented Athenian commercial and imperial leadership

A high-quality amphora, produced at the time of Pisistratus

As part of his public works program, Pisistratus converted a natural spring into an elaborate fountain house called the Enneakrounos (nine-spouter); (a) part of the feed pipe of the Enneakrounos, made of gray clay; (b) the feed pipe inscribed with the name 'Charon', possibly the name of its maker

4 His religious beliefs influenced his administration.

  (a) What was the aim of his religious policy?

  (b) In what ways did he honour the goddess Athena?

  (c) How did he promote the local rural cults of Demeter and Dionysus?

  (d) What was the significance of his purification of the sanctuary of Apollo on the island of Delos?

5 It was under Pisistratus that Athens first developed a foreign policy.

  (a) Note his relationship with

      Argos and Sparta;

      Thebes;

      Eretria in Euboea;

      the tyrant Lygdamis of Naxos;

      Thessaly and Macedonia;

      Polycrates, tyrant of Samos.

  (b) What is meant by 'many of his external connections were of a personal kind'? (Ehrenberg).[22]

Hippias and Hipparchus, 527–510

1 'On the death of Pisistratus, his sons took over the regime and continued the management of affairs in the same way' (Aristotle).[23]

  (a) What does Aristotle say about Hippias and Hipparchus?[24]

  (b) What cultural and building achievements can be attributed to them?

2 'After this the tyranny became much more cruel. Hippias took revenge for his brother's death with many executions and expulsions and became suspicious and bitter towards everyone' (Aristotle).[25]

  (a) Explain briefly the circumstances surrounding Hipparchus' death in 514. (Refer to Thucydides, VI:53–9.)

  (b) Which notable family was exiled? As a result of their failure to return to Athens, what did they do?

  (c) What actions did Hippias take in order to safeguard himself in case of revolution?

3 'Hippias held the dictatorship for three more years and in the fourth year was deposed by the Spartans and the exiled Alcmaeonids' (Thucydides).[26]

  (a) What does Aristotle say was one of the reasons Sparta invaded Attica, apart from the Delphic oracle's demand to 'first free Athens'?

  (b) How did Sparta 'free' Athens?

  (c) Where did Hippias spend the next twenty years?

  (d) What significance did this have for future events?

The importance of the Pisistratid tyranny

Read N. G. L. Hammond, A History of Greece to 322 B.C., pp. 184–5; V. Ehrenberg, From Solon to Socrates, pp. 80–1, 83; A. Andrewes, The Greek Tyrants, pp. 113–15

Explain the importance of the Pisistratid tyranny to Athens. Consider such points as

- peace and security;
- unity of the state;
- economic and cultural progress;
- the development of the idea of equality as preparation for democracy.

Part of the base of the statue to the tyrannicides, Harmodius and Aristogeiton: 'A great light shone upon the Athenians when Harmodius and Aristogeiton slew Hipparchus'

Cleisthenes' reforms — the framework of democracy

Plutarch describes Cleisthenes' achievements in the following way:

> [Cleisthenes] not only performed the noble exploit of driving out the Pisistratids and destroying their tyranny, but went on to establish laws and a constitution that was admirably balanced so as to promote harmony between citizens and security for the whole state.[27]

After the overthrow of the Pisistratid tyranny in 510 and a two-year civil war, Cleisthenes, in the face of aristocratic opposition, designed the framework of a new system of government which was to endure for centuries. His reorganisation of the whole political system was on broad democratic principles, although it took two more generations of external and internal conflicts, and the building of an empire, to perfect the system of democracy.

A new system of government devised

Cleisthenes was a practical reformer. He realised the weaknesses in Solon's system and set out to remedy these faults, although he could not have done what he did without the groundwork laid by both Solon and Pisistratus, who had been gradually moving in the same direction. These two men weakened the political hold of the aristocratic families and contributed to the growing unity of the state, but neither man had had democracy in mind. Cleisthenes himself probably became a 'democrat virtually by accident, turning to the common people when he urgently needed their support in the confused struggle to fill the vacuum left by the deposed tyrant Hippias the son of Pisistratus' (Finley).[28]

Groundwork laid by Solon and Pisistratus

Whatever his motives, Cleisthenes' measures revolutionised the state and created the machinery of local and central government which served Athens for a long time.

Rivalry for leadership

In the years following Hippias' expulsion by the Alcmaeonids and the Spartans, the noble families and their factions once again began a power struggle under the leadership of Cleisthenes and Isagoras.

Cleisthenes versus Isagoras

Isagoras defeated Cleisthenes in 508 for the archonship. Aristotle says 'As Cleisthenes was getting the worse of the party struggle, he attached the people to his following by proposing to give political power to the masses'.[29] According to Herodotus he, like all aristocrats, had previously held the common people (demos) in contempt, but now he put forward a measure by which all free people in Attica should be placed on the citizen rolls, by legislation. Many had been deprived of their citizenship after the expulsion of Hippias.

Cleisthenes appeals to the people

Table 5.5	Comparison of Cleisthenes and Isagoras
Cleisthenes	Isagoras
Member of the powerful Alcmaeonid family	'Son of Tisander, a man of reputable family' (possibly the Philaids, related to Pisistratus)[*]
Exiled under Pisistratus and organised the exiles	Probably did not oppose the rule of the Pisistratids so as to be allowed to remain in Athens
Bribed the priestess at Delphi to persuade Spartans to banish the tyrant	Personal friend of King Cleomenes of Sparta
Man of new and radical ideas	Represented the reactionary aristocrats

[*] Herodotus, *The Histories*, V:66.

Isagoras appeals to Sparta

The Assembly may have passed his measure immediately, but how this was achieved in the archonship of Isagoras is not known. However, Isagoras became alarmed and appealed to King Cleomenes of Sparta for help. Isagoras may have been concerned about the possibility of Cleisthenes being able in the future to dominate elections with the support of thousands of lower-class voters, and Cleomenes would certainly not favour any moves towards democracy.

Isagoras asserted that the Alcmaeonids, as a clan under an ancient curse (incurred during the time of the attempted tyranny of Cylon), should not live in Attica and should lose their citizenship. Cleomenes backed him up, and sent a demand that all the Alcmaeonids and their supporters should be banished forever from Athens.

Sparta demands Cleisthenes' exile

Cleisthenes left quietly, preferring to wait rather than to risk causing bloodshed. He knew the way the people felt.

Cleomenes arrived in Attica with a small force, demanding (a) the permanent expulsion of the Alcmaeonids and 700 other families, and (b) the replacement of the elected Council by an oligarchy of 300 of Isagoras' supporters.

Spartans seize Acropolis

The Council resisted, so Isagoras and the Spartans seized the Acropolis. What happened next was of great significance for the future of Athens. The Athenian people rose against the Spartans and blockaded the Acropolis for days, without any effective leadership. They were defending their legal rights. In Aristophanes' *Lysistrata*, the Chorus reminds the women that King Cleomenes could not hold the Acropolis.

The grand old Spartan king,
He had six hundred men,

He marched them into the Acropolis
And he marched them out again.
And he entered breathing fire,
But when he left the place
He hadn't washed for six whole years
And had hair upon his face.
We slept before the gates;
We wore our shields asleep;
We all of us laid siege to him
In units twenty deep.
And the King came out half starved,
And wore a ragged cloak
And 'I surrender – let me go!'
Were all the words he spoke.[30]

Humiliation of Cleomenes

After three days, Cleomenes and the Spartans surrendered their weapons and were allowed to leave Attica under a truce. Isagoras accompanied them, but his supporters were eventually sentenced to death. This was the greatest humiliation to be suffered by a Spartan king, and Cleomenes began collecting an army from every part of the Peloponnese in order to have his revenge on Athens.

The Athenians were now well aware that they were at war with Sparta. (Read Herodotus V:75, concerning the Athenians' attempts to conclude a treaty with Persia at this point.)

Athens at war with Sparta

Cleisthenes was recalled from exile and, according to Aristotle, became 'leader and champion of the people'.[31] He carried out his reforms without the benefit of the powers associated with the archonship or a tyranny, so that everything he achieved had to be confirmed by the Athenian people in their assembly.

Cleisthenes recalled

Cleisthenes' new tribal organisation

Solon had introduced many worthwhile reforms, but he had failed to alter the system of Ionian tribes which formed the basis of government. These tribes, based on ties of kinship and with regional characteristics, were dominated by the wealthy and powerful families, who disrupted the workings of government and created disunity in the state during the sixth century. For a while they were weakened by the Pisistratids, but their influence had to be broken forever without destroying the traditional organisation of religion and kinship. The state had to be able to function in a unified way without a tyrant. A new form of organisation was needed and this Cleisthenes achieved by replacing the old Ionian tribes with ten new tribes (*phylae*) determined according to territory.

A new system needed

His aims

New tribes 'to mix up the people'

Aristotle says that Cleisthenes' aim in creating ten new tribes was to mix up all the people 'so that more men should have a share in the running of the state'.[32] However, the ancient sources also say that he only turned his attention to the people because of his rivalry with Isagoras. Did he sincerely change his political thinking, believing that all citizens should participate in the working of the government? Or was he intending only to weaken his opponents while gaining and maintaining power for himself and his family?

His reforms were so well designed to give the citizens of Attica an important part to play in the running of the state that he must surely have been genuine in his desire for *isonomia* (equality of rights among all citizens).

Attempts to unify Athens

However, it is obvious that in his formation of the tribes he deliberately kept some people apart and put others together. While no doubt this benefited his own family, it also weakened the other powerful landowners. To make sure that Attica was unified and peaceful, he was forced to break the old party lines and replace allegiance to the kinship groups with allegiance to the state.

His methods

The *demes* — what were they?   Cleisthenes recognised that there already existed in the countryside of Attica a number (approximately 100 to 200) of small local districts such as towns and villages (demes). These were natural divisions, in which traditions and local loyalty were strong. In the city of Athens these did not exist, so he divided the people into an appropriate number of demes according to population. He then noted that these demes were distributed roughly in three regions: coastal, inland and city.

The importance of the demes in Cleisthenes' new system

1 The demes became the basic units around which Cleisthenes built his new tribal system. They replaced the social unit of the clan.

Unit of local government

2 Each was a unit of local government with its own assembly, officials, treasurers and annually elected leader (*demarchos*). It was through the deme that the people gained experience in participating in politics.

Citizenship based on deme

3 Cleisthenes used the criterion of residence in a deme (rather than membership of a phratry) as the basis for citizenship. At eighteen, each boy's name was entered on the deme's register and a man was now recognised by his deme-name rather than by that of his father.

Membership hereditary

4 Membership in a deme became hereditary. The deme of a man at the time of Cleisthenes' reform remained the deme of his descendants, even if they shifted away and lived elsewhere. This may have been to make sure the tribes remained equal in size.

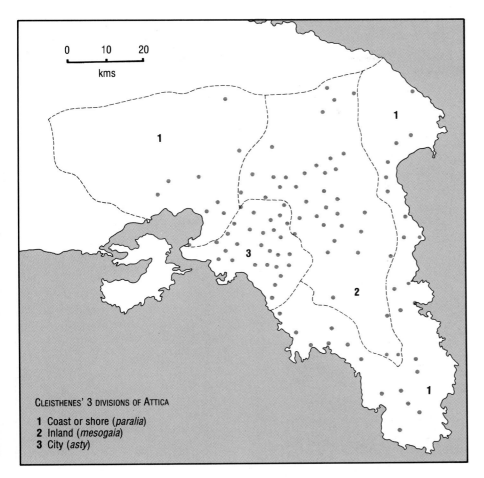

Distribution of demes in Attica

CLEISTHENES' 3 DIVISIONS OF ATTICA

1 Coast or shore (*paralia*)
2 Inland (*mesogaia*)
3 City (*asty*)

5 It was from the record of deme levels that information would come for the levy of soldiers from each tribe, candidates for office and the new Council of 500.

6 The structure of the deme emphasised the equality of its members.

The trittyes — what were they? The word *trittys* (singular) means 'a third' and these trittyes were the artificial divisions which Cleisthenes created to mix up the people. He divided the regions of coast, inland and city into ten trittyes each. In each trittys the basic unit was the deme. While some trittyes had one chief deme, others had many smaller demes.

In order to create a tribe, Cleisthenes took one trittys from each of the three regions.

The importance of the trittyes The trittyes had no independent political function; they were simply the link between deme and tribe.

Trittyes – artificial units

99

Cleisthenes' tribe and trittys
organisation

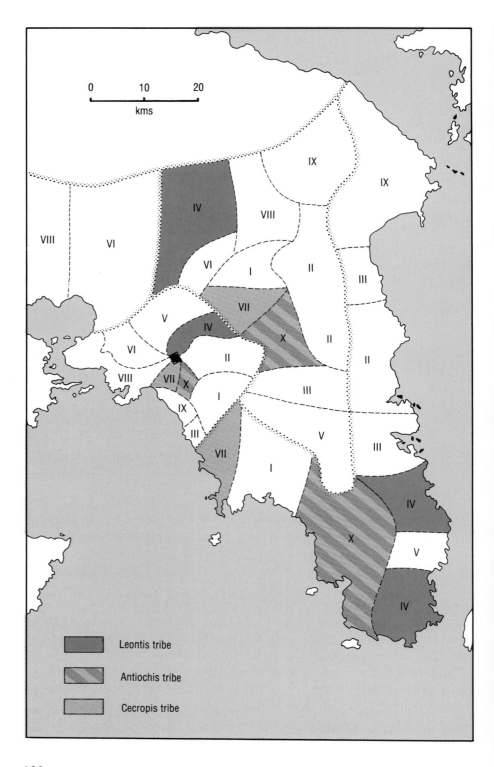

0   10   20
kms

Leontis tribe

Antiochis tribe

Cecropis tribe

The importance of the tribes

The tribes were given the names of legendary or ancient Athenian heroes, chosen by the Pythia at Delphi from a list submitted to her. Statues of these eponymous heroes were placed in the agora (marketplace of Athens).

It was as a member of a tribe that a citizen participated in the public life of the state.

- Each tribe had a shrine, and a priest who conducted sacrifices in honour of the tribe's eponymous hero.
- The tribe owned property from which came the money in the tribal treasury, and each had its own assembly and officials.

Tribes the basis of public life

- The tribe was responsible for providing a quota of men for the army, the Council of 500, boards of magistrates and the courts.
- The tribes were responsible for performing public services (liturgies) for such occasions as festivals.

The constitution of Cleisthenes

The structure of the constitution was based on the ten new tribes, although the assembly, archons, Council of Areopagus and Heliaea still functioned as they had done under Solon and Pisistratus. It was in the organisation of the new Council of 500, which became the chief organ of government, that the working of the new tribal system was most obvious. A new military organisation was also based on the ten tribes. The introduction of ostracism was attributed by Aristotle to Cleisthenes, although there is no evidence of its use before 487 B.C.

Changes in military organisation

'Then they appointed generals by tribes, one from each tribe; but the leader of the whole army was the Polemarch' (Aristotle).[33]

The use of lot

Random selection of officials was introduced by Solon, as it 'left the decision to the gods' and prevented undue influence being imposed by clans and parties. However, he usually combined it with election—at least at one level—as this would lessen the possibility of there being incompetent candidates.

Most officials selected by lot

Cleisthenes used lot far more widely, as he believed it was a more democratic method. Although it could still produce mediocre officials, Cleisthenes' system would at least mean that those who became candidates for public office would have had some political experience, either in the assembly or at the deme level. Apart from archons and generals, most officials and councillors were chosen by lot.

The year was divided into ten months, called *prytanies*

Cecropis	Acamantis	Antiochis	Hippothontis	Aeantis	Leontis	Erechtheis	Pandionis	Aegeis	Oeneis

The fifty presiding councillors were called *prytaneis* (presidents) and lived at public expense in the *tholos*

For day-to-day business a body of 500 was too large, so the fifty members of each tribe were selected by lot to act as a committee for one-tenth of the year; each prytany was called after the tribe presiding

ADMINISTRATIVE FUNCTIONS
1 Finance
2 Public works
3 Foreign affairs
4 Supervision of magistrates

COUNCIL OF 500
(represented every area in Attica)

PROBULEUTIC FUNCTIONS
All proposals considered before submission to assembly; agenda prepared for assembly

CITIZENS OVER 30   50   50   50   50   50   50   50   50   50   50   SELECTED BY LOT

Erechtheis	Aegeis	Pandionis	Leontis	Acamantis	Oeneis	Cecropis	Hippothontis	Aeantis	Antiochis

The demes which made up a tribe selected a fixed number of candidates, according to their size

NOTES:
1 There were few citizens who had not sat at least once in the council (restricted to twice in a lifetime); this gave citizens political experience.
2 Councillors took an oath on entering office to 'advise what is best for Athens' and were responsible for their acts when they finished their year's term of office.

The Council of 500

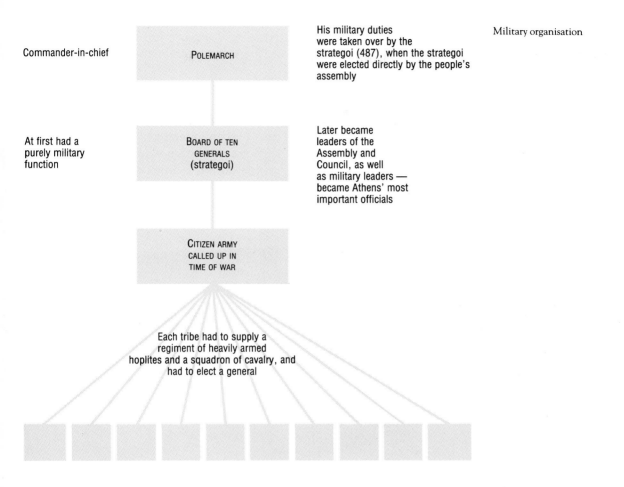

Commander-in-chief

POLEMARCH

His military duties were taken over by the strategoi (487), when the strategoi were elected directly by the people's assembly

Military organisation

At first had a purely military function

BOARD OF TEN GENERALS (strategoi)

Later became leaders of the Assembly and Council, as well as military leaders — became Athens' most important officials

CITIZEN ARMY CALLED UP IN TIME OF WAR

Each tribe had to supply a regiment of heavily armed hoplites and a squadron of cavalry, and had to elect a general

Ostracism

'Cleisthenes enacted other new laws in his bid for popular support, among them the law about ostracism' (Aristotle).[34]

Ostracism was an institution by which any Athenian who was regarded as being too powerful and dangerous to the welfare of the people was sent into exile for ten years, although his family was allowed to remain in Attica and his property was not confiscated.

In the sixth prytany of each year the people were asked in the assembly if they wanted an ostracism to be held. If the answer was in the affirmative, it was held in a later prytany (some sources say the seventh prytany while others think it was the eighth). The agora was fenced in, with ten entrances — one for each tribe. *Ostraka* (the singular is *ostrakon*) were pieces of broken pottery, or potsherds, on which the name of the person to be ostracised was scratched. A quorum of 6000 citizens was necessary for an ostracism to be valid.

Ostracism — a check on tyranny

Ostraka

Not introduced until 488

Despite Aristotle's evidence, many scholars believe that ostracism was not introduced by Cleisthenes, because it was not until 488/487 that the first ostracism occurred. However, there are several explanations that may account for this.

- After the failure of Isagoras and the Spartans, there may not have been any need to hold one for some time.
- There may have been attempts at ostracism but failure to get a quorum of voters, which would have meant abandonment of the attempt.
- Aristotle says that they held their first ostracism when 'the people were confident' after their victory at Marathon.[35] Since the institution was intended to prevent tyranny, it was held just after Hippias had accompanied the Persians to Marathon, and was directed against a member of the Pisistratids.

An ostrakon inscribed with the words 'Kallixenos [Callixenus] the traitor'

The contribution of Cleisthenes to the establishment of democracy

Government moving towards democracy

The government of Athens was not yet fully democratic, but it was moving steadily towards that goal. Cleisthenes created the framework for democracy.

1 By destroying the basis of the old jealousies and factional strife he unified the state, so that all citizens saw themselves as Athenians first, with pride in their city and state. They were now able to vote in the assembly as individuals, without the fear of outside pressure.
2 By relating local government to the central government, Cleisthenes helped the Athenians to see themselves as an integral part of the government of the state.

- At the deme level the people gained valuable political experience, which would have given them added confidence to take on the responsibility associated with the Council of 500. Twice in their lives they could take the oath 'to advise what is best for the city' as a councillor.

    All classes gained political experience

- Regardless of wealth or birth, all had equal political rights in the election of officials whether at the deme level (demarch), the tribal level (general) or the state level (archons and councillors).

3 Despite some of the problems associated with the use of lot, such as the possibility of gaining mediocre officials, Cleisthenes' wider use of this method of appointment was more democratic in that it emphasised the equality of all citizens.

    Equality of citizens emphasised

4 Ostracism, if it was introduced by Cleisthenes, weakened the Areopagus by depriving it of its most important political function — the guarding of the constitution and protecting the state against the danger of tyranny. Ostracism was intended to prevent internal strife (*stasis*). It was not until later that it became a dangerous weapon for use in getting rid of opponents.

    Checks on power

5 Cleisthenes created a number of popular courts (*dikasteria*) which functioned alongside the Heliaea. These dicasteries were in fact smaller panels of the Heliaea.

Undemocratic aspects of the constitution

The archons were still elected from the top two classes and retained their powers; the aristocratic Areopagus Council, made up of ex-archons, still had considerable powers, and the extent to which the country and poor citizens could take up public office was restricted by the fact that officials were not paid.

Democracy incomplete

These undemocratic aspects were gradually removed during the next half-century. In 487 archons were selected by lot; in 462, under Ephialtes, the Areopagus lost all its important political powers. Soon after, Pericles opened the archonship to the lower classes and introduced payment of jurors and of all officials selected by lot.

Athens threatened from outside

In 506, while still adjusting to the reforms of Cleisthenes, Athens was faced with threats from enemies on three sides.

Renewed threats from Sparta

King Cleomenes, wanting revenge on Athens for his recent humiliation, had raised an army from the Peloponnesian states and had no difficulty gaining the support of Thebes to the north and the city of Chalcis in Euboea. Both of these cities were hostile to Athens.

Cleomenes' efforts were frustrated, however, by the refusal of the

Corinthians to remain with him; they disapproved of the undertaking, and returned home. The two Spartan kings (Cleomenes and Demaratus, both of whom travelled with the army at this stage) quarrelled, and Cleomenes was forced to abandon his attempt.

Victory for Athens

The Thebans, however, had already crossed the border and the Athenians had to prevent them from joining forces with the Chalcidians. They attacked the Thebans in northern Attica, winning an overwhelming victory and taking prisoners; they then crossed to Euboea, defeated Chalcis, and took possession of part of the fertile Lelantine Plain,

First Athenian cleruchs

establishing a cleruchy (outsettlement) of 4000 Athenian citizens. These cleruchs (outsettlers) retained their Athenian citizenship but became landowners; they also acted as watchdogs for Athenian interests. The Chalcidian and Boeotian prisoners were ransomed and Athens extended her territory on the northern frontier, although the people there did not become Athenian citizens.

Herodotus summed up the victory of the new Athenian democracy:

Thus Athens went from strength to strength, and proved, if proof were needed, how noble a thing freedom is . . . for while they were oppressed under a despotic government, they had no better success in war than any of their neighbours, yet, once the yoke was flung off, they proved the finest fighters in the world.[36]

Essay topics

1 What were the problems facing Solon when he was appointed archon with extraordinary powers, in 594 B.C.? How successful was he in finding a permanent solution to them?

2 Comment on Solon's own statement: 'I stood guard with a broad shield in front of both parties and prevented either from triumphing unjustly'.

3 To what extent can Solon be regarded as 'the Father of Democracy'? Explain some of the steps he took which ultimately led to a more democratic government in Athens.

4 What lasting benefits did the Pisistratid tyranny bring to Athens?

5 What were the aims of Cleisthenes in establishing a new system of tribes? What functions did these tribes have in the working of the Athenian constitution?

6 How far were the developments towards democracy in the sixth century the by-product of struggles for personal power?

7 Write a detailed account of ostracism. Include in your essay discussion of
(a) why it was introduced;
(b) how it operated;
(c) some of the prominent Athenians who were banished during the fifth century;
(d) when and why it was discontinued.

Timeline: Athens in the sixth century

600 At this point, too, the inequalities between rich and poor had, as it were, come to a head. The city stood on the brink of revolution and it seemed as if the only way to put a stop to its perpetual disorders and achieve stability was to set up a tyranny. — Plutarch, *Solon*, 13

594 Solon appointed archon with extraordinary powers, to mediate between aristocrats and commoners; carries out economic, social and political reforms, but fails to satisfy either side satisfactorily
Political turmoil; party strife among nobles; no archons could be elected in 589 and 584 (*anarchia* — no rule)

560 First attempt at tyranny by Pisistratus, a member of a noble family

556 Pisistratus forced by his political opponents to leave Athens

550 Pisistratus' second attempt at tyranny; exiled same year

546 Third, successful, seizure of power; lays foundations for the future greatness of Athens
Pisistratus administered the city's affairs moderately and more like a citizen than a tyrant. — Aristotle, *Athenian Constitution*, 16:2

527 Pisistratus succeeded by his son, Hippias; Hipparchus (a second son) may have helped in the rule

These particular dictators, in fact, showed for a very long time both high principles and intelligence in their policy. — Thucydides, VI:54

514 Hipparchus assassinated by Harmodius and Aristogeiton. For the next four years Hippias' rule becomes harsher — a complete change of government

After this the dictatorship became more oppressive to the Athenians. Hippias was now more frightened himself, and he put to death many of the citizens. — Thucydides, VI:59

510 Hippias overthrown by King Cleomenes of Sparta, under instruction from Delphic oracle; exiled Athenian clan of the Alcmaeonids were behind this

508 Factional strife yet again
Isagoras elected chief archon
Cleisthenes (an Alcmaeonid) appeals to the people in order to get the upper hand — introduces new democratic measures
Isagoras appeals to Sparta for support — Cleomenes marches into Attica again to establish a narrow oligarchy, but fails
Cleisthenes devises a new political organisation — undermines power of the clans; democracy in more complete sense

506

Cleomenes seeks revenge for humiliation; launches combined attack on
    the new democracy with help from Boeotia and Chalcis
Athenian victory

500

Thus Athens went from strength to strength, and proved, if proof was needed,
how noble a thing freedom is, not in one respect only, but in all. — Herodotus,
V:81

Further reading

Primary sources

Aristotle. *The Athenian Constitution.*
Herodotus. *The Histories.*
Plutarch. *The Rise and Fall of Athens*, Ch. 2.

Secondary sources

Andrewes, A. *The Greek Tyrants.*
Bury, J. B. & Meiggs, R. *A History of Greece.*
Ehrenberg, V. *From Solon to Socrates.*
Forrest, W. G. *The Emergence of Greek Democracy.*
Hammond, N. G. L. *A History of Greece to 322 B. C.*
McDermott, W & Caldwell, W. *Readings in the History of the Ancient
    World.*

The conflicts between the Greeks and the Persians

6

The use of source material

Herodotus

THE GREEK word *historia* means 'research' or 'inquiry' and it is on the researches of Herodotus of Halicarnassus that we rely most heavily for our information of the Persian War period. He has often been criticised — both in the past and in the present — for his inaccuracy, bias and failure to evaluate events properly, but there is no other major ancient source against which scholars can check his facts.

Herodotus was a born storyteller and an accomplished collector of facts, and he relates what people living at the time believed about past events. His work is fascinating and essential reading for this period, but it is necessary to keep in mind some of its weaknesses.

Herodotus — a collector of facts

Who was Herodotus?

Many details of his life are uncertain, so any biography of Herodotus can only be sketchy.

A Roman copy of the fifth-century Greek bust of Herodotus (Courtesy of the Metropolitan Museum of Art, New York)

Early life in Halicarnassus

He was born in Halicarnassus in southern Asia Minor about 484 B.C., four years prior to the great invasion of Greece by Xerxes which is the culmination of his research. It is possible that as a boy he may have talked with men from Caria who had sailed and fought against the Greeks at Salamis under the leadership of Queen Artemisia.

At some time before 454 (some sources place it at about 464) he was banished by the tyrant Lygdamis, grandson of Queen Artemisia, on account of his participation in an uprising. He fled to Samos, and it is probably during these years that he began his extensive travels — certainly to the Black Sea region.

Extensive travels

He may have taken part in an attempt to free Halicarnassus and it is likely that after 454 he travelled to Egypt, Tyre, Babylon and Cyrene, after which he migrated to Athens. It was during his years in Athens that he developed his pro-Athenian attitude and composed his story of Xerxes' invasion of Greece.

Years in Athens

By a law of Pericles in 451, Herodotus was unable to become an Athenian citizen as he had hoped to do, so he joined the Athenian colony of Thurii in southern Italy. About 431–430 (the first years of the Peloponnesian War), he probably returned to Athens. Most sources believe he died (c.425) in Thurii, and was honoured by the building of a mausoleum in the market place.

Thurii in Italy

His aims in writing the history

1 'To preserve the memory of the past by putting on record the astonishing achievements both of our own, and of other peoples'.[1]
2 To outline the causes of the conflict between the Greeks and the Persians. In tracing the contacts and conflicts between the two different cultures, he reveals the contrast between oriental autocracy and the freedom of Greece.

Herodotus' sources

See Herodotus: The Histories, 6:137 (pp. 370).

Herodotus openly used the work of Hecataeus, the great traveller and geographer of Asia Minor, but there is no evidence that he used any other prose source. The fact that he does not give credit to other sources does not, however, indicate that he did not use them.

He collected material from wherever he could — speaking to people of all kinds, from soldiers to priests — and he simply repeated stories that he was told. He was informed of Athenian and Spartan family traditions and he obviously had some reliable Persian sources. 'It is my principle, that I ought to repeat what is said; but I am not bound always to believe it and that may be taken to apply to this book as a whole.'[2]

Some of his material came from his own observations of people during his travels, and from inscribed monuments.

Source of his information

See H. Histories, 7:152 (p. 421)

Weaknesses in Herodotus

His work contains errors

There are mistakes in Herodotus, because oral tradition — on which he relied for much of his information — obviously changed, and one person's view of an event did not always agree with another's. He did not sift his evidence when there were conflicting accounts, as Thucydides did.

Inaccuracies

He was writing about the history of a war and yet he was no military expert. In fact he did not have the most elementary knowledge of warfare and therefore could be misled by his sources, which Thucydides, a trained soldier, was not. Herodotus could not evaluate the military information he was given about battles, and his figures on the numbers of men and ships are suspect (usually grossly exaggerated).

No military knowledge

Treatment of causes is superficial

Although one of the aims of Herodotus was to record the causes of the conflicts between the Greeks and the Persians, he does not consider anything other than the ambitions, desires or whims of individuals. He does not delve into deeper causes.

No deep understanding of causes

He is biased, but honest about it

He openly declares his admiration for Athens and his account of the first and second invasions is written largely from the Athenian point of view. He expresses the view that the Athenians were truly the saviours of

Athenian bias

Greece, even though he knew that his opinion would be unpopular in some areas. He admired Athenian democracy, was enthusiastic about the empire, and favoured Pericles and the Alcmaeonid family in particular. He tends to express the Alcmaeonid family's picture of Themistocles and he is hostile to King Cleomenes of Sparta and to particular cities, such as Thebes, Corinth and Aegina. He is also far from fair in his treatment of Ionia, regarding the Ionian revolt. However, it must be remembered that he received his information at a time when Athens and Sparta were hostile to one another, after 464. Those reading Herodotus should be aware of his bias and should not forget that a good case can be made for Spartan heroism in the second invasion.

Hostility to
Peloponnesians

Aeschylus

Aeschylus, a dramatist of the early fifth century, presented to the Greek public in 472 a play called *The Persians*. He had fought at Marathon and probably also at Salamis and Plataea. His description in the play of the Battle of Salamis — which seems to be an eyewitness account — is very useful source material, but it should be remembered that it was intended to carry a religious message, not just to glorify the Greek victory over Persia.

Eyewitness

A religious play

The theme of the play is that human pride and arrogance (*hubris*) is punished severely and quickly by the gods, either through human hands or through nature. In this case Xerxes had gone beyond the limits set down by the gods, by crossing the Hellespont and launching his campaign in Europe.

The play contains deliberate omissions and inaccuracies in order to illustrate the theme, and the Athenian audience at the time were aware of these. Aeschylus does not mention any Greek or specifically Athenian names. The victory of Salamis was a victory for the gods.

His vivid description of this battle is very useful, despite the fact that he has streamlined his account for dramatic purposes.

Vivid description of
Salamis

The Troezen inscription — the Themistocles decree

In 1932 a Greek farmer living in the area of ancient Troezen, in the Peloponnese, found a marble slab about 60 centimetres high and 45 centimetres wide. In 1959 it was removed to a local museum where Professor M. A. Jameson, travelling through that part of the Peloponnese, saw it and realised its significance. On translation it appeared to be a copy

Discovery at Troezen

of a decree passed by the Athenian Assembly, outlining evacuation procedures in the face of the Persian invasion of 480 B.C.

It included a decision by the Athenians, on the motion of Themistocles, to evacuate their wives and children to Troezen and old men and movable possessions to Salamis, while all those of military age were to embark on their ships with any others who wished to share the danger. A detailed description is then given about the appointment of trierarchs and the exact manning of the ships; it also records the decision to send half their ships to Artemisium, while the rest were to lie in wait at Salamis. The last few lines of the inscription include the order to recall all exiles. *Evacuation decisions*

Until the discovery of the inscription, Herodotus' account of the evacuation — as a last-minute action carried out after the fall of Thermopylae and the retreat from Artemisium — was never doubted. If this stele, inscribed 150 years after the Persian invasions, was an exact copy of an early fifth-century decree, it throws a whole new light on the purpose of Thermopylae and Artemisium and the evacuation of Athens. It also validates Thucydides' verdict that Themistocles was the most far-sighted statesman of his time. Since its discovery, however, controversy as to its authenticity has raged among scholars, each one arguing convincingly one way or the other. Some believe it is a mildly edited fourth-century version of a fifth-century decree — perhaps preserved on papyrus — later paraphrased and finally inscribed. Others believe it is a total fabrication by fourth-century Troezenians to honour Athens, while still others suggest that only part of it is authentic (lines 1–18) and the rest added at some later time. It is also possible that it was a series of separate motions put forward and later set down as a memorial. *Herodotus' account*

Controversy over authenticity

Whatever the truth, there is no doubting the evacuation of the Athenian people in 480. The question is:

- Did it occur, as Herodotus says, as a desperate action, after the defence of Thermopylae and Artemisium failed and the Peloponnesians showed they were unwilling to defend Attica? Or was it a carefully thought out plan of campaign which was begun before Thermopylae, with Themistocles, as indicated in the decree, seeing that the battle would eventually have to be fought at Salamis, involving the sacrifice of Athens? *Which version is correct?*

The Greeks of Asia Minor and the Persian Empire

The map and notes on page 114 provided a summary of the events of this period up to the succession of Cambyses, son of the Persian conqueror, Cyrus.

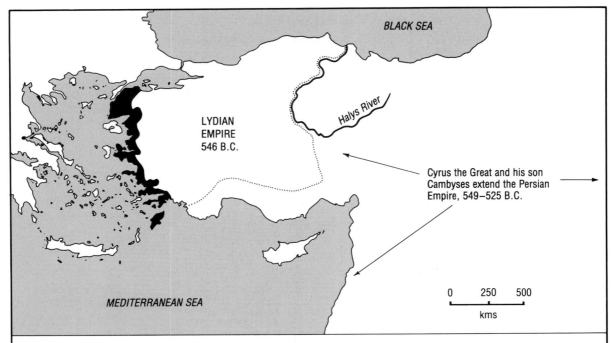

1 The Greeks, who had migrated across the Aegean during the Dorian invasions, had settled in the isolated valleys along the coast of Asia Minor. In the sixth century, Ionia (as the central part of Asia Minor was known) produced many outstanding men of intellect, such as Thales, Anaximander, Pythagoras and Xenophanes.

The freedom of these Greek cities on the fringe of Asia was precarious, particularly since they lacked unity — both politically and racially.

2 In 560 the wealthy kingdom of Lydia, led by King Croesus, subjugated all the Greeks of Asia Minor except those of Miletus. The kingdom extended from the Aegean to the River Halys.

Although Croesus was more oriental than Greek, there was a close sympathy between Lydian and Greek civilisations. The Greek language spread throughout Lydia, Greek gods were honoured, and Croesus himself gave generously to Greek sanctuaries and consulted the Delphic oracle.

The Lydians allowed the Greeks a large amount of freedom and they benefited from the introduction of the first coinage of electrum (gold and silver) and from inland trade.

3 In the east, the Median king was overthrown by Cyrus of Persia, who became one of the great conquerors in history. In 546 he captured Sardis, bringing to a sudden end the kingdom of Lydia, although Croesus was spared.

This was to have great repercussions for the Greeks, as the Lydians had acted as a barrier to the oriental kingdoms of the east; once this barrier was removed, the Greeks came into direct contact with an empire which stretched to areas unknown to them.

Cyrus went on to extend his empire, controlling Armenia, Hyrcania, Bactria, Afghanistan.

4 Cyrus had invited the Ionians in the Lydian army to change sides, but they refused. When Cyrus won the Ionians made overtures to him, but he would make no arrangements, except with Miletus, which had a treaty under Lydia and continued to have independence.

The Ionians were disunited and easy prey for Cyrus' general, Harpagus. A heavy tribute was imposed on them, and they were expected to contribute military and naval forces when needed. Two cities preferred permanent exile rather than to live under Persian rule.

Cyrus was succeeded by his son, Cambyses, who added Egypt and Greek Cyrene to his empire.

The Persian Empire, extended under Cyrus

Darius I sitting in state — a detail from the bas-relief of the treasury of Darius at Persepolis

Darius I — Persian king (521–486)

On the death of Cambyses, an impostor king ruled for seven months before being overthrown in a revolution led by members of seven leading Persian families, one of whom was Darius. From this group Darius was chosen as king in 521, but within a few months he faced revolt in many parts of his empire. The quelling of these uprisings — in Babylon, Elam,

Darius becomes king

Media and Armenia—showed his cool and ruthless determination and his ability to rule. He consolidated his hold on the empire by marrying two daughters of Cyrus.

He next organised his empire with such thoroughness and attention to detail that his arrangements lasted with little trouble for nearly 200 years.

Royal provinces

Satrapies   A satrapy was a province ruled by a governor, or satrap. Darius increased the number of these and instituted a fixed yearly tribute. The satraps had great power and independence in their regions, although the royal assent was needed for major decisions and even for minor wars of conquest. Sometimes the administrative and military commands were separated, to act as a check.

Size of empire

Royal Road   To improve communications, he developed an efficient road and courier system throughout the empire. The Royal Road was the fastest link between the satrapy of Lydia in the west, with its capital at Sardis, and the Persian capital of Susa. It followed the old caravan routes, a journey of approximately three months for a man on foot. Herodotus describes in detail the staging posts, rest houses, military and guard posts along the way,[3] and says 'there is nothing in the world which travels faster than these Persian couriers... Nothing stops these couriers from covering their allotted stage in the quickest possible time—neither snow, rain, heat, nor darkness'.[4] Obviously there were other royal roads, to the east and to Egypt. However, the extent of the empire from Egypt to India meant that it could take weeks for the king to receive and send messages. In the long run, the unity and effectiveness of the empire was due to the autocracy of Darius and to his constant inspections, either directly or through trusted agents of his far-flung governors.

Communications

The gold daric of Darius

Coinage   Darius was interested in economic matters, and introduced the Persian gold coin called the *daric*.

Darius moves into Europe

If Darius was to follow in the footsteps of Cyrus and Cambyses, Europe would be his next objective. He had already sent out an expedition to gain information on the coasts of Greece and Italy.

In 513 he crossed the Bosphorus with an army, to march through Thrace into Scythia. What his motive was is not known. It may have been to subdue Thrace in order to secure the safety of Asia Minor, or to gain a northern frontier at the Danube. Herodotus suggests it was a raid of revenge for a previous Scythian attack.

Aims of Darius' Scythian campaign

The Ionians

During this invasion the Ionians and other Asiatic Greeks were in charge of the fleet, which sailed into the Black Sea as far as the Danube and had to bridge it and await Darius' return. The Ionians waiting at the bridge were urged by the Scythians to pull it down and return home. In

Opposite: The extent of the Persian Empire at the time of Darius (490)

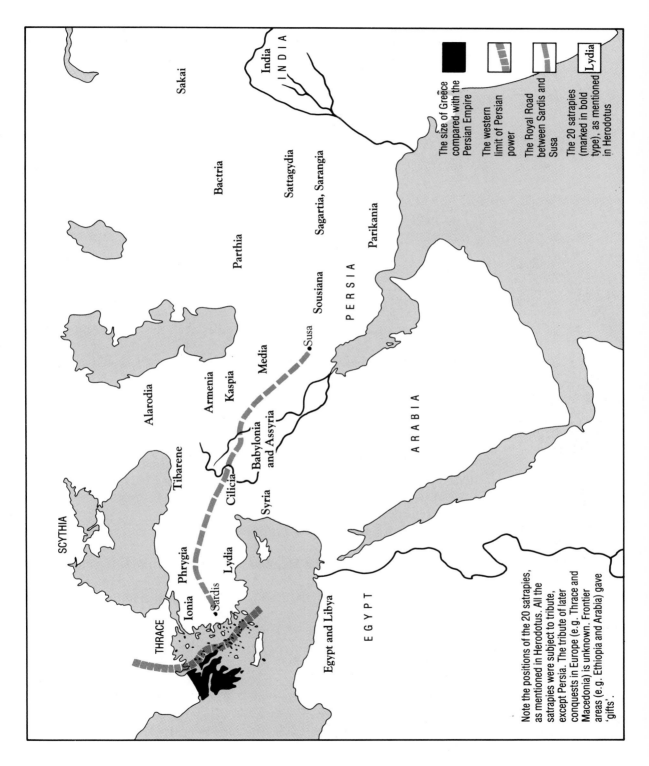

The size of Greece compared with the Persian Empire

The western limit of Persian power

The Royal Road between Sardis and Susa

The 20 satrapies (marked in bold type), as mentioned in Herodotus

Lydia

Note the positions of the 20 satrapies, as mentioned in Herodotus. All the satrapies were subject to tribute, except Persia. The tribute of later conquests in Europe (e.g. Thrace and Macedonia) is unknown. Frontier areas (e.g. Ethiopia and Arabia) gave 'gifts'.

India

I N D I A

Sakai

Bactria

Sattagydia

Sagartia, Sarangia

Parthia

Parikania

Sousiana

P E R S I A

Susa

Media

Kaspia

Armenia

Babylonia and Assyria

Alarodia

Cilicia

A R A B I A

Tibarene

Syria

SCYTHIA

Phrygia

Lydia

Ionia

Sardis

THRACE

Egypt and Libya

E G Y P T

the discussion which followed Miltiades, the Athenian ruler of the Chersonese, expressed the opinion that they should take the Scythians' advice and free Ionia, but other Greek leaders pointed out that each of them owed his position, as head of state, to Darius.

Results

Despite his failure in Scythia and the attempt by the towns around the Bosphorus to rebel, Darius did make substantial gains when he left two of his commanders to complete the conquest of Thrace. He had added two new satrapies in Europe and had secured control of the easy route through Thrace to the Strymon River, with its timber and gold mines. This area was of great strategic importance.

The Ionian revolt, 499–493

Causes

Herodotus' view

Herodotus sees the direct cause of the revolt in 499 of the Greeks of Asia Minor against Persian control as simply the ambitions and intrigues of the tyrant of Miletus, Aristagoras, and his father-in-law Histiaeus. He does not take into account that there was widespread discontent throughout the Greek cities of Asia Minor and that this had existed certainly from 545, when they became subject to Persia. Aristagoras could not have stirred up a rebellion of disunited Greek communities if they had not been unhappy with their situation.

Underlying causes

Loss of freedom

1 The Greeks had lost their autonomy or independence in deciding their own lifestyle, something which was precious to them.

Barbarian overlords

2 They were subject not only to another power, but to an oriental, 'barbarian' king to whom they paid a heavy tribute, most of which was not returned into local circulation.

3 The Persian system of local government in Asia Minor involved the use of Greek, pro-Persian tyrants who were 'puppets' of the great king. They held their position through the support of the satrap, to whom they were responsible. Tyranny had been a common form of government in Greece and Asia Minor when Cyrus conquered those areas, but in the generation which followed most states had thrown off their tyrants, and tyranny was no longer acceptable to the Greeks. In order to free themselves from it, they had to rebel against the Persian king who controlled them.

Herodotus on at least three occasions gives an indication of this underlying discontent. 'Histiaeus to Darius: "It appears that the Ionians have waited till I was out of sight to do what they have long passionately desired to do"'.[5] However, what the Greeks needed was leadership and direction, as they lacked unity.

Direct cause   Histiaeus, tyrant of Miletus and a successful commander under Darius, was summoned to Susa and detained there indefinitely by the king, who suspected his ambitions. In his place at Miletus Histiaeus left his son-in-law, Aristagoras. When he was approached by a delegation of aristocrats from Naxos, recently removed in a popular uprising and wanting help to recover their position, Aristagoras saw an opportunity to make himself ruler of Naxos. He hoped at the same time to crush Naxos commercially. Concealing his purpose, he made the Naxian exiles an offer.

Aristagoras' ambitions

Planned attempt to seize Naxos

Needing help with this plan, Aristagoras proposed to the satrap at Sardis, Artaphernes, that in returning the Naxian exiles Persia might gain control of Naxos and the other islands of the Cyclades and, using these as stepping stones, finally extend the great Persian king's empire as far as the rich island of Euboea. Artaphernes submitted the plan to his half-brother Darius, and gained his consent.

The plan, however, misfired, as the Naxians were warned of the attack and prepared for a long siege. The costly expedition failed to gain anything and Aristagoras, fearful of Artaphernes' reaction, was in a dilemma as to what step to take next.

Failure to take Naxos

According to Herodotus, 'these various causes of alarm were already making Aristagoras contemplate rebellion' when Histiaeus sent a message to Aristagoras (the famous story of the slave with the tatooed head) 'urging him to do precisely what he was thinking of, namely, to revolt'.[6] Histiaeus' motive was that he thought Darius would send him down to the coast to restore order.

Aristagoras' alarm

Aristagoras' attempts to gain support

1 He renounced his own tyranny and urged other Greek leaders to do the same. Those who did not were removed forcibly or put under threat of attack.
2 He went to mainland Greece to seek support from Sparta and Athens. The Spartans were not interested when they realised the distance of Susa from the sea. Athens and Eretria agreed to send aid, Athens contributing twenty warships and Eretria five.

Seeks support from the mainland

Why did Athens and Eretria send help to Ionia?

1 The Athenians were already on bad terms with Persia, owing to the activities of the ex-tyrant Hippias at the court of Artaphernes where, according to Herodotus, he was moving heaven and earth 'to procure the subjection of Athens to himself and Darius'.[7] The Athenians had urged Artaphernes not to listen to the exiled Pisistratid, but he had demanded that the Athenians take him back or accept the consequences. The Athenians were now openly hostile to Persia.
2 The new democracy at Athens was opposed to tyranny.

Links between Athens and Ionia

3 The Greeks, generally, were becoming alarmed at Darius' movements into Europe (Thrace).

4 Aristagoras pointed out the close link between Athens and Ionia, that 'Miletus had been founded by Athenian settlers so it was only natural that the Athenians, powerful as they were, would help her in her need'.[8]

Eretria repays debt

5 The Eretrians sent help because in a previous war with their neighbour Chalcis they had been helped by Miletus, and were now repaying 'a debt of honour'.

The part played by Athens and Eretria and its significance

'The sailing of this fleet was the beginning of trouble not only for Greece but for other peoples.'[9]

Degree of help

The Athenians and Eretrians landed at Ephesus, were joined by Ionian troops, and marched inland. They took Sardis, except for the citadel, and in the attack set fire to several thatched houses. The fire spread rapidly until the whole lower town, including the temple of the goddess Cybele, was destroyed. The Ionians, Athenians and Eretrians withdrew to the coast pursued by Persian forces, but were forced into battle near Ephesus, losing many men. The mainland Greeks sailed for home, taking no more part in the revolt.

Future trouble for Athens

Despite their limited participation, the Athenians and Eretrians were to suffer at the hands of the Persians in the years to come. Darius is said to have desired revenge for the burning of his temples so much that he prayed: '"Grant O god, that I may punish the Athenians". Then he commanded one of his servants to repeat to him the words, "Master, remember the Athenians", three times, whenever he sat down to dinner'.[10]

The course of the war

Six years of war

Herodotus' chronology is unreliable, as it often gives the impression that many battles occurred in the one year.

498   Burning of Sardis; Athenians defeated near Ephesus
497   Cyprus joins revolt
      Under siege by Persians
      Cyprus subdued
496   Revolt in Caria — fierce land fighting — great losses by Carians
      Aristagoras flees to Thrace
      Histiaeus sent down to coast — goes to Byzantium
495   No decisive operations — nothing mentioned in Herodotus
494   Only six cities on coast fight on
      Great battle at Ladé (opposite Miletus)
      Samos withdraws, followed by others
      Greeks defeated
      Miletus destroyed; people sold into slavery

493 Histiaeus killed
Miltiades escapes to Athens
492 Persians take all offshore islands: Chios, Lesbos, Tenedos
European coast of the Chersonese and Bosphorus retaken
Darius sends Mardonius with an army and a navy to retake Thrace and attack Athens and Eretria

Greeks defeated

Reasons for the Ionian defeat

1 The Persian Empire had the resources to maintain a sustained war effort.

2 The Ionians lacked unity and discipline. Herodotus describes their failure to work together under one leader[11] and suggests that the withdrawal of the Samians, who wished to save their houses and temples, encouraged others 'to become faint hearted'.[12]

Disunity of Greeks

Results and their significance

Destruction of Miletus

Miletus was destroyed, its temples burned and plundered and its inhabitants killed or taken into captivity to Susa. Miletus ceased to be a force in history, and economic supremacy passed to the mainland of Greece. The fate of Miletus had a great impact on the Athenians, as many felt that more help should have been given to Ionia. When Phrynichus some years later presented a play called *The Fall of Miletus*, the audience was moved to tears of shame. Phrynichus was fined; his play was never to be presented in public again.

Persians initiate reforms

Generally, however, the Ionians were treated with great tolerance by the Persians, and Artaphernes introduced several measures which encouraged peace. He bound the Ionians by oath to settle any future conflicts among themselves by arbitration rather than by raids, and he conducted surveys to determine a fair land tax. In the following year Darius, realising the Greeks' hatred of tyranny, sent Mardonius to the coast to set up democracies.

However, despite these improvements the Greeks were still not free; they remained under Persian control until 479, when they were liberated by the Athenians.

Escape of Miltiades to Athens

The escape of Miltiades as the Phoenician fleet approached and his return to Athens at a critical time was vital for the future defence of Greece at Marathon. He had intimate knowledge of Persian ways and military tactics.

Darius seeks revenge

The help given by the Athenians to the Ionians drew upon them the vengeance of Darius, who now set in motion his first expedition against Greece.

The Ionian revolt was the first round in the struggle between Greece and Persia.

Expedition of Mardonius, 492

Abortive expedition against Greece

Mardonius, Darius' son-in-law, gathered 'a formidable fleet and army' and 'began his march through Europe with Eretria and Athens as his main objectives'[13] but with instructions to subjugate as many towns as he could on the way. Mardonius had ordered the Ionians to contribute ships to ferry his forces across the Hellespont and to accompany the army along the coast of Thrace. Thrace and Macedonia submitted without resistance, but Mardonius suffered a serious setback when his fleet was wrecked in the stormy waters off the rugged coast of Mt Athos. According to Herodotus, many ships were lost; men drowned, were taken by 'monsters', or died of exposure. This was followed by an attack on the army by a Thracian tribe, and Mardonius was wounded.

Preparations for next attempt

This attempted invasion of Greece had to be aborted, but Herodotus probably exaggerated the disastrous nature of the campaign. It was hardly the failure he suggested, and Persian prestige did not suffer. It did not deter Darius, as his aim was obviously to conquer the divided and quarrelling Greek states, and preparations were immediately put into effect for a new attempt at invasion and conquest.

Assignment: The first Persian invasion of Greece, 490

This assignment is an essential part of the study of this chapter.

Darius' preparations

1 Demands for submission.
'Darius now began to put out feelers to test the attitude of the Greeks, and to find out whether they were likely to resist or surrender. He sent heralds to the various Greek states to demand earth and water for the King...'.
(a) What was the significance of the 'earth and water'?
(b) What was the reaction of Athens and Sparta?
(c) For what reasons did the islands of the Aegean submit?
(d) What was the significance of the submission of Aegina?
(e) How did this bring to a head internal conflict in Sparta?
(f) What was done to keep Aegina in check?
Refer to Herodotus, VI:47–52, VI:74, VII:133; Ehrenberg, *From Solon to Socrates*, p. 129; Hammond, p. 209.
2 Recruitment of an army and a fleet.
'... [Darius] sent orders to the Asiatic coast towns which were already tributary for the provision of warships and transport vessels to carry cavalry.'
Refer to Herodotus, VI:48, VI:95; Ehrenberg, op. cit., p. 130; Hammond, p. 212.

3 Selection of leaders.

'In consequence of the ill success of his previous expedition he relieved Mardonius of his command, and appointed other generals....'.

Refer to Herodotus, VI:94–5.

Darius' aims

'... Their orders were to reduce Athens and Eretria to slavery and to bring the slaves before the king.'

1 Was the punishment of Athens and Eretria the only aim of Darius? What other aims may he have had?
2 What part did Hippias, ex-tyrant of Athens, play?

Refer to Herodotus, V:105, VI:46, VI:94–5; Ehrenberg, op. cit., p. 130; Hammond, p. 212.

Developments in Athens

'While Athens and Aegina were at each other's throats, the king of Persia continued to mature his plans' and Miltiades, 'getting home to what looked like safety found his enemies waiting for him'.

1 Why were Athens and Aegina enemies?
2 What was the 'unheralded' war fought with Aegina on the eve of the Persian invasion?
3 Themistocles, the archon for 493, began his attempts to turn Athens into a naval power. What project did he carry out that later served Athens so well?
4 What was the real reason behind the impeachment and trial of Miltiades?

The nature of Greek politics in the early fifth century, in particular that of Athens, had a bearing on Miltiades' impeachment in 493 and on his later trial and sentence after Paros, and is important in understanding Themistocles' later career.

Athenian democracy was in its infancy and political events still reflected the rivalries between prominent men and families.

- They were unashamedly ambitious to rule.
- They wanted to be the best and so envied any other individual or faction that dominated the state, and attempted to have them overthrown (Miltiades and Themistocles).
- They hated being ruled by other factions and objected to democracy putting their social 'inferiors' on the same level as themselves. In time they were forced to become reconciled to democracy, and if they could preserve their dignity by leading and persuading the people, then that was second only to totally dominating the state.
- They did not object to despotic rule as a system, and could be placated by marriage links or by being promoted to positions of honour in the state.
- If they were driven into exile they did not hesitate to side with a rival state (for example, Hippias with Persia) to obtain restoration to power.
- They did not regard siding with the enemy or opening the gates to an invader as acting against the people, because their 'own' people were their family, relatives and friends.

Those who were firmest in their resistance to Persia were the middle-class people of Athens. The leading factions at this time were the Alcmaeonids, the Pisistratids and the Philaids. Themistocles was an exception who claimed that the people were his faction.[14]

The route taken by Darius

The Persians 'started at Samos and sailed across the Icarian Sea and through the islands'.

1 Draw a map showing their sea route from Asia Minor to Marathon.
2 Explain why Darius chose this route.
3 What was the fate of Naxos, Delos, the other islands and Carystus?

Refer to Herodotus, VI:95–100; Ehrenberg, op. cit., p. 130; Hammond, pp. 212–13

The fate of Eretria

'... At the news of the Persian approach the people at once called to Athens for help...Nevertheless...things in Eretria were not in a healthy state.'

1 How did Athens respond to the call for help?
2 How was opinion divided in Eretria?
3 Describe the siege and the treatment of Eretria by Persia.

Refer to Herodotus, VI:100–1; Ehrenberg, op. cit., p. 131.

The Athenian appeal to Sparta

'Before they left the city the Athenian generals sent off a message to Sparta.'

● Why were the Spartans unable to send help immediately, despite their willingness to do so?

The Carnean festival of Apollo was celebrated under the moon in the bright summer evenings of the second month of the year (beginning at the first new moon after the midsummer solstice and culminating at the second full moon). This was a month in which Dorians did not engage in warfare, and their religious principles were sincere. The week leading up to the full moon was the most sacred part of this sacred month.[15]

The Persian landing at Marathon

'Having mastered Eretria, the Persians waited a few days and then sailed for Attica, flushed with victory and confident that they would treat Athens in the same way.'

Why did the Persians choose Marathon for a landing in Attica?

Refer to Herodotus, VI:101; Ehrenberg, op. cit., pp. 132–3; Hammond, p. 213.

Athenian strategy and leadership

'Amongst the Athenian commanders opinion was divided.'

There had been serious debate at Athens. Some citizens preferred to defend the walls while others, like Miltiades, had urged the Athenians to march out and meet the enemy. A decree ('Miltiades' Decree') was known to fourth-century sources and indicates that Miltiades was able to persuade the council and the polemarch to give the orders to take food and march out if the Persians landed.

1 Who was the commander-in-chief?
2 What part did the ten generals play?
3 What arguments did Miltiades use to convince the generals they should fight at Marathon?
4 What advantages were gained by the Athenians in taking up their position at the south end of the plain?
5 Explain why the small town of Plataea sent a contingent to help the Athenians.
6 What did Herodotus mean when he said 'amongst the Athenian commanders opinion was divided'?
7 Why did the Athenians wait for some days in the foothills of Pentelicus?
8 Why did the Persians delay their attack?

Refer to Herodotus, VI:101–9; Ehrenberg, op. cit., pp. 133–5; Hammond pp. 213–15.

The Battle of Marathon and its significance

The conduct of the opposing forces at Marathon is described in the maps on the page opposite.

The immediate repercussions of the battle

1 The Athenian generals, realising the danger to Athens from Hippias' friends and the possible landing of Persian troops on the beach at

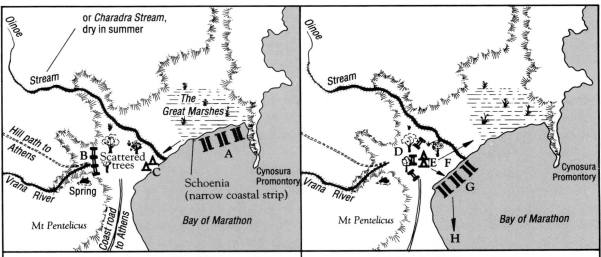

A First Persian landing and camp. Safe anchorage protected by the promontory; good grazing for horses on edge of marshes.

B Greeks had a secure defensive position — hills to the rear, scattered trees in front and good water supplies. They covered both coast road and hill path.

C The bulk of the Persian forces left their camp in the north of the plain, crossed the Charadra and took up a position within a mile of the Greeks.

Datis' aim may have been to keep the Greek army where it was while he embarked some troops, including his cavalry, and moved against undefended Athens. He was probably waiting for a signal from Hippias' friends in Athens — note Herodotus' mention (VI: 115) of the shield signal from the top of Mt Pentelicus.

He is believed to have waited until the last possible moment — the day the Spartans were due to march.

The element of surprise was necessary to successfully move against Athens; this meant getting men and horses on board at the north end, under cover of darkness.

Miltiades, informed by some Ionians of the absence of the cavalry, convinced Callimachus that the time to attack had come.

D At dawn the Greeks moved 'at a quick step' towards the surprised Persians. Miltiades' aim was to get so close that the Persian archers were ineffective. He also realised that the usual eight-deep formation of the Greeks would be outflanked by the more numerous Persians. He weakened his centre and strengthened his wings, hoping they would converge on the enemy's centre.

E The 'elite' Persians broke through the centre but were surrounded by the Greek wings. Few in the centre escaped — 6400 dead Persians were counted.

F Many of the Persians fled towards the north-east, where they were cut down in the narrow area between the sea and the marsh.

G Others fled towards the sea and were taken aboard the waiting ships. Only seven were captured by the Athenians.

H The Persians collected the Eretrian prisoners and sailed for Athens.

The Battle of Marathon

Phalerum, left Aristides and his regiment to guard the prisoners and spoil and rushed back to Athens with their regiments.

2 The Persians collected their Eretrian prisoners, appeared within sight of Athens, then turned for Asia.   *Persians return to Asia*

3 The Spartans (approximately 2000) arrived at Athens soon after and in a desire to see the site of battle, armour and weapons of the Persians,   *Spartans arrive*

marched to Marathon. They congratulated the Athenians on their victory and returned home to Sparta.

4 The Greek dead were cremated and their ashes buried under a mound (called the *Soros*), originally 12 metres high. (It was first excavated in 1890 and a flat pavement covered in bones and ashes was found, as well as a pit for sacrificial animals and a large number of funeral vessels.) On the mound were placed inscribed marble slabs commemorating those who fell, and it became the site of continued local worship.

Today the mound is still 9 metres high.

Marathon legend begins

The mound of Marathon (*soros*); originally 12 metres high, this burial mound of the 192 Athenians killed at Marathon stands near the centre of the battlefield. It has been excavated by the Greek government, revealing burnt bones, a sacrificial pit and fragments of thirty funeral urns. Today it still stands 9 metres high

Why the Athenians and Plataeans won at Marathon

Leadership and strategy   Callimachus, as elected commander-in-chief, listened to the advice of Miltiades, who had first-hand knowledge and experience of Persian methods of fighting and arms.

The political leadership of Callimachus and Miltiades in convincing the Athenian Assembly that they should send an army to Marathon prevented Miltiades' enemies from giving aid to the Persians.

Site of Marathon

The choice of Marathon proved suitable for the Athenians, as its strategic position—on the heights commanding both roads to Athens—allowed them to wait in safety until the right moment to attack.

Absence of Persian cavalry

Miltiades grasped the right time to engage the Persians, when he was informed that the Persian cavalry was absent. The fact that the expert Persian cavalry took no part in the battle was one of the significant reasons for the Greek victory.

Miltiades knew the Persians would position their best troops in the centre, and the disposition of his infantry allowed the wings to encircle the stronger Persian centre. The charge (on the run) of the Greek hoplites created surprise and confusion among the Persians, as well as allowing the Greeks to get close to the Persian bowmen before the latter could release their barrage of arrows.

Strategy and leadership

The Persians were confined between the sea and the hills and their only chances of escape were to flee to the north (where many perished on the edge of the great marsh) or to reach their ships, which were standing offshore.

Difficulty of escape

Skill, discipline and arms of the Athenian and Plataean hoplites Although only citizen soldiers, the Greek hoplites were far more disciplined than their Persian counterparts and also better protected, with their bronze-visored helmets, solid bronze breastplates, shields and javelins. The Persians were generally lightly clad, with wicker shields and bows and arrows, although sometimes Persians had body armour of scales sewn to leather vests.

Superiority of Greek hoplites

Detail from a marble relief, showing an early fifth-century Athenian hoplite

A Corinthian type of bronze helmet, inscribed with the words 'Miltiades dedicated me'. It was probably worn at the Battle of Marathon

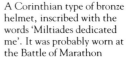

Desire for freedom

Greeks' defence of their freedom   Freedom to rule themselves in their own way — without a tyrant or an oriental 'barbarian' overlord — was the motivating factor behind the young democracy's stand. In defending their homeland, the Athenians proved more solid and united than Hippias' friends had hoped.

Fear of Sparta

Fear of Sparta's arrival   This is a point which is often overlooked. The possibility of the Spartans marching to Marathon had a real influence on the campaign by forcing the Persians and their 'friends' in Athens to hurry their operations.[16]

The significance of Marathon

For the Persians

1 The Battle of Marathon was the first real check to Persia's plans for western expansion.

Persians not deterred

2 Although it left the Persians weakened for the moment, it was only a temporary setback and did not deter them from making another attempt.

3 Darius was more determined than ever on revenge against Athens.

4 They had learnt a great deal about the Greeks, and realised the mistake in their strategy. In any future invasion they would return to the plan of Mardonius in 492; that is, a combined military and naval advance around the northern Aegean.

5 They believed that far greater forces and more careful preparations would be necessary next time. These massive preparations were put into effect almost immediately.

For the Greeks

Athenian confidence increased

1 The moral victory for Athens was far greater than the military victory. They believed 'the gods had been with them' and would continue to help them in any future confrontation. This built up their confidence.

2 The Greeks no longer believed the Persians were unbeatable and they would be more inclined to join in a common cause if the Persians attacked again. By their examination of the battlefield, the Spartans had learnt something of the conditions under which the Persian infantry could be defeated.

Greeks underestimate danger

3 However, in their optimism the Greeks underestimated the future danger to them, and continued their quarrelling. They made no plans to defend themselves, despite adequate warnings of the Persian activities. The exception to this was the Athenian statesman Themistocles who, Plutarch says, believed that Marathon 'was only the prelude to a far greater struggle'.[17]

4 Many saw Marathon as a victory for democracy. Changes occurred from 487, when the strategoi began to be elected by the whole people; the

archons from that time onwards were selected by lot. Thus, the strategoi greatly increased in importance.

5 Athens gained in prestige; it was the beginning of her emergence as the leading state in Greece, although she was forced to accept Spartan military and naval leadership until 479.

6 Marathon almost immediately acquired a mystique, and the image of the 'men of Marathon' took on heroic proportions.

Prestige of Athens and her democracy

This coin was minted in 486 to commemorate the great Athenian victory at Marathon. It is a silver 10-drachma piece, and features the 'owl of Marathon'

Fragment of a monument erected in Athens to commemorate Marathon. The inscription includes the words 'The valour of these men will shine as a light, imperishable forever'

An inscribed herm of Miltiades (c.550–489)

Profile of Miltiades

Students should build up a profile of Miltiades by referring to Herodotus. Note the following points.

Early life and career

- His arrival in the Chersonese. How he maintained his power.
- His attitude during Darius' Scythian campaign.
- Reasons why he fled from the Chersonese.
- Advantages he gained for Athens.

Arrival in Athens

- Impeachment; reasons for his trial. Result.
- His opinions about the best strategy for meeting the Persians.
- Reasons why he preferred to move to Marathon.

Marathon

- His generalship and strategy. (Do not forget that Callimachus — not Miltiades — was the overall military commander; it was not until 487 that the archons were appointed by lot — Herodotus is wrong here. If Callimachus listened to Miltiades' advice, it is to his credit).

Subsequent career

- The expedition to Paros — his intentions.
- Reasons for its failure.
- His trial by his enemies; results.
- Death.

Miltiades — hero of Marathon (c. 550–489)

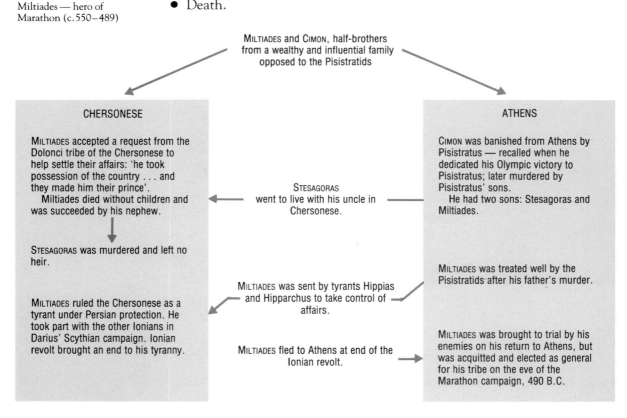

MILTIADES and CIMON, half-brothers from a wealthy and influential family opposed to the Pisistratids

CHERSONESE

MILTIADES accepted a request from the Dolonci tribe of the Chersonese to help settle their affairs: 'he took possession of the country . . . and they made him their prince'.

Miltiades died without children and was succeeded by his nephew.

STESAGORAS was murdered and left no heir.

MILTIADES ruled the Chersonese as a tyrant under Persian protection. He took part with the other Ionians in Darius' Scythian campaign. Ionian revolt brought an end to his tyranny.

STESAGORAS went to live with his uncle in Chersonese.

MILTIADES was sent by tyrants Hippias and Hipparchus to take control of affairs.

MILTIADES fled to Athens at end of the Ionian revolt.

ATHENS

CIMON was banished from Athens by Pisistratus — recalled when he dedicated his Olympic victory to Pisistratus; later murdered by Pisistratus' sons.

He had two sons: Stesagoras and Miltiades.

MILTIADES was treated well by the Pisistratids after his father's murder.

MILTIADES was brought to trial by his enemies on his return to Athens, but was acquitted and elected as general for his tribe on the eve of the Marathon campaign, 490 B.C.

130

The interwar period, 490–480

The Persian preparations

The second Persian invasion of Greece was delayed for ten years owing to the death of Darius in 486, the rebellion of the Egyptians in 486–484, the revolt of Babylon in 482 and the massive nature of the preparations needed for another invasion of Greece.

Delay of second invasion

Herodotus suggests that Xerxes was not interested at first in invading Greece. He was convinced, however, by the arguments of his cousin, Mardonius, who was ambitious and who may have envisaged himself as the governor of a conquered Greece. Mardonius, of course, played up the argument for revenge, stressing the fact that if Xerxes continued the work of his father, Darius, he would be held in great honour, and the punishment of Athens would deter others from attacking the Persian Empire. Mardonius was, according to Herodotus, helped in his attempt to convince the king by a number of Greek exiles at the Persian court at that time: Demaratus (ex-King of Sparta) and the Pisistratids of Athens, whose knowledge of Greece and the Greeks would have been very useful. Also, the powerful Aleuidae of Thessaly are supposed to have sent a message to Xerxes, offering assistance to him if he invaded Greece.

Influences on Xerxes

Just prior to the departure of the expedition, Xerxes called a conference of his commanders to explain his reasons for invading Greece and to find out their attitudes.

Xerxes' reasons for invading Greece

The desire of Xerxes to continue in the footsteps of his predecessors — Cyrus, Cambyses and Darius — and to add as much power and territory to his empire as possible was the main motivating factor. He did not want to achieve less than those who had sat on the throne before him. He also saw that after punishing Athens, the way would lie open for further conquests by which he could make the whole of Europe one country under his rule. The fact that the Persian king sent out demands for submission to most Greek cities indicates that revenge against Athens was not the major reason for the invasion.

Personal honour, imperialism and revenge

Herodotus then relates the arguments, for and against the invasion, that took place at the Persian court between the King's uncle Artabanus and his cousin Mardonius.

Mardonius urges Xerxes not to allow the Ionians of Europe to make fools of the Persians, but in his eagerness to convince the king he underestimates the fighting ability, strategy and character of the Greeks.

Divided opinion in Persian court

Artabanus, on the other hand, points out how the Athenians alone destroyed the Persian army at Marathon, and he suggests that if the Persian fleet should be defeated in Greece it would make the bridge over the Hellespont an obvious target for destruction, leaving the Persian army vulnerable. Finally, he reminds Xerxes that the gods punish severely and quickly those men who, in their arrogant pride, put themselves on a level with the gods.

Xerxes accused Artabanus of cowardice, but his uncle's speech continued to worry him until a dream he had was interpreted by the Magi as signifying Xerxes' conquest of the world.

Combined land/sea operation

The invasion was to be a combined land/sea operation, taking the same route on which Mardonius set out in 492.

The cutting of the Athos Canal

This was undertaken 'in view of the previous disaster to the fleet off Mt Athos', and preparations had been going on in the area for the previous three years. Herodotus believed that it was not really necessary and 'that it was mere ostentation that made Xerxes have the canal dug', as he wanted to leave something by which to be remembered.[18]

Bridging the Strymon River

Engineering feats

The great Strymon River was bridged near its mouth, 'a task Xerxes entrusted to the Phoenicians and Egyptians'.[19]

Supply depots

Carefully selected sites along the coast of Thrace and Macedonia were used as 'provision dumps' for enormous quantities of grain and salt meat. These were not only to feed the army in transit, but to be drawn on as the army moved further and further into hostile country.[20]

Recruiting an army and a navy

Provisioning and raising army and navy

'. . . Xerxes in the process of assembling his armies had every corner of the continent ransacked.' This continued for four years, and 'there was not a nation in Asia that he did not take with him against the Greeks'. The coastal provinces provided horse transports, crews, warships, boats for floating bridges, and other naval craft.[21]

Incredible size of forces

Herodotus mentions that Xerxes' forces were in the vicinity of 3 million, but it is more likely to have been closer to 200 000. Of these 200 000, 10 000 were the elite Immortals.

The royal family, the Achaemenidae, figures largely in the expedition, with five of Darius' sons among the thirty generals.

The size of the army and navy, and the fact that Xerxes himself accompanied the expedition, indicates how important it was for him not only to defeat the Greeks but to prove that he was the equal of Cyrus, Cambyses and Darius.

Bridging the Hellespont

The greatest of Xerxes' engineering feats were the two floating bridges, seven furlongs in length, 'constructed across the Hellespont from Asia to Europe' between Sestos and Abydos.

The bridge between Asia and Europe

Demands for submission

When the army reached Sardis, 'Xerxes' first act was to send representatives to every place in Greece except Athens and Sparta with a demand for earth and water and a further order to prepare entertainment for him against his coming'.[22]

Support in Greece

Developments in Athens

In the decade after Marathon the struggle between members of leading families to influence the assembly continued, but new leaders like Themistocles and Aristides, without powerful connections, came to dominate the political scene.

This power struggle was reflected in the repeated use of ostracism, from 488, and was part of a series of political campaigns waged by Themistocles and his opponents. An enormous number of ostraka (found singly and in groups) bore his name, as he was the outstanding personality of this period and his opponents would have gone to great lengths to stop his rise to power. One hundred and ninety-one ostraka found in a disused well on the side of the Acropolis are so similar in material, spelling and writing as to suggest that they were prepared beforehand to be distributed to his enemies' supporters. The fact that he was not exiled during this period indicates his ability to organise his supporters to concentrate their votes against first one and then another of the leaders of the Philaid, Pisistratid and Alcmaeonid factions.

Factional struggles — ostracism

Victims of ostracism, 488–482

488 Hipparchus, son of Charmus, leading Pisistratid
487 } Megacles, son of Hippocrates   leading members of the
486 } Callixenus, son of Aristonymus   Alcmaeonids
485 Xanthippus, prosecutor of Miltiades, married to an Alcmaeonid
484(?) Hippocrates, son of Alcinaeonides
483 }
482 } Aristides

Prominent men exiled

Ostrakon inscribed 'Out with Themistocles'

133

This painted clay plaque from the Athenian Acropolis originally bore the inscription 'Megacles is handsome'. This was erased and replaced with the name 'Glaukytes' — some time after Megacles was ostracised in 486

Constitutional changes

Archons and generals

Major constitutional changes occurred in 487. The archons were now selected by lot and in time the ten popularly elected generals became the chief officers of the state. This meant that the archons were now dependent on the advice of others and in the long term this had an effect on the composition of the Council of the Areopagus.

The war with Aegina

Need for a navy

The war continued. The Aeginetans' request for the return of their citizens — held as hostages by Athens during the first invasion — was refused. In retaliation they attacked a sacred Athenian galley; the Athenians in turn supported a proposed rebellion in Aegina, which failed. The Athenians, whose navy was no match for the powerful Aeginetan fleet, had been forced to borrow twenty ships from their ally, Corinth.

Themistocles and Athenian sea power

Themistocles was the most brilliant and innovative leader of Athens (with the possible exception of Pericles) during the fifth century, a fact which was recognised by the impartial historian Thucydides, who said of him:

A Roman copy of an original sculpture of Themistocles (c.470–450)

Themistocles was a man who showed an unmistakable natural genius; in this respect he was quite exceptional, and beyond all others deserves our admiration. Without studying a subject in advance or deliberating over it later, but simply using the intelligence that was his by nature, he had the power to reach the right conclusion in matters that have to be settled on the spur of the moment and do not admit of long discussions, and in estimating what was likely to happen, his forecasts of the future were always more reliable than those of others . . . He was particularly remarkable at looking into the future and seeing there the hidden possibilities for good or evil. To sum him up in a few words, it may be said that through force of genius and by rapidity of action this man was supreme at doing precisely the right thing at precisely the right moment.[23]

Thucydides' verdict on Themistocles

135

Hostile tradition

However, tradition generally was hostile to him. Herodotus was friendly with the Alcmaeonids, one of whom later charged Themistocles with treason. His other informants, as well as later Greek writers, were generally conservatives who disliked the radical democracy which Themistocles, as the founder of sea power, promoted. However, despite their prejudice Herodotus and Plutarch fail to hide the greatness of the man.

Background

Themistocles was born about 524, of mixed parentage. His father was Neocles, a lesser aristocrat, and his mother was believed to be non-Greek — possibly Thracian. Had it not been for the reforms of Cleisthenes he would not have been a citizen of Athens, and he certainly would not have qualified for citizenship at the time of Pericles.

According to Plutarch, 'he was seized with the desire to win the leading place in the state, and so he accepted without any hesitation the hostility of those who were already established at the head of affairs'.[24]

Ambition

The earliest record of his rise to power was his election in 493 to the archonship. He was extremely ambitious but had no political backing from any faction, and to have reached this position in the state is an indication of his ability. Plutarch says that he was held in affection by the people, knew everyone by name and had a fair reputation as an arbitrator in commercial disputes.[25]

Archonship, 493

As archon, in order to establish both a naval base and a commercial harbour, he began the fortification of the rocky bays of Piraeus, five miles from Athens, instead of the unprotected beaches of Phalerum. 'It was his ambition to unite the whole city to the sea',[26] but his project was halted by the first Persian invasion; it was later completed in the interwar period.

He served at Marathon and realised that despite Athens' victory the danger from Persia was not past, and that Marathon was simply 'the beginning of far greater conflicts'. He believed that when the Persians came in greater force the only way to defeat them would be to cut off their supply lines by defeating them at sea. Also, he knew that Athens' future lay with the sea, as no army could hope to compete with Sparta. The development of a strong Athenian navy would also help in the war with Aegina. From 493 he led the people, increasing in popularity and benefiting from the ostracism of his opponents, and little by little turning the thoughts of the Athenians in the direction of the sea.

Naval policy

Opposition from Aristides

For the implementation of his naval policy he needed more warships than Athens had, but he was opposed by Aristides and the wealthy, landowning hoplite class, who saw that the lower classes as rowers in a fleet would increase in status, and that the wealthy would be responsible for maintaining the warships. Tradition depicts Themistocles as the clever, unscrupulous, radical opposed by the good, just, conservative Aristides. According to Plutarch, Aristides opposed Themistocles as he 'was constantly introducing sweeping reforms and inciting the people to fresh enterprises'[27] and at the same time 'checking and obstructing him at every step in the business of government'.[28]

The two politicians faced each other in the assembly over the question of what to do with the surplus produce of the silver mines at Laurium, where an unprecedentedly rich vein had recently been discovered. It was proposed that the surplus be shared out among the Athenians at a rate of 10 drachmas a man, but Themistocles was able to persuade the assembly to use the money to build 100 new triremes (Herodotus says 200). In his arguments he did not stress the need for a navy to face the danger of the Persians, but played on the anger felt by the Athenians against the Aeginetans. As Herodotus comments, 'the outbreak of this war [with Aegina] at that moment saved Greece by forcing Athens to become a maritime power'.[29]

Debate on wealth from Laurium

New ships built

By careful use of propaganda, Themistocles was able to persuade the people to ostracise Aristides, and the ships were built. Thus the navy, which ultimately was not used against Aegina, was at the disposal of Greece in her hour of need.

Ostracism of Aristides

An ostrakon inscribed with the name of Aristides

Greek preparations

The congress at the Isthmus, 481 B.C.

In 481 invitations were sent out to patriotic Greek states to attend a conference at the Isthmus of Corinth. It is believed that thirty-one states—willing to help in the defence of Greece—attended. It was the first time they referred to themselves as 'the Greeks'.

The Greek congress formed

The representatives agreed on the following points:

1 Sparta was to be given the high command in both military and naval spheres. Athens, with her navy the size of the combined Peloponnesian fleet, probably hoped for leadership at sea, and Themistocles should have had that command. However, the Greeks believed that military power was more important than naval strength, and no Greek city liked putting its men and ships under another's command. The Peloponnesians trusted Sparta and preferred that she, though a minor naval power, should give the orders. 'The Athenians waived their claim in the interest of national survival, knowing that a quarrel about the

Leadership

command would certainly mean the destruction of Greece' (Herodotus).[31]

Feuds cease

2 All feuds and disputes would end. This put an end to the thirty years' hostility of Athens and Aegina, and combined their two large navies.

Spies sent out

3 Spies would be sent to Asia, to estimate the strength of Xerxes' forces and to report on his invasion preparations.

4 Envoys were to be appointed to negotiate with other Greek states 'in the hope of uniting, if it were possible, the whole Greek world and of bringing all the various communities to undertake joint action in face of the common danger' (Herodotus).[32] Envoys were sent to Corcyra, Syracuse, Argos and Crete.

Gelon, the tyrant of Syracuse, offered a large fleet and military force in return for the overall command. This was refused, and a second demand for either naval or military command was also blocked. Negotiations broke down, but he did send a representative — plus a large treasure — to Delphi to see how the fighting in Greece went.

Negotiations with the western Greeks

Corcyra agreed to help by sending sixty ships, but delayed deliberately and then sailed only as far as Pylos in the Peloponnese to await the result of the fighting.

The cities of Crete sent a delegation to Delphi and were encouraged to remain neutral, while Argos, Sparta's traditional enemy, at first demanded equal command with Sparta. The Delphic oracle's advice to Argos, however, was not to get involved.

Many of the Greek states, particularly the smaller ones, feared destruction at the hands of the Persians if they openly assisted Persia's enemies.

Fines for 'medisers'

5 States which voluntarily submitted to Persia were to be tithed or fined. Individual 'medisers' were to face trial.

Greek strategy

Themistocles' strategy

The Greek strategy, thought to have been devised by Themistocles, was based on the belief that the Greeks would not be able to defeat the Persians on open ground. The enormous Persian army and huge fleet

Restricted areas

would need to be contained in restricted areas (such as mountain passes and narrow waterways), and their cavalry strength minimised. Such a large force would need an extended supply line, and if this could be interrupted the Persians would be weakened.

The Peloponnesians of course wanted to defend the Isthmus, but this selfish attitude did not prevail and the first line of defence agreed upon was the valley of Tempe in Thessaly. This decision was probably due to a request by envoys from Thessaly; however, before Xerxes had reached Macedonia, the Greek force sent north had already withdrawn. The

Withdrawal from Tempe

reason given by Herodotus was the discovery that the position could not be held because of alternative passes which the Persians could take over the mountains. Thessaly could not be defended, but a second line of defence at the narrow pass at Thermopylae and the straits at Artemisium could save central Greece.

Consultation of the Delphic oracle

The Greeks asked for religious guidance from the Delphic oracle, which consistently advised nonresistance; it was obvious the oracle intended to remain neutral. Athens and Sparta, committed to resist the enemy, received depressing prophecies. The Spartans were told that their city would be sacked or a Spartan king would be killed. The Athenians received two prophecies. The original one was so gloomy that the Athenian *theopropoi* (oracle-seekers) would not return home until they received a better oracle. The original prophecy told them to flee westward, as their city would be totally destroyed by the Persians. After appearing as suppliants, the Athenians were given a second, milder reply, which caused a division of opinion at Athens over its meaning. They were told, reports Herodotus,

Delphic oracle's neutrality

> that the wooden wall only shall not fall, but help you and your children. But await not the host of horse and foot coming from Asia, nor be still, but turn your back and withdraw from the foe. Truly a day will come when you will meet him face to face. Divine Salamis, you will bring death to women's sons when the corn is scattered, or the harvest gathered in.[33]

Negative oracles for Athens

The return of the Athenian exiles

In 480 Themistocles, aware that Greek exiles (for example, Hippias and Demaratus) often joined the enemies of their cities in order to be restored to power, considered the question of those who had been ostracised in the previous ten years. According to the Troezen inscription, the exiles were recalled and ordered to Salamis to await the people's decision about their future. This was so that 'all Athenians may in unity ward off the Barbarian'.[30] Xanthippus and Aristides both returned, and played a significant role in the defence of Greece.

Return of exiles

The second invasion of Greece, 480–479

The defence of Greece

The annotated maps on pages 140 and 141 described the tactics of both Greeks and Persians in the battles of Thermopylae and Artemisium.

Marble statue of a warrior, believed to be King Leonidas of Sparta

139

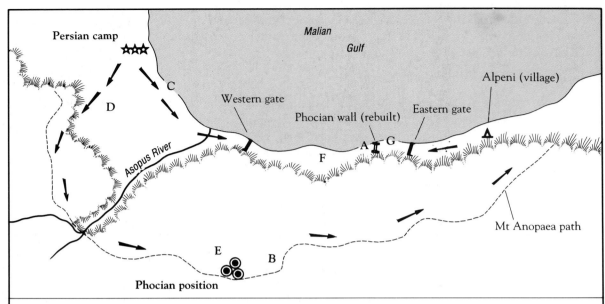

A Leonidas, the Spartan king, with an advance force of approximately 7000 soldiers (300 Spartans, plus Peloponnesians, Phocians, Thebans, Thespians and Locrians), took up a position near the ancient wall, which he rebuilt. He held the narrow passage (about 1.5 kilometres in length) through which he could advance and retire. The village of Alpeni was his supply base.

B It was believed the Greeks' position could not be reached by any detour, but Leonidas on arrival was informed of a mountain path. The 1000 Phocians volunteered to hold the path, as they knew the country well.

C The Persians, before attacking, waited four days for the remainder of their army. Then for two days Xerxes sent his infantry unsuccessfully against the Greeks.

Even the famed immortals had no success, because of the Greeks' strategic position, the Spartan strategy of first feigning retreat and then wheeling around and charging, and the inability of Xerxes to use his cavalry.

D Ephialtes, a native of the region, told Xerxes of a mountain path which bypassed the Greeks' position. He guided Hydarnes and the immortals over it during the night.

E The surprised Phocians guarding the path prepared to fight, but the Persians moved quickly on. Deserters from Xerxes' army (probably Greeks) informed Leonidas of the attempt to encircle him and this was reinforced at daybreak by Phocian lookouts.

F Leonidas sent most of the troops away, keeping only his 300 Spartans, the Thebans (kept as

hostages) and the Thespians, who volunteered to remain. They moved out into the wider part of the pass, fighting with great courage and inflicting further heavy losses. Leonidas was killed, and a battle ensued over possession of his body.

G When Ephialtes and Hydarnes arrived, the Greeks retired to the narrow section and took up a position on a mound. There they were completely surrounded, defending themselves with anything at hand. The Spartans and Thespians died fighting; the Thebans surrendered. Xerxes committed several barbarities, including the mutilation of Leonidas' body.

The Battle of Thermopylae

Results of Thermopylae and Artemisium

Losses

The Persian losses of soldiers at Thermopylae were far greater than those of the Greeks. It has been suggested that the Greeks lost approximately 4000, of whom a large percentage were helots, while the Persian loss was

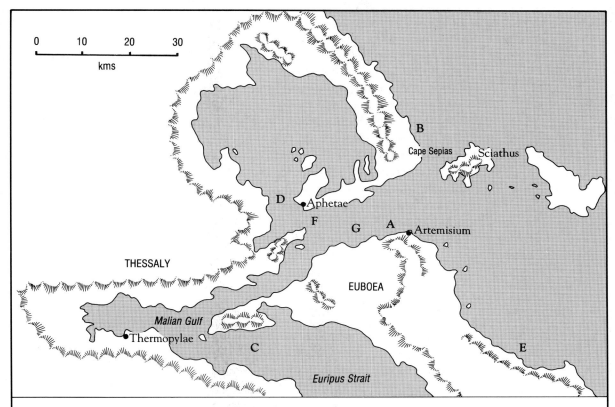

A A Greek fleet of 271 triremes (more than half of them Athenian) under Eurybiades and Themistocles chose Artemisium as its anchorage. The location was ideal, covering the entrance to the channel between Euboea and the mainland. It gave the Greeks a sheltered line of retreat and communications, the narrows would restrict the larger Persian navy, and the Greeks could stop the Persians making contact with their army. To cut off the Greeks, the Persians would have to circumnavigate Euboea, losing contact with the army.

B The Persians waited off the Magnesian coast, near Cape Sepias, for the army to reach Thessaly. There were too many ships to beach, so they anchored eight lines deep. A storm raged for three days, hitting the exposed fleet. Persian losses were great, with wreckage spread for 80 kilometres along the coast.

C The Greeks rode out the storm in the lee of Euboea, but left lookouts on the headlands of Sciathus and Euboea. After the storm they returned to Artemisium.

D The Persians made their headquarters at Aphetae.

E Two hundred Persian vessels were sent south, to round Euboea, but were destroyed on the rugged south coast. Fifty-three Athenian vessels, on the lookout for the squadron, arrived with news of their destruction.

F The Athenians made two raids on the enemy, inflicting heavy losses.

G The Persian fleet received a message from Xerxes to break through, as they were held up and running out of food. The Persians took up battle position in the straits, and the two great fleets met face to face. Soldiers on deck fought through the day and the Persian ships crowded and fouled each other. The battle was indecisive but the Greeks suffered severely, and when news reached them of the defeat at Thermopylae, the decision was taken to withdraw under cover of night.

The Battle of Artemisium

in the vicinity of 20 000. This is probably exaggerated. In three naval battles and two storms, the Persian fleet was greatly reduced—perhaps by half.

Greek fleet retires to Salamis

With the news of the loss of Thermopylae, Eurybiades and Themistocles, choosing the right moment, had the men light their fires as usual and sail down the Euripus at night, towing their damaged hulls and captured ships. The Athenians brought up the rear, and Themistocles used the opportunity to inscribe propaganda messages to the Ionians of the Persian fleet, suggesting that they defect or fight half-heartedly. Despite the indecisive nature of the battle at Artemisium the morale of the Greeks was high, and the Athenians were given the prize for valour.

Central Greece submits

The Persian fleet did not hurry after them, but moved slowly along the coast, sacking the coastal villages and arriving at Phalerum at about the same time as the army entered Attica. Three days after the battle the Persian army moved through central Greece, which now lay wide open. Boeotia submitted, having little choice, while the Plataeans and Thespians fled to the Peloponnese and their cities were burnt. A detachment of Persians is said to have approached Delphi, but it was not sacked.

Evacuation of Athens

A general evacuation was ordered in Athens. Whether this had been agreed to before Artemisium (as the Troezen decree suggests) and was only put into effect hurriedly when it was realised that the Peloponnesian army had no intention of meeting the enemy in Boeotia, or whether partial evacuation had occurred before Artemisium, is not known. However, Themistocles had about six days in which to supervise such a massive movement and the ex-archons of the Areopagus are said to have distributed money to the generals to pay each man 8 drachmas a day to buy food for a month. Many people had to be persuaded to leave; Herodotus tells us that they were encouraged to do so by the priestess of the temple where the sacred snake, guardian of the Acropolis, was believed to dwell. It no longer took the offerings left for it and so was assumed to have fled, thus setting a wise example for the citizens of Athens.

Some remain on the Acropolis

The evacuation was incomplete and a number of people garrisoned the Acropolis. The Themistocles decree suggests that the priests and priestesses were to remain to guard the sacred property, with some old men 'whose poverty prevented them seeking shelter in Salamis with the rest...'.

Themistocles' interpretation of the oracle

The Delphic oracle had advised the Athenians to put their trust in the wooden wall. Many Athenians believed this meant that they should defend themselves behind wooden walls on the Acropolis. Themistocles, however, believed that the wooden walls referred to ships and that the words 'divine Salamis' meant that the enemy would be destroyed at Salamis. The oracle experts had suggested taking to the ships and sailing away, but Themistocles persuaded the Athenians to remain with their ships and meet the invader at sea, after evacuating the Athenian women and children to Troezen, Salamis and Aegina.

The importance of Thermopylae and Artemisium

The loss of Thermopylae, the strongest position for defence north of the Isthmus, forced the submission of most of Boeotia and the loss of central Greece. The government of Sparta must take some blame for this, being too slow in mobilising the Peloponnesian forces and failing to bring reinforcements to Leonidas. Although Peloponnesian participation in the sacred Olympic and Carnean festivals should be considered, it may have been a convenient excuse, as many Peloponnesians did not approve of Themistocles' northern strategy.

Loss of central Greece

Leonidas and his small force deserve an honoured place among military heroes, despite their failure. Their rearguard action prevented the Persians overtaking the rest of the retreating forces. However, for a Spartan king there was no other choice of action, and Leonidas died according to Spartan law.

Valour of Leonidas

Themistocles' plan to hold the Persian fleet at Artemisium played a decisive role in the outcome of the war. The difficulties faced by the fleet at Artemisium — the weather, Greek raids, and restricted fighting in the straits — all had contributed to the loss of a large portion of it. This meant that the Persians would not be able to divide their fleet and make raids against the Peloponnese for the purpose of creating diversions and seizing strategic points. They could not afford to risk the defeat of the fleet and the loss of the whole campaign, so were forced now to concentrate at one point only.

Loss of Persian ships

Fragment from a relief on the Erectheum in Athens, showing the front section of the hull of a trireme

Salamis

Threats to Greek unity on the eve of the battle

War councils at Salamis

According to Herodotus, the Greek commanders held a series of war councils, which centred around the question of whether to keep the navy at Salamis or move it closer to the army at the fortified Isthmus. Yet Herodotus' account is not altogether reliable, as his informants would at the time (thirty years previously) have been only young soldiers and could not have known exactly what was said at the meetings of the generals. His treatment of the Peloponnesians is biased, especially his slanderous attack on the Corinthians and their commander, Adeimantus. He depicts Eurybiades and the Peloponnesian generals as cowardly and foolish.

Peloponnesians prefer defence of Isthmus

There is no doubt that the Peloponnesians would have preferred to have defended the coastline closer to the Isthmus, and it may have required a great deal of argument on the part of Themistocles to convince Eurybiades and the other commanders that the best place to fight was at Salamis. Perhaps bitter words were spoken in the heat of the arguments, and some jealousy may have been involved. No doubt some of the Peloponnesian commanders had a difficult time persuading their men to stay and fight in the straits after news of the fall of the Acropolis reached them. Also, the Persian army had made a demonstration as far as Megara which increased the nervousness of the army manning the Isthmus wall, and the feverish activity of the army may well have made many sailors in the fleet feel that Eurybiades was foolish in making a stand at Salamis.

The army at the Isthmus wall

Importance of the fleet

Whether the story of Themistocles' threat to put all the Athenians aboard their ships and sail for Siris in Italy is true or not, Eurybiades must have known that without an Athenian contingent, he would not have had sufficient strength to go into battle.

The advantages of Salamis as put forward by Themistocles

Salamis versus the Isthmus

1 Fighting in the narrows would favour the smaller and heavier Greek fleet. Fighting in open sea near the Isthmus would favour the greater numbers of Persians.
2 A defeat for the Persians at Salamis would stop the army advancing to the Isthmus.

When they were persuaded to fight at Salamis, the Peloponnesians stood loyally by their decision; their performance in the battle is evidence of this.

Themistocles' part in drawing the Persians into the narrows

Themistocles' plan of deception

Herodotus informs us that while the Peloponnesians were still arguing about withdrawing, Themistocles slipped out and put into effect a plan to deceive the Persians. He sent a personal slave with a message to the enemy. Aeschylus, in his play *The Persians*, also refers to this.

A Hellene from the Athenian army came and told
Your son Xerxes this tale: that, once the shades of night
Set in, the Hellenes would not stay, but leap on board,
And by whatever secret route offered escape,
Row for their lives.[34]

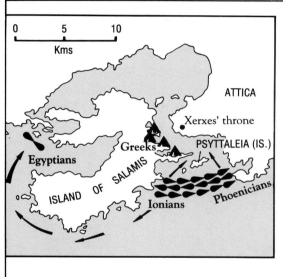

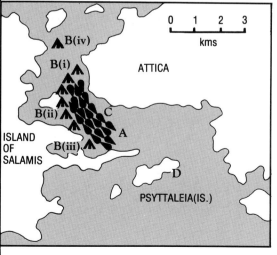

A The Phoenicians led the Persian fleet into the narrows, with the Ionians at the rear. There was much confusion as the ships passed into the strait (only about a kilometre wide), as they had to get out of line to make room for those behind.

B (i) The Ionians opposed the Phoenicians, but held back until they passed the narrows.
 (ii) Eurybiades and his squadrons moved down the channel to overlap the Phoenicians and line up with the Ionians.
 (iii) The Aeginetans and Megarians may have been positioned to strike at the flank of the Ionians.
 (iv) The Corinthians (who Herodotus said sailed away in panic) may have been sent to guard against the Egyptians entering the western end.

C The Persian ships, in their confusion, rammed each other. The Greeks waited until a south wind brought a heavy swell that turned the higher Phoenician ships broadside, enabling the lower Greek triremes to ram them. Some Phoenicians, unable to escape, ran aground on the coast of Attica. The Ionians fought well. The Aeginetans prevented the Persian centre escaping by ramming the fugitives. The fighting went on all day, until a west wind allowed the remainder of the Persian ships to flee down the coast of Attica. Many Persians drowned.

D Amid the confusion Aristides, with a force of Athenian hoplites, landed on Psyttaleia and cut to pieces the Persian forces stationed there.

The Battle of Salamis

145

Herodotus adds that the slave, Sicinnus, informed the Persians that the Greeks were 'at daggers drawn with each other'[35] and would offer no opposition; that in fact there were many pro-Persians amongst them.

Whether Themistocles was responsible alone or in conjunction with the other commanders, the deception worked.

Persian reaction

Persians divide their fleet

The Persian admirals were given the following orders:

> When the sun no longer flames to warm the earth and darkness holds
> The court of heaven, range the main body of our fleet
> Threefold, to guard the outlets and the choppy straits.[36]

It has been suggested that the Egyptian squadron, which played no part in the battle, was sent to guard the western exit from the bay of Salamis. Xerxes also ordered troops to be landed on the tiny island of Psyttaleia, in order to save shipwrecked Persians and to kill any Greeks trying to land. The Persians then advanced into the straits in two divisions, on either side of Psyttaleia.

Persians drawn into the straits

The Greek commanders were made aware of the situation when Aristides (recently returned from exile and elected general) crossed over from Aegina. The news was supported by a ship from Tenos which deserted to the Greeks.

The immediate results of Salamis

Persian fleet withdraws

The Persian fleet sailed for Asia without delay and made its headquarters at Samos. It was vital for Xerxes to prevent a rebellion in Asia Minor and to protect his line of retreat.

The Greeks followed only as far as the island of Andros. Their intention was to punish Andros—together with other neighbouring islands and Carystus in Euboea—for aiding the Persian fleet. Although unsuccessful at Andros, they devastated the territory of Carystus and collected fines from some of the other islands.

Xerxes returns to Asia

Xerxes was escorted to the Hellespont by Artabazus and 60 000 Persian troops. These soldiers later returned to join Mardonius after besieging Olynthus and Potidaea, which had revolted against Persia. This was extremely dangerous, as they were close to Mardonius' line of communication and could set an example of revolt to others.

Mardonius remains

Mardonius moved north, to winter in Thessaly until the next campaigning season. He made plans to attack the Peloponnese and to detach Athens from her Greek alliance.

The Greeks give thanks

The Greeks made dedications to the gods and awarded the prize for valour to the Aeginetans, with the Athenians second. Themistocles, who should have received the individual prize, was the subject of envy and it was not awarded.

The importance of Salamis

Although Salamis was a decisive battle it did not end the war, because the Persian army remained undefeated and all of Greece north of Attica was under Persian control. Xerxes had not given up his intentions of subduing Greece.

However, it was the turning point in the second invasion, as it ended the Persian strategy of combined naval and military operations and left the Persian army without a supply line.

Turning point in the war

Salamis weakened the allegiance of the Greeks of Asia Minor and paved the way for the revolt in 479.

According to Thucydides, the Battle of Salamis saved the Peloponnese, as

Peloponnese saved

> 'it prevented the Persians from sailing against the Peloponnese and destroying the cities one by one; for no system of mutual defence could have been organised in face of the Persian naval superiority...the fate of Hellas depended on her navy'.[37]

Herodotus says: 'Themistocles' name was on everyone's lips and he acquired the reputation of being by far the most able man in the country';[38] he received great honour from the Spartans.

His policy of establishing Athens as a sea power had been justified, and the naval policy of the Delian League (formed in 478) was an extension of that success.

Themistocles' naval policy justified

Salamis was a victory too for the Athenian system of government. It proved to the Greek world that a democratic system could defeat an autocratic power.

Victory for democracy

The victory of the Greeks inspired great works of art, literature and drama.

Inspired works of art

Greek unity threatened

Mardonius spent the winter in Thessaly and in the spring moved into Boeotia, where Thebes gave him active support against Athens and Sparta. He made diplomatic moves to detach Athens from the Greek League, using as his intermediary Alexander of Macedon, an ally of Athens. Athens was promised, if she would join the Persians, not only her autonomy, but any land she wished and the rebuilding of her temples. If she would not, the city would be once again occupied and devastated. At the same time gold was sent to Sparta's enemies in the Peloponnese — notably Argos — in the hope of undermining Sparta's resistance.

Mardonius attempts to break up League

Athens' anger at Sparta's selfishness

Athens refused Mardonius' offer and once again her people evacuated to Salamis, from where they denounced Sparta for failing to move north with an army. They threatened the Spartans that they would withdraw from the war. The Spartans, who had once again been holding a religious festival, made counter offers to help protect the Athenians. It would not have taken a great deal to convince the Spartans that if the Athenians withdrew, 'the back door' to the Isthmus would be open. There were also those in Sparta anxious for a campaign—notably the king, Pausanias, regent for his child cousin Pleistarchus, the son of Leonidas.

Athens threatens to side with Persia

Angered at the hesitation of the Peloponnesians, the Athenians warned the ephors that they would make terms with Persia, but were told that an army of 5000 Spartiates—accompanied by 35 000 helots—was already on the move. Other Peloponnesian contingents joined in the march north. Mardonius, on receipt of this news, evacuated Athens, but destroyed it as thoroughly as before. He then moved into Boeotia.

Peloponnesians mobilise

Sparta's policy appears selfish, short-sighted and isolationist, but in view of the fact that within fifteen years she was faced with a full-scale helot rebellion in Messenia and Laconia, her reluctance and nervousness about moving beyond the Isthmus is understandable. Once the decision to move had been given the Peloponnesians, led by Pausanias, moved with great speed and determination. They were joined at Eleusis by the Athenians, led by Aristides.

The Battle of Plataea

Tactics of the Greeks and the Persians in three stages of the Battle of Plataea are illustrated in maps on pages 149 to 151.

Results of the battle

Great Persian losses

The Persian losses were great. According to Herodotus, except for the 40 000 who fled with Artabazus, no more than 3000 out of the 300 000 Persians escaped. The Greek loss of hoplites was very low in comparison and Herodotus' figures are not to be trusted.

Greek dedications

The Greek troops camped on the battlefield for ten days. During this time they collected and distributed the enormous spoils of which they dedicated one-tenth to Apollo at Delphi. The symbol of the alliance against the Persians was a gold tripod resting on the bronze coils of a three-headed serpent, inscribed with the names of the thirty-one cities which had contributed to victory both at Salamis and at Plataea.

Plataea honoured

The dead were buried outside the city of Plataea and the Plataeans were given the privilege of celebrating a four-yearly festival of freedom in their honour.

148

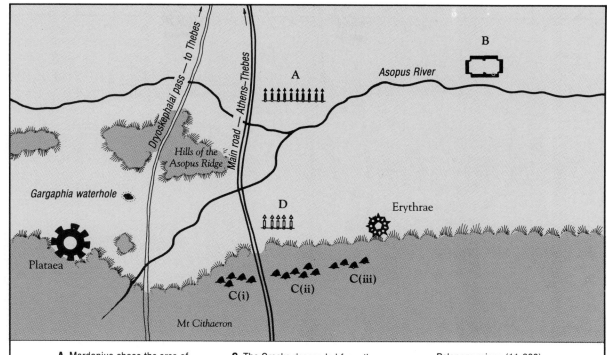

A Mardonius chose the area of Plataea because it was cavalry country and Thebes was an allied city. He camped his troops along the line of the river Asopus facing the passes by which the Greeks emerged.

B The Persians built a huge stockade (approximately 900 acres) to serve as protection in case of defeat in the field. The stockade was sited to make it possible to keep in touch with Thebes.

C The Greeks descended from the Cithaeron ranges, spread out along the lower slopes, and would go no further. The total armoured strength of the Greeks was approximately 38 700.
 (i) On the left wing were the Athenians and Plataeans (approximately 8600).
 (ii) At left centre was a miscellaneous group including forces from Megara, Aegina, Eretria, Chalcis and the western Greeks (7300). At right centre were the

Peloponnesians (11 300).
 (iii) On the right were the Lacedaemonians (Spartans) and Tegeans (11 500).
 Light armed troops brought total strength close to 100,000.

D Mardonius decided to harass them with his cavalry under their brilliant leader, Masistius. The fighting continued for some time but the Greeks would not move into the plain. Masistius was killed and the cavalry fell back, leaderless.

The Battle of Plataea — original position of troops

Ten days after the battle the Greeks marched on Thebes, besieged it and demanded that the leaders be handed over to be tried for medising. The Greeks, however, did not wish to spend the time or suffer further loss of life in carrying out the terms of their oath 'to punish all medisers and tithe them'. The Theban leaders did not stand trial, but were taken back to the Isthmus and put to death.

Thebes punished

The significance of Plataea

Plataea was a decisive battle which put an end to the invasion of mainland Greece. However, much of northern and eastern Greece was

End of Persian occupation

149

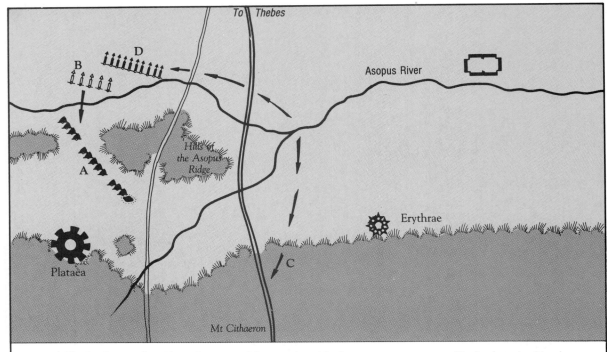

A The Greeks moved west towards Plataea by way of the foothills, to take up a position near the chain of hills called the Asopus Ridge. This position gave the troops room to move around, allowed food convoys to unload safely behind the lines, and had plenty of water. It meant leaving the main pass from Athens uncovered, but they thought they could still cover the other route by which reinforcements and food wagons could reach the troops.

B Mardonius made life difficult for the Greeks, as he had to protect his allies, the Thebans. The Persian cavalry prevented the Athenians drawing water from the Asopus River. This forced the whole army to rely on the spring.

C Acting on advice from the Thebans, Mardonius sent his cavalry to waylay the food wagons. The Persians slaughtered 500 animals and their escorts as they were converging onto the plain.

D The Persian infantry still did not cross the Asopus River, but the cavalry rode around the Greek forces and fouled the Gargaphia spring — their last source of water — near the Spartan position.

The Battle of Plataea — the Greeks' second position

still occupied and so the Greeks continued the struggle, but now took the offensive.

Example of Greek unity

Plataea is often cited as one of the best examples of Greek unity. Approximately twenty-three states had taken an oath of comradeship to fight together until the barbarian invaders were destroyed, and for approximately three weeks over 100 000 Greeks had faced extreme difficulties and delays together and had resisted the attacks of the Persians and their allies. There were threats to unity during those weeks, but it was a national alliance — however shortlived.

Spartan victory

The discipline and prowess of the Spartan hoplites were once more revealed, as they and the Tegeans bore the brunt of the fighting.

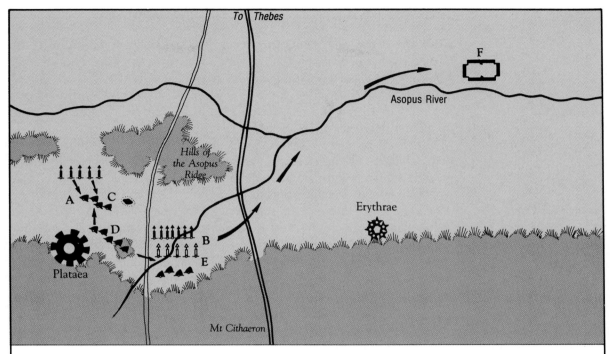

A Pausanias and the generals had a council of war, as the Asopus Ridge could not be held, and decided to move during the night. The centre moved closer to Plataea, the Spartans kept to the higher ground and the Athenians, with further to go, moved along the low ground.

B When Mardonius saw that the Greeks had moved he led his troops across the Asopus, believing that they were fleeing. His front faced the Spartans and Tegeans — he had not seen the Athenians. His cavalry was already harassing the Spartans. Pausanias sent a message for the Athenians to hurry and join the line.

C Aristides, leading his Athenian troops to link up with the Spartans, was overtaken by the medising Thessalian cavalry and Boeotian infantry, fighting on the side of Persia. He was forced to form in battle order.

D The centre divided into two, with the Megarians and non-Peloponnesians helping the Athenians, and the Peloponnesians (led by Corinth) closing the gap between the Athenians and Spartans. Many of those helping the Athenians were cut down.

E The Spartans waited behind their shields, showing great discipline as the arrows poured down on them. Finally, Pausanias charged. Mardonius was killed and his troops fled to the stockade. Artabazus, the other Persian commander, retreated with his troops, eventually returning northwards to Asia.

F When the other Greeks — including the Athenians — arrived (the Boeotians had withdrawn when news of Pausanias' victory reached them), the stockade was taken and the Persians slaughtered.

The Battle of Plataea — battle positions

Herodotus grudgingly admits that Pausanias 'won the most splendid victory which history records'.[39]

The success of Plataea brought new supporters to the alliance. Samos had already revolted against Persia, and was soon followed by the Ionians and Aeolians.

New supporters for alliance

The Battle of Mycale and the recapture of Sestos

Greek fleet at Delos

Persian fleet at Samos

Samos joins Greeks

After the battle of Salamis the Greek fleet, only about one-third of its former strength, assembled at Aegina. The Spartan king Leotychides, admiral of the fleet, was approached by refugees from Chios (in Ionia) asking that the fleet sail to Ionia as it was ready to revolt, but the request was refused. However, the Greeks sailed as far as Delos, where they took up a defensive position.

The Persian navy, much reduced in size, made its headquarters at Samos where, according to Herodotus, it 'remained to guard against a possible Ionian revolt' and 'it never entered their thoughts that the Greeks would undertake an expedition to Ionia... so far as naval operations were concerned the Persians had completely lost heart'.[40] To the Greeks at Delos came representatives of a resistance group from Samos, with information that the Persians were in poor condition and that the mere sight of the allied fleet off the coast would encourage the Ionians to revolt. The Council of War decided to take the offensive, and sailed to Samos to find that the Persians had retreated to the mainland, beaching their ships along the narrow coastal area of the Mycale promontory. The Persian land forces in the area, many of whom were Greek or subject peoples whose loyalty would waver if things went wrong, joined the fleet on the shore and built a stockade. The Milesians were sent to guard the paths leading inland.

Greeks land at Mycale

Persian army and navy destroyed

Second Ionian revolt

Leotychides sailed his flagship close to shore, proclaiming freedom to the Greeks in the hope that they would mutiny, then landed his troops further down the coast. Half the Greeks (led by the Athenians) faced the Persians, who had formed a strong rampart with their wicker shields, while the Spartans made their way over hilly ground to attack the Persians from inland. The Persians held out for some time, but the Athenians doubled their efforts, broke through and stormed the stockade; the Spartans, making their way over the hills, arrived in time to join in finishing off the work. The Ionians among the Persian forces changed sides, and the Milesians in the hills 'joined in the slaughter and proved their [Persians] bitterest enemies. Thus this day saw the second Ionian revolt from Persian domination'.[41] The Greeks then burnt the ships and the fort, and retired to Samos to debate the future of Ionia.

Results of Mycale

Problem of the future of Ionia

Peloponnesian solution

The revolt of the Ionians presented the Greeks with a serious problem. How were they to protect the Greeks of Asia Minor? A debate followed. The Peloponnesians, not wishing to keep troops permanently in the area, suggested a massive evacuation of Ionians to the trading towns of those Greeks who had medised. This was not only impracticable but was opposed strenuously by the Athenians, led by Xanthippus, who would never approve of the forced migration of Athenian colonists. The Spartans gave way to the Athenian arguments and enrolled the island states that had cooperated—for example, Chios, Samos and Lesbos—into the Hellenic League, with an oath binding them to its support. For the moment the Greeks of Asia Minor were left without the protection of an alliance.

Hellenic League enlarged

The fleet (with Ionian reinforcements) now sailed to Abydos in the Hellespont to destroy Xerxes' bridge, but it had already gone. The Persians in the surrounding area congregated in the city of Sestos when news of the Greeks' approach reached them. The Peloponnesians, satisfied that the bridge was gone, sailed home, but the Athenians under Xanthippus, with Ionian and Hellespontine allies, attacked Sestos. The city was not only the main Persian base in the Chersonese, it had been under Athenian control before—during the time of Miltiades—and was strategically located for entry to the Black Sea with its precious grain products.

Peloponnesians return home

Despite protests from his men, Xanthippus refused to leave until Sestos was taken and the Persians killed, or captured and ransomed. In the words of Herodotus, 'This done, the fleet set sail for Greece with all sorts of stuff on board, including the cables of the bridges, which the Athenians proposed to dedicate as an offering in their temples'.[42]

Xanthippus and Athenians remain

The significance of Mycale and Sestos

Mycale ended the defence of the mainland, freed some of the Ionian cities and gave the Greeks supremacy in the Aegean, but the war with Persia was not yet over. Despite the fact that Herodotus ends his history of the Persian Wars at this point, further military and naval action was taken against Persia until 448, but it now entered a new phase under Athenian leadership.

Greeks control Aegean Sea

The leadership shown by Athens at Sestos was the first step in the establishment of an empire, towards which she had been moving slowly under the influence of such leaders as Pisistratus, Miltiades and Themistocles.

Athenian leadership of Greece

Using evidence

The following illustration is part of the 'Serpent Column', erected at Delphi by the Greek states as a memorial to the Persian Wars. The three twining serpents originally supported a gold tripod on their heads. (What remains of the column can now be seen in the Hippodrome in Istanbul.) The inscription on the column lists the Greek allies who participated in

153

Part of the 'Serpent Column' at Delphi

the war against the Persian invaders in the years 480–479. This was not the original inscription, however.

   As well as the information on the 'Serpent Column', a second inscription on a bronze statue of Zeus at Olympia was reported by Herodotus and Pausanias[43] (not the Spartan King of the same name, but the traveller in the second century A.D.). Herodotus and Thucydides add further information about (a) the number of states taking part in the defence of Greece, (b) the booty taken from the Persians after the Battle of Plataea (from which this dedication was made), (c) the original inscription on the column and (d) details of the reasons for some states being included in the list of participants even though they had submitted to Persia.

(a) The monument was dedicated in 479, sometime after the Battle of Plataea but before the Battle of Mycale in the same year. This is known, because the campaign of Mycale included a number of new allies whose names were not on the list.

(b) The 'Serpent Column' was made from the booty collected after the Battle of Plataea. Herodotus describes the tents full of gold and silver furniture, jewellery, weapons, bowls and cups and sacks of gold which the Persians left behind when they fled the field of battle.

> When all the stuff had been collected, a tenth was set apart for the God at Delphi, and from this was made the gold tripod which stands next the altar on the three-headed bronze snake: portions were also assigned to the Gods at Olympia and the Isthmus, and from these were made, in the first case, a bronze Zeus, fifteen feet high, and, in the second, a bronze Poseidon, nine and a half feet high.[44]

(c) Thucydides records some details about the original inscription on the column. He says that Pausanias, the King of Sparta and overall commander at Plataea, 'on his own responsibility' had the following couplet inscribed:

> Leader of Hellenes in war, victorious over the Persians,
> Pausanias to the god Phoebus erected the trophy.

> Since Pausanias 'departed from the accepted rules of behaviour', the Spartans had it erased immediately and 'inscribed by name all the cities who had joined in defeating the Persians and who were making the dedication'.[45]

(d) The members of the Greek alliance are listed on the column in the following order:

1 Sparta	17 Ceos	
2 Athens	18 Melos	
3 Corinth	19 Tenos	[this was added after the others, in a different hand]
4 Tegea		
5 Sicyon	20 Naxos	
6 Aegina	21 Eretria	
7 Megara	22 Chalcis	
8 Epidaurus	23 Styra	
9 Orchomenus	24 Elis	
10 Phileious	25 Potidaea	
11 Troezen	26 Leucas	
12 Hermione	27 Anactorium	
13 Tiryns	28 Kythnos	
14 Plataea	29 Siphnos	
15 Thespiae	30 Ambracia	
16 Mycenae	31 Lepreon	

● There are a few differences in the list of states inscribed on the bronze Zeus at Olympia, as reported by Pausanias (Thespiae, Eretria, Leucas and Siphnos were not included) and by Herodotus (he does not mention the cities of Euboea). However, it is believed that the 'Serpent Column' list was the original.

- Sparta's position in the list indicates that her leadership was never contested throughout the war. It was not until after Mycale and the later behaviour of Pausanias, the Spartan King, that the Athenians had an excuse 'for depriving the Lacedaemonians of the command'.[46]

- Athens was second in command, owing to the size of her navy. She had given up her claim for command of the fleet 'in the interest of national survival' when the other Greeks 'had stipulated for a Lacedaemonian commander'.[47]

- Corinth, mentioned third in the list, was an influential member of the Peloponnesian League but also a minor leader in her own right, since she was able to bring into the conflict some of her important colonies.

- According to Wade-Gery in *The Athenian Tribute Lists*, the names on the list fall into three main categories:

    Sparta and her Peloponnesian allies
    Athens, her allies and the Aegean states
    Corinth and her colonies

    There are five cities which do not appear to be in the right categories and it is suggested that they may have been added as an afterthought, since their claims as allies in the second invasion may have been questionable.

- Two interesting names appearing on the list are those of Naxos and Tenos. (Tenos appears to have been added later.)

    Naxos and Tenos had been mobilised for Xerxes, but Herodotus records how some of their ships were brought over to the other side. Four of the Naxian triremes destined for Xerxes' fleet were brought over to the Greek side by the trierarch Democritos, who later distinguished himself at Salamis, destroying five enemy ships.[48]

    Herodotus explains why Tenos was added to the list of allies later.

    But while they still doubted, a Tenian warship commanded by Panaetius, the son of Sosimenes, deserted from the Persians and came in with a full account. For this service the name of the Tenians was afterwards inscribed on the tripod at Delphi amongst the other states who helped to defeat the invader.[49]

- The Corinthian colony of Potidaea in the northern Aegean was originally part of Xerxes' force but when he was defeated at Salamis, the Potidaeans revolted from Persia in late 480 and contributed 300 hoplites for the Battle of Plataea. (Refer to Herodotus, VII:123, VIII:129, IX:27.

Table 6.2	Conflicts between Greeks and Persians	
Events	Dates	Personalities
Lydia and Greeks of Asia Minor fall under control of Persia	c.545	Cyrus (Persian king) Croesus (Lydian king)
Darius' Scythian campaign and conquest of Thrace — first movement into Europe	c.516–512	Darius (Persian king)
Ionian Revolt — preliminary round in conflict between Persians and Greeks	499–493	Aristagoras (Greek tyrant of Miletus) Artaphernes (Satrap of Sardis)
First expedition against Greece; reached Macedonia — failed	492	Darius (Persian king) Mardonius (Commander of Persian forces)
First Persian invasion of Greece; invasion by sea via the Aegean islands; landing at Marathon	490	Darius (Persian king) Datis — Persian Artaphernes — commanders Miltiades (Athenian general) Callimachus (polemarch) Hippias (ex-tyrant of Athens — guided Persians)
Second invasion of Greece — combined land/sea operation: (a) Thermopylae (military) (b) Artemisium (naval) (c) Salamis (naval) (d) Plataea (military) (e) Mycale (naval)	480–479 480 480 480 479 479	Xerxes (Persian king) Mardonius (Persian commander) Themistocles ⎫ Aristides ⎬ Athenians Xanthippus ⎭ Leonidas ⎫ Leotychides ⎟ Spartans Eurybiades ⎟ Pausanias ⎭

Essay topics

1 Why did the Persians invade Greece in 490? How did the Athenian victory at Marathon affect the preparations made by each side for the second invasion?

2 How important was naval power in the second Persian invasion?

3 To what extent were the Greeks united in the defence of their homeland in 480–479?

4 Comment on Thucydides' statement that 'Themistocles was a man who showed unmistakable natural genius'.

5 Why did Persia fail in its attempts to conquer Greece between 490 and 479?

6 Discuss the careers of Miltiades and Themistocles, with particular reference to their role in Athenian politics.

157

Further reading

Primary sources

Aeschylus. *The Persians.*
Aristotle. *The Athenian Constitution.*
Herodotus. *The Histories.*
Plutarch. *The Rise and Fall of Athens*, Chs 3 & 4.
Thucydides. *The Peloponnesian War.*

Secondary sources

Burn, A. R. *Persia and the Greeks.*
Bury, J. R. & Meiggs, R. *A History of Greece.*
Ehrenberg, V. *From Solon to Socrates.*
Hammond, N. G. L. *A History of Greece to 322 B.C.*
Kagan, D. *Problems in Ancient History*, vol. 1.
McDermott, W & Caldwell, W. *Readings in the History of the Ancient World.*

The rise to power of Athens, 478–445 B.C.

7

Sources for the period

The Delian League, 478–461

Relations between Athens and Sparta, 478–461

The imperial policy of Athens, 460–445

T HE FIFTY YEARS between the Persian Wars and the Peloponnesian War—referred to in Thucydides as the *Pentecontaetia* (half-century)—saw the rise to power of Athens, first as the leader or hegemon of a group of allies in the Delian League and then as the head of a powerful empire, which reached its political, economic and cultural peak at the time of the brilliant statesman, Pericles. The period is marked also by the gradual deterioration of relations between the two leading Greek states due, according to Thucydides, to the fear and jealousy that Athens' power inspired in Sparta and her allies. The outstanding Athenian personalities of this period—Themistocles, Aristides, Cimon and Pericles —had a direct bearing on the relationship between Athens and Sparta.

Chief developments of the period 479–445

Sources for the period

Literary sources

Thucydides, who wrote *The Peloponnesian War*, is one of the chief sources for this period, 479–445 B.C. (see Chapter 8 for more detail), as he digresses from his main narrative to write an account of the growth of

Thucydides' theme

Athenian imperial power between the Persian and the Peloponnesian Wars. Unfortunately his *Pentecontaetia* is brief and sketchy, as he was interested only in those events which illustrated his theme, and anything that was not related to the growth of Athenian imperial power was regarded as irrelevant. He also found it unnecessary to give more than a few examples to prove his point.

Historians have to fill in the gaps in Thucydides' account by using other material.

Diodorus unreliable

Diodorus lived in Sicily 400 years after this period and wrote a *Universal History*, from the earliest times down to the time of Caesar. The value of his account of fifth-century Greece is limited, as he summarised his sources and omitted detail. He also had a tendency to colour his work with patriotic exaggerations of Athens' part in events, and often turned Athenian defeats into victories.

Tragic and comic poets such as Aeschylus and Aristophanes are useful, particularly since their works were written for the common people and not for an intellectual elite.

Aeschylus gives some indication of his political sympathies, which tended to veer towards the radicals, while Aristophanes, using subjects from contemporary life, is a valuable source for the social historian.

Bias of pamphlet writers

There were in fifth-century Athens a number of writers who, through political pamphlets and biographies, give a good deal of information about the lives of leading personalities and other areas of 'human interest'. They do not refrain from using local gossip and the political mudslinging of the time. Considered together with Aristophanes, they give an idea of Athenian society. Much of their work is lost, but Plutarch used them in writing his *Lives*.

About 430 B.C. a twelve-page political pamphlet in speech form, by an anonymous author, appeared in Athens. This document, *The Constitution of the Athenians* or *Athenaion Politeia*, is sometimes referred to as the work of 'the Old Oligarch', or Pseudo-Xenophon. It is a critical comment on the radical democracy of the day, and attempts to show the working of the Athenian constitution. It must be treated cautiously because of its anti-democratic bias, although Thucydides himself was no lover of radical democracy.

Only fragments survive of atthidographers' records

Atthidographers were a group of local historians writing in the fourth century. They generally gave an accurate and unadorned account of the history of Athens in the fifth century. The most noteworthy of these was Philochorus, but unfortunately only fragments of his work survive. Later, ancient writers used the work of these atthidographers.

Aristotle's political bias

Aristotle's *Athenian Constitution* gives a summary of Athenian political history down to 403, but it reflects Aristotle's oligarchic leanings.

Plutarch wrote in the first century A.D.; his biographical essays on Aristides, Themistocles, Cimon and Pericles reflect a great deal of literary evidence not available to the historian today. His *Lives* should be used as a useful complement to Thucydides. Plutarch mentions quite important events not recorded in Thucydides; however he was not critical enough of his own sources and often had difficulty sorting out conflicting viewpoints, particularly in the case of Pericles.

Much detail in Plutarch, but not critical

Archaeological evidence

The material remains of the fifth century, such as buildings, coins, artefacts and inscriptions, are used by historians to complement the literary evidence.

Of these, the epigraphic remains — the inscriptions on stone — are the most valuable. These inscriptions include dedications to the gods, lists of casualties in war, public accounts, decrees passed by the Assembly and, most important, the Athenian tribute lists.

Epigraphic remains valuable but fragmentary

Athenian tribute lists

These inscriptions, though in a fragmentary state, have been restored by epigraphists; they are the best documentary evidence for these years and can be used to test Thucydides' view on Athenian imperial power. However, epigraphic material suffers from the drawbacks associated with its fragmentary nature and with the fact that there are obviously forgeries and later copies.

The Delian League, 478–461

'The Delian League' and 'the Confederacy of Delos' are modern terms for an organisation which was referred to in the fifth century as 'The Athenians and their Allies'. It grew out of the Hellenic League, but unlike that league it was led not by Sparta, but by Athens.

A naval organisation

Reasons for Athenian leadership

Thucydides suggests that Athens became the leader because of the arrogant and harsh behaviour of Pausanias (the Spartan king) towards the Ionians and other recently liberated Greeks. Pausanias had been sent out in charge of an allied fleet in 478 to resume operations against the Persians and to free those Greek states still under Persian control. He had retaken Byzantium and it was while there, as Plutarch says, that he 'treated his own allies harshly and arrogantly and scattered insults far and wide with his officiousness and absurd pretensions'.[1] Read also Thucydides, I:

Actions of Pausanias

125–35. His behaviour caused resentment among the Ionians, who made overtures to the Athenians suggesting that the latter should assume leadership. Pausanias was recalled by his own government and replaced by another commanding officer, Dorcis, whom the Ionians also rejected.

Greeks of Asia Minor take initiative

Thucydides stresses that it was the allies who took the initiative in transferring the leadership from Sparta to Athens, although some sources indicate that Aristides instigated their defection from the Hellenic League. This is not generally accepted, although Athens would have been glad of the move and Thucydides says that they had already made up their minds to remove Pausanias 'and to arrange matters generally in a way that would best suit their own interests'.[2]

Sparta's lack of interest in the Aegean

The Spartans were content to give up the leadership. They had previously shown their lack of interest in the future of the Aegean and Ionia, when they returned home after Mycale. 'We did not gain this empire by force. It came to us at a time when you were unwilling to fight on to the end against the Persians'.[3] These words were spoken by the Athenians to the Spartans in the debate preceding the declaration of war in 432.

Sparta's domestic problems

Sparta had domestic problems. There was the continuing fear that the helots would revolt, and the need to consolidate her position as leader within the Peloponnese. Her political horizons were bounded by the coasts of the Peloponnese and she was becoming increasingly isolationist and inward-looking.

According to Thucydides, the Spartans were afraid of being disgraced again by high-ranking officers sent abroad. Plutarch adds to this view; they 'ceased to send generals to carry on the war, preferring to have their citizens behave with moderation and abide by their traditional customs instead of lording it over the rest of Greece'.[4]

Athens' qualifications for leadership

The Athenians, who shared a common descent with the Ionians, were held in high regard after Salamis and had a large and experienced navy—essential for leadership of any league of coastal and island states. Thucydides says that the Spartans, who were friendly with Athens at the time, believed the Athenians were quite capable of conducting the war with Persia.

The Athenians accepted the *hegemonia* (leadership), and set about implementing the allies' proposals.

The organisation of the League

League organised by Aristides

Aristides was probably now commander-in-chief, and plans were laid for a meeting to be held at Delos of all Greeks of the Aegean and coastal regions.

The aims of the League

The official aim was 'to compensate themselves for their losses by ravaging the territory of the King of Persia' (Thucydides).[5] It is this immediate aim of an aggressive, offensive war against Persia which may have initially attracted states to the Congress at Delos. The Greeks of Asia had to be liberated, and in order to achieve this purpose the king would be made to pay. The long-term objective was to maintain the freedom of the Greeks — to organise a defensive alliance so that in any future attacks upon their territory, the Greeks would be well prepared to resist.

The objectives therefore were both offensive and defensive.

Immediate and long-term purposes

Finances

To carry out its aims, the Delian League needed to have a strong fleet and adequate funds. It was decided that some states were to provide money and some were to provide ships.

A regular system of contributions had to be devised, and at the request of the allies this was entrusted to the Athenian Aristides. Plutarch explains that since they wanted each city to be fairly assessed, they asked Athens for Aristides' help 'and appointed him to survey the various territories and their revenues, and then to fix their contributions according to each member's worth and ability to pay'. He drew up a list of assessments not only with fairness and integrity but also with kindness and goodwill.[6] The total assessment of the contributions amounted to 460 talents, which was to be collected and supervised by Athenian officials called *hellenotamiae* (treasurers of the Greeks).

Fair assessments made by Aristides

Once the assessment was made it was probably clear which states could afford to provide ships and which states were unable to do so.

Ship contributors

Those who contributed ships — such as the large islands of Chios, Lesbos, Samos, Naxos and Thasos — retained control of them; they were expected to serve in the League fleet for only a portion of each year. However, it was expensive to maintain and provision these ships, the crews faced the dangers associated with long campaigns, and casualties among both men and ships occurred. It was no wonder that later many members became tired of service and preferred to stay safely protected at home, accepting assessment in money instead of in ships.

The *phoros* (money payment) collected by the hellenotamiae from the second class of members went directly into the League's treasury at Delos.

Money contributions (phoros)

Delos as headquarters

Delos was to be the site of the treasury and the meetings of the allies.

Delos was selected not only because it was the ancient centre of Ionian culture and religion based on the cult of Apollo, but because it was midway between Athens and the coast of Asia Minor, it had a good harbour, and it was politically insignificant.

Delos most suitable site

163

Delos

Autonomy of allies

Initial independence of members

The allies were initially independent states with their own particular forms of government. It was not long, however, before rebellious states lost their autonomy, and became subject to Athens.

Council (Synod) of the League

Athenian influence in Council

It is not certain whether all members (including Athens) had equal voting power, but it is probable that Athens — as the leader and most influential state — could control the vote by her patronage or intimidation of smaller states who would follow her lead. The Synod decided League policy and strategy, and Athenian officials carried them out.

Oath to indicate permanence

The oath   Thucydides does not directly mention the oath of allegiance taken by members, but both Aristotle and Plutarch do. Aristotle says that it was Aristides . . . 'who swore the oaths to the Ionians that they should have the same enemies and friends, to confirm which they sank lumps of iron in the sea'.[7] This oath, sworn bilaterally between the Athenians and the allies, indicated that Athens was to be the hegemon for as long as the League continued, and the League was meant to be permanent. This implies that secession would be seen as rebellion. Thucydides says that when Naxos revolted, she was forced back into allegiance.

Original extent of the League

League membership widespread

The number of original members is not known, but the extremities of the area the League covered in the first year were Byzantium in the Propontis,

164

the Aineum promontary in the north-west, Rhodes in the south-east and Siphnos in the south-west.

Athens' position

From the beginning, Athens had considerable power:
1 She was the permanent leader.
2 As *hegemon*, she had executive powers. Aristides assessed the tribute, ten Athenian officials collected and supervised the contributions, and Cimon was the leader of the fleet.
3 She presided over the Synod and could influence policy and strategy.
4 She contributed the largest number of ships and men.

Athens dominant from the beginning

Although individuals may at an early stage have seen the potential for empire, there is no real evidence to suggest that the Athenian people aimed at making Athens an imperial power.

Table 7.1	A comparison of the Delian and Peloponnesian Leagues*	
Similarities	Differences
Both were organised as permanent leagues.	Athens had one vote in a single council. Sparta's assembly made up one half of the decision-making process. In the Assembly of Allies, each state had one vote. A majority vote in both was required for a decision to be carried out.
Allies of both were autonomous.	Peloponnesians levied men and sometimes money only in time of war. Contributions ceased with the war. The Delian League had a permanent war fund; money contributions never ceased.
In each, the most powerful state was recognised as *hegemon*.	The Peloponnesian League had no specific enemy; it was aimed at stability within the Peloponnese. The Delian League was aimed at opposing a specific enemy and establishing eventual peace in the Aegean.
Each league was both offensive and defensive in its aim.	The Peloponnesian League tolerated members' wars with each other and with outsiders. The Delian League generally did not; the Synod decided foreign policy.

* Based on the original constitution and the intention of both organisations—not on the way they always operated in practice.
Source: The Athenian Tribute Lists, Vol:III.

The career of Cimon

Cimon, son of Miltiades

War service

Influential in Athens and leader of League fleet

Leader of Delian League forces

Aristocratic and conservative

Actively 'philo-Laconian'

Rich, but generous

Refer to Plutarch, *Cimon*, 5, 6, 15, 16.

Cimon was the son of Miltiades and as a young man he paid his father's heavy fine of 50 talents for the unsuccessful attack on Paros in 489.

He served in the Persian Wars and according to Plutarch 'in all the qualities that war demands he was fully the equal of Themistocles and his own father Miltiades'.[8]

He entered politics at a time when the people 'had had enough of Themistocles and they proceeded to promote Cimon to the highest honours and offices in the State'.[9] However, it was as a protégé of Aristides that he advanced in politics. Aristides is said to have recognised in Cimon an ability that would be a match for the cleverness and audacity of Themistocles. In the years between the ostracism of Themistocles in 472 and his own loss of prestige and power in 461, he was the most influential Athenian.

From 478 until 461 he led the Delian League forces. He was originally sent out as one of the commanders of the Greek expeditionary force when it was still under the orders of Pausanias. 'By virtue of his character and his skill in handling men',[10] he gained the support of the allies at a time when Pausanias' behaviour was causing offence. After the latter's expulsion, Cimon took over the command and in the next ten years freed the Aegean of Persians.

He was a member of the aristocratic group of families, and as such was conservative and oligarchic in sympathy. During his career he attempted to prevent the 'encroachments of the people upon the prerogatives of the aristocracy'[11]. In this he failed.

Cimon was actively pro-Spartan and his policy rested on the belief in a dual hegemony, in which Sparta maintained the military leadership of Greece and Athens had supremacy at sea. He went so far in his Spartan sympathies as to name one of his sons Lacedaemonius, and he 'enjoyed a privileged position with the Spartans'.[12]

He was rich and lived lavishly but was extremely generous to the people.

The activities of the League under Cimon

Thucydides describes three fronts on which the League forces fought. They mounted operations 'against the Persians, some against their own allies when they revolted, some against the Peloponnesian powers with whom on various occasions they became involved'.[13]

In the first ten years of the League's existence its main actions were directed against the Persians, but during this time some action was taken against its own members and this increased in frequency after this period. Operations against Sparta and the Peloponnesians did not really begin until after 460.

Table 7.2 Activities of the Delian League	
Activities against Persia	*Activities against its own members, and use of coercion against others*
Byzantium retaken, 479–478	Island of Scyrus cleared of pirates — Athenian cleruchy established, 474–473
Eion, on Strymon River, recaptured, 476–475	Coercion of Carystus — forced to join League, 472
Southern Asia Minor (Caria) delivered from Persians	Revolt of Naxos, 469
Battle of Eurymedon River in Pamphylia, 468	Revolt of Thasos, 465–463

The capture of Byzantium, 478–477

The Persians were cut off from their garrisons in Thrace once Byzantium was captured, and access to the valuable trade of the Black Sea was again available to the Greeks.

The siege and capture of Eion, 476–475

Eion, on the mouth of the Strymon River, was of great economic and strategic importance; it dominated the main east-west land route and was a natural centre of exchange for a hinterland rich in precious ore (gold and silver), timber and corn. The famous gold mines of Mt Pangaeus were nearby. Eion had been a supply depot for the Persian forces, and was its strongest garrison west of the Hellespont.

The Persian commander, Boges, heroically defended the city; when defeat was imminent he killed his family, destroyed his possessions and committed suicide.

Cimon's actions here had removed a potentially dangerous base from which new Persian offensives could have been launched against Greece.

The conquest of Scyrus, 474–473

Scyrus was a relatively poor island north-east of Euboea which was inhabited not by Persians, but by non-Greek pirates, whose activities had been disrupting trade. Why the League forces were used to conquer Scyrus is not certain, as the attack seems to have had nothing to do with its stated aims. Plutarch says that Cimon and the fleet were urged to capture

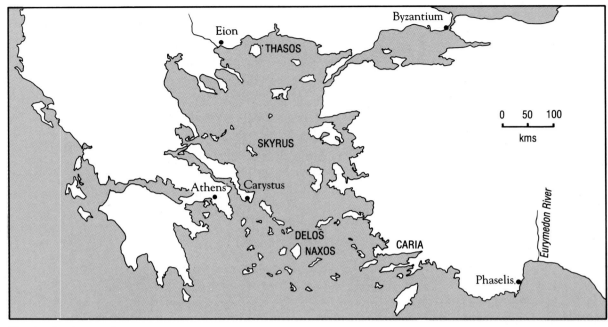

Map showing the area of operations of the Delian League fleet, 478–465 B.C.

the island and that an oracle bade them bring home the bones of the legendary Athenian hero, Theseus, who was believed to have been killed there. Its capture and enslavement may have guaranteed the freedom of the seas for trade, as it was on the main trade route from Athens to western Thrace.

Athenian cleruchy on Scyrus

However, its inclusion in Thucydides' account is probably due to the fact that the Athenians colonised the island themselves. This cleruchy, a settlement of Athenian citizens, served two purposes. It solved the land shortage in Attica and watched over Athens' interests in the area. Cleruchies came to be a feature of later imperial policy.

The coercion of Carystus, 472

Neutral Carystus posed a threat

Carystus, on the southern tip of Euboea, had been unwilling to join the Delian League, but in 472, out of a fear that it might collaborate at some time in the future with the Persians, the League forces coerced it into joining. Its position — close to Athens and dominating the strategic waterway between Andros and Euboea — made this possibility of collaboration extremely dangerous. However, to make war on a state which desired to remain neutral, and to deprive it of its independence, was an outrage to most Greeks. The only justification the League could give was one of political necessity, since the Persians were still a real threat in the Aegean. If Carystus became a Persian stronghold, the interests of all the League members would be threatened.

The revolt and subjugation of Naxos, 469

Naxos—one of the largest islands in the Aegean and an important ship-contributing member of the League—wished to secede, and revolted in 469. The rebellion was put down by siege and Naxos lost its autonomy, although it is not certain whether it had to surrender its fleet as well. Neither is it clear from the evidence whether it became a tribute-paying subject at this point, but this is likely. Despite the harshness of the treatment the League had the right to insist that a member fulfil its obligations, for once it had joined, its contribution to the war effort was no longer voluntary, but compulsory, and Naxos had acted in defiance of the League's constitution. Naxos was a test case and it was apparent that in the future Athens, as the leader of the League, would not hesitate to use force to make sure that obligations were fully met.

Naxos—first member to rebel

Subject, tribute-paying state

The Battle of Eurymedon, 468

The coast of Caria south of Miletus was still in Persian hands and Cimon 'sacked or destroyed some cities and induced others to revolt or annexed them, until not a single Persian soldier was left on the mainland of Asia Minor from Ionia to Pamphylia' (Plutarch).[14]

The city of Phaselis, which was Greek, refused to revolt against Persia and refused to join Cimon in his campaign against the Persians in this area. Cimon attacked the walls and devastated the countryside until Phaselis came to terms, and was enrolled in the League.

The Persians had a large fleet and army at the mouth of the Eurymedon River in Pamphylia, and Cimon, in the most ambitious and costly campaign ever undertaken by the League fleet, hoped to strike a mortal blow at the Persians so that they would not dare to enter the Aegean again.

Combined naval and land attack on Persians at Eurymedon

He not only inflicted a crushing defeat on the Persian navy, but, as Plutarch records, on the same day 'he threw back the barbarians with great slaughter and captured the army and its camp which was full of all kinds of spoil'.[15] He followed up this double victory by intercepting and capturing eighty Phoenician ships sent from Cyprus to reinforce the Persian navy. This was Cimon's greatest victory, and justified the existence of the League up to this point: it had carried out its objectives by freeing Greek cities and towns still under Persian control, by making the Aegean once again secure from attack and by capturing Persian wealth and resources.

Existence of League justified

The captured spoils from Eurymedon were used to construct the southern wall of the Acropolis and to begin the Long Walls of Athens.

The question now was: Had the League completed its work? Many members probably felt that the League had achieved its purpose. The price of membership, the continuing payment of tribute or contribution of

Should the League now continue?

169

ships, may have seemed unnecessarily burdensome. On the other hand, there were obviously still many advantages to be gained by remaining in an alliance. What direction would it take now? The initiative lay with Athens.

The revolt of Thasos, 465

The situation at Thasos revealed the direction Athens intended to take in her future relations with the allies.

Thasos — a test case

Thasos was the richest island in the northern Aegean; it had a strong fleet, and extensive mining and trading interests on the adjacent mainland of Thrace. It was also one of the largest ship-contributing members of the League, and came into conflict with Athens over gold mining and trade in the area. It is believed that Athens claimed a share in these. A dispute broke out and Thasos seceded from the League. This revolt was significant for three reasons:

A private dispute but the League involved

1 Even though the Battle of Eurymedon had been fought three years earlier and had removed any threat from Persia in this area, Athens showed that she had no intention of allowing members to leave the League.
2 It was the first time that Athens had used the League's power against a member state in a private quarrel.
3 For the first time a conflict between League members involved a Peloponnesian state, namely Sparta.

Sparta's offer of help

Cimon's fleet besieged Thasos, which looked for help to Macedonia and Thrace — also anxious to keep Athens out of the area. More importantly, Thasos sought aid from Sparta. The Spartans agreed to attack Attica, but Athens was unaware of this offer of help until later. However, the

Siege of Thasos

Spartans were prevented from sending assistance by a disastrous earthquake that destroyed much of the city and simultaneously by a revolt of the helots of Messenia, who held out in the mountainous country around Mt Ithome until 460. The siege of Thasos lasted for two years. The Athenians confiscated the Thasians' navy, demolished their walls, closed their mint and annexed their possessions on the mainland. They were forced to pay an indemnity immediately; they lost their independence and became a tribute-paying subject state dependent on the will of Athens.

Thasos' subject status a warning to others

Athens had given fair warning to other members. At much the same time, she made an unsuccessful attempt to establish a cleruchy of 10 000 Athenians at a place on the Strymon River called 'The Nine Ways', later known as Amphipolis. Cimon on his return to Athens was accused by his

Cimon on trial

enemies, the radical democrats, of having been bribed by King Alexander of Macedon to refrain from invading and annexing part of Macedonia. He was acquitted of the charge, but this incident revealed the growing strength of the opposition in Athens to the conservative policies which Cimon represented.

Relations between Athens and Sparta, 478–461

Thucydides saw the period from the revolt of Thasos in 465 to the ostracism of Cimon in 461 as a chain of events leading to a break with Sparta which was to have serious repercussions in the future. If this was the first real collision with Sparta, what had Athenian–Spartan relations been like in the preceding fifteen years while Athens was organising and leading the Delian League?

465–463: break begins between Athens and Sparta

The 'inactive' alliance

Athens and Sparta were still in alliance with each other during this period, as the Hellenic League formed against Persia still existed and was never formally dissolved. The relations between Athens and Sparta seemed cordial enough, but Thucydides may have gone too far when he said that 'this was a time when Sparta was particularly friendly to Athens because of the courage displayed by Athens against the Persians'.[16] There were several hints of ill-will and jealousy.

Early relations cordial

Themistocles' anti-Spartan policy, 478–472

The first cause of friction concerned the rebuilding of the walls of Athens. After the Persians were expelled from Greece, Themistocles supervised the rebuilding and the fortification of Athens. This alarmed the Spartans and their allies, who suggested that the Athenians should refrain from rebuilding their walls and join with Sparta in 'pulling down all the fortifications which still existed in cities outside the Peloponnese'.[17] They concealed their real fear, which was the sudden growth of Athenian sea power, and used the pretext that a fortified Athens could be a base for the Persians if they came again. Themistocles went to Sparta, denied that the walls were being built and suggested that envoys be sent to see for themselves. In this he completely outwitted the Spartans, because the envoys were held as hostages until the walls were high enough. He then announced that the walls were finished and that in the future Athens was capable of making up her own mind about what was in her own interests.

Spartans object to rebuilding of Athens' walls

Themistocles' anti-Spartan actions

According to Thucydides, the Spartans had not intended to stop the building and were merely offering advice. They showed no open signs of displeasure with Athens, but concealed their resentment.

Sparta's resentment concealed

Immediately after the Persian Wars, the Greek states met at the Amphictyonic Council (a religious organisation which controlled Delphi). The Spartans suggested that all those Greeks who had remained neutral or had helped Persia should be expelled from the Council. Themistocles

Spartans offended over medisers

realised that if the Thessalians, Thebans and Argives were removed, the members of the Peloponnesian League would dominate the Council. He said it would be intolerable if it was controlled by two or three large states. Plutarch says that this 'gave particular offence to the Spartans, and made them try to strengthen Cimon's position by showing him favours and thus establish him as a political rival to Themistocles'.[18]

Themistocles ostracised

In 472 Themistocles was ostracised, as he had made many enemies due to his radical policies, his outspokenness and vanity, and his continuous opposition to Sparta. Many envied him his success and sought to bring him down. He moved to Argos, Sparta's traditional enemy, and from there he spread anti-Spartan propaganda throughout the Peloponnese. The Spartans wanted him removed, and when he became implicated in the intrigues of Pausanias (of which there was no real proof) he was accused of high treason and pursued by both Spartan and Athenian officials. It is hardly likely that he was communicating with Persia, but he may well have been plotting against the Spartan constitution.

*Themistocles'
anti-Spartan
propaganda from
Argos*

Sparta's acceptance of Athenian leadership at sea

*Sparta's naval
weakness*

Sparta was forced to accept Athenian leadership of the Delian League because she realised her own unfitness to conduct a war by sea in the eastern Aegean and because she was faced with many problems within the Peloponnese. If she felt any real antagonism towards Athens it remained dormant for some time, except for one occasion in 478.

There were those in Sparta, particularly of the younger generation, who were so upset by the loss of leadership that they demanded a war to reinstate Sparta as leader of the Greek League by sea. It took all the effort of the old men in the gerousia to make them see reason. They pointed out that Sparta's traditions and institutions revolved around the army, and that sea power was incompatible with them. Thus a period of dual leadership resulted, which was promoted also by Cimon.

*Sparta's internal
stability undermined
by Persian wars*

The internal stability of Sparta was adversely affected by the Persian Wars. Her citizens, perioeci and helots were exposed to wealth in the form of spoils while the royal family's prestige suffered severely, owing to the questionable activities of its members. Cleomenes was believed to have been engaged in revolutionary activities against Sparta; Demaratus, in exile at the Persian court, accompanied Xerxes to Greece; while Pausanias was charged with treason and Leotychides was found guilty of corruption. The power of the ephors grew at the expense of the kings and there was a tightening up of the Spartan system to prevent any liberalising effects on the people.

*Loss of influence in
Peloponnese*

Sparta had also lost much prestige in the eyes of her allies and needed to concentrate on maintaining her position as head of the Peloponnesian

League. In 472 she faced Argos and Tegea in battle, and in 471 was concerned when the cities of Elis, Mantinea and Argos adopted a democratic form of government.

The pro-Spartan policy of Cimon, 471–462

After the ostracism of Themistocles, the Spartans showed goodwill towards Athens because of Cimon, to whom they gave honours and favours. He was described by some as more of a Peloponnesian than an Athenian. He aimed at maintaining good relations with Sparta by emphasising the dual hegemony of Greece. Cimon's policy helped to postpone a rift between Athens and Sparta.

Cimon promoted dual hegemony

However, he was not a democrat at heart and although the Athenian government was a moderate democracy, it was moving towards a fuller and more radical form. It was unlikely that Cimon, with his more conservative sympathies, would remain influential for much longer.

Spartan offer of help to rebels at Thasos

Why Sparta offered help to the rebellious Thasians in 465 is not really known, but it was a serious blow to the policy of Cimon. Perhaps the great success of Cimon and the League at Eurymedon released the dormant jealousy Sparta had felt all along towards Athens. Certainly the internal politics of Athens had changed, and by 466 a new, radical democratic opposition to Cimon and the conservatives — in the hands of Ephialtes and Pericles — was gaining the confidence of the people.

Sparta's dormant jealousy of Athens emerged

Sparta's secret offer of help to invade Attica never eventuated, as she faced a disastrous earthquake and a more dangerous helot revolt.

Athens sends help to Sparta — Cimon versus the radical democrats

The helots of Laconia, with help from sympathisers, revolted after the earthquake but were forced to withdraw under Spartan pressure to Messenia, where they took up a strong position on the fortified hill of Ithome. Sparta appealed to her allies of the Persian War, as the Hellenic alliance of 481 still existed.

Earthquake and helot revolt in Sparta

A public debate, recorded in Plutarch, reveals that Cimon — with his policy of conservative politics at home and cooperation with Sparta — was opposed by Ephialtes, who was not only a radical democrat but who saw Sparta as a rival and possible enemy. The fact that Cimon succeeded in

Athens sends help to Sparta

persuading the Assembly to send a large force of hoplites to Sparta's aid indicates that the majority of Athenians still supported a policy of friendship and cooperation with Sparta.

Sparta's rejection of Athenian aid

Radical democrats in Athens — fear in Sparta

At some point the Spartans regretted asking Athens for help, and of all the allies besieging Ithome only the Athenians were told by Sparta that their help was no longer needed and they must return home. Thucydides said it was the Spartans' fear of the bold and revolutionary ideas of the Athenians that led to this decision. The Spartans had obviously become aware of the radical political changes that were taking place in Athens during Cimon's absence in the Peloponnese.

Powers of Areopagus reduced

The Areopagus council was deprived of all its political power and its jurisdiction as a court of law was reduced. Its powers were divided between the Council of 500, the Assembly and the Heliaea (court). Plutarch records the words of Plato in regard to this reform: 'Ephialtes poured out neat a full draught of freedom for the people and made them unmanageable'.[19] Thucydides says that the Athenians who returned home 'were

Humiliation of Athens and ostracism of Cimon

deeply offended considering this was not the sort of treatment they deserved from Sparta'.[20] They broke the alliance with Sparta and joined with Argos, Sparta's traditional enemy, and with Thessaly. The rebuff of the expeditionary force brought a humiliating end to Cimon's career and to his policy of joint leadership of Greece. He was ostracised in 461 and during his ten-year absence the radical democracy asserted itself.

An ostrakon inscribed with the name 'Kimon' (Cimon)

The imperial policy of Athens, 460–445

After the humiliation and ostracism of Cimon and the weakening of the conservatives as a result of Ephialtes' attack on the powers of the Council of the Areopagus, the radical democrats gained the ascendancy in Athens and embarked on an aggressive imperial policy, which involved

1 a commitment to the continuing existence and expansion of the League, which saw Athens becoming more ruthless in her treatment of her allies and following a policy more in her own interests than in theirs;
2 exploiting the weaknesses of Sparta by building up a land empire in central Greece;
3 continuing Athens' hostility to Persia.

Refer to Table 7.3.

Table 7.3 Athen's foreign relations, 460–445		
With Sparta and Persia	*Date*	*With her allies*
Broke long-standing alliance with Sparta Joined Argos, Sparta's enemy	460	An important stage in the transition from League to Athenian Empire (460–454)
Drew Megara into League, causing bitter hatred of Corinth		New members enrolled, e.g. Megara
League expedition to Cyprus diverted to Egypt after appeals from Egyptians		More allies chose to deprive themselves of the ability to resist by contributing money instead of ships; Athens' naval strength increased at their expense
Began building the Long Walls, fortifying and connecting Athens and Piraeus		
		Allied council at Delos was dominated by the policy of Athens
War with Aegina, who was forced into League as subject state	457	More members were reduced to the status of subject, tribute-paying states, e.g. Aegina
Defeated at Tanagra by Spartans; won control of Phocis, Locris, and Boeotia — Battle of Oenophyta		Allied contingents used in interests of Athens, e.g. in Boeotia at Battle of Tanagra; this revealed that the original objectives of the League had been left far behind
Carried out offensive against coasts of Peloponnese — attacked Cythera, Methone and dockyards at Gytheum		

175

Table 7.3 (cont.)		
With Sparta and Persia	*Date*	*With her allies*
Settled helots at Naupactus, at the mouth of the Gulf of Corinth		Allies carried the main burden of the Egyptian campaign
Gained control of south side of Corinthian Gulf — cities of Achaea joined alliance		
Disastrous defeat of Greeks in Egypt by Persia	454	After failure in Egypt, allied treasury moved from Delos to Athens
Cimon returned from exile; five-year truce with Sparta and resumption of war with Persia		League finances were in the hands of Athens
Cimon and League forces started to liberate Cyprus but Cimon died of disease; the allies defeated the Persians off Cyprus and on the coast of Cilicia		At some point the allied council at Delos ceased to meet. Athens no longer consulted allies; they had little or no control over their own foreign affairs
Persia began negotiations; Peace of Callias, 448, marked end of war with Persia and beginning of consolidation of Athens' Empire	448	Decrees affecting relations with individual allies were issued by the Athenian state; degree of control over allies increased
Pericles proposed a Panhellenic conference at Athens — no response from the Peloponnesians led to the failure of any diplomatic offensive		Control over allies took various forms: • oaths of loyalty • cleruchies established at strategic points • garrisons stationed in member states • compliant or democratic governments installed • use of Athenian system of weights, measures and coinage obligatory • use of Athenian law courts to hear cases concerning allies
Lost control of Boeotia, Phocis and Locris (448–447)		
Megara and Euboea revolted, 447–446; Athens lost Megara, but crushed Euboea — this delayed further revolts in the Aegean		
Thirty Years' Peace signed — this created for a time a balance of power in the Greek world; ill-will between Athens and Corinth continued, although Corinth free for the time from the danger of being encircled by Athens	445	

The transformation from league to empire

At what point did Athens' leadership of a league of allied states become rule over subject states? From the point of view of individual allies it would have occurred at different times, depending on when they felt the use of Athenian force against them.

From the Athenian point of view, it is harder to say. There is certainly no evidence to suggest that the Athenians had any long-term plans, in the years 479 to 470, to change the League into an empire, although from the beginning the potential to develop into an imperial power was there.

Transformation from league to empire gradual

It is difficult to point to any one particular year in which this change occurred, although there were certain events, such as the subjugation of Naxos and Thasos, which focused on the changing relationship of Athens and her allies. However by 446–445 there is no longer any doubt or pretence about Athens' imperial position. The Chalcis Decree, issued after the Euboean cities—of which Chalcis was the largest—revolted, required the inhabitants to take an oath 'not to revolt against the Athenian demos' and 'to be obedient to the Athenian demos'.

Athens' changing relations with her allies

First subject states—a third type of member (472–469)

Thucydides says that Eion, Scyrus (setting up of a cleruchy), Carystus (forcing an independent and unwilling state to join the League) and Naxos (reducing a rebellious member to subject status) were stepping stones to Athens' rise to power, but he was looking back from a time when Athens was at the height of that power. In the beginning Athens had tied herself to a group of allies in the anti-Persian cause, and in order to make sure she was not left to fight the Persians alone, she insisted that the allies honour their obligations. Those cities which did not, such as Naxos, paid the penalty for revolt—a reduction to the status of tribute-paying subjects. Within a few years of the formation of the Delian League there were three types of members: those contributing ships; those contributing money; and the more recent, subject members paying tribute. Those in the first two categories were independent allies, while the members of the third group had lost their autonomy.

Thucydides' view of first steps to power

Insistence on obligations being met

Subject, tribute-paying members added

Thucydides says 'it was the actual course of events which first compelled us to increase our power to its present extent: fear of Persia was our chief motive...'.[21]

Indication of change in nature of League—Thasos, 465

As early as 465, the use of League forces to reduce a member state (Thasos) to subject status because of a personal quarrel with Athens

Athens used League for own purposes

177

indicated a change in the nature of the League, and its possible use to promote Athens' interests in the future.

Increased demands on allies as Spartan–Athenian relationship deteriorated, 462–461

Athens' relations with allies changed

An important turning point in Athens' relations with her allies occurred in the years 465 to 460 with a change of direction in Athenian internal politics — the growth of radical democracy. This caused a deterioration in the relationship between Athens and Sparta, resulting in an open break in 462–461. Athens realised the importance of keeping her alliance together in the face of future Spartan hostility. Also, she was now aware that she faced opposition on two sides — from the Persians and from the Spartans. It was imperative to keep her allies bound to her, and so throughout the years 459–450 Athens' demands on her allies increased.

Allies preferred to contribute money

Athenian navy grew at allies' expense

Apart from the burden of the continued assessment for tribute, which many allies came to resent after 468 (Eurymedon), the prospect after 460 of being forced to fight against other Greeks — particularly against Sparta — must have caused much discontent. It was during this period that more allies — reluctant to face military service, and to avoid serving abroad — 'had assessments made by which instead of producing ships, they were to pay a corresponding sum of money' (Thucydides).[22] This suited Athens, who may have even encouraged it, as her navy grew at the expense of the allies. The allies also became increasingly ill-prepared for and inexperienced in war. When members failed to honour their contributions — either in money or in ships — and revolted against the alliance, the Athenians were easily able to force them back into the League as subjects. Thucydides' conclusion was that 'for this position it was the allies themselves who were to blame'.[23] The process of reducing previously independent allies to subjects of Athens continued, and in this Athens claimed she had no choice. The Athenians explained their point of view to the Spartans, as reported by Thucydides:

Not safe for Athens to let allies secede

> There came a time when we were surrounded by enemies, when we had already crushed some revolts, when you had lost the friendly feelings that you used to have for us and had turned against us and begun to arouse our suspicion: at this point it was clearly no longer safe for us to risk letting our Empire go, especially as any allies that left us would go over to you.[24]

Allies forced to further interests of Athens — influence of Pericles

Naval allies involved in furthering Athens' own interests

Under the influence of Pericles, an avowed imperialist, the allies of the League were required to support Athens in pursuing her own interests during the years 459–454.

- The war between Athens and Aegina, in which the allies of the Delian League probably participated, was a flagrant act of aggression on Athens' part. The crushing defeat and subsequent reduction of Aegina

—'that eyesore of the Piraeus', which was forced to pay the largest single contribution of any subject in the League (30 talents)—must have created fear and resentment among many of the members of the League.

- In Athens' attempt to build up a land as well as a naval empire, the maritime allies were expected to play a part. The Delian League allies sent military contingents to fight the Peloponnesians in Boeotia at the Battle of Tanagra (457).

Allies fought at the Battle of Tanagra

The naval allies were now governed by the policy of Athens, which bore no resemblance to the original purpose of the League. Pericles never doubted that Athens' greatness depended on her maintaining and extending her control over her allies and subjects.

Allied treasury controlled by Athens, 454

In 454, the allied treasury at Delos was moved to Athens on the excuse of a possible Phoenician raid into the Aegean. The Athenians and their allies had just suffered a disastrous defeat in Egypt at the hands of a Persian army and a Phoenician fleet, with great losses in both ships and men. Although reasons of safety could be justified, the move was a significant step in the evolution of the League into an empire.

League treasury removed to Athens

Prior to this, the Congress of the Allies had controlled the treasury, but after 454–453 the Congress ceased to meet and the League revenue became part of Athens' own treasury. The Athenian Assembly decided without consulting the allies how the funds were to be used, and the Athenian Council supervised and checked the annual income and assessed the amount of tribute that was due from each state.

Allies not consulted about revenue

One sixtieth of the tribute was paid into the sacred treasury of Athena, and Pericles proposed the diversion of 5000 talents from it into a building fund. It is from this period that the fragments of the Quota Lists (Tribute Lists) come. From 454, the contributions of member states were inscribed on stone.

Part of League funds paid into Athenian treasury

'These are the first fruits of the goddess paid by the Hellenotamiae, whose secretary was . . . and audited by the thirty state-Accountants, from the tribute which the cities paid in, when Ariston was archon of the Athenians. There is a mina for every talent'.[25] [There were sixty minas to every talent in Athenian currency.]

Control over allies tightened, 453–449

In 451 Athens, under the influence of Cimon (recently returned from exile), signed a five-year truce with Sparta. This gave Athens an opportunity to continue consolidating her League into an empire. Not only did Cimon renew Delian League attacks on Persian-held territory, but Athens reasserted her position of command throughout the Aegean. The number of tribute-paying states increased during this period, particularly in the

Athens' truce with Sparta

Increase in number of subject states

Decrees — Athens tightens control over allies

south-east Aegean, where the danger from Persia was the greatest.

Evidence of the methods she used to exert her control over and regain the allegiance of rebellious states is contained in a number of inscriptions, dated approximately from 453 to 449. Although fragmentary, the decrees relating to Erythrae, Miletus and Colophon give enough details to indicate the tightening up of Athens' control. Of the three inscriptions, the Erythrae Decree is by far the most detailed and outlines some of the methods by which Athens controlled her allies.

Fragment from a marble stele inscribed with the quota figures for the allies, 451–450

Part of the text of an Athenian decree of 451–450, in which the Athenians extended a vote of praise to the city of Sigeum on the shores of the Hellespont

Evidence from inscriptions

Garrisons   Athens did not hesitate to place garrisons in rebellious cities. Erythrae is the first known example of this, but it may have occurred earlier. These garrisons not only served a military purpose but were a political device as well. Their job was to protect the Athenian inspectors or commissioners (*episkopoi*) sent out to install 'puppet' governments, or at least governments favourable to Athens. '. . . the Council installed by the [Athenian] inspectors and garrison commander, and in future by the [outgoing] council and the garrison commander'.[26]

Garrisons served military and political purposes

Democratic forms of government   In most cases Athens set up a democratic form of government closely modelled on her own, only smaller. Councillors of the Boule were over thirty years of age, selected by lot and liable to prosecution if they did not abide by the oath they swore on taking up office.

Democratic governments usually replaced oligarchic or Persian-inspired tyrannies. Although this imposition of an altered constitution favourable to Athens was imperialistic, generally the majority of people in the state favoured a democracy. However, in the case of Miletus Athens appears to have first supported an oligarchic government in place of a tyranny, but when these oligarchs revolted against Athens and slaughtered the democrats, Athens installed a more reliable democratic government.

Oligarchies and tyrannies replaced by democracies

G. E. M. de Ste Croix has argued that in fact a state only revolted against Athens if there was a chance of an oligarchic faction gaining control there.

Oaths of loyalty

'I will perform my duties as councillor to the best of my ability and faithfully to the people of Erythrae and of Athens and the allies. I will not revolt from the people of Athens nor will I permit another to do so . . .'.[27]

'I shall neither desert nor disrupt the democracy of Colophon'.[28]

Oaths sworn in support of Athens

Interference in the law   Athenian involvement in the judicial affairs of her allies may have begun quite early. A decree relating to Phaselis, probably passed after 462, clearly defines the judicial relationship between Athens and Phaselis.

In the Erythrae Decree there is the beginning of interference by Athens in legal matters, but it concerned only political cases, such as persons accused of treason against Erythrae or Athens. Seven years later, with the issuing of the Chalcis Decree (446–445), much greater interference by Athens occurred and the actions of local courts were restricted severely.

Interference in legal affairs by Athens increased

As time went by, Athens demanded that many trials concerning allies should be referred to Athenian law courts. Although usually fairly treated, the allies became discontented at this further loss of independence. The use of Athenian law courts in political cases was an effective method of democratic control, as most of those brought to trial were oligarchs.

Subject states contributed to Athenian religious festivals

Religion   The subject status of Erythrae is clearly emphasised when the people are instructed to send envoys with offerings to the great Panathenaic Festival, held in Athens every four years. A minimum value 'of not less that 3 minae' was set for their sacred contribution.[29]

Establishment of cleruchies

Cleruchies at strategic locations

Between 450 and 446 Athens inaugurated a system of cleruchies, which were settlements of Athenian citizens abroad. These strengthened Athens' hold on her empire, as they were located at strategic points in the Aegean. There had already been some cleruchies established earlier, such as those on the land of the Chalcidians in 506 and at Scyrus after the Persian wars. Some, like Lemnos and Imbros, were later reinforced, but this was the first time that Athens planted settlements on the territory of her allies. This policy was associated with Pericles and — although popular with Athenians — caused more bitterness and resentment than any other aspect of Athenian imperial policy. The bitterness was greatest in the islands, where the amount of good land was limited. The best land was taken by the Athenian cleruchs, dispossessing a local population often three or four times as numerous as the newcomers. These local people often became quite destitute.

Created great bitterness amongst allies

Relieved unemployment

The Athenian settlers, drawn from the two lowest classes, were raised to hoplite status by the grant of land. Not only did this system relieve 'the city of a large number of idlers and agitators and raise the standards of the poorest classes', but at the same time it implanted amongst the allies 'a healthy fear of rebellion' (Plutarch).[30] These settlements became the watchdogs of the empire and provided safe ports of call for the fleet, as well as being an important part of Pericles' social policy to relieve unemployment.

In 450 Naxos (500 cleruchs), Andros (250 cleruchs) and possibly Carystus were settled. These areas were rebellious, and needed close supervision.

Cleruchs acted as watchdogs for Athens

It is believed that Tolmides, the Athenian general, led some cleruchs to the Dardanelles area, and in 447 Pericles himself led 1000 cleruchs to re-establish Athenian control in the Chersonese. This was vital to Athens' corn trade from the Black Sea, which was being threatened again by warlike tribes. Plutarch says that these 1000 cleruchs 'provided the cities there with fresh strength and vigour but he [Pericles] also secured the neck of the Isthmus'.[31]

The northern frontier of the Chalcidic region was secured against the Bisaltian tribes by settling 1000 cleruchs in the area.

Plutarch records that after Euboea revolted against Athens in 447–446,

Pericles 'transplanted the whole population of Histiaea from their territory and replaced them with Athenian colonists'.[32] These cleruchs were not colonists in the strict sense, as they were still Athenian citizens and could be called up for military service.

Peace of Callias

After the death of Cimon in Cyprus and a victory against the Persians and Phoenicians off the coast of Cilicia, both the Persians and the Greeks were ready to negotiate for peace. Under the leadership of the Athenian Callias, an embassy was sent to Susa to bring the war with Persia officially to an end.

In 449 the Persians agreed not to come within three days' march of the coast of Asia Minor and not to send warships into the Aegean and Propontis. The Greeks of Asia Minor were to be autonomous, and Athens agreed not to attack Persian territory. However, she abandoned her allies in Cyprus and Egypt.

Did this peace end Athens' claims over her allies? Since ships were only contributed in time of war, those allies contributing money would also expect to pay only in time of war. There is one tribute list missing from the records at this time and it is believed that the allies may have refused to pay their contributions in the first year of peace.

Hostility of allies to continued contributions

Pericles' imperial policy

The end of the war with Persia and the five-year truce with Sparta confronted Pericles with a major problem. Thousands of soldiers and sailors, previously away on summer campaigns and supported by League funds, were now unemployed.

At the same time Pericles had a vision of Athens as the capital of Greece, graced with buildings worthy of that position. The temples on the Acropolis had been in ruins since the second Persian invasion and he now saw the solution to both problems: a massive building program. However, this required funds.

Pericles' building and employment policy needed funds

A Panhellenic conference of all Greek states of the mainland and the Aegean was planned by Pericles to discuss (a) the rebuilding of all temples destroyed by the Persians and (b) the security of the Aegean Sea. However, the underlying intention was to get general support for the rebuilding of Athens' temples (which were the only areas destroyed) and for the recognition of the Athenian navy as protector of the Aegean.

As the response to his invitation was negative, Pericles took it as an excuse to force the allies to continue their contributions in order to further his policies of carrying out a building program, developing democracy, and maintaining Athenian forces over a wide area.

Failure of Panhellenic conference

Under Pericles, the Athenian demos exploited its leadership over the allies. However, there were critics within Athens of this policy and

Allies forced to continue contributions — Pericles opposed

Plutarch records how Pericles' enemies, led by Thucydides (son of Melesias, not the historian), denounced his actions as 'barefaced tyranny'. Pericles replied that 'the Athenians were not obliged to give an account of how their [the allies'] money was spent', and as long as Athens provided the services paid for [that is, protection] she could use the surplus any way she wished.[33]

Many allies refused to pay

The tribute list for 448 revealed the opposition and hostility to continued payment, since many important members (for example, Miletus and Aegina) were missing from the list and others, such as Thasos, paid only part of what they owed.

The Cleinias Decree, passed about 447, informed the cities of the League of the decision by Athens to continue exacting contributions, and outlined details for their annual collection. Those who refused to pay or reduced their payments would have to plead their cases in the Athenian law courts. The tribute was reassessed every four years and published at the great Panathenaic Festival, when each state sent delegates.

Coinage Decree further restricted allies

Somewhere between 450 and 446 a Coinage Decree was passed in Athens, enforcing uniformity of coinage, weights and measures among the members of the League. Athenian silver coins were to be used throughout the area under her control. Local currencies had to be melted down, and mints closed. Although this measure undoubtedly made trade easier, it was a further example of the allies' loss of freedom.

Revolt of Megara and Euboea — the Chalcis Decree

Chalcis Decree revealed Athens' imperialism

In 447–446 the island of Euboea revolted against Athens at the same time as Megara destroyed her Athenian garrison. The loss of Megara was disastrous, but Pericles subdued the whole island of Euboea and soon after issued a decree relating to the Euboean city of Chalcis. This decree leaves no doubt that the original members of the League were now very much subjects of an imperial power. The citizens of Chalcis were required to swear an oath which included the following statements:

1 'I will not revolt against the Athenian people by any art or device, either in word or in deed'.
2 'I will pay the tribute to the Athenians'.
3 'I will aid and succour the Athenian people if any one wrongs the Athenian people'.
4 'I will be obedient to the Athenian people'.[34]

Benefits for Athens from the empire

Thucydides records the Athenians' explanation for their empire.

We have done nothing extraordinary, nothing contrary to human nature in accepting an empire when it was offered to us and then in refusing to give it up. Three very powerful motives prevent us from doing so — security, honour and self-interest.[35]

The Athenians received great benefits from their empire. The funds collected were used for the payment of state officials and jurors, for the maintenance of the fleet and payment of the rowers and soldiers, for the building of temples and to subsidise festivals.

Athenian society and government subsidised by allied contributions

Aristophanes describes the sources of the imperial revenue as coming not only from tribute but from 'percentage deposits', court fees, mine rents, market and harbour dues, rents and confiscations, and according to him they totalled not much less that 2000 talents. Between 447 and 432 the Athenians did not need to pay any direct taxes to the state.

Advantages and disadvantages for member states

Membership of the empire provided advantages such as peace, better protection, democratic governments, and prosperity through increased trade. However, the loss of the members' independence in domestic and foreign affairs, their economic dependence on Athens and her high-handed actions towards them far outweighed any advantages gained. They saw her becoming a tyrant state.

Allies benefited from peace and protection

The treatment of Samos, which in 440 stood up for its right to go to war with another state, was an example of this 'tyranny'. A dispute had broken out between Samos and Mytilene, both members of the empire. Samos had been a reliable, ship-contributing, independent member and would not have expected Athens to intervene in the dispute. When Samos refused to abide by Athens' demands that she cease fighting and accept Athenian arbitration, Pericles with forty ships sought to reassert Athenian control by seizing hostages, establishing a garrison and setting up a democratic government. During the absence of Pericles and the Athenian navy, the escaped leaders returned and overthrew the newly-established democracy. This was a test of Athens' power and it was crucial that Samos be subdued before the Persians intervened and other allies followed her example. Byzantium had already revolted and seized the Bosphorus. The Athenian navy — reinforced with ships from Chios and Lesbos — eventually defeated the Samians at sea, and a nine-month siege ended Samos' independent existence. She was forced to pull down her walls, surrender her fleet, pay a sum of 1276 talents and swear an oath of loyalty.

Athens seen as a tyrant state

Samos reduced to subject status

Some years later, Pericles reminded the Athenians that they had incurred hatred in administering their empire and that it was like a tyranny. However, according to Thucydides he said that although 'it may have been wrong to take it; it is certainly dangerous to let it go'.[36]

Athens incurred hatred of allies

Assignment: Athens' relations with Sparta and the Peloponnesian League, 461–445

Hostility of Corinth to Athens

Of all the members of the Peloponnesian League, the one with the most reason to fear and hate Athens after 460 was Corinth. During the ten years of Athens' expansion on the mainland, it was Corinth who was placed in the greatest danger. As Athens drew Megara into her alliance, settled the helots at Naupactus and extended her control to both sides of the Corinthian Gulf, Corinth was encircled and her valuable trade with the west threatened. Her bitter hatred of Athens continued even after the Thirty Years' Peace was signed, which relieved her for a time from the danger she had faced since 458.

Corinth's size, wealth, strategic position and large navy made her a vital member of the Peloponnesian League; her influence within that organisation contributed to the breakdown of the peace between Athens and Sparta.

Megara and Aegina

1 Why did Megara join the Athenian alliance in 459?
2 What advantages did Athens gain?
3 What effect did this have on Corinth's relations with Athens?
4 Why did war with Aegina break out and what part did Corinth and Epidaurus play in attempting to help Aegina?
5 What effect did the war in the Megarid have on Corinth?
6 What was the fate of Aegina?

Central Greece

1 What was Sparta's pretext for marching into central Greece?
2 What was her real aim?
3 Why did Sparta and Athens clash at the Battle of Tanagra?
4 How effective was this victory for Sparta?
5 What was its significance for Athens?

Naupactus

Explain the significance of the settlement of the Messenian rebels at Naupactus for
1 Athens
2 Sparta
3 Corinth

Peloponnesian coasts and the Corinthian Gulf

1 What setbacks did the members of the Peloponnesian League suffer between 455 and 453 at the hands of the Athenian navy?
2 Why was Corinth in a position of great danger at this time?

Alliances in the west

What was the significance for Corinth of Athens' alliances with the towns of Sicily and southern Italy?

Five-year truce, 451

Why was a five-year truce concluded between Athens and Sparta?

The loss of Athens' land empire

1 How did Boeotia, Phocis and Locris regain their independence?
2 How serious were these losses to Athens?
3 Who helped Megara revolt against Athens? Why was this disastrous for Athens?
4 What part did Sparta play in the Megarian revolt?

The Thirty Years' Peace, 445

1 What were the terms of the peace signed between Athens and Sparta?
2 What was left to Athens of her former land empire?
3 What was the significance for Corinth of the peace?
4 What is meant by the term 'balance of power'? How did this now apply to the Greek world?
5 How long did the peace last?

Essay topics

1 What was the relationship between Athens and her allies in the first ten years of the Delian League's existence?
2 What effect did Themistocles, Pausanias and Cimon have on Athenian–Spartan relations between 479 and 461?
3 Assess the part played by each of the following in the formation of the Athenian empire:
   (a) Themistocles
   (b) Aristides
   (c) Cimon
   (d) Pericles
4 Explain the change in Sparta's attitude to Athens after 462–461 and show how Sparta and members of the Peloponnesian League reacted to Athens' territorial expansion between 461 and 445.
5 Using as much documentary evidence as possible, explain what benefits Athens gained from her empire and what grievances the members of the empire suffered after 454.

Further reading

Primary sources

Aristophanes. *The Wasps.*
Aristotle. *The Athenian Constitution.*
Athenian Tribute Lists, ed. B. D. Merritt, H. T. Wade-Gery & A. F. McGregor.
Plutarch. *The Rise and Fall of Athens*, Chs 3, 4, 5, 6.
Thucydides. *The Peloponnesian War.*

Secondary sources

Burn, A. R. *Pericles and Athens.*
Bury, J. B. & Meiggs, R. *A History of Greece.*
French, A. *The Athenian Half-century.*
Hammond, N. G. L. *A History of Greece to 322 B. C.*
Hill, G. F., Meiggs, R. & Andrewes, A. *Sources for Greek History from the Persian to the Peloponnesian Wars.*
Horsley, G. H. R. *Some Aspects of the Athenian Empire.*
Lewis, N. *The Fifth Century B.C.*
Meiggs, R. *The Athenian Empire.*

8 *Periclean Athens*

Pericles — a profile
The agora in the fifth century
Periclean democracy
Athenian women in the fifth century

*Pericles — a profile**

Pericles — a Roman copy of a Greek original, c.440

CONSIDERING that the rise and predominance of Pericles coincided with the period of Athenian greatness, it is surprising that much of his life is so thinly documented. Plutarch's biography of Pericles is based only on the last twenty years of his life, and Plutarch was not critical enough of his sources. Although he mentions twenty authorities, eight of which were contemporaries of Pericles, only the works of Thucydides and Aristophanes survive today.

Thucydides, who saw Pericles as the greatest of all the leading figures of the Peloponnesian War, chose to reveal only those characteristics which had a bearing on the main issues of the war. He omitted much biographical and anecdotal detail which must have been known to him.

Aristophanes' references to Pericles must be treated cautiously, since an integral part of the comic poet's work was caricature and personal ridicule of leading citizens.

---

* Read Thucydides, Plutarch and Aristophanes for more detail on the life of Pericles. Secondary sources such as A. R. Burn's *Pericles and Athens* can be used to supplement the primary sources.

188

Background and education

Refer to Plutarch, *Pericles*, 4–6; Burn, *Pericles and Athens*, pp. 17–26.

He was born about 494 into a distinguished family. His mother was Agariste, one of the Alcmaeonids; Cleisthenes was his great uncle and Xanthippus his father, a notable politician and general during the Persian Wars.

His childhood and youth were spent during the Persian Wars. His father's ostracism and the evacuation of Athens must have affected him.

He came under the influence of two distinguished teachers, to whom he owed much.

1 Anaxagoras, the great Ionian intellectual, whose scientific ideas freed Pericles from the superstitions held by the people he guided.
2 Damon, his music teacher, who had an interest in politics and philosophy. It was probably due to him that Pericles entered politics as a radical.

He was very close to Protagoras, the greatest of the sophists, and was a friend of the dramatist Sophocles and the sculptor Phidias.

Characteristics and abilities

Refer to Plutarch, *Pericles*, 39; Thucydides, II:65.

An outline of the character of Pericles would reveal the following attributes:

- intelligent, rational thought;
- aloofness;
- persuasive oratory, great skill in debate, having no need to use flattery;
- determined, firm leadership of an indecisive people;
- moderation, and a sense of justice;
- reserve and dignity, with a 'serene temper';
- great integrity, unable to be bribed;
- farsightedness;
- intense patriotism and idealism.

The early years, 471–461

Refer to Burn, pp. 33–46; Plutarch, *Pericles*, 7.

1 He served with Cimon and the Delian League fleet.
2 He first spoke in the assembly on the side of the radical democrats in 469; he was associated with Ephialtes from 463 to 461.

His position within the democracy

Refer to Plutarch, *Pericles*, 9.15; Thucydides, II:65; Burn, pp. 56–60.

Pericles' great influence over the Athenian people, especially after 454, was based on two factors:

1 his position as general
2 his personal abilities

His position as a general

- He was elected as one of ten generals—the military and political leaders of Athens.
- He had the same rights as every other citizen.
- People could and did refuse to listen to a general's advice.
- A general's duty was to carry out the policy decided by the people, even if he regarded it as unsound.
- A general could be re-elected, but could also be brought to trial or fined if any aspect of his work was called into question or if he was unsuccessful in a campaign.
- After 445, Pericles was re-elected general fifteen times in succession.
- It is possible that a change in the system of electing generals favoured him; one general, elected from all Athenians—not from an individual tribe—became the general-in-chief (*strategos autocrator*).

His personal abilities

Aspects of his character have already been mentioned in the previous section. According to Thucydides, when Pericles was at the head of the state it was wisely led and firmly guarded. His position, his intelligence and his known integrity enabled him to respect the liberty of the people and at the same time to hold them in check.

However, he was not without his opponents.

- Thucydides (son of Melesias) was his most outspoken critic, especially over the funds of the empire and Pericles' building program.
- Pericles' friends and associates were attacked by his opponents and prosecuted in the courts, or ostracised.
- The ostracism of Thucydides removed effective opposition to Pericles, but he was still vulnerable to attack. In 430 the people deposed and fined him, but later reinstated him. He was the constant butt of the comic poets.

Thucydides the historian, who disapproved of democracy but admired Pericles, has also said that it was he who led the people rather than they who led him, and that in what was nominally a democracy, the power was really in the hands of the first citizen.

His contribution to Athens

He completed the steps to democracy

Refer to Aristotle, *The Athenian Constitution*, 26–7; Plutarch, *Pericles*, 9; Burn, *Pericles and Athens*, pp. 75–8.

1 The Areopagus was further stripped of its powers, which were transferred to the Heliaea.
2 Payment of jurors was introduced.
3 State pay also was introduced for other officials — archons, councillors.
4 Chief archonships were opened to smallholders, and later to the thetes.
5 Citizenship was restricted; this was tied to the question of state pay for services — there should be as few citizens as possible to enjoy the new privileges and profits of citizenship.

Choice by lot and payment for services enabled the poorer classes to take a larger part in public affairs, but there was considerable criticism of state pay for services (for example, later by Plato). It was said to corrupt the people, to make them idle and open to political bribery by manipulative politicians.

Why did this Athenian aristocrat devote himself to shaping so complete a democracy?

C. M. Bowra, in his book *Periclean Athens*, argues that Pericles completed the work started by Themistocles because he was so intensely patriotic, and believed in Athens. If Athens was to be the great city he envisaged, every citizen had to play his part to the full extent of his ability. Plutarch suggests another reason — empire.

He promoted the Athenian Empire

Refer to Plutarch, *Pericles*, 11, 19, 20; Burn, *Pericles and Athens*, Chs 6, 7.

The transformation of the League into an empire revealed the guiding hand of Pericles. By concentrating control in Athenian hands, he made Athens truly imperial. He regarded the empire as not only indispensable for the growth and maintenance of Athens, but as a noble achievement for which his countrymen deserved the greatest praise.

- He took steps to make the League more manageable — democratic governments were set up, garrisons were established in allied cities, more court cases involving allied states were now heard in Athens and oaths were taken and treaties signed with individual League members.
- He fostered a new wave of colonisation in the form of cleruchies. Approximately 6000 cleruchs secured the waterways and ensured Athenian grain supplies and raw materials. Colonists were sent out to Thurii in southern Italy and Amphipolis in the northern Aegean.
- Treaties and alliances signed with the cities of Sicily extended Athenian influence to those areas not within the borders of her empire.

- Pericles' later policy was to consolidate the empire rather than to expand it.

He carried out an ambitious building program

Refer to Plutarch, *Pericles*, 12–13; Burn, *Pericles and Athens*, Ch. 9.

His aims were (a) to glorify Athens and (b) to ensure that the unskilled masses, who had no military training, should not be debarred from benefiting from the national income and yet should not be paid for sitting about and doing nothing.

His building achievements included the Parthenon, the statue of Athena, the Temple of Athena Nike, the Temple of Hephaestus, the Temple of Poseidon at Sunium, the Hall of Mysteries at Eleusis, the Propylaea and the Odeon. (These are treated later in this chapter.)

This small fragment concerns the building of the Propylaea. It outlines the number of drachmas and obols spent in the fourth year of building

He promoted economic growth

1 The Piraeus was improved as a port and a market — its defences were completed. Pericles
   - built another Long Wall from Athens to Phalerum;
   - constructed dry docks;
   - built storehouses around the wharves;
   - rebuilt the Emporion (this was a showplace where merchants displayed their wares);
   - laid out the town on a rectangular (grid) street pattern — this was the work of the Milesian architect, Hippodamus.

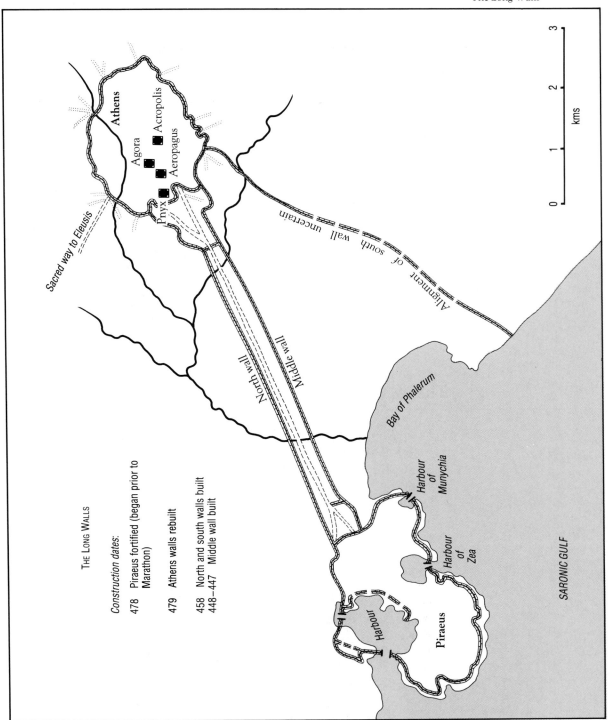

The Long Walls

Athens

Agora
Acropolis
Aeropagus
Pnyx

Sacred way to Eleusis

Alignment of south wall uncertain

North wall
Middle wall

Bay of Phalerum

Harbour of Munychia

Harbour of Zea

Harbour

Piraeus

SARONIC GULF

0   1   2   3
kms

THE LONG WALLS

Construction dates:

478   Piraeus fortified (began prior to Marathon)

479   Athens walls rebuilt

458   North and south walls built
448–447   Middle wall built

2 With the decline of the cities of Ionia and Phoenicia, Athens became the centre of trade in the Aegean. A strong line of communication was secured between Athens and the Black Sea. Pericles visited the area in 436.

3 Athens entered the trade of the western Mediterannean.

His leadership in the first years of the Peloponnesian War

Refer to Plutarch, *Pericles*, 29, 30, 33; Thucydides, I:127, 139–46, II:59–65, 122; Burn, *Pericles and Athens*, Ch. 12–13.

In the first three years of the war, Pericles

1 stood firm against Peloponnesian demands to give the allies their freedom and to revoke the Megarian Decrees;

2 gave Athenians hope of victory and outlined a strategy which if adhered to, could have won the war, namely, to (a) abandon their lands and farms, (b) remain within the city—rely on their ships, (c) fight no pitched battles with Spartans, and (d) make no new conquests;

3 supervised the evacuation of Attica;

4 remained immovable in the face of the complaints of the people and denunciation by his enemies.

The agora in the fifth century

The agora ('gathering place') was the centre of political, social and commerical life in Athens. In Pericles' day it was still an open, tree-lined square with markets, specialist shops, shrines, law courts and other public buildings.

Excavations of the agora have been carried out by the American School of Classical Studies in Athens. Some of the School's publications deal in detail with the material remains which have thrown so much light on life and politics in the fifth century; for example, *The Athenian Citizen* and *Inscriptions from the Athenian Agora*.

Material remains excavated from the Athenian agora of the fifth century: allotment tokens — small clay plaques for choosing jurors

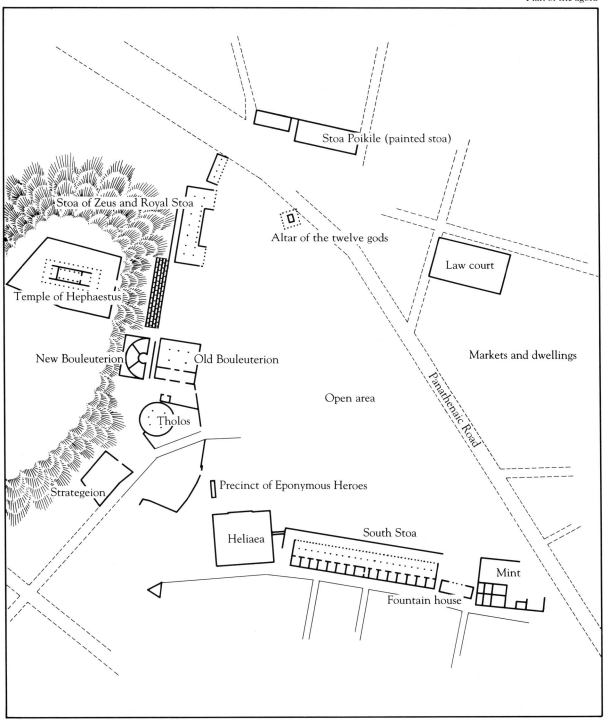

Stoa Poikile (painted stoa)

Stoa of Zeus and Royal Stoa

Altar of the twelve gods

Law court

Temple of Hephaestus

Markets and dwellings

New Bouleuterion

Old Bouleuterion

Open area

Panathenaic Road

Tholos

Strategeion

Precinct of Eponymous Heroes

Heliaea

South Stoa

Mint

Fountain house

Major features	Material remains	Major features	Material remains
The New Bouleuterion } Council **The Old Bouleuterion** } House The New Bouleuterion — meetings of the Council of 500. The Old Bouleuterion — storage of state archives, such as decrees written on papyrus or parchment. This building was later replaced by the Metroon. It also housed the Shrine of the Mother of the Gods.	• Allotment tokens — small clay plaques cut into two like jigsaw pieces, bearing name of tribe and deme • Klepsydra — water clocks for timing speeches • Decrees inscribed on stone honouring individuals or groups, such as the poletai (lessors of public contracts)	**South Stoa** **Stoa of Zeus** and **Royal Stoa** **Stoa Poikile** (painted stoa) Stoas were porches — roofed promenades which contained offices and other apartments. The South Stoa held the offices of the magistrates.	• South Stoa — long double-aisled colonnade fronting a row of sixteen square rooms
Tholos — Housed the prytaneis and their secretaries while on duty. Also used as a repository for official weights and measures.	• Remains of a kitchen; cups and vessels used by prytaneis, marked as public property; shopping lists • Square bronze weights inscribed with symbols and letters • Terracotta measures, dry and liquid; bronze measures were found near the mint	**Fountain house**	• Potsherds — pieces of the pitchers broken by the women at the well • Terracotta pipes
		The Mint	• Furnaces and water basins • Blanks of coins • Coins — Attic 'owls' • An inscription nearby dealing with coinage
Strategeion — Headquarters of the generals.	• Identified by an inscription containing directions that it be set up in front of the headquarters of the generals	**Altar of the twelve gods** — Focal point of the Agora. Distances were measured from it.	• Stone sill carried a parapet • Base of statues — one bearing a dedication to the twelve gods
		Markets and dwellings	
Precinct of the eponymous heroes — Bronze statues of ten heroes from whom the ten tribes took their names, and therefore the basis of an individual's citizenship. This was the information centre, where notices were posted.	• A long rectangular enclosure around a very long base; part of the fence has been reconstructed	**Open area** — Used for holding ostracisms once a year; it was then fenced off, with ten entrances.	• Large numbers of ostraka bearing victims' names and sometimes comments; large deposits in S.W. corner used to fill potholes in the roads
The Heliaea — From the 6th century. **Law Court** — Predecessor of the later square peristyle.	• Kleroterion — an allotment device for selecting jurors • Ballots used by jurors to record verdict • Ballot 'box' • Bronze and wooden jurors' tickets • Klepsydra — water clock	**The Panathenaic Road** — Sacred way, which wound its way from Eleusis to the Acropolis.	• Hard-packed earth and gravel • Larger stones producing a cobbled effect • Evidence of width — 10–20 metres
		The Temple of Hephaestus — Outside the Agora; may have been built as a dedication by the metal workers to their patron god.	• Evidence of metalwork around the hill

Fifth-century artefacts
excavated from the agora:
(a) an official liquid
measure;
(b) a council cup used by
officials on duty in the
tholos;
(c) a bronze standard weight

Assignment: Using literary and archaeological evidence

The following assignment has been devised to develop skills in using both literary and archaeological evidence.

Literary evidence

The Wasps *of Aristophanes*

Produced in 422, at a time when Athens was involved in the Peloponnesian War with Sparta, the *Wasps* is a useful source for an understanding of Athenian society and domestic politics, the administration of justice, Athens' relations with her allies, and army life. Since Aristophanes' intention was to show how the jurors (the 'wasps') were being exploited and manipulated by the popular leaders (the demagogues) for their own ends, there are many useful references to the law courts.

- What can be inferred about the functioning of the Athenian law courts in the fifth century?

Find references to the following:
1 number of jurors;
2 admission of jurors to courts;
3 number of courts operating at any one time;
4 courtroom procedure:
   (a) time of start
   (b) duration of cases and speeches
   (c) prosecutors, sycophants
   (d) methods used by defendants to sway jurors
   (e) methods of voting
   (f) registering sentences
5 jurors' pay, poverty of jurors, jurors' 'power';
6 weaknesses of the system.

Take care to note exaggerations and distortions of the truth, remembering that Aristophanes' first aim was to entertain his audience.

Archaeological evidence

The buildings on the Acropolis

'Mighty indeed are the marks and monuments of our empire which we have left.' — Thucydides[1]

197

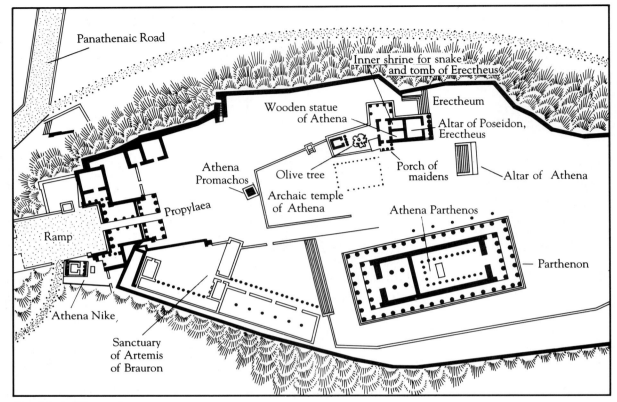

Plan of the buildings on the
Acropolis

1 The Parthenon
 (a) What is the meaning of the word
  'Parthenon'?
 (b) When was the Parthenon built and who
  were its architects and its sculptor?
 (c) What was its purpose?
 (d) Make a note of its main architectural
  features.
 (e) What do you learn about Athenian
  public religion from the sculptures on
  the metopes, pediment and frieze? Give
  some details of the Panathenaic Festival.
2 The Statue of Athena Parthenos
 There are no remains of this, except for
 small copies. Find Pausanias' description of
 it. What were the meanings of the symbols

(snakes and wings) carried by Athena?
3 The Temple of Athena Niké
 (a) What is the meaning of the word 'Niké'?
 (b) What was the purpose of this small
  temple?
 (c) Who was its architect?
 (d) What was depicted on its frieze?
4 The Statue of Athena Promachos
 (a) Who built this huge bronze statue?
 (b) What was its significance?
5 The Propylaea
 (a) What was the Propylaea?
 (b) Who was its architect?
 (c) Describe the architectural details.
 (d) Why was the original plan not fully
  implemented?

6 The Erechtheum
  (a) When was this built?
  (b) Why was it such an irregular shape, unusual for a temple? Make reference to
    (i) the site;
    (ii) earlier shrines and relics.
  (c) To whom was the temple dedicated?
  (d) What was the legendary contest between Athena and Poseidon?
  (e) What are the building's main architectural features? What are the caryatids?
  (f) Detailed accounts have been found relating to costs and wages. Give some examples of these.
  (g) What does the rebuilding of this temple, in a period of dire need, indicate about the Athenian people?

The Parthenon

Athena Nike

The Erectheum

The Propylaea

Parthenon sculpture: Lapith and centaur (the metope)

Parthenon sculpture: horse of Selene, from the east pediment, 438–431

Parthenon sculpture: maidens from the frieze, 442–438 (Courtesy of Musée du Louvre)

Periclean democracy

The government of Athens in the time of Pericles is generally regarded as the best example of direct democracy.

DEMOKRATIA	
DEMOS (people)	KRATEIN (to rule)

The nature of Periclean democracy

Pericles' Funeral Oration *(epitaphios)*

Refer to Thucydides, II:34–46.

The ideal of the Athenian democracy was expressed by Pericles in his famous *Funeral Oration*, delivered at the end of the first year of the Peloponnesian War to honour those who had died for Athens. Pericles appealed to the patriotism of his listeners by describing the great qualities of their way of life and the unique advantages of Athenian citizenship. Thucydides recorded Pericles' speech years after it was spoken, and it is possible that he may have heard it delivered. Although his usual method was to compose speeches from the general drift of what was said, they did reflect the expression of the character of the speaker, which in the case of Pericles revealed his abiding passion for Athens and his idealism. The fact that Thucydides recorded the speech—when he was no supporter of democracy and when it had nothing to do with the course of the war—indicates that he wanted to make a statement about the ideals of a man whom he greatly admired.

Pericles' ideal of democracy

Thucydides' motive in recording the Funeral Oration

Features of the democracy   The democracy, as idealised by Pericles, comprised the following features:
1 It possessed an original constitution, not a copy—rather was it a pattern for others.
2 Equal rights existed for all citizens in the law courts.
3 Positions within the administration were based on a man's ability, achievements and character, not on wealth or class—poverty was no bar to involvement.
4 It offered political, social and individual freedom. Freedom of speech was prized, and tolerance of others' way of life.
5 It demanded respect for authority and public opinion, and obedience to the laws, both written and unwritten.

201

Freedom, balance and moderation

6 Citizens maintained a proper balance between public duties and private business.

7 Citizens had time and opportunity to enjoy their leisure and recreation.

8 Citizens delighted in beauty and tasteful things without ostentation, in moderation.

9 People pursued knowledge without 'becoming soft'.

10 Athens was open to the world, and felt no fear of strangers.

11 Education in Athens was not restrictive.

12 Citizens were not preoccupied with war and laborious training, yet still faced danger with skill and courage.

Well-informed and involved citizens

13 Citizens were obliged to be well informed on politics so that they could contribute to intelligent debate before any decisive action was taken.

14 Wealth was an opportunity for service to the state; poverty was no disgrace, but the poor citizen was expected to work to improve his lot.

15 Athens was a free society which knew its restraints and responsibilities and as such was an education to the rest of Greece.

Contrast with Sparta

Pericles contrasted the Athenian way of life with the rigid military oligarchy of Sparta, and although the picture presented is idealised, it could not have been too far from the truth, as those listening to his speech would have seen his appeal as a mockery. The democracy certainly had its weaknesses and problems and a large body of critics, both contemporary and in the fourth century.

Criticisms of democracy

There were many contemporary critics of the ideal of democracy and the way it operated, but it must be remembered that most were oligarchs and that they were writing in the decades after Pericles' death, when the people were suffering the stress and disillusionment of war. This situation revealed weaknesses in the democracy and those who led the people were not always the best qualified men, but men of ordinary backgrounds, with little culture or statesmanship. They whipped up the passions of the urban masses by means of flattery and clever arguments; the people appeared fickle in their support, and interested in selfish advantage rather than in the welfare of the state.

Weaknesses in democracy revealed by war

Anonymous pamphleteer criticised equality of and exploitation by masses

The Old Oligarch (or pseudo-Xenophon) was the name given to the author of an anonymous pamphlet on the Athenian Constitution which appeared five or ten years after the death of Pericles. He began his attack on democracy with the words 'As for the Constitution of the Athenians I do not approve, for in choosing thus, they chose that rascals should fare better than good citizens.'[2] However, he does state that it is perfectly fair that the poor and commons have 'advantages over the well-born and wealthy, as it is the commons which mans the fleet and has brought the state her power'.

He claims that everywhere 'the best elements are opposed to democracy'[3] because it favours exploitation of the better classes for the advantage of the poorer masses. He complains that slaves are undisciplined and placed on an equal footing with free men.

Herodotus, although an admirer of Athens and a democrat, complained that there is nothing worse than the masses when they act without enough knowledge on an issue. In fact, he says that the lack of restraint—or excesses—of the people is worse than the violence of despots.

Herodotus criticised lack of restraint

Aristophanes condemns the democracy for its apathy and choice of leaders in the *Knights*, and the manipulation of the demos by their leaders in the *Wasps*.

Comic poets criticised demagogues

Thucydides approved of the Athenian democracy while it was guided by Pericles, but after the latter's death he describes it (in the words of Cleon and Alcibiades) as incompetent, easily deceived and fickle. Thucydides recognised that the Athenian democracy was quite unsuited to governing an empire; he reports Cleon as saying 'Personally I have had occasion often enough already to observe that a democracy is incapable of governing others'.[4]

Thucydides approved while it was guided by Pericles

The democracy was also easily mislead: 'Any novelty in an argument deceives you at once, but when the argument is tried and proved you become unwilling to follow it.'[5] And as Alcibiades explained to the Spartans: 'Nothing new can be said of a system which is generally recognised as absurd.'[6]

Aristotle and Plato criticised democracy for giving the kind of freedom where each person lives as he likes and where equality is given indiscriminately, regardless of status or class.

Philosophers disapproved of excessive freedom

The views held by the critics, however, did not represent public opinion and the majority of Athenians were proud of their form of government and way of life.

The truth about democracy in the late fifth century is probably somewhere between the ideal of Pericles and the views of the Old Oligarch.

Features of democratic government in Athens

1 All adult male citizens had the right to propose legislation, to debate and to vote.
2 All such citizens had the right to stand for office.
3 Most official positions within the state were determined by lot (sortition). The chief magistrates, who were now the generals, were elected by vote of the whole people.

Allowed complete involvement of citizens

4 Annual tenure of office—and in some cases rotation of office—gave citizens an opportunity to gain political experience.

5 There was careful supervision of all officials during and after their tenure of office.

6 People's courts had almost total jurisdiction.

7 There was payment for officials and jurors.

Qualifications for citizenship

Athenian citizenship   In order to become an Athenian citizen, a young man had to qualify in the following ways:

1 Both parents must have been Athenian citizens, legally married.

2 The deme members must have been satisfied (a) that the boy had reached the age of eighteen and (b) that he was freeborn.

3 He had to be registered on the deme roll.

4 He had to be scrutinised by the councillors.

5 He had to spend two years in the army as a cadet, prior to becoming a member of the assembly.

The assembly — ecclesia

Aristophanes' *Ecclesiazusae* (*Females in the Assembly*) reveals something of the procedure of the Ecclesia.

Assembly — sovereign body

- It was the sovereign political body, which included all citizens over eighteen.

- It was well organised to deal with business speedily. There were four meetings each prytany—forty a year. (A year was divided into ten prytanies, or committee periods, each lasting about thirty-six days.) The agenda was fixed by law. The first meeting of the month voted confirmation of the magistrates and discussed issues of food supply and defence. The second meeting allowed petitions to be presented; anyone who wished, after informing the Council of 500, could speak to the people about any matter. The third and fourth meetings dealt with all other business, but had to include three sacred matters, three audiences for heralds and embassies and three secular matters. Emergency meetings could also be called.

Agenda

Pnyx — meeting place

- The assembly met on the Pnyx at dawn, but the number in attendance at any one time varied according to the degree of public interest. Farmers from outlying districts in Attica would find some difficulty in attending all meetings. A quorum of 6000 was needed for important business.

- Scythian archers, who were public slaves, acted as policemen and roped people into the assembly if they were found idling in the city rather than attending an assembly meeting.

- The assembly began with an announcement by a herald, and one of the prytaneis (from the Council) would be chosen by lot to preside. A secretary kept records.

- A report was read from the Council of 500, after which generals could speak, followed by other magistrates and then people according to age. The issues were debated freely and any citizen could amend or initiate legislation, but new proposals had to be submitted to the Council and an individual was responsible for his proposals. Once a law had been in effect for a year, the people took responsibility for it.
- Voting was by show of hands, except in cases of treason or of an ostracism.
- Administrative decrees passed by the people were called *psephismata*.
- Laws were reviewed by the *thesmothetae* (judges) before the people and if they were found to be out of date, or needed changing for any reason, a special jury was selected and the law was put on trial. Those who proposed changes were the prosecutors, and five people acted as defenders. A majority vote from jurors determined whether the law was to be changed or not.

Debate and proposals

Decrees and laws

The Council of 500 — Boule

- It consisted of 500 councillors, fifty from each tribe, selected by lot annually.
- Councillors had to be over thirty years of age and could hold office only twice in a lifetime.
- The Council was in continuous session under the prytany system. Each tribal group of fifty acted as an executive committee (prytaneis = presidents) for one-tenth of the year, and one-third of their number was constantly on duty and in residence in the round house (tholos), next to the council house (the Bouleuterion). They lived during this time at public expense.
- Councillors took an oath and submitted both to scrutiny prior to taking office and to an examination of their work at the end of their year in office.
- Councillors were paid 1 drachma a day.
- Each day a foreman was drawn by lot from the fifty prytaneis, and could preside for that day. During this time he had control of the seal of the city and the keys to the temples.
- The prytaneis dealt with routine daily matters, prepared the agenda for the Council and reported daily to the Council as a whole.
- Councillors discussed all matters of importance and prepared motions, (*probouleuma*), which were placed on the agenda for the assembly.
- They saw that decrees were carried out, managed public property and supervised the collection and expenditure of public money and the building of public works, as well as supervising the army and navy.
- They supervised the election of generals and examined the qualifications of new councillors before they took office.

Committee system provided continuity

Prytaneis

Preparation of agenda and administration

The magistrates

The generals

Election of generals

- Ten generals (*strategoi*) were elected annually by the assembly, which tended to choose men whose opinion they respected. Often they were men of wealth and social standing.
- Generals were unpaid, except when on active military service.
- They could be re-elected.
- Constitutionally all ten were equal, but sometimes a more forceful personality, an outstanding orator, or one with greater experience might have more influence over the people.
- They could be fined for failing to carry out their duties adequately and if there was a breach of discipline or negligence while on campaign they could be fined, exiled or (in extreme cases) sentenced to death.

Civic and military leaders

- They controlled the Athenian navy, army and cavalry. One general was appointed to the heavy infantry and commanded foreign expeditions, one was sent to the country, two to the Piraeus and one to enrol captains for the triremes; the others were assigned as needed.
- Meetings of the assembly were called by them, and they dealt with the city's foreign policy.

The archons

Selected by lot

- The nine archons and their secretary were chosen annually by lot.
- They were generally of mediocre ability.
- They received 4 obols a day while in office.
- They were not eligible for re-election, but became life members of the Areopagus.
- They were merely religious officials and magistrates in the courts.
- The chief archon — the 'eponymous' archon after whom the year was named — presided over the Great Dionysia festival and dealt with cases concerning family matters.

Religious and legal duties

- The king-archon (*basileus* means 'king') had jurisdiction over religious cases and conducted the mysteries and other festivals.
- The polemarch (originally the military leader) conducted certain rites connected with war and presided over cases involving foreigners.
- The six thesmothetae (judges) guarded the laws and prepared all the other cases for trial.

Other officials   There was a large number of officials involved in running the state. The majority were selected by lot and often worked together in boards of ten.

Often worked in boards of ten

A few financial officers were elected, but these were restricted to the top two classes.

There were ten treasurers of the sacred money of Athena and ten treasurers of the sacred money of other gods. They kept the books, and paid out money as ordered by the people. Money could be borrowed from these funds.

Other financial boards included *exactors*, who exacted fines on instruction from the courts; *sellers*, who sold confiscated estates at auction; *receivers*, who allocated funds every prytany to various boards and groups, and *auditors*, who checked accounts.

Religious officials organised all festivals, whether dramatic, musical or athletic.

Market controllers — five for Piraeus and five for the city — superintended all merchandise and prevented the sale of shoddy articles or adulterated food.

Controllers of the measures — five for Piraeus and five for the city — superintended the weights and measures in the marketplace.

Ten corn wardens checked that corn was sold at the correct price.

Port superintendents kept a watch over the harbour.

Prison officers could punish those who confessed their guilt. Those who professed innocence went before the courts.

Each tribal regiment of the army and the cavalry had a commander.

Temporary boards of ten were selected for special duties.

Hundreds of official jobs available

Religious, financial, military, legal positions

The law courts — dikasteria

Aristophanes' *Wasps* gives much valuable information on the law courts.

The law courts were highly democratic institutions with no interference by the magistrates who presided.

All citizens over thirty were eligible to enrol for jury duty.

At the beginning of each year, 6000 jurors (dikasts) were selected (600 from each tribe) by lot from those who presented themselves. The 6000 were divided into ten sections and each citizen was given a bronze or wooden ticket on which was inscribed his name and a letter indicating to which section he belonged.

On the day a trial was being held, members of the jury panels who wished to participate presented themselves at dawn and placed their tickets in boxes denoting their sections. An official would randomly place them into an allotment device called a *kleroterion*, of which there was one for each tribe, and from this determined who was selected for the day. They were then alloted to a particular court, as there could be many courts in session at any one time.

Juries tended to be large (ranging from 201 to 501 jurors), the size depending on the importance of the case.

In the time of Pericles the pay for jury service was 2 obols a day, but this was increased to 3 obols under Cleon. Although this was not quite enough to live on, it was attractive to the old people and the very poor.

Jurors took an oath to judge cases according to the laws of Athens.

When a person was summoned to appear in court, only one person was

Courts very democratic

Jury corps

Allotment system

Large juries

Payment

Summonses

required to act as witness to the summons. The summons had to specify the offence that was alleged, the magistrate who would preside at the case and the date on which the accused had to present himself.

The plaintiffs and defendants usually conducted their own cases. In public cases, the plaintiff could be a magistrate or advocate appointed by the people. It was common for a defendant to arrange for one or more speakers to plead for him and if they were good orators, or popular, the jury would applaud and look more kindly on the defendant's case. Many techniques were used to gain the jurors' sympathy and approval. The use of character witnesses was often vital for the defendant's case, for even a guilty man could be acquitted if the jury could be persuaded that his past services to the state far outweighed his crime.

Techniques used by defendants

The speeches and pleas were limited in time according to the seriousness of the crime or the amount of money involved. A water clock (*klepsydra*) was used to time the speeches.

Timing of cases and speakers

In the fifth century, the method of registering a vote was with a small stone or shell placed into one of two urns set up in the court—one for acquittal, one for condemnation. In the fourth century the 'ballot' was a metal disc with a hub, which was either hollow (condemnation) or solid (acquittal). The idea was that the juror would hold a hub in each hand with his thumb and forefinger covering and hiding the ends of it. When he went to vote, nobody could tell which one he put in the voting receptacle and which one he placed in the discard urn.

Verdicts and sentences

A verdict of guilty was followed by a second action. The plaintiff and defendants submitted alternative verdicts and the jury chose between them, indicating their choice by scratching a line on a wax tablet. A short line indicated the lighter sentence, while a longer line recommended a heavier penalty.

The court official then made a formal announcement of the penalty to be imposed.

The very size of the juries made bribery difficult, but one of the weaknesses of the Athenian jury system was that jurors had only a vague idea of the law. Another problem was that precedents were not observed, so there was often no consistency in the verdicts.

Liturgies — public burdnes

Public duties of wealthy citizens

A liturgy was a public duty imposed on wealthy citizens. There were various kinds of liturgies.

Manning and outfitting a trireme

Trierarchoi Trierarchoi were rich citizens accepting financial and general responsibility for a ship in the Athenian navy. At the beginning of each year the state selected certain men from the top class to act as trierarchs, or commanders of triremes. The state provided the hull and a supply of canvas and rigging, but the trierarch purchased the rest of the equipment and engaged and trained the crew. They paid bonuses to attract skilled officers and good rowers, and were responsible for maintaining the ships' fighting efficiency. They usually took a pride in their ships, and competition for prizes—such as the golden crown offered to the first trierarch to have his ship ready to sail—stimulated them to spend more than the minimum required. Trierarchs usually commanded the ships themselves.

Thucydides describes the competition between trierarchs on the eve of the Sicilian campaign (415) during the Peloponnesian War.

> The captains, too, offered extra pay, in addition to that provided by the State to the *thranitae* [skilled rowers] and the rest of the crews, and they went to great expense on figure-heads and general fittings, everyone of them being as anxious as possible that his own ship should stand out from the rest for its fine looks and for its speed.[7]

Choregoi   Choregoi were rich citizens who, on a rotation basis, took financial and general responsibility for a chorus participating in a festival. Their duties included choosing, training and outfitting the chorus. According to Aristotle, some of the choregoi were chosen by the archon and some were selected by the tribes.

Organizing and financing a chorus

A person chosen for a liturgy could claim exemption if he had performed that liturgy before or if he was already performing another one.

A choregos whose chorus won a comic or tragic competition was awarded a crown and a specially inscribed bronze tripod, which he was permitted to set up on a pillar.

When a city sent a religious delegation (for example, to Delphi or Delos), a wealthy citizen was expected to equip it with the magnificence worthy of the occasion and to lead the deputation.

Equipping religious delegations

One rich citizen accused of bribery used the professional speech-writer Lysias (later fifth and early fourth centuries) to list in his defence the amount of money he had spent on liturgies.

> I won first prize at the festival of the [Greater] Dionysia in the men's chorus; that cost me 5000 drachmae, including the cost of the commemorative tripod... And as soon as I got back home (from five years as trierarch overseas) I financed a team of torch-racers for the festival for Prometheus and won first prize again; that cost me 1200 drachmae... The following year I financed Cephisodorus in the contest for comic dramas and won the first prize again; that cost me 1600 drachmae including the dedication of the properties.[8]

Competition among wealthy

Finances

By far the largest portion of the state revenue came from the tribute paid by Athens' subject states, but other sources of income included the state-owned mines, which were leased to contractors, and rents from state-owned properties; the sale of confiscated property; port and market dues; sales tax; duties on imports and exports, and court fees and fines.

Sources of state revenue

Taxes

Athenian citizens did not pay tax on their earnings, but a tax was collected from the resident aliens (the metics).

In wartime a special tax called *eisphora* was levied on tribes and collected from citizens according to the value of their property.

State expenditure

The chief items of expenditure were for war, payment of public officials and jurors, religious festivals, processions and sacrifices, public works, public gifts, assistance to the poor who could not afford a ticket to the theatre, and the one area of social welfare in Athens: the support of orphans of citizens killed or invalided in war.

> There is a law which prescribes that men who possess less than three minas and are so maimed in their bodies that they cannot do any work are to be scrutinised by the Council and given a public maintenance grant of two obols a day each.[9]

The army and navy

Citizen army

The army   All citizens between the ages of eighteen and sixty, of zeugitae class (small landholders) or above, were liable for military service. A muster roll was kept by the tribal commanders.

Knights — cavalry

The first two classes made up the cavalry. They provided their own horses, but were given an allowance for the animals' upkeep and received special training. Membership of the cavalry was an honour and the knights took part in public processions such as the Panathenaea. They and their horses were annually inspected by the Council, 'and if it finds that any man has a good horse but is not maintaining it well, it punishes him by withholding the fodder grant'. The councillors vote as to whether a man is fit to serve in the cavalry and if they reject him, 'his service is at an end'.[10]

Hoplites
Cadet training

Members of the zeugitae class served as hoplites.

- After an eighteen-year-old boy was registered in his deme, he entered a two-year period of military training as a cadet (*ephebe*,) supervised by three elected members of the tribe over forty years of age. They first took the cadets on a tour of the sanctuaries and then proceeded to the Piraeus, where they did guard duty. During this first year, two elected trainers gave them instructions in weapon-handling and drilling. The supervisors of the cadets were paid 1 drachma and the ephebes 4 obols each. At the end of the year the cadets displayed to the people in the assembly the skills they had acquired, and received from the state a spear and a shield. Their second year was spent patrolling the frontiers of Attica.

Provision of own equipment

- All Athenian citizens were on active service between the ages of twenty and sixty, and they provided their own armour and weapons. Only those orphaned by war were *given* a full set of armour. When called up for service, the hoplites were expected to report with at least three days' rations.

- The thetes provided the light-armed troops and bowmen.
- Metics, the resident aliens, were also enrolled on the military registers.

The navy   The Athenian navy comprised approximately 300 triremes at the beginning of the Peloponnesian War, with a reserve fleet of 100 ships to defend the Piraeus. Each trireme had a crew of oarsmen recruited from thetes, metics and allied subjects. The thetes, who were the lowest class of citizens, were paid more than the others since they were the upper row of oarsmen. There were skilled seamen who navigated and hoplites who acted as marines on board, as well as the trierarch.

Thetes as rowers

Table 8.1	Rights and duties of an Athenian citizen	
	Rights	*Duties*
Legislative	The right of citizens over eighteen to vote for legislation, initiate or amend legislation, make decisions on war or peace, elect generals, speak in the assembly and confirm magistrates.	To take an intelligent interest in political affairs, to attend the assembly as frequently as possible and to take individual responsibility for their proposals.
Administrative	The right of citizens over thirty (a) to stand for election to the Council of 500 twice in a lifetime, and to gain experience on an executive committee; (b) to be president of the prytaneis once and (c) to be paid for service.	To show political responsibility in the day-to-day running of the state; to see that no unworthy or unqualified person was selected for office; to see that public property and money were not squandered; to act as a check on irresponsible acts of the assembly; to inspect the cavalry and ships and to work closely with various boards.
Administrative	The right of citizens over thirty to stand for election as one of ten generals (if experienced and competent), to be chosen for any one of hundreds of official and administrative tasks, and to be paid for these.	To fulfil administrative positions on orders of the people — religious, financial, military or economic — and to obey the commands of magistrates.
Legal	The right of all citizens to equality under the law and of every citizen over thirty to be empanelled as a juror and to be paid for jury service.	For jurors, to take an oath to judge cases according to the laws of Athens.
Economic	The right of the rich to claim exemption from liturgies if they had performed them before or if	For rich citizens, to take financial and general responsibility for the outfitting, maintenance and

Table 8.1 (cont.)		
	Rights	*Duties*
Economic	they could prove that they were unable to afford them. The right of the poor to be subsidised by the state if unable to afford tickets for the theatre during religious festivals. The right of orphans and widows of those killed in action and those invalided in war to receive a pension.	command of a trireme, and the selection, training and outfitting of a chorus. To contribute to a war tax (*eisphora*) in emergencies, according to value of property.
Military	The right of all citizens to protection. The right of those in the first two classes to become a knight in the cavalry, to get an allowance from the state for maintenance of a horse and to take part in public processions. The right of those of zeugitae class to serve as hoplites, and to be presented with a spear and a shield by the state on completion of a two-year military training period. The right of the thetes to be enrolled as oarsmen in the fleet and as light-armed troops.	For citizen soldiers, to fight for their gods, homes and laws and not to abandon fellow soldiers in battle. For knights, to provide their own horses and to accept annual scrutiny as to suitability. For all boys of eighteen to twenty years, to complete military training involving frontier duty. For all citizens between twenty and sixty years, to be ready for active service, to provide their own armour and equipment and to report to duty with three days' rations.
Religious	The right to worship.	To participate in religious festivals and sacrifices, and to respect religious customs, e.g. burial rites.

Note: This list is incomplete. Other rights and duties — for example, the right to own property — can be added from the sources and from wider reading. A similar chart should be built up for the Spartan citizen, as a means of comparison and contrast.

Athenian women in the fifth century

The women of fifth-century Athens were in marked contrast to the women of Sparta, who lived in a warrior society and were known throughout Greece for their freedom and social and legal equality with men. Historians have not always been in agreement about the position of Athenian women because the evidence can be easily misinterpreted.

- All literature about women in the fifth-century was written by men.
- Plays depicting women were meant to entertain and teach a lesson.
- Women described in literature tended to be from the 'better' classes rather than the lower classes.
- Women shown on pottery were usually hetairai (female companions).

Source material easily misinterpreted

The status of a woman was determined by her class. The women held in most respect were priestesses, while those with the greatest social freedom were the *hetairai*. They were not simply prostitutes, but often intelligent women who mixed freely with the men, attending symposia (drinking parties), discussing philosophy, drama and politics. Aspasia, the mistress of Pericles, was the most famous hetaira. A poor woman had greater social freedom than a middle-class girl or matron, since she had no choice but to go to the market and fountain herself and she often ran a small stall in the agora.

Status depended on class

Most evidence and debate about women centres around those of the 'better' classes. The most commonly held view is that these women lived in total seclusion, were subservient and were treated with indifference in the male society of Athens where men preferred cultured foreign women or other men as companions. That this picture is not complete is obvious from the works of some of the painters and sculptors who depict scenes of affection between husband, wife and children on funerary urns, pottery and sculptured gravestones.

View of women as subservient questioned

Evidence from pottery

Also, the heroines of both tragedy and comedy are often shown as strong, aggressive and often smarter and more enterprising than the men. If any of the traits revealed by women like Sophocles' Antigone, Aristophanes' Lysistrata and Euripides' Medea were recognisable in the women of fifth-century Athens, then there is some doubt about their subservience.

Heroines of tragedy and comedy

Male attitudes towards women

Evidence

Pericles in his *Funeral Oration* described the duty of women in one sentence: 'The greatest glory of a woman is to be least talked about by men, whether they are praising you or citicising you.'[11]

Hypocrisy of Pericles' view of women

Detail of a flute girl — she wears the ungirt chiton of such artists (c.450)

Stele of a woman (c.400) (Courtesy of the Metropolitan Museum of Art, New York)

Girls at a fountain (From a vase painting)

Yet Pericles divorced his wife and lived with one of the most talked-about women in Athens.

In *Women of Troy*, Euripides has Andromache say that the greatest source of scandal for a woman is 'when she won't stay indoors and when she practises saucy speech'. She therefore offered her husband 'a silent tongue and gentle looks'.[12]

Expected to keep silent

Xenophon in *Economicus* describes a conversation between Isomachus and Socrates about a wife's duties.

> You will stay inside and help in sending out the servants with outdoor tasks. You must supervise the indoor servants, and receive any revenues; from these you must meet any necessary expenses and look after the surplus providently so that you don't spend the whole year's budget in a month. When wool is brought to you, you must see the right clothes are made for those who need them. And you must see that the dried corn remains fit for consumption.[13]

Expected to be a good household manager

Lysias wrote a speech for a husband whose wife was in court on a charge of adultery, in which he says 'At first, Athenians, she was the best of wives; she was a clever and economical manager of the house, running everything meticulously'.[14]

On the whole it would be fair to say that women were urged to keep a low profile and were expected to master the arts of spinning, weaving, making clothes, managing the home, cooking and preserving food, and supervising the children and servants. An Athenian woman gained great esteem from running an efficient household where she held supreme authority. The keys to the cellar and store-room, which she carried around with her at all times, were an indication of that authority.

However, a woman's social contacts were limited as she was married at a very early age (twelve to fifteen years) to a husband much older (thirty); she ate in the women's quarters, with the children and slaves, while the men entertained friends, and she was not permitted to leave the house without a male chaperone. The shopping was done by the husband or a slave. Only at family festivals did men and women mingle.

Social contacts limited

Middle class women and girls went out occasionally during the important religious festivals. It was the greatest honour that could be bestowed on a girl to be selected to take part in the procession of the Panathenaic Festival. Women attended the Thesmophoria, a festival reserved for married women.

Women's festivals

There is evidence to suggest that women attended the theatre but it is unlikely that women from the 'better' classes sat through the rather bawdy comedies.

It is possible that there may have been a few women who felt frustrated by their restricted lifestyles. Euripides' Medea complained that when a man became bored with home life he could escape depression by going out and meeting a friend. She said that she would rather go out to battle than remain safely at home, and would certainly 'rather stand to arms three times than bear one child'.

Some resented their exclusion

215

It was the greatest honour that could be bestowed on a girl to be selected for the Panathenaic Festival. Women were also involved in the rites of Dionysus and Demeter and the Festival of Artemis, held every four years.

Political and legal status

No political or legal rights

Athenian women had no political rights at all, and legally they were under the control of men all their lives. They had no choice of a husband and in legal disputes could act only through men. The Athenians were very concerned with the disposal of property and the fate of heiresses. A man's nearest male relative could claim an heiress in marriage, to ensure that the estate stayed in the family. Men had the right to divorce their wives even if they had no valid reason for doing so. Women, however, found it virtually impossible to get a divorce no matter what the husband's offence. Unlike Sparta, where women became substantial landowners, land and property were exclusively male-owned in Athens. However, there is evidence that among the working class women could own and operate small businesses.

Although women may have had no political rights, very few legal rights and limited social contact, and may have spent much of their time in the home managing domestic affairs, evidence suggests that on occasion they did show an independence of spirit.

Assignment: Athenian and Spartan women

Compare the lifestyles of Athenian and Spartan women, emphasising such features as social freedom, education, legal and economic rights, and main duties.

Further reading

Primary sources

Aristophanes. *The Wasps.*
_____. *Ecclesiazusae.*
_____. *Lysistrata.*
Aristotle. *The Athenian Constitution.*
The Old Oligarch. *The Constitution of the Athenians.*
Thucydides. *The Peloponnesian War.*

Secondary sources

The Athenian Citizen.
Barrow, R. *Athenian Democracy.*
Jones, A. H. M. *Athenian Democracy.*

The Peloponnesian War, 431–404 B.C.

9

The historians of this period

Thucydides

A contemporary account

THE MAIN SOURCE for this period is Thucydides' famous history of the Peloponnesian War, which was written about 404 B.C. It is therefore a contemporary account, not only of the war itself but of the Athenian people and what they thought about current affairs. As Thucydides says, 'I lived through the whole of it, being of an age to understand what was happening, and I put my mind to the subject so as to get an accurate view of it'.[1]

Background

- He was born in Athens sometime between 460 and 455, and died about 400.

Thucydides (in the
Capitoline Museum, Rome)

- He seems to have been connected with the family of Miltiades and Cimon, and had property in Thrace.
- When the war broke out he was a young man; he may have taken part in some of the early actions of the war.

Early years in Athens

- In 427 he caught the plague, which he describes graphically in Book II, and was one of the few to recover from it.
- He played some part in public life, reaching the rank of general (*strategos*) about 424.
- As general, he was in charge of an Athenian fleet, in the northern Aegean, sent to help the city of Amphipolis which was besieged by Brasidas the Spartan. His failure to save the city — through no fault of his own, since he had only seven ships at his disposal — led to his exile from Athens for twenty years.
- He used his time in exile in Thrace — and his travels to the Peloponnese and possibly to Sicily — to research his history, speaking to people from both sides.

His exile

219

- He returned to Athens in 404 when Athenian exiles were recalled at the end of the war, but he had then only about four years to live. He had written his history as far as the year 411. The period between 411 and 404 was covered by Xenophon and Theopompus.

Influences on his writing

His early life in Athens developed in him a concern for the problems of government and an appreciation of the policies of Pericles. The years he spent in exile gave him a clear grasp of the vital issues of the time, and since his exile was associated with the emergence of a new aggressive imperialism in Athens, he became aware of Athens' errors in strategy.

Reasons for writing his history

His aim

He wrote his history because he believed it 'was the greatest disturbance in the history of the Hellenes, affecting also a large part of the non-Hellenic world, and...the whole of mankind'.[2] His work was written to last forever—not just to appeal to the people of his day—and he hoped that those who in years to come read his record of these tragic events would learn something that might help them in similar circumstances.

His method

Evidence treated critically

Thucydides has often been regarded as the first 'scientific' historian because of the rigorous methods he used to establish the truth. He investigated his facts meticulously and would not accept any evidence uncritically.

> I have made it a principle not to write down the first story that came my way, and not even to be guided by my own general impressions; either I was present myself at the events which I described or else I heard of them from eye-witnesses whose reports I have checked with as much thoroughness as possible.[3]

Some bias

He admits, however, that it was difficult to discover the truth, as eyewitnesses often gave conflicting reports of the same event, either through partiality or through imperfect memories. He was aware that what people left out of their accounts sometimes revealed prejudice. His attempts to be objective sometimes faltered, as he revealed a partiality to Brasidas and quite obviously hostile feelings towards Cleon.

Speeches used

Thucydides made use of speeches and dialogues, many of which he himself listened to either before or during the war. He admits he had difficulty in remembering the precise words spoken, and because his informants had the same problem he kept as closely as he could to the words spoken, making the speeches contain what in his opinion was called for in each situation.[4]

Reliability

Since Thucydides lived through the war, discussed the events with those who were present and was critical in his approach, his opinion is likely to be close to the truth.

Xenophon

Xenophon lived at the end of the fifth and the beginning of the fourth century. Although he was born in Athens, he found life difficult during the oligarchic revolution and eventually left the city, in 401, to enter the service of Cyrus of Persia as a mercenary. He was exiled from Athens, fought under the Spartan king Agesilaus, and ended his days on an estate in the Peloponnese.

His many works include the *Hellenica*, a history of Greek affairs in seven books (411–362) of which the first two cover the years 411 to 403 and are a continuation of Thucydides' work.

Xenophon's Hellenica

The drift to war, 445–431

The Peloponnesian War, which broke out between Athens and Sparta in 431, was—according to Thucydides—inevitable because of 'the growth of Athenian power and the fear which this caused in Sparta'.[5] He believed that (a) since 479 Athens had been growing more powerful and had given offence to many states, (b) from 460 a noticeable rift had occurred between Athens and Sparta, and (c) between 456 and 446 Athens had incurred the hostility of Sparta's most influential ally, Corinth.

Thucydides' long-term cause

However, in 445 Athens and Sparta signed the Thirty Years' Peace, which established a balance of power. Greece was divided into two great rival systems of alliance, involving the states of both continental Greece and Asia Minor. In this situation neither side could tolerate any action that would threaten the stability of its alliance, and so any minor conflict involving members of one alliance or the other could lead to war.

Balance of power in 445

The peace broke down after only fifteen years, and this period (445–431) is often referred to as the 'drift to war'. Yet it cannot be said that either side was busily preparing for war or provoking the other. Both states seemed to recognise that a workable balance might be maintained.

No obvious war preparations

Pericles for more than ten years proved remarkably successful in directing the energies of the Athenians into fields other than expansion. It was a period of consolidation of the empire and of an ambitious building program in Athens, and suggests that Pericles was not anticipating war, in the 440s at least. The Athenians appeared to be far too busy with their rich and varied lifestyle to be plotting a war with Sparta.

Although Spartan citizens lived in a state of readiness for war, they knew that they lacked the funds and the seapower available to Athens and they seemed ready to keep the peace. Sparta made no attempt to strike at Athens when Samos revolted in 440. King Archidamus was a friend of

Peace maintained in 440s

221

Pericles, and caution seemed to outweigh the jealousy and fear that also existed because of Athens' power and prosperity.

Immediate incidents leading to the breaking of the Thirty Years' Peace

Immediate causes

Thucydides distinguishes between the long-term cause (growth of Athenian power), which made war inevitable, and a number of disputes or grievances which he believed were the reason for the outbreak of the war at that time. These disputes involved Sparta's powerful ally, Corinth, and brought to the surface again the fear and hatred that Corinth felt for Athens.

The dispute between Corcyra and Corinth over Epidamnus

A local dispute between Corinth and her prosperous colony Corcyra had the potential to upset the balance of power in the Greek world.

Corcyra and Corinth quarrel

Corcyra, on the trade route to Italy, had established a colony of her own at Epidamnus. When in 435 a revolution broke out there between oligarchs and democrats, Corcyra was asked to intervene on behalf of the democrats, who were being besieged in their city. Corcyra refused to send help, but Corinth despatched a force to defend Epidamnus. This resulted in a quarrel between Corinth and Corcyra, and a naval battle ended in a victory for Corcyra, whose navy was large and powerful. Corinth spent the next two years building a large fleet of ninety-five triremes—and collecting another forty from her colonies and allies—for a confrontation with Corcyra. Athens and Sparta remained neutral in this local conflict, although Sparta did try to restrain Corinth from war.

Corcyra's need for an ally

Corcyra, fearing the revenge of Corinth, needed an ally. She sent an embassy to Athens asking for an alliance, and Corinth sent a counter-delegation urging Athens not to cause a rupture with the Peloponnese.

Corcyra's appeal to Athens

The Corcyraeans pointed out that it would be in Athens' interest to agree to an alliance, since
1 Corcyra was the largest naval power in Greece, after Athens;
2 war was inevitable, because Sparta was frightened of Athens and Corinth was her enemy;
3 Corcyra's position on the coastal route to Italy and Sicily would enable her to prevent reinforcements coming to the aid of the Peloponnesians if war broke out;
4 it would not break the Thirty Years' Peace between Athens and Sparta, since Corcyra was neutral and entitled to join whichever side she chose.

Corinth stresses the danger in an alliance

The Corinthian envoy's speech was less forceful, recalling Corinth's aid to Athens in the past and stressing the danger to the peace if she became an ally of Corcyra. Corinth could not afford to be cut off from her westward trading area (Sicily and Italy), which would mean ruin for her. Pericles' previous attempts to encircle her and cut her off from the Corinthian Gulf and the west were still fresh in her mind.

The Athenians could not, however, sit by and see the naval and shipbuilding potential of Corcyra added to that of Corinth and Sparta. Having the largest fleet was vital to the Athenians. Yet Pericles knew that if they concluded an alliance with Corcyra, war was bound to occur sooner or later.

The Athenian Assembly met twice, since the issues involved were so important. The citizens voted for an impossible compromise: an alliance for defensive purposes only, which would operate if Athens and Corcyra were attacked from outside.

Athenians compromise

A squadron of only ten Athenian ships — led by Lacedaemonius, the son of Cimon and a pro-Spartan — was sent to watch events closely but to refrain from action unless Corcyra was attacked directly by Corinth. For the moment, the peace of 445 was preserved.

In the battle which followed, at Sybota, the ten Athenian vessels participated only when it appeared that Corcyra was in trouble. When twenty more Athenian vessels arrived, the Corinthians abandoned their plan for a second attack and sailed home. The Athenians made no attempt to pursue them.

Battle of Sybota

Although this had been a purely defensive action on the part of Athens, according to Thucydides it 'gave Corinth her first cause for war against Athens'.[6] She maintained that the peace had been broken, but neither Athens nor Sparta considered it so.

'First cause' for war

Corinth's reaction — Potidaea

The Corinthians now sought some means of striking at Athens. They could not appeal to Sparta, which had urged Corinth to make peace with Corcyra and did not regard the peace of 445 as broken. They had to find some way of involving Sparta and the Peloponnesian League in a war with Athens, and in an angry and humiliated mood they retaliated by causing trouble in Athens' sphere of influence.

Corinth stirs up trouble for Athens

Potidaea, an old Corinthian colony, was a member of the Delian League but had maintained its right to receive magistrates from its mother city every year. Corinth often kept her colonies in this state of semidependence. Athenian rule in Potidaea was resented since Athens had more than doubled the tribute and Corinthian magistrates, now acting as agents of Corinth's hostility to Athens, supported Potidaea's planned revolt, which broke out in 432. Trouble spread to the whole Chalcidic area; Athens made two demands of Potidaea: first, to give up her Corinthian magistrates and second, to pull down her city walls on the southern side. The Potidaeans refused.

Corinth and Athens at 'war' over Potidaea

Both the Athenians and the Peloponnesians sent forces to Potidaea, where the Peloponnesians, led by a Corinthian general, Aristeus, were defeated. Potidaea was then placed under siege by the Athenians.

This was Corinth's second grievance against Athens, and there were only two alternatives.

Unlikely solutions

1 Sparta could lead the Peloponnesians in a general war against Athens or else risk the defection of her most powerful ally.
2 Athens could abandon her attempt to subdue Potidaea, at the risk of losing her empire.

Athens' reaction – The Megarian Decree, 432

While the situation hovered between peace and war, Pericles prepared for a war.

Reorganisation of Athens by Pericles

1 He reorganised the states' finances in 434–433 by means of two special decrees which established two funds.
   (a) After all outstanding debts were paid, the surplus from the Athenian imperial revenue and internal revenue was to be deposited in a special fund for the maintenance of the walls and navy.
   (b) The building program was brought to an end (the Propylaea was never completed), but enough money was put aside for urgent repairs.
2 He renewed Athens' alliances with the towns of Leontini in Sicily and Rhegium in Italy.
3 He issued the Megarian Decree. This harsh edict excluded Megara from the markets and ports of the Athenian empire and meant starvation and ruin for its people.

What reasons did he have for issuing this decree and why did he choose Megara as his victim?

1 Since Pericles probably believed that a war was now unavoidable, a show of strength was needed to demonstrate to Corinth and the Peloponnesians the power of Athens. By issuing these economic sanctions against Megara, he was not breaking the Thirty Years' Peace. Professor F. E. Adcock believes that this decree against Megara was not a *cause* of the war but an *operation* of war.

Megarian decrees — a show of strength

2 Why Megara became the victim is not really known, but a number of reasons have been suggested.
   (a) Relations with Megara had been poor since the Athenian garrison had been murdered there in 447, and a recent protest had been made about the trespassing of Megarians on sacred ground.
   (b) Pericles had a private quarrel with Megara.[7]
   (c) Pericles wanted to recover control of Megara and bring her to the dependent position of Aegina, so that the Megarid could be used to block the land route between Boeotia and the Peloponnese and

224

secure a direct access to the Corinthian Gulf for Athens' commerce or her troops.

Thucydides has made it clear that Pericles now saw that war was inevitable and seems to have considered it better that it should occur while he was still there to control it, as his real fear was of the erratic and overoptimistic behaviour of the Athenians themselves.

War inevitable

Assemblies at Sparta

Refer to Thucydides, I: 66–88, 118–25.

The first assembly at Sparta was called to hear the complaints of Sparta's allies and 'anyone who had claimed to have suffered from Athenian aggression'. Many (including Megara and Aegina) came forward, while the Corinthians were the last to speak, 'having allowed the previous speakers to do their part in hardening Spartan opinion against Athens'.[8]

Grievances aired by Sparta's allies

The Corinthians denounced Athenian imperialism.

> Athens has deprived some states of their freedom and is scheming to do the same thing for others, especially among our own allies and . . . she herself has for a long time been preparing for the eventuality of war'.[9]

For this situation the Corinthians blamed Sparta, whose attitude after the Persian Wars allowed Athens to build up her present strength and power. The most significant aspect of the speech was Corinth's threat: 'Do not force the rest of us in despair to join a different alliance'.[10]

Corinth's threat

Athenian delegates at Sparta also addressed the assembly, and their speech was boastful and provocative. They justified the existence of their empire and warned the Spartans to take time over their decisions, since war very rarely goes as expected. They urged the Spartans to settle the differences between them by arbitration; if they refused to do this, they must accept responsibility for the war.

The Spartans discussed the complaints of their allies among themselves, but opinion in Sparta was divided, since Athens' alliance with Corcyra could not be considered illegal in the light of the Peace of 445, and Potidaea was a complicated issue — if there was any blame there, Corinth was the aggressor.

King Archidamus, 'a man who had a reputation for both intelligence and moderation',[11] pointed out the dangers involved in rushing unprepared into a war against a much wealthier, better-armed naval power. He suggested that the Spartans should not declare war immediately, but should approach Athens with their allies' grievances and in the meantime make new allies with financial and naval resources.

King Archidamus and the peace party

Sthenelaidas — one of the ephors and the leader of the war party — dismissed the idea of any further discussions and urged the Spartans to help their allies immediately: 'cast your votes for the honour of Sparta and for war'.[12]

Influence of the war party

The majority of Spartan votes indicated their belief that the Thirty Years' Peace had been broken. However, war could only be declared by a majority decision of the Peloponnesian League and this was immediately called.

Spartan concern for her prestige

There were no legal grounds for Sparta to declare war, since Athens did not break the treaty in the Corcyra affair and Corinth was the aggressor at Potidaea. Certainly, Athenian ambitions were to be feared and Athens had shown her unfriendly attitude towards Megara, but as J. H. Finley says, none of these factors influenced Sparta. What was important was Sparta's need to maintain her own prestige with and ascendancy over her allies. Ultimately the point was reached where her allies were so insistent that Sparta could no longer remain inactive if she were to continue to lead the Peloponnesian League. The fact that the vote for war in the Spartan Assembly was carried by such a large majority reveals the bitterness and resentment that was felt towards Athens.

Oracle's support of Sparta

After having sent to Delphi to seek divine approval and support, the allies met yet again, and after an optimistic speech by the Corinthians they voted for war. However, they decided that since they were not adequately prepared, they should not attack immediately.

Ultimatums issued

Once war had been declared, Sparta issued an ultimatum: Athens was 'to expel the curse' of the Alcmaeonidae and thus send Pericles into exile. It was common to seek a religious reason for war. Athens rejected further demands — to call off the blockade of Potidaea, restore Aegina's autonomy and repeal the Megarian Decree. The Spartans had made it clear that the war could be avoided if the Megarian Decree was revoked, but Pericles was not fooled by this, as he knew Sparta would have to satisfy Corinth in some way. He urged the people not to make any concessions under the threat of force, because once they gave way on any issue, further demands would follow.

Athens' refusal to make concessions

The Athenians sent the Spartan envoys away with the message that they would give the Megarians access to their markets when Sparta ceased expelling strangers from her cities and restored full independence to her own allies. They also offered to accept arbitration on the various complaints under the terms of the Treaty of 445, on a fair and equal basis. The Spartan envoys never returned, since Sparta could not submit to arbitration as she had already declared that the treaty was broken, and would not risk the loss of her allies by taking such a step.

War finally began in 431, when the Thebans attacked Athens' ally, Plataea. 'In this affair of Plataea the treaty had quite obviously been broken, and now the Athenians made ready for war, as did the Spartans and their allies.'[13]

Thucydides and the causes of the war: some criticisms

Thucydides spends most of Book 1 developing the idea that the real cause of the war, Athenian imperialism, could be traced back fifty years and that the incidents at Corcyra and Potidaea were only of secondary importance. They rather determined *why* the war occurred when it did.

Thucydides has often been accused of misunderstanding the causes of the war; that is, of not estimating accurately the relative seriousness of the incidents leading to it and not giving enough emphasis to the Megarian Decree as a cause.

Although no modern historian would overlook economic causes, Thucydides did not regard the Megarian question as relevant to the outbreak of war. To him, Corinth was the main instigator of a war that was bound to occur at some time, and for Corinth the most important issues were the alliance of Athens and Corcyra and the Potidaean incident, not the independence of Megara.

Megarian issue not seen as relevant by Thucydides

As J. B. Bury points out in *The Ancient Greek Historians*, the Megarian Decree did not determine Corinth's action and it was Corinth's action which was decisive. However, once war was declared, Athens' act of cruelty against Megara formed an important item in the list of grievances, and in the final negotiations it was given prominence because the other two incidents were easier for Athens to justify.

Aristophanes and Plutarch suggest that the outbreak of war was due to the Megarian Decree.

Plutarch's view of Megarian Decree

> In fact it seems likely that the Athenians might have avoided war on any one of the issues if only they could have been persuaded to lift their embargo against the Megarians and come to terms with them.[14]

There is no evidence to suggest that if there had been no Athenian/Corcyraean alliance or siege of Potidaea, the Megarian issue by itself would have caused the outbreak of war at the time.[15]

Thucydides' explanation of the long-term cause of the war—Sparta's jealousy and fear of Athens' growing power—is regarded by some historians as far too simplistic. They see other issues as playing a significant part in the conflict:

Other elements which caused mistrust

1 opposing political beliefs—that the war was basically a conflict between the supporters of oligarchy and democracy;
2 racial and cultural differences between Ionians and Dorians;
3 commercial and economic rivalry;
4 personal motives of Pericles.

The first three can be regarded not as causes but as elements which added to the mistrust between the members of the two alliances. However, the view that Pericles provoked the Peloponnesian War to restore his position—which suffered as a result of attacks on his friends and

227

accusations against him of embezzlement—cannot be justified. It is based on the mistaken belief that all the attacks on Pericles' friends occurred in the year 432 (when in fact they took place years before) and that attacks on Pericles' administration of finance took place before war broke out, when it is known that this occurred in 430. Those who wished to blacken the character of Pericles accepted the inventions of the comic poets. Aristophanes, ten years after the outbreak of war, suggests in his play *Peace* that Pericles brought about the war in alarm caused by the disgrace of his friend Phidias, who was prosecuted for embezzling gold and ivory to be used in making the statue of Athena. However, Thucydides stresses that at the beginning of the war Pericles' position as the leader of Athens was as strong as ever.

Criticism of Thucydides' view

Professor F. Adcock does not believe that Thucydides' explanation of the cause of the war—Sparta's fear of Athens' growing power—can be justified by the history of the ten years preceding the outbreak.

The opposing sides

Characteristics

In Book 1:69–71 Thucydides, through the words of the Corinthian spokesman at the debate at Sparta, distinguishes between the democratic Athenians and the oligarchic Spartans.

Table 9.1	
Athenians	*Spartans*
Swift to take action 'They are quick to form a resolution and quick at carrying it out.' 'They never hesitate.'	**Slow to take action** 'You wait calmly on events relying for your defence, not on action, but on making people think that you will act.' 'You hang back.'
Innovative and creative 'Each man cultivates his own intelligence, again with a view to doing something notable for his city'.	**Lacking in initiative** 'You never originate an idea.'
Daring and impulsive 'Athenian daring will outrun its own resources; they will take risks against their better judgement.'	**Cautious and conservative** 'You do less than you could have done, mistrust your own judgement, however sound it may be.'
Always abroad 'They think that the farther they go the more they will get.'	**Parochial** 'You think that any movement may endanger what you have already.'

Athenians	Spartans
Optimistic and confident 'Suppose they fail in some undertaking; they make good the loss immediately by setting their hopes in some other direction.'	**Pessimistic** 'You assume that dangers will last forever.'

Allies and subjects

The map on page 230 shows the position of the allies and subjects of the Athenian Empire and of Sparta and the Peloponnesian League.

Resources and strategy

Read Thucydides, II:13 for an account of the resources and strategy of Athens.

Table 9.2	Resources of Athens and Sparta	
	Athens	*Sparta*
Infantry and cavalry strength	13 000 front-line hoplites and garrisons of city, Piraeus and frontiers; 1200 cavalry (Thessaly sent cavalry), 200 mounted archers conscripted from colonies and cleruchies	30 000 (approx.) hoplites; 2000 cavalry, mainly from Boeotia, Phocis and Locris; skilled and experienced
Naval strength	300 triremes, the fleets of Corcyra, Lesbos, Chios, and rowers from the empire Naval tactics better Naval bases available at Naupactus, Acarnania, Zacynthus and the Cyclades	100 triremes — relied mainly on Corinthian navy; trouble recruiting trained rowers Suffered owing to defection of Corcyra but had powerful Dorian naval power in the west — Syracuse, a colony of Corinth
Finances	Reserve fund of 6000 talents and annual income of 1000 talents, 600 of which were from tribute	Limited funds; relied on Corinth's wealth and hoped for help from Persia

Table 9.3	Strategy of Athens and Sparta	
	Athens	*Sparta*
Basis of strategy	Naval superiority, walls, fortification of Piraeus and resources of empire making Athens	Military superiority Naval and financial limitations

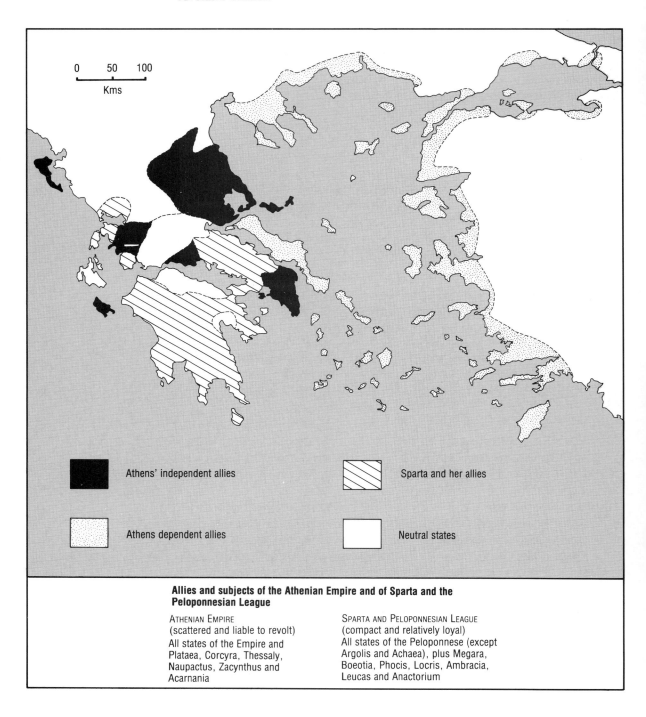

0   50   100
Kms

■ Athens' independent allies

▨ Sparta and her allies

░ Athens dependent allies

□ Neutral states

Allies and subjects of the Athenian Empire and of Sparta and the Peloponnesian League

ATHENIAN EMPIRE
(scattered and liable to revolt)
All states of the Empire and
Plataea, Corcyra, Thessaly,
Naupactus, Zacynthus and
Acarnania

SPARTA AND PELOPONNESIAN LEAGUE
(compact and relatively loyal)
All states of the Peloponnese (except
Argolis and Achaea), plus Megara,
Boeotia, Phocis, Locris, Ambracia,
Leucas and Anactorium

	Athens	Sparta
Basis of strategy	able to withstand siege and starvation Military inferiority Need to keep empire under control	
Aims	To avoid direct military conflict with Sparta To abandon lands and farms and withdraw within the walls of Athens sending livestock to Euboea To keep the sea lanes open To harass the enemy by sea raids on towns and coastline of the Peloponnese To encourage revolts among helots To refrain from making new conquests	To offer decisive land battle or to wear Athens down by annual invasion and ravaging of Attica To avoid any engagement with Athenian fleet until naval policy could be put into effect To enter the Aegean in strength later and to instigate and support revolts among Athens' subjects so as to dissolve the empire

Major incidents and personalities of the Archidamian War, 431–421

First invasion of Attica, 431

When King Archidamus of Sparta led the Peloponnesians into Attica for the first time, the Athenians took Pericles' advice and brought their women, children and household property into Athens, where most of them 'had to settle down in those parts of the city that had not been built over and in the temples and shrines of the heroes except the Acropolis, in the temple of Eleusinian Demeter, and some other places that were strictly forbidden . . .' A number also settled in the towers of the walls, between the Long Walls and in the Piraeus.[16] They sent their livestock to Euboea.

Evacuation of Attica

However, when they saw that 'their land was being laid waste in front of their very eyes', they felt outraged—especially the young, who wanted to march out and stop it.[17] Violent discussions ensued and the city was in a thoroughly excited state. The Athenian people were furious with Pericles.

According to Plutarch, Pericles

'. . . behaved like the helmsman of a ship, who, when a storm sweeps down upon it in the open sea, makes everything fast, takes in sail and relies on his own skill and takes no notice of the fears and entreaties of the sea-sick and terrified passengers'.[18]

Opposition to Pericles in Athens

Thucydides said that Pericles was so 'convinced of the rightness of his views about not going out to battle'[19] that he endured the criticisms calmly and did not summon any assemblies for fear the people would make some foolish decision in their anger. He then sent out minor cavalry patrols, saw to the defences of the city and sent off a fleet of 100 ships to raid the coast of the Peloponnese.

Athenian horseman
(Courtesy of Musée
du Louvre)

Between 430 and 425 the conduct of the war followed a basic pattern.
- Sparta used her superior military forces in land-based actions, including the annual invasions of Attica (except in 429 and 426).
- Athens, following Pericles' strategy of relying on her long walls and her navy, refused to meet Sparta on land, but made raids on the coast of the Peloponnese and on the coasts of Sparta's allies. The fleet, active on the coasts of western Greece, won over Cephallenia and some coastal towns of Acarnania.

232

The plague, 430

Plutarch describes how 'an act of heaven' now 'intervened to upset human calculations'.[20] A plague broke out among the Athenians, having originated in Ethiopia—according to Thucydides—and spread to Egypt and North Africa. Thucydides gives a graphic account of the symptoms and progress of the disease, which caused suffering 'almost beyond the capacity of human nature to endure'.[21] It is estimated that approximately one-third of the Athenian population died, and many of those who survived were permanently weakened. It particularly affected the number of fighting men available, 'as it devoured the flower of their manhood and their strength'.[22]

Origin of plague

Effects of plague

The despair of the people made them indifferent to the laws, whether civil or religious, and when overtures of peace to Sparta were rejected they turned on Pericles. He was suspended from his post of strategos and his accounts were called for and examined by the Council. However, although he was condemned and fined, the people soon discovered that there was no one else with his qualities of leadership and he was re-elected strategos. In the following year, 429, he contracted the plague and died. 'After his death, the course of events soon brought home Pericles' worth to the Athenians and made them sharply conscious of his loss.'[23]

Pericles' death

A new type of politician now emerged to lead the people. These new leaders were less aristocratic. They were often tradesmen, like Cleon the leather merchant, Lysicles the sheep dealer and Hyperbolus the lamp maker, and were more inclined to pursue an aggressive war. The fickle city masses were easily swayed by their clever speeches, and their policies appealed more to the sailors, craftsmen and traders for whom the continuance and expansion of the war meant pay and profit. On the other hand the richer classes, who carried the financial burden of the war, and the small farmers whose lands were devastated year after year by the Peloponnesians, were more inclined to follow the advice of Nicias, a wealthy, conservative land and slave owner. He wished to see the war come to an end, and tended to follow the policy of Pericles.

New type of leader

This divergence of opinion meant that Athenian policy and strategy suffered a lack of continuity in the years after Pericles' death.

Opposing views on strategy

Epitaph for the Athenians who fell at Potidaea (original in the British Museum)

Cleon

Cleon came to the forefront of Athenian politics after the death of Pericles and by 425 was the unofficial leader of the assembly. Cleon was a demagogue, a popular leader who appealed to the emotions, self-interest and prejudices of the people.

Very little is known of his early career, except that he was the son of a rich tanner and his first-known action in politics was to attack Pericles, in 431. What is known of him comes chiefly from his enemies. His reputation suffered from the criticisms of Aristophanes and the bias of Thucydides.

Thucydides and Cleon

Thucydides' usual practice was to allow the words and actions of the personalities featured in his work to speak for themselves, but in his presentation of Cleon he departs quite noticeably from his normal procedure. Far from maintaining an objective view of Cleon, he shows a distinct animosity, condemning both his character and conduct.

There are four episodes in which Cleon was the major participant — the Mytilenian debate, the speech of the Spartan envoys during the Pylos campaign, the debate on Pylos and the military campaign against Brasidas at Amphipolis.

In the Mytilenian debate he is described as a violent man. Thucydides shows him playing on the anger of the people and suggesting the most brutal of penalties. In general, Thucydides wanted to show the influence of demagogues like Cleon on the people.

The debate over the Spartan peace proposals shows Cleon attacking the Spartan envoys, accusing them of insincerity. Thucydides wished to condemn the part played by Cleon in the breakdown of discussions with the Spartans and their allies. Cleon is featured on a more personal level in the second debate on Pylos, where Thucydides attempts to suggest that his appointment as commander at Pylos was an act of irresponsibility, and exposes his unworthiness.

Finally, in the campaign in the Chalcidice Cleon is contrasted unfavourably with the Spartan commander, Brasidas. The defects in his personality were the cause of the Athenian defeat, according to Thucydides, who convicts Cleon of incompetence and cowardice.

Why did Thucydides condemn Cleon?

Despite Thucydides' disapproval of democracy, he greatly admired Pericles and his leadership of the people. He was therefore highly prejudiced against the type of politician represented by Cleon, who succeeded Pericles and whom he blamed for the downfall of his city. He was bitter against the régime that allowed them to have such influence. Also,

Thucydides was banished in 423 for failing to take Amphipolis when he was strategos and it is possible that Cleon had something to do with his indictment. Thucydides depicts Cleon as brutal, dishonest, unscrupulous, misguided and incompetent.

Aristophanes and Cleon

Aristophanes does not spare Cleon in his plays, particularly in the *Knights* and the *Wasps*.

In the *Knights* he describes him 'as a leather seller...a robber and a shrieker, with a voice like an overloaded sewer',[24] while in the *Wasps* he attempts to expose Cleon as a profit-making plunderer who was making money out of the war at the expense of the people of Athens. The innuendoes in Aristophanes suggest that he was involved in bribery and embezzlement, and had too much influence over the people.

Butt of comic poet

The portrait of Cleon in Aristophanes perhaps carries no more historical weight than a modern political cartoon.

Aristotle and Cleon

'Cleon, it seems, more than anyone else corrupted the people by his wild impulses, and was the first man who, when on the platform, shouted, uttered abuse and made speeches with his clothes hitched up, while everyone else spoke in an orderly manner.'[25]

Vulgar speeches and behaviour

Plutarch and Cleon

Plutarch describes the 'intolerable arrogance' and audacity of Cleon, which no one could restrain and which 'brought many disasters on the city'. He

> broke down all conventions of decent behaviour in the Assembly by shouting, abusing, striding up and down the platform and slapping his thigh as he spoke...his habits produced among the politicians an irresponsibility and a disregard for propriety which before long were to throw the affairs of Athens into chaos.[26]

Neither Thucydides nor Aristophanes reveals the complete picture of Cleon.

He belonged to the merchant class, believed in a radically democratic government—although he knew its weaknesses—and followed a policy of aggressive imperialism, seeing the empire for what it really was.

An aggressive imperialist

He was a clever orator, but his speeches were not dignified and intellectual; rather they played on the disturbed emotions of the people, appealing more particularly to the instincts of the lower classes.

Played to the lower classes

He was a demagogue, not a statesman. His repeated refusals of peace offers, and his great increase in the tribute at a time when the allies' help was vital, were not the acts of a statesman.

Man of action

He showed courage, determination, leadership and initiative, and was a man of action who stood behind his decisions and carried them through.

He was not the ridiculous, corrupt brute Aristophanes would have us believe and it would not be possible to account for his long survival and predominance in a city with the political outlook of Athens if there had been no integrity in the man.

The revolt of Lesbos

Stalemate

By 428 the war had reached a stalemate. Athens had a number of successes in the north-west of Greece and the Peloponnesians continued their regular invasions of Attica, but many actions were indecisive. Plataea was still under siege by the Spartans and Boeotians, and Athens was too weak from the effects of the plague to take the initiative.

Revolt led by Mytilene

However, in 428 Lesbos — the largest and richest of Athens' allies in the eastern Aegean — revolted, led by the city of Mytilene. Lesbos was still independent, did not pay tribute and maintained its own fleet, part of which contributed to Athens' naval strength in the Peloponnesian War.

The oligarchs of Mytilene had been planning for some time to unite the rest of Lesbos under their control and had already approached Sparta for help, but the Spartans had been unwilling to receive them into their alliance at that time. The Athenians, warned of the planned secession by the loyal city of Methymna (in the north of Lesbos), sent a small fleet to demand that the oligarchs cease their activities, but the ultimatum was rejected. The Athenians laid siege to the city and awaited reinforcements from Athens, in the meantime gaining help from the cleruchies in Imbros and Lemnos.

Envoys from Mytilene evaded the Athenian ships, reached the Peloponnese and successfully convinced the Peloponnesians — at a gathering at Olympia — of the benefits to be gained by supporting Lesbos.

Appeal to Sparta

It is not in Attica, as some people think, that the war will be won or lost, but in the countries from which Attica draws her strength... If you give us your wholehearted support you will gain for yourselves a state which has a large navy (which is the thing you need most); you will be in a much better position for breaking the power of Athens by detaching her allies from her, since the others will be greatly encouraged to come over to you... Once you come forward in the role of liberators, you will find that your strength in the war is enormously increased.[27]

Lesbos joined Spartan alliance

The Mytilenians were welcomed into the Spartan alliance and the Peloponnesians agreed to attack Athens simultaneously by land and by sea and

236

to send a fleet to the aid of Lesbos, in the belief that Athens was weakened by the plague and temporarily inactive.

Although Athens had 100 ships in reserve for such an emergency, she had difficulty getting rowers from the thetes, whose ranks had been thinned out by the plague. Every available citizen of hoplite class was recruited as a rower, with the addition of some metics. Although suffering acute financial strain, the Athenians were determined to find the funds necessary to carry on a siege of Lesbos, and imposed on the rich a property tax which brought in 200 talents. The Peloponnesians, in the middle of their harvest time, responded with reluctance and resentment to Sparta's order to muster for a second attack on Attica. Ships for the naval attack on Athens began to be hauled over the Isthmus from the Corinthian Gulf to the Saronic Gulf. However, when the Athenians with great energy attacked the lands along the Peloponnesian coast that had been left unharvested, the Spartan plan to invade Attica was abandoned.

Crisis handled quickly by Athens

Peloponnesians reluctant to invade Attica twice

Athens dispatched more ships and 1000 hoplites to Lesbos under the command of Paches, and throughout the winter the Athenians besieged the island by both land and sea. The desperate Mytilenians waited for the promised Spartan help, which did not come. One week after the Mytilenians were forced to surrender, a Peloponnesian fleet under the admiral Alcidas reached Asia Minor. Although the appearance of an enemy fleet in the Aegean caused widespread alarm and anger among the Athenians, the Peloponnesians achieved nothing. Alcidas neither attacked the Athenians nor took any initiative among Athens' subjects which could have raised a general revolt. Lacking any resolution, he withdrew and sailed for the Peloponnese, pursued for a time by Paches. The ringleaders of the revolt were sent to Athens to await their fate.

Surrender of Mytilene — Spartan arrival too late

The handling of this crisis by Athens, and the mishandling of a great opportunity to do serious damage to the Athenians by Sparta, revealed once again the difference between the two cities.

The Mytilenian debate

The Athenians, in a mood of anger, decided in their Assembly to put to death not only the ringleaders but 'the entire adult male population of Mytilene and to make slaves of the women and children'. They were influenced in this decision by Cleon, a man 'remarkable among the Athenians for the violence of his character'.[28] However, on the following day this ferocious decree was reconsidered, and the debate between Cleon and Diodotus (an unknown Athenian) dealing with the punishment of the Mytilenians was also used by Thucydides to comment on the character of Athenian democracy and the contrasting views of imperialism.

Death penalty for Mytilenians

Table 9.4	Thucydides' comparison of views of Cleon and Diodotus	
	Cleon	Diodotus
Second Athenian Assembly held	The people were unable to make a decision and keep to it. They were influenced by each new and clever argument.	Frequent discussions on matters of importance were necessary. Decisions made in haste and anger were never wise decisions.
	The revolt of Mytilene was an act of calculated aggression by an ally who took sides with their bitterest enemies in order to destroy them.	Despite the guilt of the Mytilenians, Athens would not benefit in the future from the indiscriminate slaughter of innocent and guilty. Such action would alienate the democrats and other cities of the empire.
Cleon — harshest penalty proposed *Diodotus — moderate behaviour suited Athens' interests*	Since the Athenian empire was a 'tyranny', they could only succeed in holding it together by force. 'Your leadership depends on superior strength, not on any goodwill of theirs'. The city of Mytilene should suffer the severest penalty: the death sentence for all citizens of military age and the enslavement of the women and children.	The death penalty would not deter cities from rebellion in the future and the leader of an empire should take care of her allies before they came to feel the need to revolt. Moderation would benefit Athens, since it would give the rebels a chance to atone for their guilt and allow Athens to make full use of the indemnity now and tribute in the future.
	This would serve as harsh warning to other allies and would prevent Athens having to neglect the war with her real enemies in order to fight her own allies.	

Demos easily led

The vote was taken and the decision, although very close, favoured the moderate view of Diodotus. The ringleaders were put to death (approximately 1000), the walls were dismantled and the fleet surrendered. Instead of imposing tribute, the Athenians divided up the land—except for that of loyal Methymna—into 3000 holdings, which were distributed to Athenian cleruchs.

The destruction of Plataea and civil war in Corcyra, 427

Growing violence

The leadership of Cleon and the original decision of the Athenian Assembly to put to death all adult male inhabitants of Mytilene revealed a growing violence associated with the war. Two further incidents emphasised this trend.

The destruction of Plataea

Refer to Thucydides, III:51-68.

238

The small Boeotian city of Plataea, a loyal ally of Athens for many years, was besieged by the Spartans and their allies the Thebans from 431 to 427. The enmity between Plataea and Thebes had existed for a long time, with the Thebans committing frequent acts of aggression against Plataea. The Spartans, who considered the Thebans useful to them in the war, destroyed Plataea in 427. They killed all adult males, made slaves of the women and children, razed the city to the ground and leased out the land to Theban cultivators. 'This was the end of Plataea, in the ninety-third year after she became an ally of Athens'.[29]

Plataea totally destroyed

Civil war in Corcyra

Refer to Thucydides, III:69–85.

In the same year there was a civil war in Corcyra between the democrats, supported by Athens (with whom Corcyra was allied), and the oligarchs, who were connected with Corinth.

Thucydides records the horrible excesses of cruelty committed by both sides. 'There was death in every shape and form. And as usually happens in such situations people went to every extreme and beyond it'.[30] This revolution was so savage — as were those which broke out later in other Greek states — that there seems to have been a general deterioration in standards of conduct throughout the Greek world.

Brutal revolutions

Power, greed and personal ambition were the cause of these revolutions. Both the democrats and the aristocrats, while professing to serve the public interest, were in fact seeking their own ascendancy, and they stopped at nothing to achieve this.

The Athenian seizure of Pylos and Sphacteria, 425

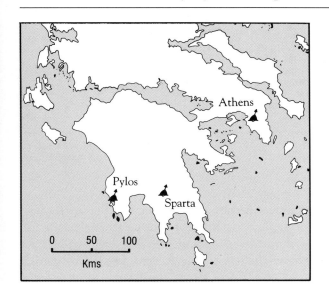

Map showing the position of Pylos

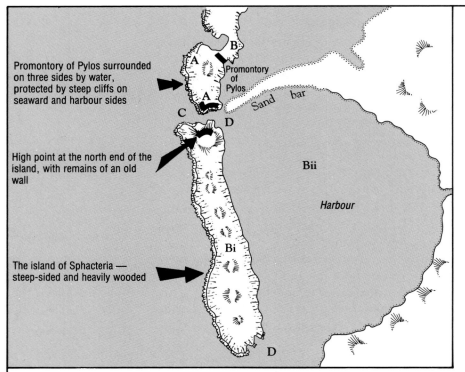

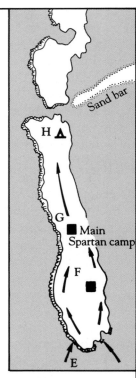

Promontory of Pylos surrounded on three sides by water, protected by steep cliffs on seaward and harbour sides

High point at the north end of the island, with remains of an old wall

The island of Sphacteria — steep-sided and heavily wooded

A Walls were built by the Athenians on the promontory.

B A Spartan force arrived and made camp in the north of the promontory. They also landed 420

Bi Lacedaemonians on the island of Sphacteria to prevent the Athenians using it as a base. The

Bii Spartans recalled their fleet from Corcyra.

C Demosthenes repelled several attempted landings by the Spartans on the south-west coast of Pylos.

D Athenian naval reinforcements arrived from Zacynthus and entered the harbour.

E With Cleon's arrival, the Athenian troops (approximately 14 000) landed in the south from the sea and from the harbour.

F The Spartan outpost was taken by surprise and the men killed. The main body of Spartan hoplites advanced against the Athenians but could not cope with the light-armed troops on the high ground on their flanks. The arrows pierced their helmets and cuirasses and they could not see for the clouds of dust caused by the recent fire.

G This was no pitched battle, and unable to move freely they fell back to the fort at the north of the island which was garrisoned.

H The Athenians had no success in dislodging the Spartans until a Messenian captain led a small force up the sheer cliffs which had been left unguarded by the Spartans. Exposed on both sides, the Spartans (after much deliberation with their leaders on the mainland) surrendered.

The Athenian capture of Pylos and Sphacteria (first stage)

The Athenian capture of Pylos and Sphacteria (second stage)

Pylos fortified by Demosthenes

In 425, an Athenian fleet commanded by Eurymedon and Sophocles was on its way to Sicily on a diplomatic mission. Demosthenes, one of Athens' most enterprising commanders, accompanied the fleet but had no definite command. Demosthenes believed that Athens needed to gain a base in enemy territory and when a storm forced the fleet to shelter for a time, he saw the opportunity to fortify the promontory of Pylos. Refer to points A, B, Bi, Bii, C and D on the map opposite.

The Spartan fleet, sheltering in the harbour and unprepared for battle was attacked by the Athenians. The Spartan forces on Sphacteria were cut off, causing grave alarm in Sparta. A truce was called, and Spartan ambassadors were sent to Athens to seek peace and to get back their men as soon as possible.

Their assumption was that Athens had wanted to make peace even earlier, had only been prevented from doing so by Spartan opposition, and would now gladly embrace the opportunity offered and return the men. The Athenians, however, aimed at winning still more, and, as for making peace, they considered that while they had men on the island they could do so whenever they liked. The man who, more than the others, encouraged them in this attitude was Cleon, the son of Cleaenetus, a popular figure of the time who had the greatest influence with the masses.[31]

Athenian refusal to make peace

The Spartans achieved nothing, and the truce ended. The Athenians refused to give back the Spartan ships they had been holding during the truce and the Spartans, after making a formal protest, went back to attacking the northern wall. The Athenians kept up a continuous blockade of Sphacteria, day and night. This became increasingly difficult, owing to bad weather and lack of food and water. The Spartans on the island were supplied by volunteers who employed every method they could think of for importing provisions.

Blockade of Sphacteria

The Athenians were concerned that the blockade was taking so long and feared that with the onset of winter they would have to end it without having achieved anything. The demos now regretted not making peace and Cleon, the instigator of this policy, lost his popularity.

Cleon	Nicias
Cleon blamed Nicias, as one of the generals, claiming that if they were 'real men it would be easy to take out a force and capture the Spartans on the island'. He would do it himself if he were in command, he said.[32]	Nicias, sensing that the people were annoyed at Cleon's claim, offered Cleon his command and told him 'to take whatever forces he liked and see what he could do himself'. He had called Cleon's bluff.[33]

Debate in Athens

Cleon, unable to back out of this situation, claimed he would bring back the Spartans alive within twenty days or kill them on the spot. The claim, though appearing irresponsible and causing much ridicule in Athens, was based on the fact that he had heard that Demosthenes had already begun to implement a plan for landing on the island. A fire on the island had cleared the heavy tree cover, enabling Demosthenes to see the number and location of troops as well as the best landing sites. Now refer to points E-H.

The Spartans on the island had been told to make their own decisions but to do nothing dishonourable. Their surrender

Surrender of Spartan hoplites

caused much more surprise among the Hellenes than anything else that happened in the war. The general impression had been that Spartans would never surrender their arms whether because of hunger or any other form of compulsion.[34]

The importance of Athens' success at Pylos

The capture of Pylos and of the Spartan hoplites at Sphacteria was a turning point in the first phase of the war.

Athenian outpost in enemy territory

Military significance   From Athenian-held Pylos, the Messenians made raids on the surrounding territory whenever they wished and encouraged the desertion of helots, providing them with a refuge. The Spartans became more apprehensive than ever of a widespread helot revolt. Although unintentionally, the seizure of Pylos justified Pericles' original strategy.

Spartan hostages in Athens

The prisoners held at Athens were used to put pressure on the Spartans to cease their annual invasions of Attica, the Athenians threatening to kill the hostages if the raids continued.

Spartan surrender encourages further aggression

The surrender by Spartan hoplites after a defeat was unheard of, and in a mood of overconfidence the war party in Athens looked further afield and initiated more aggressive campaigns, disregarding the sound policy laid down by Pericles. Although they did regain the Megarian port of Nisaea (lost at the time of the Thirty Years' Peace), the daring scheme to regain Boeotia resulted in their disastrous defeat at Delium in the following year.

Increase in Cleon's popularity

Cleon's unexpected success at Pylos led Nicias to attempt to retrieve his military reputation. He gained control for Athens of the Methana Peninsula (between Epidaurus and Troezen) which was walled and garrisoned, and in the following year he secured the island of Cythera, from which the Athenians could attack Laconia. Athens now had three vital bases in the Peloponnese: Pylos, Cythera and Methana.

Opposition to peace — Cleon

Political significance   Cleon's reputation was enhanced by the victory at Sphacteria and at the height of his popularity and power he was able to persuade the Assembly to oppose the peace party of Nicias and refuse Sparta's continued offers of peace. The Athenians believed that the 120 Spartiate prisoners gave them the means by which to make an advantageous settlement whenever they chose.

Cleon re-elected

Despite Aristophanes' criticism of him in the *Knights*, Cleon was re-elected as general.

The Assembly, under the influence of Cleon, passed a decree providing for a reassessment of the tribute. This strengthened Athens' financial situation, as in some cases the tribute was doubled or trebled and names appeared on the tribute lists which had not been there before. At the same time the pay for jurors was increased from 2 obols to 3 obols a day. This may have been not simply a ploy to win greater popularity for Cleon, but a genuine attempt to relieve the distress caused by higher living costs and loss of harvests.

Reassessment of tribute

The Thracian campaign, 424–422

Brasidas, the Spartan general, with a Peloponnesian force of 1700 hoplites (including 700 helots), marched north to Thrace in 424 at the request of Perdiccas of Macedonia and the Thracian towns, who were alarmed at the Athenian success.

Sparta saw this as an opportunity to divert the attention of the Athenians from their direct attacks on the territory of Sparta; it also gave them a reason to send some helots along with the army, 'since in the present state of affairs, with Pylos in enemy hands, they feared a revolution'.[39] As well, the Spartans wanted to have places to offer in exchange for the hostages in Athens when peace terms were arranged.

Thracian campaign — Spartan response to Pylos

Brasidas won over the town of Acanthus by oratory and diplomacy; he then took the important Athenian city of Amphipolis by offering moderate terms, guaranteeing the people full political rights and continued possession of their property. Any who wished to leave were free to do so within five days.

Amphipolis taken by Brasidas

Thucydides, who at the time was an Athenian general stationed at Thasos, was keeping an eye on Athens' interests in the north-west when Brasidas made his attempt on Amphipolis. Thucydides failed to prevent this and the Athenians banished him, but his exile enabled him to write his great history of the Peloponnesian War.

Exile of Thucydides

The fall of Amphipolis caused great alarm in Athens because of the city's strategic and economic value. The area was rich in resources, such as gold, and timber for shipbuilding. The Athenians also feared that the example of Amphipolis would encourage the other allies to revolt, with a resultant loss of revenue to Athens. Athenian garrisons were sent to the various cities; Brasidas appealed for reinforcements, and began building triremes.

Importance of Amphipolis

Torone went over to Sparta by treachery, but once Brasidas entered the city he guaranteed the citizens their civil rights, with no reprisals.

In 423 an armistice was signed between Athens and Sparta.

The Athenians calculated that in this way Brasidas would not be able to win over any more of their dependencies before they had had time to take measures for their security.[40]

Truce

However, while these negotiations were in progress, the people of Scione revolted against Athens. Brasidas praised them for their courage and resolution and assured them that as such loyal friends of Sparta, he would honour them in every way.

Infringement of truce by Brasidas

When news of the truce arrived Brasidas refused to give up Scione, even though it had been taken after the armistice was signed. The Athenians were furious; Cleon proposed that it should be recaptured and the death penalty imposed upon the inhabitants.

Mende also revolted against Athens and Brasidas accepted the citizens as allies, despite the infringement of the truce. The Athenians made preparations, under Nicias, to attack both cities. Mende was retaken (the Athenian troops had to be restrained from slaughtering the inhabitants) and Scione was placed under siege.

Cleon in Thrace

After the armistice, Cleon sailed out with a force of 1500 against the Thracian towns. During Brasidas' absence, he took Torone and made slaves of the women and children, while the men were sent to Athens.

Deaths of Cleon and Brasidas

The battle for Amphipolis was lost by Cleon and the Athenians, who were disorganised, panic-stricken and thrown off balance by the audacity of Brasidas. Both Brasidas and Cleon died — the one in battle and the other, according to Thucydides, fleeing from the scene.

Now 'Cleon and Brasidas were dead — the two people who on each side had been most opposed to peace'.[41]

Brasidas

'Un-Spartan'

Brasidas, the outstanding Spartan general of the Archidamian War, was not a typical Spartan. Bury refers to him as 'a Spartan by mistake'.[35]

Thucydides presents him in a very favourable light — particularly when comparing him with Cleon — and he is easily the most attractive personality, except for Pericles, in Thucydides' work.

Daring

Although the courage and skilful strategy he displayed were expected of a Spartan commander, his initiative and resourceful daring were not typical. When the Athenians were attempting to take Megara Brasidas, on his way to Thrace, saw the danger, took the initiative and formulated a plan to outwit the Athenians and save Megara.

His attractive personal qualities brought him the support of Athens' allies in Thrace:

Energetic

- The Chalcidians asked particularly for Brasidas to lead an army into Thrace, because 'he had a great reputation for energy in every direction'.[36]

Gallant and diplomatic

- His gallantry, diplomacy and persuasive oratory won over the cities of the Chalcidice, for 'he was not at all a bad speaker either, for a Spartan'.[37]

- His upright and moderate conduct created a lasting pro-Spartan feeling in the area. *Moderate and just*
- He was seen as a liberator and honoured as a hero; the city of Scione had heaped honours on him, presenting him with a gold crown. On his death, Amphipolis worshipped him as the new founder of the city, making annual sacrifices and holding games in his honour.

His restless talents inspired envy in his own Spartan peers; they wanted him operating out of the Peloponnese and failed to support him in Thrace.

> The Spartans, however, did nothing for him, partly because their leading men were jealous of him, partly because what they really wanted was to recover the prisoners made on the island and to end the war.[38]

His personal ambition was one of the chief obstacles to peace. He overlooked the truce between Athens and Sparta, signed in 423, and continued to support revolts of Athens' allies.

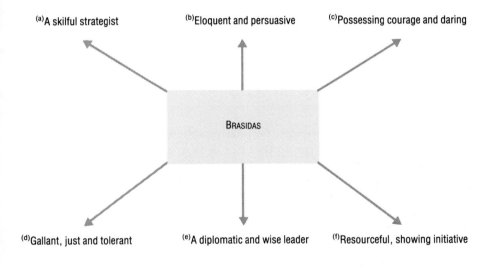

(a)A skilful strategist   (b)Eloquent and persuasive   (c)Possessing courage and daring

BRASIDAS

(d)Gallant, just and tolerant   (e)A diplomatic and wise leader   (f)Resourceful, showing initiative

Refer to Thucydides: (a) IV: 124, 126; (b) IV: 83–7, 121, 126; (c) IV: 11, 79; (d) IV: 83, 104, 108; (e) IV: 83, 87; (f) II: 24, 93, IV: 69.

The qualities of Brasidas

The peace of Nicias, 421

Nicias knew 'that the Spartans had for some time been anxious for peace, while the Athenians no longer had the same appetite for war' and so he made every effort to reconcile them.[42] Both sides now wanted peace. Their reasons are shown in Table 9.5.

Table 9.5	
Athenian reasons	*Spartan reasons*
Loss of confidence over recent defeats. Delium and Amphipolis	Anxiety to get back Spartan prisoners taken during Pylos campaign
Apprehensive about allies — fear of revolts	Sparta's territory was being raided from Pylos and Cythera
Regretting their rejection of peace after Pylos	Helots likely to revolt
	Thirty Years' Peace with Argos coming to an end

Terms of peace
1 It was to last fifty years.
2 Delphi was to be free.
3 Disputes were to be settled by law and alterations to the treaty made by mutual consent.
4 Chalcidice was to be independent.
5 Amphipolis and Panactum were to be given back to Athens.
6 Pylos, Cythera and Methana were to be returned to Sparta.
7 All prisoners were to be exchanged.

Nicias

Nicias — represented conservatives

'After the death of Pericles the distinguished were championed by Nicias'.[43] In fact he drew his support not only from the rich, but from the small landowners and refugees from Attica who wanted peace. He was a conservative, who tended to follow Periclean strategy, and he sought to make a reasonable peace with Sparta without surrender or the empire being broken up. For these reasons, 'Cleon regarded Nicias as his actual enemy'.[44]

Great wealth and generosity

His great wealth — from silver, mined by an enormous labour force of slaves — was used, according to Plutarch, to win the favour of the people by financing dramatic and gymnastic exhibitions on a grand scale and by making lavish offerings to the gods. This was more likely to have been an act of devotion, as he was a pious man and 'stood in great awe of the supernatural and he was particularly subject, as Thucydides tells us, to the influence of divination.'[45]

Successful, but cautious

According to Thucydides, at the time of the Peace of 421, it was 'Nicias, the son of Niceratus, who had done better in his military commands than anyone else of his time'.[46] He was consistently successful, although he lacked flair and daring and, as Plutarch remarked, 'he did his best to evade any difficult or lengthy enterprise and whenever he served as general, he played for safety'.[47] Although he was an experienced and trusted commander, he was naturally cautious, timid and inclined to defeatism.

In the early part of the Peloponnesian War, Nicias stood out against the aggressive policy of Cleon and the war party, but 'even when Nicias was free of Cleon he had no time to stabilise Athenian politics or to compose the differences within the city'[48] because of the ambitions of Alcibiades.

Opposed by Cleon and Alcibiades

The period of changing alliances, 421–416

Problems associated with the peace

Members of the Spartan alliance — such as Corinth, Megara, Boeotia, Elis and Mantinea — refused to ratify the treaty. Corinth had lost many of her possessions in the north-west (Corcyra, Sollium, Anactorium and Corinthian colonies in Acarnania) and was expected to accept their loss without any compensation. Megara's chief harbour of Nisaea was still in Athenian hands and Boeotia refused to give back the frontier post of Panactum.

Discontent of Sparta's allies

In alarm at the refusal of her allies to sign the peace treaty, Sparta formed an alliance with Athens.

Alliance between Athens and Sparta

The treaty was never implemented completely, since Amphipolis was not returned to Athens (owing to the objections of its inhabitants) and Pylos was not restored to Sparta.

The resentment on the part of Sparta's allies led to political upheaval and a general reshuffling of alliances in the next few years. They joined in a secret and unofficial alliance with Argos, Sparta's traditional enemy.

New alignment of powers

Sparta, aware of the coalition, implemented a number of plans to win back her former allies even at the risk of breaking the alliance with Athens, but was unsuccessful. She did, however, form a separate alliance with the Boeotian League. Thus the Athenians felt that they had been cheated.

Nicias attempted to preserve the peace between Athens and Sparta, but Alcibiades, the son of Cleinias, had other ideas. He wished to discard the alliance and win over Argos, even at the risk of war with Sparta. Plutarch suggests that Alcibiades aimed to violate the treaty out of sheer jealousy of Nicias' success, while according to Thucydides Alcibiades believed the Spartans could not be trusted.

Treaty undermined by Alcibiades

Alcibiades arranged an agreement between Athens, Argos, Mantinea and Elis. Corinth and Megara rejoined the Spartan alliance, preferring the protection of Sparta, their former leader. Thucydides says

Athenian/Argive alliance

> It would certainly be an error of judgement to consider the interval of the agreement [peace] as anything else except a period of war... It is hardly

possible to use the word 'peace' of a situation in which neither side gave back or received what had been promised.[49]

The Battle of Mantinea

The Spartan alliance and the Athenian/Argive coalition met on the battle field near Mantinea in 418, where Spartan military superiority was demonstrated once more.

Sparta and Argos concluded a fifty-year alliance and the Mantineans rejoined the Spartan alliance, which by 417 was as strong as ever.

Athens' aggression against Melos, 416

Alcibiades' success in undermining the peace treaty was followed by a policy of increased aggression by Athens.

In 416 the Athenians launched an expedition against the neutral island of Melos, which had refused to become part of the Athenian Empire. Thucydides used the incident to show the real character of Athenian imperialism.[50] The Melians wanted to remain free and neutral, but the Athenians believed that they had the right to conquer other states simply because they were more powerful. 'The strong do what they have the power to do and the weak accept what they have to accept.'[51]

The nature of Athenian imperialism

In a dialogue between the Athenians and the Melians the question of freedom and independence was discussed, and the Athenians expressed sentiments that were evidence of just how aggressive their imperial policy had become.

> It is for the good of our own empire that we are here... you, by giving in, would save yourselves from disaster; we, by not destroying you, would be able to profit from you.[52]

The Athenians believed that the hatred which the Melians felt for them was evidence of Athens' power, which rested on the rule of the sea. Since Melos was a weak island state, it was particularly important to the Athenians that she should not escape Athens' control.

The destruction of Melos

The Melians refused to give up the freedom they had enjoyed for 700 years, knowing, however, that the refusal would lead to their destruction. Melos was eventually reduced by siege; all men of military age were put to death, the women and children were sold into slavery and the Athenians set up a cleruchy there.

The expedition against Melos was totally against what had been Pericles' policy for Athenian success in the war. He had told the Athenians to wait quietly, to pay attention to their navy, to attempt no new conquests and not to risk the safety of the city itself.

However, the expedition to Melos was of minor significance to the outcome of the war when compared with the Athenian enterprise under-taken next — the massive campaign against Syracuse in Sicily.

Alcibiades

Alcibiades is first mentioned by Thucydides in his account of the negotiations between Athens and Argos in 420. He continued to play a vital role in both Athenian and Spartan affairs during the war, until 406.

Plutarch remarks that 'public opinion found it difficult to judge Alcibiades because of the extreme inconsistency of his character'.[53] However, this was to be expected in a career which 'was spent in the midst of great enterprises and shifts of fortune'.[54]

Inconsistency

- Alcibiades, as a relative and ward of Pericles, was blessed with birth, wealth and prestige as well as good looks, grace and charm.

Natural attributes

- There was a darker side to his nature as well. He was often accused of drunkenness, lawlessness, debauchery and insolence; apparently he spent extravagantly and dressed effeminately.

- He was personally ambitious, 'desiring to gain the upper hand over his rivals'[55] and to win fame and distinction.

Ambitious

- As well as his qualities as a statesman, Alcibiades had the ability to win over the people — particularly the young — by his eloquence. Many found his charm to be irresistible and admired his versatility and cleverness. One such admirer was Tissaphernes, the Persian satrap.

- He was an opportunist. He served first Athens and then Sparta, he worked alongside the Persians, he supported first the oligarchs and then the democrats and he ended his days in Persia.

An opportunist

- 'He could assimilate and adapt himself to the pursuits and manner of living of others'.[56] When he renounced Athens, he lived in Sparta according to Spartan customs — wearing his hair long, eating black broth and coarse bread, and taking cold baths.

Adaptable

- He was the most enterprising and experienced general Athens produced during the war; his ability to turn events around caused the Athenians, in the darkest days of the Thirty and the Spartan occupation, to believe 'that the cause of Athens could never be utterly lost so long as Alcibiades was alive'.[57] For this reason Lysander demanded that Pharnabazus, the Persian satrap in whose province Alcibiades was living, should order his execution.

An enterprising commander

The Sicilian expedition, 415–412

This was the greatest Hellenic action that took place during this war, and, in my opinion, the greatest action that we know of in Hellenic history — to the victors the most brilliant of successes, to the vanquished the most calamitous of defeats.[58]

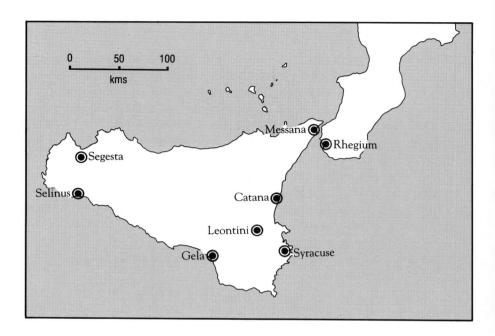

Sicily and southern Italy

Background to the Sicilian campaign

Early Athenian
interest in west

There had been a growing Athenian interest in western trade and colonisation from the time of Themistocles. By 446 there was considerable discontent within the Athenian empire (Megara and Euboea had revolted) and many politicians believed that Athens should make its political influence felt among the Ionian cities of Sicily and Italy.

In 443–442 Athens concluded alliances with Rhegium in Italy and Leontini in Sicily, to keep a check on Syracuse. There were city-state rivalries in Sicily between Dorians led by Corinthian Syracuse and Ionians led by Leontini.

Athens founded the colony of Thurii (in southern Italy) in 444, and this caused alarm in Syracuse.

Western trade rivalry with Corinth had been one of the significant causes of conflict leading up to the outbreak of the Peloponnesian War.

More aggressive
attitude after Pericles

First expedition to
Sicily

With the death of Pericles there was a much more aggressive attitude to the west, and in 427 an embassy from Leontini appealed to the Athenians for help against Syracuse. In the hope of preventing the unification of Sicily under Syracuse, and to stop western help to Sparta, cut off supplies to the Peloponnese and strike a blow at the trade of their hated rival

Corinth, the Athenians agreed. Laches led the expedition, but achieved little beyond patrolling the straits and renewing the old alliance with Segesta.

Two years later another expedition was dispatched, under Pythodorus, Sophocles and Eurymedon. It was delayed for some time at Pylos. Hermocrates, one of the most distinguished figures in Sicilian history, appealed to the Sicilians for unity and in 424 a conference was held at Gela, where the cities agreed on peace. The Athenians were no longer needed, and returned home. However, public opinion in Athens, influenced by Cleon, fined Eurymedon and banished his colleagues for dereliction of duty.

In 416 Segesta appealed to Athens for help in her dispute with Selinus, an ally of Syracuse, and offered to supply the funds to finance the expedition. Athenian envoys, sent to investigate the claims of the Segestaeans concerning their wealth, returned with 60 talents as payment for a fleet and with considerable enthusiasm about Segesta's resources. They had been deceived.

Athenians deceived

The Athenian Assembly's decision

The radical Assembly was easily influenced by Alcibiades, who 'persuaded them [the demos] to abandon these piecemeal attempts, sail out to Sicily and try to subdue the island completely by means of an invasion on the grand scale'.[59]

Alcibiades' influence in favour of expedition

The people were influenced by

1 the thought of rich rewards (corn, wheat, minerals);
2 the hope of striking a decisive blow against the Peloponnesians by cutting them off from valuable supplies and naval support;
3 the possibilities of the conquest of the whole of Sicily; many, like Alcibiades, saw Sicily as a stepping stone to further conquests in the western Mediterranean.

The Assembly voted a fleet of sixty ships under the joint command of Nicias, Alcibiades and Lamachus. Plutarch says that the people believed that the experience and caution of Nicias would combine well with the daring of Alcibiades and the forthrightness of Lamachus.

Further debate in the Assembly

Nicias attempted to divert the Athenians from the campaign by stressing the following:

Nicias' opposition to expedition

251

- the danger at home, as many important states such as Corinth had not accepted the peace and were still openly at war with Athens;
- the instability of the empire — 'We get only a grudging obedience from our subjects';[60]
- the need for Athens to recuperate from the plague and the financial strains of the war;
- the danger involved in distant alliances and the difficulties of controlling Sicily if the Athenians should be successful;
- the folly of listening to an ambitious and reckless young spendthrift who hoped to make great profit out of his appointment.

Alcibiades stressed the following points:

Action urged by Alcibiades

- the prospect of becoming the leader of all Greek cities, by using what was gained in Sicily;
- lack of unity among Sicilians, and their limitations in terms of military resources;
- the danger to Athens of an 'inactive' policy and the setting of young against old.

Estimates of army, navy exaggerated

Nicias attempted once again to deter the people, by exaggerating the estimates of ships and men needed, but the Athenians 'far from losing their appetite for the voyage because of the difficulties in preparing for it, became more enthusiastic about it than ever'.[61] They voted for more than double that which was originally requested. A total force of over 30 000 set out, including 5100 hoplites, 134 triremes and 130 supply ships.

'Our country is now on the verge of the greatest danger
she has ever known.' Nicias[62]

The mutilation of the hermae

Damaged hermae — Alcibiades accused

Just prior to the fleet sailing an event occurred which the superstitious masses saw as a bad omen for the expedition. It was the mutilation of nearly all the stone busts, or hermae (originally of the god Hermes), which stood outside the entrances to private houses and shrines. The angry populace were convinced that it was 'evidence of a revolutionary conspiracy to overthrow the democracy'.[63]

The enemies of Alcibiades accused him of instigating this, because he is believed once to have taken part in mock celebrations of the Eleusinian mysteries, and because of his unconventional character. There were those (such as Androcles and Pisander) who were envious of his leadership of the people, and wanted to get rid of him. It is also possible that the whole affair may have been instigated by Corinth, to cripple the Sicilian enterprise.

A herm (a marble or bronze column, with sculpted head). Herms were found at the entrances of streets and homes

Alcibiades denied the charges and demanded an immediate trial so that his enemies could not build up an unfair case against him while he was in Sicily. However, he was popular with the soldiers and sailors and had procured the contingents from Argos and Mantinea for the campaign; his enemies believed they would stand more chance of condemning him if they recalled him at the right moment. To Alcibiades this was a serious blow, but he could not delay the expedition. Thucydides gives a vivid description of the preparation and departure of the fleet. 'Certainly this expedition that first set sail was by a long way the most costly and finest looking force of Hellenic troops that up to that time had ever come from a single city.'[64]

Assembly's refusal to try Alcibiades

Strategy

When the fleet reached Rhegium (in southern Italy) it received a cool reception; the people of Rhegium refused to join forces with the Athenian fleet. The Athenians were further discouraged to find that they had been deceived about the wealth of Segesta and that she was unable to finance the expedition as she had promised. Nicias, of course, was not surprised at this news.

Disappointing reception by allies

The aims of the expedition had been only vaguely defined in the assembly prior to departure, and this now led to disputes among the generals over strategy. (Nicias could not have been more unlike the other two generals, and had disapproved of the enterprise from the start.)

- Nicias advised that they should try to settle the difference between Segesta and Selinus, sail around the coast (making a demonstration of their strength) and then return to Athens.
- Lamachus, who was a courageous and honest soldier, urged immediate battle with the real enemy, Syracuse, as this would catch them unprepared and would encourage the rest of Sicily to come over to the side of Athens.
- Alcibiades advocated that they should first send heralds to all Sicilian cities except Selinus and Syracuse, urging them to revolt and thus detaching them from Syracuse. They could then make their attack on Syracuse, which would be left without allies.

Lamachus eventually gave his vote to the plan of Alcibiades.

Recall of Alcibiades

When diplomacy failed to win over Sicilian allies, a bold attack was the only alternative, but the effectiveness of the expedition was lost as the Athenians delayed.

Alcibiades' enemies in Athens had succeeded in having him recalled to stand trial, and sent a ship to escort him home. Lamachus 'was a commander of warlike spirit and great personal courage, but he lacked authority and prestige because he was poor',[65] and Nicias was therefore left to conduct the war as he wished.

Effects of the recall   The recall of Alcibiades removed the one person who could have spurred the Athenians into action. The men were discouraged at his departure and 'foresaw that under Nicias' command the campaign would drag on endlessly with long periods of delay and inactivity.'[66]

Nicias frittered away the rest of the year, sailing around the coast of Sicily and marching back through the centre of the island with only minor successes and nothing to justify the loss of precious time.

The Syracusans, far from showing concern, became increasingly confident and contemptuous of the Athenians and made up their mind to attack the Athenian base at Catana. Nicias did, however, show that he could act; he tricked the Syracusans into believing that if they marched to Catana they would find it undefended, and so drew the whole of the enemy's strength away from Syracuse. He then sailed to Syracuse, made himself master of the harbour and secured a strong position for a camp. 'This was the best stroke of generalship that Nicias achieved in the entire Sicilian campaign'.[67]

He was now free to occupy the plain, but instead the whole army — minus a garrison — returned to Catana.

Alcibiades escaped from his Athenian escorts at Thurii. From there he proceeded to Argos and then to Sparta. He was condemned to death in absentia, and his property was confiscated.

Alcibiades' escape to Sparta

He now turned his brilliant initiative against Athens and offered to render the Spartans great service. An opportunity came with the arrival of a delegation of Corinthians to persuade Sparta to send a force to Italy. The Spartans, unwilling to send military assistance, were roused to action by Alcibiades, who suggested a threefold attack on Athens:

1 A Spartan commander should be sent to Sicily to organise the troops already there and to force others into action.

Alcibiades' advice to Spartans

2 The war in Greece should be prosecuted more openly, in order to prevent Athens sending reinforcements to Sicily.

3 The Spartans should fortify Decelea (in Attica). A permanent enemy base close to Athens was what the Athenians feared most, as it would deprive them of the use of their lands and of their mines (and the revenue from them), and also would cut them off from their food supplies in Euboea. Such an act might even encourage their allies to refuse to pay tribute.

Sparta immediately appointed Gylippus to be the commander of the Syracusans, with the power to take reinforcements into Sicily. In addition, the Spartans prepared to invade Attica and fortify Decelea.

Appointment of Gylippus

Alcibiades had justified his help to his former enemies in the following way: 'The Athens I love is not the one which is wronging me now, but that one in which I used to have secure enjoyment of my rights as a citizen'.[68] He declared that he would shrink from nothing to restore his country to what it had been, even if it meant siding with its enemies.

Attempted siege of Syracuse by Athenians, 414

The Athenians had spent the previous winter awaiting a cavalry force and money, which they had requested from Athens. Their plan was to attack Syracuse by gaining control of the heights of Epipolae, a steep plateau lying directly north of the city. Refer to the map on page 256 for details of the attempted Athenian siege, noting the reasons for its failure.

Athenian plan to take the heights of Epipolae

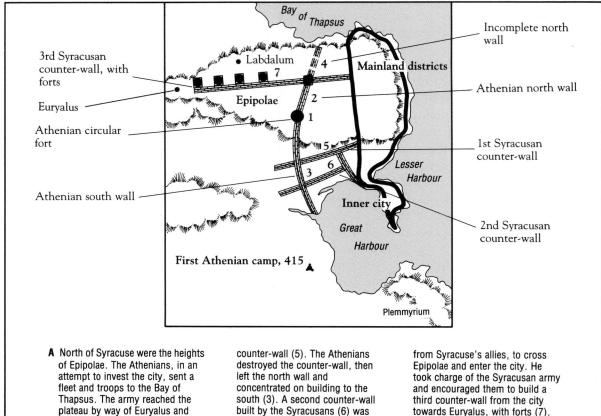

3rd Syracusan counter-wall, with forts

Euryalus

Athenian circular fort

Athenian south wall

Bay of Thapsus

Labdalum

7

Epipolae

Incomplete north wall

4

Mainland districts

Athenian north wall

2

1

5

6

3

First Athenian camp, 415

Lesser Harbour

Inner city

Great Harbour

1st Syracusan counter-wall

2nd Syracusan counter-wall

Plemmyrium

A North of Syracuse were the heights of Epipolae. The Athenians, in an attempt to invest the city, sent a fleet and troops to the Bay of Thapsus. The army reached the plateau by way of Euryalus and fortified Labdalum.

B The Athenian plan was to run a wall north-south from sea to sea cutting off communications by land, while the fleet entered the harbour and cut them off by sea.

C They began by building a circular fort (1) and concentrated on the north wall (2), while the Syracusans built their first

counter-wall (5). The Athenians destroyed the counter-wall, then left the north wall and concentrated on building to the south (3). A second counter-wall built by the Syracusans (6) was attacked by the Athenians led by Lamachus, who lost his life in the battle. The Syracusans could not stop the Athenians building a double wall down to the harbour

D However, Nicias failed to complete the north wall (4) and this allowed Gylippus, the brilliant Spartan general who had raised forces

from Syracuse's allies, to cross Epipolae and enter the city. He took charge of the Syracusan army and encouraged them to build a third counter-wall from the city towards Euryalus, with forts (7).

E This deprived the Athenians of any chance of besieging the city and Nicias could see that since the arrival of Gylippus, their prospects of a naval victory were greater than their chances on land.

F The headland of Plemmyrium was fortified by the Athenians; the fighting ships, merchant vessels and stores were located there.

The Athenian siege of Syracuse, 414

Nicias' appeal to Athens

Despite their fortification at Plemmyrium, the crews stationed there suffered great hardship due to lack of water and fuel and to attacks by the

Syracusan cavalry stationed nearby. Gylippus had left Syracuse to raise more troops from the rest of Sicily, another delegation had been sent to Sparta for more troops, and the Syracusans were training crews to mount a challenge to the Athenians at sea.

Nicias, realising that the Athenians were in a very dangerous position, sent off an urgent letter to the Athenian government. He informed them that the Athenians were besieged and outnumbered, that the foreigners in their service were deserting, that the ships were rotting and the crews were low in morale. His dispatch recommended that they either recall the expedition to Athens immediately or send out another force as big as the first, together with large sums of money. As he himself was ill with a disease of the kidneys, he requested that he be allowed to return home.

Nicias' urgent message for help

Athenian situation desperate

Nicias' letter reveals his frame of mind and the utter lack of contact between the army and the Athenian people. A general in the field never escaped the fear of ignorance and abuse at home.

The Athenians refused to recall Nicias, but voted to send another military and naval force led by Demosthenes and Eurymedon. This was an enormous effort, considering the Spartan occupation of Decelea.

Reinforcements sent from Athens

Map showing the position of Decelea

The effects of the occupation of Decelea

Under the command of King Agis III the Spartans fortified Decelea, which was visible from Athens and controlled the routes to Boeotia and Euboea. As a result of maintaining this hostile post in Attica, Athens suffered greatly. In fact, according to Thucydides, it was 'one of the chief reasons for the decline of Athenian power'.[69] The occupation of Decelea meant that

Athenian difficulties with Decelea occupied

- Athenian lands could no longer be farmed;
- food supplies had to be brought the long and expensive way by sea from Euboea;
- more than 20 000 slaves deserted, many of whom had been mining the silver at Laurium;
- with the loss of revenue from the mines and the effort of carrying on two wars at one time, Athens suffered acute financial strain.

The Athenian reaction to the seizure of Decelea was to occupy a post in Laconia, opposite the island of Cythera, where they hoped to undermine Sparta's hold on her helots.

The arrival of Demosthenes and Athenian reinforcements

Athenian naval reverses

By the time Demosthenes arrived with seventy-three triremes, 5000 hoplites and large numbers of light-armed troops, the Athenians had suffered two more defeats which adversely affected their naval strength. Gylippus had urged the Syracusans to try their fortune in a battle at sea, saying that 'the effect of this on the war in general would be, he expected, something well worth all the risks involved' (Thucydides).[70]

The capture of the Athenian forts on Plemmyrium with the resultant loss of ships, equipment and stores caused a feeling of bewilderment and a decline in morale. Convoys with supplies were intercepted at the entrance to the harbour and the constant vigilance necessary put a tremendous strain on the army. They had moved their fleet further into the harbour, to a less protected site.

The Athenians were defeated in a naval contest in the Great Harbour. The method used by the Athenians—of ramming the sides of the enemy's ships—required speed and space and necessitated only a light prow. However, the Syracusans had perfected a new type of ship—first used by the Corinthians—with a heavily reinforced prow. This enabled them to ram head-on in narrow, crowded spaces such as the harbour of Syracuse.

New Syracusan naval tactics

Despite these losses Demosthenes' plan was to make full use of the fear caused by the arrival of the Athenian reinforcements, by immediately attacking the cross-wall on Epipolae. If this was successful, they could take Syracuse. If it failed, they could still withdraw the army and the fleet and return to Athens without further squandering men and resources.

Failure of Demosthenes' night attack

The night battle on Epipolae, which resulted in the total confusion, defeat and withdrawal of Demosthenes and his troops, is described by Thucydides.[71] Demosthenes now urged an immediate retirement from Sicily while they still had the ships to return to Athens.

Nicias' failure to retreat

Nicias refused to lead the army away. Firstly, he was afraid what the soldiers would say of him when they returned to Athens, and

> knowing the Athenian character as he did, rather than be put to death on a disgraceful charge and by an unjust verdict of the Athenians, he preferred to take his chance and if it must be, to meet his own death himself at the hands of the enemy.[72]

Secondly, he believed a revolutionary party in Syracuse would betray the city to the Athenians.

He even refused to move to a safer location. Two further events happened which sealed his fate:

- Gylippus returned with a large army raised in Sicily, together with reinforcements from the Peloponnese;
- an eclipse of the moon was taken by most of the Athenians as a warning from the gods, and Nicias' soothsayers advised delaying action for a complete lunar month; he waited, and his last chance of escape passed.

Nicias' refusal to leave

Syracusan naval victory, 413

While Nicias delayed, Eurymedon was killed and the Athenians lost eighteen more ships. The Syracusans began to blockade the mouth of the harbour with a line of anchored triremes, merchant ships and any other craft available.

The Athenians, realising the danger, abandoned the upper walls and built close to their ships a wall behind which they put their stores, the sick and a detachment of soldiers as a garrison. The rest of the army was to man every ship in an attempt to break out of the blockade. If they failed, the plan was to burn the ships and march overland to the nearest friendly place.

No description of Thucydides equals his vivid account of this battle in the Great Harbour.[73]

Syracusan blockade of the harbour

Athenian disaster in the harbour

The retreat of the Athenians

After the disastrous Athenian defeat the remaining ships were beached; the men fled to the camp and wanted to retreat at once. A further delay of two days gave the Syracusans and Gylippus a chance to build road-blocks and post ambushes.

The retreat of 40 000 men, without food and full of shame and distress at leaving behind the dead unburied and the sick and injured begging to

Suffering of retreating Athenian troops

be taken, caused 'sufferings too great for tears'. Thucydides claimed that 'no Hellenic army had ever suffered such a reverse'.[74]

Death of Nicias and Demosthenes

Nicias, even in the most terrible retreat, saw the suffering of his men and did his best to encourage and comfort them, but they were eventually worn down and captured. Nicias surrendered himself to Gylippus, since he trusted him more than the Syracusans, but despite Gylippus' objections Nicias and Demosthenes were put to death. Thucydides said: 'of all the Hellenes in my time, [Nicias] least deserved to come to so miserable an end, since the whole of his life had been devoted to the study and practice of virtue'.[75]

Enormous losses

The captured Athenians (approximately 7000) were put to work in the quarries, where they suffered terribly and where many died. '... their losses were, as they say, total; army, navy, everything was destroyed and, out of many, only few returned.'[76]

The mistakes made by the Athenians during the Sicilian campaign

Pericles had once said that he did not fear the enemy's strategy, but rather the Athenians' mistakes. No part of the war justifies this view more than the Sicilian expedition.

The Athenian Assembly

Poor decisions by Athenian Assembly

- The Assembly ignored Nicias' sound arguments against sending out the expedition.
- It had a vague idea of Sicily and its resources, and relied on Segesta to partially fund the expedition.
- It voted too large a force and did not define the expedition's aims clearly.
- Nicias was elected as commander of an expedition of which he so vehemently disapproved.
- Joint leadership was given to three very different personalities.
- It was wrong to send a commander with a charge hanging over his head.
- It made a mistake in recalling Alcibiades, thereby depriving the expedition of the one person who could have brought success. As a result, Alcibiades gave vital help to Sparta.
- It refused to listen to Nicias' plea for withdrawal of the expedition, and failed to replace him when he was so sick.
- It should not have sent major reinforcements when the Athenians were suffering the effects of the occupation of Decelea.

Nicias

- Nicias' temperament was not suited to a bold and daring enterprise.
- He wasted time and resources for little or no gain.
- He delayed when immediate action was required.
- He failed to complete the north wall, so allowing Gylippus to enter Syracuse.
- He refused to retreat after the defeat of Demosthenes on Epipolae.
- He allowed the excessive superstition and fear on the part of the Athenian people to affect his judgment.

Nicias' temperament unsuitable

Effects of Athens' failure in Sicily

Athenian reaction

After the initial disbelief that such total destruction could have occurred, the Athenians were alarmed at the possibility of the Syracusan fleet appearing off the Piraeus, as they were depleted of men of military age, ships, crews and finances.

However, despite feelings of despair, they decided not to give in. The Athenians

- replaced the Council with a Board of Ten Commissioners (the *Probuli*) to be chosen annually (this smaller, permanent body would assist in the reorganisation of the Athenian state after the Sicilian disaster);
- used the 1000 talents, wisely set aside by Pericles for a naval crisis, to rebuild their navy (the plan was carried out so vigorously that within a year they had 150 new triremes);
- carried out strict economic measures to conserve finances;
- withdrew their garrison from Laconia;
- fortified Sunium, to give security to their corn ships rounding the promontory;
- imposed a 5 per cent tax on imports and exports in all ports of the empire, which replaced the tribute;
- attempted to keep a close watch on their allies.

A decadrachm of Syracuse, minted after the Syracusan victory over the Athenians in the Sicilian campaign (c.413)

Spartan reaction

The Spartans' confidence was at a high level, particularly since they believed that they would soon be joined by their allies from Sicily. They now began to throw themselves into the war without any reservation.

They implemented a shipbuilding program, aiming initially at 100 triremes, and King Agis set out to raise money from their allies for this purpose.

Increase in Spartan confidence

Revolt of Athenian allies

First signs of revolt by allies

Euboea and Lesbos communicated with King Agis at Decelea, indicating their willingness to revolt; at the same time, Chios and Erythrae applied directly to Sparta for help in their planned defection from Athens.

The beginning of Persian intervention

The weakening of Athenian naval power gave the Persians, under King Darius II, the opportunity to support a Spartan/Persian attempt to undermine Athenian control in the Aegean and to regain the cities of Asia Minor.

Persian offers of help to Sparta in Aegean

Tissaphernes, Satrap of Lydia, Caria and Ionia, and Pharnabazus, Satrap of Phrygia and Bithynia, both promised Persian financial support to Sparta in return for help in their territories. They wanted the tribute from the cities in Ionia and the Hellespont, which was being paid to Athens. Each satrap attempted to make his own arrangements with Sparta, but the members of the Spartan alliance agreed on a policy which they thought would satisfy them both. They decided to sail to Chios first, then to Lesbos and finally to the Hellespont.

The last phase of the war — the Decelean War, 412–404

The last phase of the war was fought almost entirely at sea in the eastern Aegean, and Alcibiades' influence was felt in many ways on both sides. As Plutarch said, he had the manner of submitting himself 'to more startling transformations than a chameleon'.[77]

Alcibiades' role in the allies' revolts

When the Peloponnesian fleet sailed for Chios, Alcibiades accompanied it in order to incite the Ionian cities to revolt. Chios' secession was followed by Erythrae, Clazomenae and Ephesus, and the movement spread rapidly. Miletus was won over, and it was here that an official alliance between Sparta and the King of Persia was drawn up.

The Treaty of Miletus, 412

Sparta's betrayal of Asiatic Greeks

The significant clause in this treaty was the surrendering to Darius of the Greek communities of Asia Minor. This was a treacherous betrayal of the Greeks by Sparta in return for gold with which to build and man a navy. It undid all the work of the Persian Wars and the Delian League. The states of Asia Minor would not have known of this transaction.

The war against Athens was now to be carried on jointly by the Persian king and the Spartans and their allies.

Samos — Athenian naval headquarters

Athens' counterattack revealed her old energy and determination.

The Athenians chose as their naval base in Asia Minor the island of Samos, which had lost its independence when it revolted in 440. The Athenians restored the island's independence, after helping the people put down a rising by the aristocracy, and Samos remained loyal to the bitter end.

Restoration of Samian independence

From headquarters at Samos, the Athenians recovered Lesbos, Teos and Clazomenae, and attacked Chios.

Alcibiades and Tissaphernes

Alcibiades by this time was regarded with suspicion by the Spartans, and as the personal enemy of King Agis he feared for his safety, so he fled to the Persian satrap Tissaphernes, with whom he found great favour. He abandoned the Spartan cause and persuaded Tissaphernes to adopt a policy of preserving the naval balance in the Aegean 'by stinting whatever help he gave'.[78] He neither helped the Spartans totally nor finished off Athens completely, but hoped that by letting both wear themselves down until exhausted, the Persians could impose their will on Greece.

Tissaphernes' friendship with Alcibiades

Alcibiades' aim was now to use his influence with Tissaphernes to secure his recall to Athens. He made contact with the officers of the fleet who favoured oligarchy, and alleged that he could win over Tissaphernes and Persian support for Athens if there were an oligarchic government in Athens. He did not believe that the existing democracy would forgive his past offences and recall him. Plutarch says that 'Alcibiades cared no more for an oligarchy than for a democracy, but was ready to follow any course of action to get himself recalled from exile'.[79]

Alcibiades' plan for his recall to Athens

He won the support of some of the leaders at Samos who in turn presented the idea to the rank and file, to whom the prospect of support and pay from Persia appealed. They agreed to send Pisander to Athens to attempt to encourage the aristocratic leaders to overthrow the democracy, as well as to recall Alcibiades.

Support of army leaders for Alcibiades

Oligarchic revolution in Athens, 411

The Athenians sent ten negotiators with Pisander to make arrangements with Tissaphernes, but he made such demands in return for his friendship that the envoys 'saw no good purpose in going on with the discussions and, considering that they had been deceived by Alcibiades, went away in

Breakdown of Athenian negotiations with Persia

263

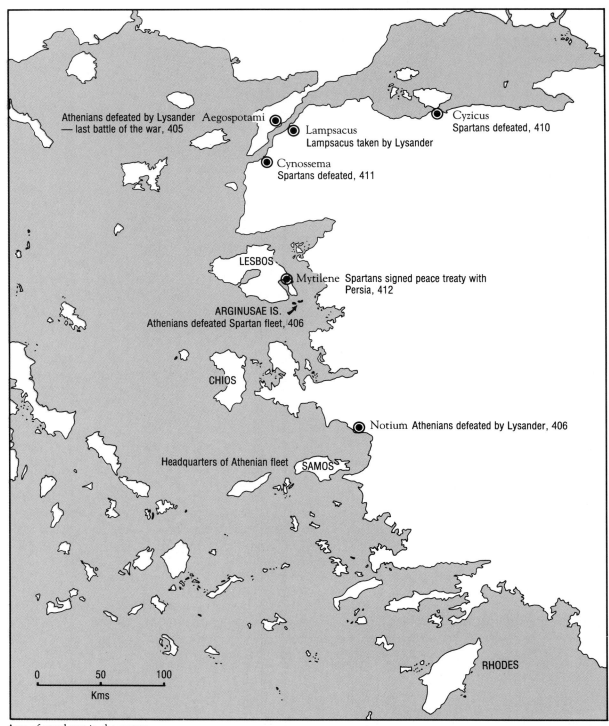

Athenians defeated by Lysander — last battle of the war, 405 Aegospotami

Lampsacus
Lampsacus taken by Lysander

Cynossema
Spartans defeated, 411

Cyzicus
Spartans defeated, 410

LESBOS

Mytilene Spartans signed peace treaty with Persia, 412

ARGINUSAE IS.
Athenians defeated Spartan fleet, 406

CHIOS

Notium Athenians defeated by Lysander, 406

Headquarters of Athenian fleet SAMOS

RHODES

0   50   100
Kms

Area of naval war in the eastern
Aegean

an embittered frame of mind and returned to Samos'.[80] Tissaphernes was still hoping to play off Athens and Sparta against each other.

Although Alcibiades was unable to fulfil his promise, the conspiracy continued in Athens, as the ground had been prepared for some time for an overthrow of the radical democracy. There were strong reasons for hatred of the democrats.

1 The extreme democrats and their demagogue leaders had proved inefficient in handling the Sicilian campaign and had failed to prevent the occupation of Decelea.

2 There had always been in Athens secret political clubs which worked for the overthrow of the government. There was the sinister figure Antiphon, a speech writer, who was the ruthless, ambitious leader of the extreme oligarchs.

Oligarchic clubs in Athens

3 There were moderate men of property who particularly felt the disastrous effects of the war in the loss of income from their ruined estates, the escape of slaves and the closure of the mines, as well as bearing the financial burdens demanded by the state. In their fear of a Spartan/Persian alliance, they were prepared to join with the oligarchs to form a government with restricted franchise. Their leader was Theramenes.

Moderates' support of revolution

The revolution occurred in 411, with the intimidation of the democrats by terror and violence. An assembly was called some distance from the city in the hope that the urban masses would be too afraid to venture outside the walls and would not attend. A list of 400 names was already prepared for a new council (to replace the existing Council of 500), and to placate the moderates, an assembly of 5000 propertied citizens was to be formed. However, the extreme oligarchs had no intention of establishing the Assembly of 5000.

The 400 oligarchs selected for the new council seized control by entering the Council House in force and ejecting the whole Council of 500. A reign of terror was then implemented as they prepared to come to terms with Sparta.

Council of 400 extreme oligarchs

Because of King Agis' suspicions the oligarchs failed to make peace with Sparta, but they built a fort at the western entrance to the Piraeus supposedly as protection from the Athenian fleet presently at Samos. Their real intention was to cut off supplies, starve the population into submission and then hand over the fleet to the Spartans.

Plan to betray Athens

A Spartan fleet appeared off the Piraeus and the treachery was revealed. This alienated the moderates under Theramenes, who led a general revolt of the people.

When the sailors and soldiers of the fleet at Samos became aware of the reign of terror at Athens, they made it quite clear that Samos was to have a democratic government, and dismissed from office any general or officer suspected of having oligarchic sympathies. They refused to recognise the oligarchic government in Athens and declared themselves the legitimate

Moderates urged to take over

265

government of the Athenians. Alcibiades, after restraining the fleet from sailing for Athens to overthrow the oligarchs, sent a message to the moderates in the Council of 400 to assert themselves, put an end to the Council and establish the 5000.

The Peloponnesian fleet which had appeared at the Piraeus sailed to Euboea, where it defeated an Athenian squadron and helped Euboea to revolt. If the Spartans had then anchored off Piraeus and at the same time attacked from Decelea, the fleet at Samos would have been forced to withdraw from Asia Minor. 'However, on this occasion, as on many others, the Spartans proved to be quite the most remarkably helpful enemies that the Athenians could have had.'[81] With the general uprising of the people under Theramenes, the oligarchic leaders escaped to Decelea and Antiphon was put to death. A moderate democracy was restored, with the franchise restricted to those who could provide themselves with hoplite equipment. According to Thucydides, this government 'was a reasonable and moderate blending of the few and the many'[82] and was the best government Athens had ever had. Civil disturbance came to an end. The Athenians voted for the return of Alcibiades, but it was another three years before he entered Athens again.

Escape of oligarchs

Democracy restored

The full democracy was restored in 410 under the leadership of Cleophon, a lyre-maker in the same mould as Cleon.

Successes of Alcibiades in the Hellespont, 411

Dissatisfied with Tissaphernes' support and suspicious of his motives, Mindarus, the Spartan admiral, had moved the scene of conflict from Ionia to the Hellespont. For the Spartans owed Pharnabazus, the satrap in the Hellespont region, the help they had promised.

Athenian naval victories

Alcibiades used this situation as an opportunity to achieve a number of naval victories before returning to Athens. With Thrasybulus and Thrasyllus, Alcibiades recovered Athenian control of the Hellespont and secured their vital corn route in battles at Cynossema, Abydos and Cyzicus. Mindarus was killed, the Spartan fleet destroyed and Pharnabazus defeated on land.

Effects of his success

Refusal of Spartan peace offer

The Spartans offered peace on the basis of the status quo; that is, as things were at the time. Although Decelea would be given up in return for the evacuation of Pylos, it meant that Athens would lose permanently all those allies who had revolted, including Euboea. Due to overconfidence from their recent naval victories, it was inevitable that the Assembly, dominated by Cleophon, would scorn the peace proposal.

After further successes in the Propontis and Bosphorus region,

Alcibiades returned to Athens as a hero and was elected in 408 as commander-in-chief, with absolute powers both on land and sea. Plutarch suggests that many of the leading citizens — knowing Alcibiades' character and reputation — were so afraid he might become a dictator that they wanted him to sail as soon as possible.

Return of Alcibiades to Athens

Turning point in the war

The Persian king appointed his son, Cyrus, as governor-in-chief of Asia Minor, with the necessary funds to build a new Spartan fleet. The jealousies of individual satraps were no longer to interfere with the prosecution of the war and the all-out support of Sparta.

Cyrus' support of Sparta

Lysander, appointed as admiral of the Peloponnesian fleet, was a skilful organiser with the ability to win and maintain support. He was a thorough and enterprising leader who Alcibiades realised was a danger, since 'he inspired such fear that all orders were promptly carried out'.[83] He was a keen strategist, but used intrigue to achieve his ends and 'disguised most of his actions in war with various forms of deceit'.[84]

Lysander — Spartan admiral

Lysander, stationed at Ephesus, was provided with money to secure ships, sailors and supplies from the cities of the coast.

Alcibiades, with a fleet of 100 ships, took up a position off Notium which controlled the passage in and out of Ephesus, but he left his lieutenant, Antiochus, in charge while he supported Thrasybulus in a brief land operation. Antiochus disobeyed orders not to engage in battle with Lysander, and lost a large number of ships. The defeat caused the downfall of Alcibiades who was relieved of his command and denounced by his political enemies. Once again the Athenians removed their most brilliant and experienced general and the only man who could have saved them at this critical time in the war. He feared for his life if he returned to Athens, so retired to his castle in Thrace where he took no further active part in the war.

Alcibiades relieved of command after Notium

The Battle of Arginusae

Since Lysander's term as admiral was over, he was recalled to Sparta and replaced by Callicratidas, who defeated Alcibiades' successor Conon off Lesbos and defeated the Athenian fleet at Mytilene. The Athenian people responded to this crisis with resolution, raising money and manning their ships with citizens from the most humble to the class of knights, and including subjects, metics and slaves.

The Battle of Arginusae was fought in 406 in the waters between Mytilene and the mainland and the Athenians were led by eight of their

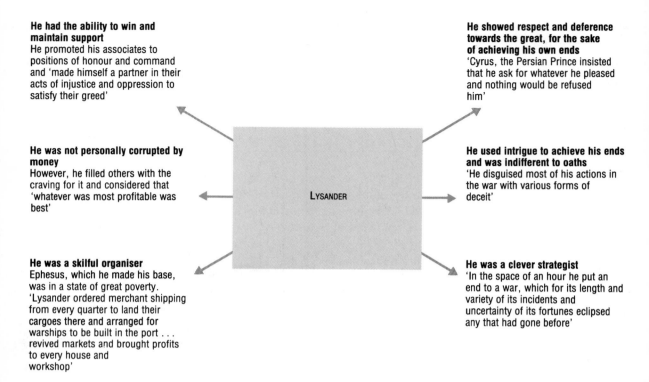

He had the ability to win and maintain support
He promoted his associates to positions of honour and command and 'made himself a partner in their acts of injustice and oppression to satisfy their greed'

He showed respect and deference towards the great, for the sake of achieving his own ends
'Cyrus, the Persian Prince insisted that he ask for whatever he pleased and nothing would be refused him'

He was not personally corrupted by money
However, he filled others with the craving for it and considered that 'whatever was most profitable was best'

He used intrigue to achieve his ends and was indifferent to oaths
'He disguised most of his actions in the war with various forms of deceit'

LYSANDER

He was a skilful organiser
Ephesus, which he made his base, was in a state of great poverty. 'Lysander ordered merchant shipping from every quarter to land their cargoes there and arranged for warships to be built in the port ... revived markets and brought profits to every house and workshop'

He was a clever strategist
'In the space of an hour he put an end to a war, which for its length and variety of its incidents and uncertainty of its fortunes eclipsed any that had gone before'

Plutarch's view of Lysander the Spartan

Deaths of Athenian generals

ten generals, including Pericles, the son of Pericles and Aspasia. It was a disaster for the Spartans, with the loss of seventy ships and approximately 14 000 men. However, in the stormy seas the Athenian generals were unable to rescue their shipwrecked crews, which doubled the Athenian casualties. The generals were charged by the resentful masses with negligence, and despite their victory were sentenced to death on a single ballot. As under Athenian law each man was entitled to a separate trial, this was an act of senseless and violent injustice. The six generals who returned to stand trial — two had gone into voluntary exile — were put to death without mercy.

Effects of the battle

Offers of peace refused again

The Athenians once again foolishly discarded valuable leaders at a time when they needed to conserve all their resources.

If Sparta were to recover, it would be as a dependant of Persia and to avoid this, the Spartans again offered to make peace with Athens. The Athenians, led by Cleophon, again refused and must be condemned for their utter stupidity, since Athens was physically and financially exhausted and Lysander had appeared in the Aegean again.

The final defeat of Athens at Aegospotami, 405

At the request of Cyrus of Persia and the Greek cities of Asia Minor to reappoint Lysander as admiral, the Spartans sent him out as a deputy, since it was their law not to allow the same man to hold the position twice.

Lysander sailed to the Hellespont and captured the city of Lampsacus in order to intercept the Athenian corn ships, while Conon and the other Athenian generals with the entire fleet of 180 ships took up a position on the opposite shore at a place called Aegospotami.

Lysander's strategy at Lampsacus

Observing Lysander's strategy day after day from his stronghold nearby, Alcibiades realised that the Athenians were unaware of their danger. However, when he attempted to warn them and suggested that they move to a safer location along the coast, they rudely rebuffed him.

Alcibiades' advice ignored

Each day the Athenians' fleet had crossed over to offer battle and each day Lysander had refused, but on the fifth day, as the Athenians were disembarking for their evening meal, Lysander attacked. It was not a battle, but a slaughter.

He captured 160 Athenian ships and put to death over 3000 Athenian prisoners.

The end of Athens at sea

Effects of the defeat

The long war was over. Athens had no choice but to surrender or be starved into submission—she had no men, ships, money, food or allies (except Samos).

Lysander blockaded the Piraeus while the Spartan kings Agis and Pausanias approached the city by land. Provisions began to fail, so the Athenians at last made proposals for peace, but Sparta intimated that the terms would include the destruction of the Long Walls. It was stupidity to resist, but this the Athenians did. Cleophon had twice before hindered the conclusion of peace when it might have been made with honour (after Cyzicus and Arginusae), and he now hindered it again when it could only be made with humiliation. An absurd decree was passed, that no one should ever propose to accept such terms.

Athens starved into submission

Starvation was imminent when Theramenes and nine others went to Sparta to accept peace terms. Meanwhile, at Athens Cleophon was put to death on a charge of desertion.

Peace terms accepted by Athens, 404

1 Destruction of the Long Walls and the fortifications at Piraeus.
2 Loss of all foreign territories, including their cleruchies at Imbros, Lemnos and Scyrus.

Humiliation for Athens

3 The return of all exiles to Athens.
4 Surrender of all triremes except twelve.
5 Athens to become an ally of Sparta, pledged to accept her leadership.

The rule of the Thirty

A commission of thirty oligarchs, set up to draft a new constitution based on the 'ancient' type, was supported by a Spartan garrison which occupied the Acropolis.

Reign of terror

Critias (a returned exile) and other extreme oligarchs in the Thirty had no intention of framing a constitution, and implemented a policy of violence against the democrats. The chief democrats were charged with conspiracy, and many thousands of innocent citizens were killed and their property confiscated. Others fled into exile, from where they organised opposition, and when the democrats seized the Piraeus a destructive civil war resulted in which Critias lost his life.

Full democracy restored

After the loss of influence of Lysander in Sparta, Pausanias the Spartan king and Thrasybulus the Athenian democrat achieved a reconciliation which brought an end to the one and a half years of tyranny, bloodshed and foreign occupation. In 403–402, full democracy was re-established on a base firmer than ever.

Reasons for the defeat of Athens

Athenian defeat due to own mistakes

At the beginning of the war, led by Pericles, Athens was at the peak of her power. Her military, naval and financial resources together with the strategy laid down by Pericles should have carried her through to victory. Yet in 404, physically and financially exhausted and with her fleet destroyed, she was starved into submission and was forced to accept the humiliation of a Spartan garrison occupying the Acropolis.

Thucydides outlines what he regards as the main reasons for Athens' failure in the war.[85]
1 The death of Pericles early in the war.
2 Changes in his strategy.
3 Self-interest and ambitions of leaders after Pericles' death.
4 The Sicilian campaign.
5 The revolt of Athens' allies.
6 Persian involvement on the side of Sparta
7 Athens' internal strife

Further factors to be considered

The Athenian demos

- Fickle, easily influenced by demagogues.
- Unwise choice of leaders, both political (Cleon, Cleophon) and military (Nicias).
- Greed for war plunder (Sicilian campaign, 415).
- Repeated failure to make peace — after Pylos, Cyzicus, Arginusae and Aegospotami.
- Internal political dissensions. The oligarchic faction and coup of 411 disrupted the war effort and weakened Athens. The war-party was overconfident.
- Deliberate rejection (twice) of Alcibiades' leadership and the death penalty imposed on the generals after Arginusae wasted valuable human resources.
- Change in attitude as the war progressed — increasing brutality alienated allies.
- Refusal to withdraw from Sicily.

Blunders by Athenian people

Leadership

Cleon

- Abandoned Pericles' policy and adopted an aggressive expansionist policy.
- Refused to accept peace after Pylos.
- Expressed brutality in the Mytilenian debate.

Policies of leaders often misguided

Nicias

- Was unable to counter Cleon's and Alcibiades' influence with the Athenian people (see section entitled 'Mistakes made by the Athenians during the Sicilian Campaign', page 260).

Alcibiades

- Reversed Nicias' peace — made alliance with Argos.
- Instigated disastrous Sicilian campaign.
- Defected to Sparta — advice concerning Gylippus and Decelea.
- Detached Ionians from Athens.
- Supported oligarchic coup.

Cleophon

- A radical democrat — continued to refuse Sparta's offer of peace.

Instability of the Athenian Empire

- Athens was always fighting on two fronts — there was constant fear of revolts.
- Her allies — for example, Mytilene, Chios, Erythrae and Euboea — revolted.
- She suffered loss of manpower, revenue and raw materials.

Problems with allies

Loss of several navies **Continued loss of Athenian ships**   Athens found increasing difficulty in rebuilding her fleet.

Plague **Unforeseen problems**   The outbreak of the plague so early in the war had an effect on morale and manpower. This, however, should not be overestimated.

Sparta

Sparta's advantages
- Sparta had the advantage of a more stable alliance.
- She had leaders such as Brasidas, Gylippus and Lysander.
- She had help from Alcibiades and from Persia.

Persian involvement in the war

Persian aid
- Tissaphernes and Pharnabazus gave support to rebellious Athenian allies and to Sparta.
- Persian gold was provided to build a Peloponnesian fleet and to pay the crews.
- Cyrus supported Lysander wholeheartedly.

The results of the Peloponnesian War

Great suffering throughout Greece

The Peloponnesian War ... not only lasted a long time, but throughout its course brought unprecedented suffering for Hellas. Never before had so many cities been captured and then devastated, whether by foreign armies or by the Hellenic powers themselves (some of these cities, after capture, were resettled with new inhabitants); never had there been so many exiles; never such loss of life — both in the actual warfare and in internal revolutions.[86]

Enormous Athenian losses

Athens' losses were formidable. Her population was depleted by war, plague, exile and deliberate massacre. The plague alone is said to have killed 17 000 soldiers, and approximately 40 000 men were lost in Sicily. Citizen manpower was cut by almost half and many of the older aristocratic families were practically wiped out. Loss of wealth (owing to war costs), loss of imperial revenue and interruption to trade and farm production led to bankruptcy. At the beginning of the war there had been a surplus of 6000 talents and an annual imperial revenue of 1000 talents. It has been estimated that approximately 35 000 talents were lost during the war. Her navy and her command of the sea were gone, and agriculture in Attica never really recovered from the ravages and neglect caused by the almost annual invasions of her territory and the occupation of Decelea.

Yet despite the sufferings caused by the war, it was a time of intellectual and artistic triumphs, exemplified by the works of such men as Thucydides, Sophocles, Euripides and Aristophanes.

Sparta, although the victor and the military and political hegemon of

Greece for a generation after the war, was on the brink of a decline. Victory brought with it internal decay. The number of Spartans with full citizenship was reduced to approximately 2000; this was due not only to war but to the influx of money and the spoils of foreign conquest. According to the Lycurgan system it was illegal to use gold and silver in Sparta, but individuals amassed gold and many grew rich at the expense of their poorer peers, who often bartered away their land. Without land a Spartan was unable to pay his annual dues to his mess, and this led to disfranchisement. The number of inferiors increased. Wealth corrupted the Spartans, who lost their self-control and became indulgent and increasingly inefficient. The discontented inferiors, perioeci and helots remained a constant danger to Sparta's authority both within and outside the Peloponnese.

Decline in Sparta — influx of wealth

Plutarch recounts the disgrace and exile of Gylippus, the Spartan commander in Sicily. He had been entrusted by Lysander with what remained of the Athenian public funds, but instead of handing it all over to the ephors, he stole a large supply of 'Attic Owls' (coins) and hid them under the tiles of his roof. 'He tarnished his brilliant reputation by this mean and ignoble action'.[87]

Corruption and disgrace of Spartan leaders

Lysander's subsequent career (after Aegospotami) reveals an extreme ambition and arrogance; according to Plutarch, he planned to abolish the claim of the two royal houses to the throne and open it to the whole Heraclid tribe. 'Lysander hoped that if the throne were to be disposed of on this principle, no Spartan would be chosen before himself'.[88]

As a result of their success, many Spartans were corrupted not only by money but by power.

The end of the Peloponnesian War did not bring peace to the Greeks. The fifty years after Aegospotami were marked by continuing interstate wars, factional fights, imperial aggressions, futile peace settlements and the interference of Persia in Greek politics, which further divided and weakened their cities.

Further fifty years of fighting

Sparta and Thebes each held military supremacy for a short time, but neither was capable of holding together the disunited Greek cities or of leading them peacefully. Each state attempted to hold power at the expense of its neighbours; few lessons had been learnt by either. For a time Athens recovered her sea power and prestige and formed a new Athenian Confederacy.

The war resulted in the rise of the mercenary soldier. The substantial number of exiles — due to economic dislocation and internal political struggles — and a large body of runaway slaves provided armies not only for adventurers such as Jason of Pherae (Thessaly) but also for Carthage, Persia and the Greek cities themselves. The existence of these armies prolonged wars and mercenary soldiers were always a problem in time of peace.

The rise of the mercenary soldier

Xenophon's Anabasis

The *anabasis*, or the march of the so-called Ten Thousand Greeks, recorded by the soldier-historian Xenophon is a dramatic example of the use of mercenaries. Cyrus, the younger son of Darius II, raised an army of somewhere between 11 000 and 13 000 Greeks from all over the Greek world—but particularly from the Peloponnese—in order to take the throne of Persia from his brother, Artaxerxes. Xenophon recounts their expedition to Babylon, the death of Cyrus and the strenuous 1600 kilometre retreat to the Black Sea, from where they enrolled in the service first of a Thracian leader and subsequently of Sparta against Persia. This incredible episode was the forerunner of Alexander the Great's expeditions, and its significance is that it revealed the military weaknesses of the Persian Empire.

Athens — financial and cultural centre in the fourth century

Despite the tragedy suffered by Athens in the last years of the fifth century and the loss of her political pre-eminence, she remained the centre of learning and intellectual creativity and developed into the financial and banking centre of the Greek world in the fourth century.

Phases of the Peloponnesian War — a review

		Events	Personalities
Archidamian War	431	Thebans attack Plataea Spartan King Archidamus leads invasion of Attica; evacuation of Attica to Athens	Pericles (Athens)
	430	Spartans invade Attica Athenian fleet under Pericles raids coast of Peloponnese Plague hits Athens Surrender of Potidaea	King Archidamus (Sparta)
	429	Plague — death of Pericles Spartans besiege Plataea Victory of Phormio in north-west	
	428	Spartans invade Attica Revolt in Lesbos (Mytilene)	Phormio (Athens)
	427	Cleon comes to the fore — Spartans invade Attica Capture and destruction of Plataea Surrender of Mytilene Laches' mission to Sicily	
	426	Demosthenes' defeat in Aetolia Peloponnesian unsuccessful offensive in the west.	Cleon (Athens)

		Events	Personalities
Archidamian War		Death of Spartan King Archidamus Demosthenes' victory at Olpae	
	425	Spartans invade Attica Cleon gains ascendancy over Nicias Expedition to Sicily detained at Pylos Demosthenes occupies Pylos Demosthenes and Cleon capture Spartans on Sphacteria Allied tribute doubled	Nicias (Athens)

	424	Operation against Boeotia fails
		    — Athenians defeated at Delium
		Athenians capture port of Megara but lose
		    Amphipolis in Thrace — Thucydides
		    banished
		Brasidas successful in Chalcidice
			Demosthenes
			    (Athens)
			Brasidas (Sparta)

	423	Temporary truce for one year	
	422	Battle of Amphipolis — Brasidas and Cleon killed	
	421	Peace of Nicias — fifty-year treaty between Athens and Sparta	

Interlude	420	Reshuffling of alliances — Sparta had
		    ignored allies in peace of Nicias;
		    Corinth, Elis and Mantinea join with
		    Argos
		Alcibiades persuades Athens to join
		    Argos
			King Agis (Sparta)

	418	Alcibiades persuades Argos to go to war
		    with Sparta, with Athenian support
		Athens and Argos defeated at Mantinea;
		    Sparta recovers leadership of
		    Peloponnese
			Alcibiades (Athens)

	416	Segesta appeals to Athens for help against
		    Syracuse
		Alcibiades with support of commercial
		    interests carries recommendation for
		    expedition to Sicily
			Nicias (Athens)

Sicilian campaign	415	Mutilation of hermae — Athenians
		    outraged
		Expedition to Sicily under Nicias,
		    Alcibiades and Lamachus
		Indecision loses Athenian advantage
			Alcibiades (Athens)

		Events	Personalities
Sicilian Campaign		Alcibiades recalled to Athens for trial; escapes to Sparta Nicias defeats Syracusans, winters in Catana Alcibiades in Sparta persuades Spartans to send Gylippus to organise and lead Syracusans	Nicias (Athens)
	414	Athenians take the heights of Epipolae and begin building a wall to cut Syracuse off on landward side Part left unfinished — Gylippus slips through with reinforcements Lamachus killed — Nicias sole commander Athenians confined to camp by Gylippus' cross-wall	Lamachus (Athens)
	413	Athenian naval base captured Reinforcements arrive from Athens under command of Demosthenes Demosthenes fails in attempt to take Epipolae. Need to withdraw but Nicias delays due to an eclipse Indecisive naval battle in Syracuse Harbour — Athenian fleet unable to escape Retreat of forces — killed, captured Loss of Nicias, Demosthenes, 40 000 men and 240 ships	Gylippus (Sparta) Demosthenes (Athens)
Decelean War	413	Athens' condition critical as Spartans occupy and fortify Decelea Ten commissioners appointed to take charge Tribute of allies changed to avoid revolt	Tissaphernes (Persia)
	412	Revolt of Athens' allies supported by Persian satraps Persians offer to finance Spartan fleet in return for Asia Minor Athens recovers some allies; Samos loyal, becomes headquarters of Athenian fleet Plans in Athens to overthrow the democracy and set up oligarchy. Moderates want reform. Alcibiades intrigues for oligarchy	Antiphon (Athens) Theramenes (Athens)
	411	Oligarchs led by Antiphon replace Council with new Council of 400 — no intention	

		Events	Personalities
Decelean War		of working with moderates led by Theramenes Democratic fleet replaces commanders and governs from Samos Oligarchs prepare to negotiate with Sparta Counter-revolution of moderate democrats depose Council of 400 — oligarchs flee	Alcibiades (Athens)
	411	Limited vote — rule of the 5000 (temporary) Alcibiades pardoned — remains with fleet which defeats Spartans under Mindarus at Cynossema	Thrasybulus (Athens)
	410	Spartan fleet annihilated at Cyzicus, with help from Alcibiades Full democracy restored	
	408	Alcibiades returns to Athens — appointed Commander-in-Chief of fleet Lysander (Spartan admiral) arranges Persian 'gold'	Mindarus (Sparta)
	406	Alcibiades' lieutenant defeated by Spartans at Notium — Alcibiades removed from office — goes into exile Athenian fleet successful at Arginusae, but generals executed for actions at end of battle Spartan offers of peace rejected	Lysander (Sparta)
	405	Lysander reappointed by Spartans — annihilates Athenian navy at Aegospotami; revolt of allies Peace negotiations	Cyrus (Persia)
	404	Spartan blockade — Athens' surrender — becomes subject ally of Sparta	Cleophon (Athens)

Revision questions

The Archidamian War

1 Which of the two sides was better equipped to carry on a long war? Explain.
2 What was the reaction of (a) the Athenian people, (b) Pericles, to the first invasion of

Attica by the Spartans?
3 What were two important effects of the plague on the future of the war?
4 What was Thucydides' view of Cleon?
5 What were three important results of the

Pylos campaign affecting the future conduct of the war?

6 List five personal qualities of Brasidas that contributed to his success in Thrace and the Chalcidice.

7 Which two groups of people in Athens supported Nicias, and what aspect of his policy made Cleon regard him as an enemy?

8 Give five reasons for the breakdown of the Peace of Nicias.

The Sicilian campaign

1 Why did Nicias oppose the sending of an expedition to Sicily in 415?

2 Describe the incident of the mutilation of the hermae.

3 What were the effects of Alcibiades' recall from Sicily?

4 Explain briefly the quote from Thucydides:

'No Hellenic army had ever suffered such a reverse'.

5 List some of the mistakes made by the Athenian Assembly with regard to the Sicilian campaign.

The Decelean War

1 Explain the reasons Sparta and Persia signed the Treaty of Miletus in 412.

2 Why did Alcibiades fall out with Sparta? Whose support did he then seek?

3 Why did an oligarchic uprising occur in Athens in 411?

4 Give two examples of the stupidity of the Athenian demos in wasting valuable human resources at a very crucial stage in the war.

5 Outline some of Lysander's qualities that helped him defeat the Athenians.

6 Who were 'The Thirty'?

Essay topics

1 To what extent was the outbreak of war between Athens and Sparta inevitable?

2 To what extent were the policies of Pericles responsible for the outbreak of the Peloponnesian War?

3 Account for the Athenian success at Pylos and Sphacteria. What effect did the campaign have on the course of the Peloponnesian War?

4 Compare Thucydides' views of Cleon and of Brasidas.

5 How important was the Sicilian expedition in bringing about the eventual defeat of Athens in the Peloponnesian War? What other factors contributed?

6 How significant for the outcome of the war was the part played by Nicias and Alcibiades?

7 How capable was the Athenian Assembly in directing affairs throughout the war?

8 To what extent was Sparta's victory due to her own strategy rather than to Athens' mistakes?

Timeline: The fifth century

This time line presents an overview of the major events in fifth-century history — covering the content of the preceding four chapters.

Persian Wars	500	
	499	Ionian revolt
	492	First expedition of Persians against Greece
	490	First invasion at Marathon
		Themistocles and Athenian naval development Further cemocratic changes in Athens Spartan leadership of Greek league
	480	Second invasion — Thermopylae and Salamis
	479	End of Persian wars — Plataea and Mycale
Delian League	478	Formation of the Delian League — naval league under Athens' leadership. Cimon commands League fleet. Sparta reluctantly accepts Athens' leadership
	468	Battle of Eurymedon — immediate threat of Persia in Aegean ended. Existence of the league perhaps not justified beyond this point
Growth of Athenian empire	461	Ostracism of Cimon and rise to power of radical democrats in Athens — Ephialtes and Pericles Democracy in Athens becomes more complete Gradual transformation of the Delian League into an empire — beginning of an Athenian land empire (at the expense of the Peloponnesian League) under leadership of Pericles
Periclean Athens — architecture, art, drama, philosophy	445	Thirty years' peace with Sparta signed (lasted fifteen years). Pericles undisputed leader of Athens — responsible for extensive building program (e.g. Parthenon). Democracy functions well under his guidance
Peloponnesian War	431	Events involving Corinth (member of Peloponnesian League) and Athens result in declaration of war between Athens and Sparta and their respective allies First phase of the war — Archidamian War Plague in Athens — death of Pericles

Peloponnesian War	421	Peace of Nicias
		Interval — a period of changing alliances
		Disastrous Sicilian campaign of Athens
	413	Last phase of the war — Decelean war
Defeat and decline of Athens	411	Athens' position critical as she faces a revolt of her allies, internal revolution, defeat and blockade
	404	Pro-Spartan oligarchy set up in Athens
		Reign of terror
	400	Full democracy restored but Athens no longer a great political force

Further reading

Primary sources

Aristophanes. *The Knights.*
_____ . *The Wasps.*
Aristotle. *The Athenian Constitution.*
Plutarch. *The Rise and Fall of Athens.*
Thucydides. *The Peloponnesian War.*
Xenophon. *Hellenica.*

Secondary sources

Adcock, F. E. *Thucydides and His History.*
Burn, A. R. *Pericles and Athens.*
Bury, J. B. *The Ancient Greek Historians.*
Bury, J. B. & Meiggs, R. *A History of Greece.*
Cambridge Ancient History, vol. 5.
De Ste Croix, G. E. M. *The Origins of the Peloponnesian War.*
Hammond, N. G. L. *A History of Greece to 322 B.C.*
Kagan, D. *The Archidamian War.*
_____ . *The Outbreak of the Peloponnesian War.*
_____ . *Problems in Ancient History*, vol. 1.

Spartan and Theban leadership of Greece

10

Spartan and Theban leadership

Sparta's failure to maintain her leadership, 404–371 B.C.

Spartan leadership — first phase

404

A FTER THE DEFEAT at Aegospotami, the Aegean cities passed under the control of Sparta. Lysander set up decarchies (Boards of 10) supported by Spartan garrisons and *harmosts* (military governors), and exacted tribute.

> He also suppressed both the democratic and other forms of government in the Greek cities of Asia Minor and left one Spartan administrator in each, and under him ten magistrates chosen from the political clubs which he had established everywhere. — Plutarch[1]

Thirty pro-Spartan oligarchs were set up in Athens, with a Spartan garrison.

403

Democracy was fully restored in Athens in 403.

In 402 Lysander was deposed; he travelled to Egypt, where he carried on intrigues calculated to change the Spartan constitution.

400

The Spartans, who had ceded Ionia to Persia in return for Persian support, were now called in to protect the Asiatic Greeks. Agesilaus, who came to

281

the Spartan throne with the help of the returned Lysander, led a fleet to Asia Minor. Lysander

> wrote to his friends in Asia Minor asking them to invite the Spartans to send Agesilaus as commander-in-chief in their war against the barbarians. — Plutarch[2]

> Agesilaus now re-established order among the cities of the coast and restored to them the constitutional forms of government... Next he determined to advance further into the interior and to transfer the theatre [of war] from the Greek seaboard to the heart of Persia. — Plutarch[3]

395

The Persians stirred up opposition to Sparta in the cities of mainland Greece through a Persian agent, Timocrates, who had been given gold to distribute to states hostile to Sparta. Thebes, Corinth, Argos and Athens were already alienated by Sparta's abuse of authority. Thebes led a revolt against Sparta; Lysander was killed leading a Spartan attack on Thebes.

394

King Agesilaus was recalled from Asia in 394.

> The gold coins of Persia at this time were stamped with the figure of an archer, and Agesilaus declared that the king was driving him out of Asia with the help of ten thousand archers: this was the sum of money which had been sent to Athens and Thebes and distributed to the demagogues, and it was for this reason that their peoples now went to war with the Spartans. — Plutarch[4]

So developed the Corinthian War — Athens, Argos, Thebes and Corinth gathered at Corinth, but were defeated by Sparta at Nemea. A second defeat occurred at Coronea, inflicted by the returning army of Agesilaus. Corinth was blockaded, and for three years the war around Corinth was a stalemate.

> How else can one describe that spirit of envy which now diverted the attention of the Greeks to forming alliances and conspiracies against one another... and which turned against themselves the very weapons that had been trained on the barbarians.... — Plutarch[5]

Persian money now enabled the exiled Athenian, Conon, to man a large squadron and defeat the Spartan fleet at Cnidus. Persians now had control of the Aegean and expelled Spartan garrisons.

393

Conon sailed back to Athens under a Persian flag, and with Persian funds the Long Walls were rebuilt and the Piraeus refortified. The naval power of Athens revived in the Aegean — Lemnos, Imbros and Scyrus were recovered.

390

In the years 390–389 Athens made alliances with Thasos and Samothrace, the Chersonese, Byzantium, Chalcedon and many other cities of Asia Minor.

In the following year Sparta made overtures to Persia, through Antalcidas.

Spartan leadership — second phase

387

The Persians were becoming concerned about Athens' naval revival. An alliance with Sparta resulted in defeat for the Athenian fleet in the Hellespont.

386

In 386 Persia summoned the Greek states to meet at Sardis to sign a peace, the so-called 'King's Peace'. Persia was to keep all states in Asia, including the islands of Clazomenae and Cyprus; all states in Greece were to be autonomous except Lemnos, Imbros and Scyrus, which belonged to Athens. Sparta was to be the enforcer of the Peace. Thebes was no longer able to preside over the Boeotian League, as all states took the oath separately.

> However it is he (The Persian King) who controls the destinies of the Hellenes, who dictates what they must each do, and all but sets up his viceroys in their cities. For with this one exception what else is lacking? Was it not he who decided the issue of the war, was it not he who directed the terms of peace and is it not he who now presides over our affairs? — Isocrates[6]

382

Sparta treacherously seized the citadel of Thebes in 382, and in 379 she destroyed the powerful Chalcidian League, for infringing the King's Peace.

The Thebans recovered their city under Pelopidas in the years 379–378, and subsequently Athens established the Second Athenian Confederacy, to oppose Spartan aggression.

> 'If any of the Greeks or of the barbarians dwelling on the mainland, or of the islanders, except such as are subjects of the King, wish to be allies of the Athenians and their allies, they may become such, while preserving their freedom and autonomy, using the form of government that they desire without either admitting a garrison or receiving a commandant or paying tribute upon the same terms as the Chians, Thebans and the other allies'.[7]

Theban leadership

The Spartans were defeated by the Athenians at sea off Naxos, in 376.

371

In 371 the Peace of Callias was signed. A repetition of the 'Kings' Peace', it declared the independence of all states and a policy of nonaggression. Thebes was excluded when Epaminondas claimed to sign for all of Boeotia. Sparta supported independence of Boeotian cities.

At the Battle of Leuctra, between Sparta and Thebes, Epaminondas unexpectedly defeated Sparta, with great slaughter; the Thebans thus extended their leadership over central Greece.

In the following year the influence of Thebes was further extended, over Thessaly and Macedon. She interfered in the Peloponnese; she invaded Laconia, and liberated and restored Messenia.

366

She next attempted to surround Sparta with enemies by supporting an Arcadian League, with Megalopolis as its centre — Sparta was now no longer leader in the Peloponnese.

362

By 362 Thebes had lost the support of some of the Arcadian cities, so marched into the Peloponnese to aid those who remained loyal. At the subsequent Battle of Mantinea, Epaminondas defeated a combined Spartan, Athenian and Mantinean force, but was himself killed. His death marked the end of Theban supremacy, based as it was on the skill and leadership of one man.

Both sides claimed the victory, but it cannot be said that with regard to the accession of new territory, or cities, or power either side was any better off after the battle than before it. In fact, there was even more uncertainty and confusion in Greece after the battle than there had been previously. — Xenophon[8]

Sparta's failure to maintain her leadership, 404–371

Alcibiades had assured the Spartans, in 414, that once they had destroyed the future prospects of Athens they would live in safety and become the leaders of the whole of Hellas, whose people would follow them voluntarily — not from coercion but from goodwill.[9]

By 404 they were the leaders of Hellas, but they had neither freed the Hellenes — which had been their avowed intention for entering the war—nor were likely to be able to lead them with goodwill or without resorting to force. There were contradictions between Sparta's so-called aim to liberate the Greeks, her agreement to hand over the Asiatic Greeks to Persia and her replacing Athens as the chief Aegean power.

Conflict between aims and methods

If her desire to free the Greeks was to be considered genuine, she should have retired to Sparta and left the states recently freed from Athens to decide their own governments and futures, but she had already established, through Lysander, firm military despotism in those states. The puppet governments, based on the political clubs established by Lysander, comprised ten pro-Spartan oligarchs and a Spartan *harmost* (military governor). They initiated reprisals against democrats, and the Spartan military governors, free of control from home, were rapacious and tyrannical. Lysander had

'Puppet' governments of Lysander

'complete autonomy over cities; . . . untold numbers of the democratic parties were massacred, for Lysander had men put to death, not only to settle his personal scores, but to gratify the greed and hatred of his friends in each city.[10]

If Sparta was to fulfil her contract with the Persians she could not be regarded as a liberator, and if she aimed to protect the Greeks of Asia Minor from Persia, then she was faced with a war for which she would need allies, naval bases in the Aegean, and tribute.

In 404 Sparta entered on an imperialistic course for which she was entirely unsuited and for which there was no justification at that point, since—unlike the Athenians seventy-five years earlier, in 479, who had taken up the cause of the eastern Greeks against Persia—the Spartans had treacherously betrayed the Asiatic Greeks to Persia. Also, unlike Athens in and after 479, she had no common economic ties with her allies and subjects.

Sparta's imperialistic course

Internal conditions and problems

In 479, when Sparta had had the opportunity to become hegemon of the Greeks both on land and sea, she had given up the leadership of the maritime Greeks in favour of Athens, since she was not a naval power and was unsuited to controlling territories far from Sparta. Was she any different in 404? Only a complete revolution in her institutions and her way of life could have prepared her for the job of an imperial power.

No more suited to rule in 404 than in 479

- The number of full Spartan hoplites with full citizenship had been reduced drastically. More *neodamodes* (freed helots) made up the army, and as Sparta pursued a more imperialistic policy, mercenary troops had to be recruited.
- An enormous body of discontented inferiors (those who had lost their citizenship), perioeci and helots increased the possibility of conspiracies

against the government such as the conspiracy of Cinadon, in 397.

- Spartan officers and leaders frequently abused their powers—for example, Gylippus and Clearchus (Byzantium), Callibius (Athens) and Lysander.

Problems—decline in numbers, corruption and conservatism

- Inequalities of wealth led to a decline in the number of Spartan citizens, while greed, indulgence and corruption increased.
- The financial and political responsibilities were in the hands of the gerousia (a body of old men) and the annually elected ephors. The gerontes were conservative and lacked the imagination that was essential in guiding an imperial state. New ideas were treated with suspicion.
- Sparta failed to adapt to changing military tactics.

Persia's role

Dependence on Persia

The success of Sparta's leadership of Greece depended to a large extent on the continued support of Persia. However, for a time the Persians backed Sparta's opponents in Greece, providing funds to encourage Argos, Corinth, Thebes and Athens to start a counterwar—although they did not need much encouragement.

The Spartan navy was defeated in the Aegean by the Athenian commander, Conon, with the backing of Persia, and the Athenian Long Walls and fortifications at Piraeus were rebuilt with the help of Persian funds.

However, the Spartan admiral, Antalcidas,

> succeeded in coming to an arrangement by which the King (of Persia) would join in the war on the side of Sparta, unless the Athenians and their allies would accept the peace which he, the King, was dictating.[11]

The Athenians were anxious to make peace, since they were afraid—now that the Persians had decided to throw their weight behind Sparta—that they would be overwhelmed.

When the King's Peace (Peace of Antalcidas) was signed in 386 Sparta become the enforcer, doing the Persian king's bidding by breaking up any dangerous alliances or groupings of states.

Betrayal of Greek freedom

Any state which put the friendship of Persia ahead of the interests of the Greek states could not lead by goodwill.

Alienation of former allies

From the beginning Sparta acted as if she alone had won the Peloponnesian War, rather than it being a victory of the Spartan alliance. Boeotia, Megara, Corinth and others had contributed the bulk of the military and naval resources to the Peloponnesian effort and had suffered severely. The first cracks appeared in the alliance when peace was signed, as the allies had wanted a harsher treatment for Athens. Sparta, not the alliance, controlled Athens and received tribute from her, and the spoils of war were not divided among the victorious allies.

Opposition of former allies

Corinth and Thebes had already indicated their resentment by supporting Athenian exiles during the rule of the Thirty, and after ten years of Spartan misrule her former allies were prepared to meet her in a trial of strength.

Strong anti-Spartan parties were organised in the cities of Boeotia, and in 395 Thebes and Athens joined in a defensive alliance 'for all time'. In the conflicts of the so-called Corinthian War between Sparta and the city-states of Thebes, Corinth, Argos and Athens, Sparta's two victories—at Corinth (Nemea) and Coronea—were not as significant as the disastrous defeat they suffered at the hands of the Athenian, Iphicrates. He revolutionised Greek military tactics by using *peltasts* (more mobile, lighter armed troops) alongside the heavy-armed hoplites. One whole division of Spartan hoplites was wiped out and this defeat was a forerunner to the Battle of Leuctra, which took place some years later.

Anti-Spartan activities

Increased political and military intervention after the King's Peace

Sparta's leadership after 386 was marked by increased repression, brutality and separatism. She made sure that no other Greek state or combination of states was strong enough to oppose her, and any that refused or hesitated to adopt oligarchic governments were severely disciplined.

Repression and brutality to weaken opponents

In a series of incidents between 386 and 379 she weakened Mantinea and Phlius, broke up the Boeotian and Chalcidian Leagues and established garrisons in central Greece.

- Democratic Mantinea refused to raze her walls and Sparta laid siege to her, eventually dividing the city into five separate villages which joined the Spartan alliance.
- In 382 Leontiades, an oligarchic leader of Thebes, betrayed the city to Sparta, who seized the Theban acropolis (Cadmea) and garrisoned it.
- The cities of the Chalcidice were experimenting with federalism. A group of settlements centred on the city of Olynthus formed themselves into a single state with Olynthian citizenship, and these—in combination with other towns in the region—made up the Chalcidian League. When overtures were made by the cities of the Chalcidian League to Athens and Thebes, two Spartan forces were sent against Olynthus, which was forced to surrender; the League was dissolved in 379.
- The town of Phlius refused to accept an oligarchic government, to

Destroyed attempts at unity — leagues, federalism

which Sparta retaliated by starving the population into submission, garrisoning it for six months and giving the fifty oligarchs the right to try and execute any citizens.

Second Athenian Confederacy

- When Sphodrias (the Spartan commander of Thespiae) decided to march by night, seize the Piraeus and threaten Athens, the Athenians became increasingly hostile to Sparta. Although Sphodrias failed in his attempt, Athens sided more openly with Thebes and in 378 began to form the Second Athenian Alliance (Confederacy).

The Second Athenian Confederacy, the growth of Thebes and the futile attempts at peace

The new Athenian Confederacy (established in 377) invited all states to join in free alliance for mutual defence against Sparta. Although the Confederacy carried out a naval war against Sparta in the Aegean, the strain on its resources was too great.

Leadership in Thebes of Epaminondas and Pelopidas

Under the able leadership of Epaminondas and Pelopidas the Thebans had regained control of their city, which was swiftly growing more powerful; Thebes was the equal of Sparta in heavy infantry and her superior in equipment, tactics and cavalry. It was the age of scientific warfare and the Spartans were to find themselves handicapped by out-of-date tactics. The cities of Boeotia formed a single state, with Thebes as the centre of government. They had been prepared to sacrifice some of their independence for the unified whole.

Peace of Callias — Thebes excluded

In 371, when the growing power of Thebes seemed more of a menace than Sparta, Athens called for a peace settlement (the Peace of Callias) which, if successful, would prevent Greece from disintegrating any further and would put a stop to Persian interference in Greek affairs. Athens and Sparta signed on behalf of their allies, but when Epaminondas insisted on signing for Boeotia and not just for Thebes, King Agesilaus of Sparta acted in a manner contrary to Hellenic interests by refusing to accept Epaminondas' signature, so cutting Thebes out of the peace settlement.

The Battle of Leuctra, 371

Myth of Spartan invincibility destroyed

In 371 the Spartans sent an army under King Cleombrotus to teach Thebes a lesson, but Epaminondas led the Boeotians to victory at Leuctra despite the Spartan superiority in numbers. Epaminondas used his cavalry and superior tactics to end once and for all the supremacy of Spartan hoplites. King Cleombrotus and 400 Spartiates died, and with the end of Spartan military domination the Peloponnesian League fell apart, as the Peloponnesian states revolted against their pro-Spartan oligarchs.

Epaminondas' policy in the Peloponnese

Epaminondas' policy after Leuctra was to undermine the economic base of the Spartan state and isolate Sparta within the Peloponnese.

In 370 Boeotia was called to aid the Arcadian cities, as the Peloponnese was in violent turmoil. Epaminondas raided Laconia as far as the Eurotas Valley—threatening Sparta herself—and liberated Messenia. The helots who had been enslaved by Sparta for over two hundred years were helped to organise a free state, with its capital on the stronghold of Ithome. The loss of the helots and the richest half of her land was not only economic disaster to Sparta, but undermined her whole social and political way of life.

Economic disruption to Sparta

Independent Messenia

The city of Mantinea, destroyed by Sparta in 386–385, was rebuilt and reorganised; the cities of Arcadia formed themselves into a league, and with the help of Epaminondas founded and fortified a new city, called Megalopolis, as their capital.

Isolation of Sparta

Sparta's attempt at leadership failed partly because her rigid conservatism hindered her from developing an imaginative and efficient way of dealing with her subjects and allies. She was unable to organise them into any long-lasting union, and offered them few advantages. Her success as a leader in Greece had depended on the continued support of Persia, and her military supremacy was lost once and for all at Leuctra because of her inability to adapt to changing military tactics.

Sparta's failure to adapt military techniques

For a brief period after Leuctra, Thebes (under Epaminondas and Pelopidas) led a strong confederacy of Phocis, Locris, Aetolia and Euboea, with Thessaly and Macedon temporarily under their leadership. It was during this time that the young Philip of Macedon spent three years as a hostage in Thebes, where he learnt the military tactics of Epaminondas.

Brief Theban hegemony under Epaminondas

Thebes did not have the resources to compete with Athens at sea and Epaminondas' hopes of building a Theban empire with Persian backing came to nothing. Theban policy in the Peloponnese was divisive and the slaughter of all the male inhabitants of the city of Orchomenos for suspected disloyalty (364) aroused anti-Theban sentiments in Arcadia and led to the formation of a hostile alliance centred on Mantinea. Epaminondas entered the Peloponnese for the last time and offered battle to the opposing alliance on the Plain of Mantinea in 362. He used the same winning strategy he had employed at Leuctra, but despite the Theban victory, Epaminondas fell in battle. His last words to his countrymen were that they should make peace.

Anti-Theban movement in Peloponnese

The sudden collapse of Thebes, following the death of Epaminondas, indicated that Thebes was even less suited than Sparta to lead Hellas.

Theban collapse with death of Epaminondas

The city-states of Greece had destroyed themselves with their petty quarrels, selfishness and insistence on absolute independence for themselves while failing to grant the same freedom to others. No state had been strong enough to dominate Greece and bring unity and peace.

Further reading

Primary sources

Isocrates. *Panegyric.*
Plutarch. *The Age of Alexander (Agesilaus, Pelopidas).*
_____ . *The Rise and Fall of Athens (Lysander).*
Xenophon. *Hellenica.*

Secondary sources

Bury, J. B. & Meiggs, R. *A History of Greece.*
Cambridge Ancient History, vol. 6.
Hammond, N. G. L. *A History of Greece to 322 B.C.*
McDermott, W. & Caldwell, W. *Readings in the History of the Ancient World.*

The rise of Macedon under Philip II, 359–336 B.C.

11

Summary of assignment
Macedonia — the land and the people
Aims and organisation of Philip II
Demosthenes of Athens
Achievement of Philip — evaluation

DURING the fourth century B.C. some of the original features of the Greek poleis (city-states) underwent certain changes. These included

- a decline in self-sufficiency, due to increasing wealth and trade;
- the growth of the professional soldier—generals were no longer politicians, and vice versa;
- a decline in the city-state as the centre of the individual's life and loyalty, due to the spread of philosophy and mystery religions.

After the Battle of Mantinea there was more confusion and disorder than ever in the city-states of Greece; this created a power vacuum into which stepped Philip II of Macedon. In contrast to the system in many Greek states such as Athens, whose democratic institutions made swift and decisive action difficult, Philip was an absolute commander and was able eventually to do for the Greeks what they could not do for themselves. He imposed a degree of unity upon them.

ANCIENT GREECE

Assignment: Philip of Macedon

Completion of this assignment is an essential part of the study of this period.

Table 11.1	Summary of assignment	
	Skills	*Material*
Part A	Comprehension Mapping Creating a time line	Macedonia: ● the geography ● the people Philip's background, abilities and character Philip's aims Events of Philip's rule
Part B	Note-making and using summaries	Organisation of a national army Access to the sea Opposition from Athens Interference in Greek politics Demosthenes' first oration Fall of Olynthus Peace of Philocrates Destruction of Phocis

Part C	Using source material — written evidence
	
	Discussion
		Demosthenes' contribution to Athenian
		    political life: Plutarch's *Demosthenes*,
		    Demosthenes' *Philippics*
		Demosthenes' attitude to Philip

Part D	Interpretation Evaluation	Philip in the Chersonese Second Sacred War — Battle of Chaeronea First and second congresses of Corinth Philip's achievements

Part A

1 *The geography of Macedonia*
   With reference to the map on page 293:
   (a) Name the areas adjacent to Macedonia (A, B, C, D and E) and the Greek states (F, G and H).
   (b) What was the name given to the area marked I?
   (c) Name Philip's capital (a) and the Greek cities (b, c, d and e).
   (d) What advantages did the Greek cities

(b, c, d and e) have, and what effect did they have on Macedonia?
   (e) Explain the importance of ✱ and ✩.
   (f) What resources would the fertile coastal plains and the mountainous uplands provide?
   (g) Find out the relationship between the geography and the political situation in Macedonia prior to the accession of Philip.

292

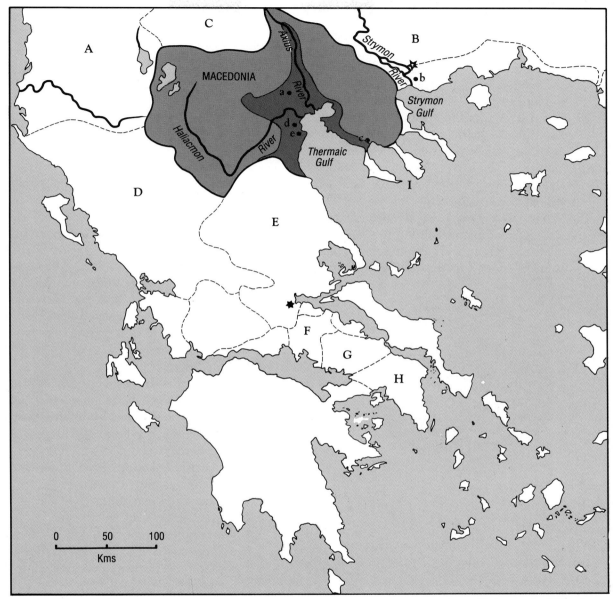

The geography of Macedonia

2 *The Macedonian people*

(a) The Greeks regarded the Macedonians as barbarians. On what grounds did they base this opinion?

(b) What was the Macedonian attitude to Hellenic society and culture? Refer to the period of King Archelaus (413–399).

(c) Macedonia was a disunited country. Explain this in reference to the monarch, clan chiefs and hill tribes.

293

3 *Philip's background, succession, character and abilities*

(a) From the age of fifteen Philip spent three years as a hostage in Thebes. What did he learn in those years that would affect Macedonia and the Greek cities in the future?

(b) The Macedonian monarchy was marked by dynastic quarrels and assassinations. A strong king was necessary if Macedonia was to develop into a powerful state. Explain how Philip, at the age of twenty-three, gained the throne.

(c) What were the characteristics and abilities that enabled Philip to seize and maintain power and within a few years to make himself master of Greece?

A gold coin of Philip II

4 *Philip's aims*

What were Philip's aims in reference to

(a) Macedonia

(b) Greece

(c) Persia

5 *Events of Philip's rule*

Draw a time line from 359 B.C., when Philip seized the throne, through to his assassination in 336. On it show the main events of his rule.

Part B

In order to carry out his aims Philip had to

- develop a powerful national army;
- gain access to the sea;
- secure funds — for example, gain control of the gold mines of Mt Pangaeus;
- find an excuse to be invited into Greece.

The following summary should be used as a guide in making notes on these topics.

1 *The organisation of a national army*

Philip organised the first truly national army. He had studied tactical innovations in Thebes; he built on the work already done by King Archelaus (413–399) and made his first experiments in the closing years of the reign of Perdiccas (365–359). The perfecting of the new Macedonian army must have taken some years, and Philip would have continued to aim at greater efficiency.

(a) The Greek cities, in contrast, were now using mercenaries.

(b) The Macedonian phalanx

- differed from the usual Greek phalanx;
- had individual battalions based on local divisions — loyalty to the group was the starting point for loyalty to Macedon;
- in its armour and weapons possessed a new, longer spear (*sarissa*);
- included the hypaspists.

(c) The Companion Cavalry

- was recruited from landed aristocracy;
- was organised into smaller territorial squadrons — loyalty was directed towards Philip;
- included the royal guard — an elite corps (100).

(d) Ancillary units consisted of

- light cavalry
- peltasts
- slingers
- engineers
- sappers

(e) Training, drill and manoeuvres were carried out.

(f) Roads and fortified posts were built.

(g) Campaigning was continued throughout the year.

(h) Philip used his army to
- protect his frontiers against attack by northern neighbours;
- cripple the Odrysian kingdom of the Thracians — his most serious rival;
- check the disruptive tendencies in his own country;
- inflict blows on the Scythian kingdom, which was expanding south and west;
- continue his attempts to annex Thessaly.

2 *Access to the sea and control of the gold mines of Mt Pangaeus*

Philip needed access to the sea to build a fleet and to have a vantage point against Athenian naval power. He also needed funds with which to finance his national army, equip a fleet and bribe various political factions in other city-states.

Amphipolis guarded the way to Mt Pangaeus and Philip was bound to come into conflict with Athens and the Chalcidic League (centred on Olynthus), but he was not anxious to provoke direct conflict. The next few years were marked by complicated diplomacy, force and concessions. In this period, Philip

(a) besieged and took Amphipolis (357), the most important port in the northern Aegean (he countered Athens' protests by promising Amphipolis to her if she handed over Pydna, but had no intention of keeping his promise — Amphipolis was declared independent);

(b) attacked Pydna in complete disregard of Athens — thus Athens lost her bargaining power;

(c) secured the support of the Chalcidian League by promising Potidaea to Olynthus (it was duly captured and handed over in 356);

(d) appeased the Chalcidian League, which allowed him to move further into Thrace — he settled Macedonians at Crenides and renamed it Philippi;

(e) isolated the Athenian base of Neapolis and held Abdera and Maronea in Thrace (355);

(f) attacked Methone, the last Athenian base on the coast of Macedonia (353).

By playing off Athens against the Chalcidian League, Philip gained
- control of the Thermaic Gulf;
- outlets to the sea along the Thracian coast;
- the mines of Mt Pangaeus, which yielded 1000 talents of silver and gold a year;
- Philippi, which became the centre of a flourishing gold-mining industry.

3 *Opposition from Athens half-hearted*

Athens was in no position to oppose Philip, for the following reasons:

(a) the revolt of Athenian allies: Chios, Rhodes, Byzantium and Cos (357);

(b) financial exhaustion and weariness of war;

(c) hopeless division of policy and lack of solidarity and civic spirit;

(d) Isocrates' urge to accept Philip's leadership and Athens' withdrawal from her naval league and peace;

(e) the young Demosthenes' (in the assembly) urging that careful preparations be made against any menace to freedom — his earliest speeches on foreign policy make no mention of Macedon.

4 *Interference in the complicated politics of Greece — The Sacred War, 356*

(a) The Amphictyonic League.

(b) Phocis, under Philomelus, seized Delphi (356).

(c) 'Sacred' War—Phocis versus Thebes, Locris and Thessaly—using a religious pretext for political purposes.

(d) Funds 'borrowed' from Delphi. Philomelus and 10 000 mercenaries defeated at the Battle of Neon (354).

(e) The Thessalian League appealed to Philip for help against Phocis—Philip eventually inflicted a crushing defeat on Phocian forces in Thessaly.

(f) Philip prepared to march through Thermopylae, punish Phocis and free Delphi. Athenian opposition forced his withdrawal to Macedon. He could afford to wait and concentrated for the next three years on strengthening his hold on Thrace.

5 *Demosthenes' first oration against Philip*
The first 'Philippic' (351) advocated an anti-Macedonian policy for Athens.

6 *Fall of Olynthus, 349–348*
(a) Philip dropped all pretence and attacked the Chalcidic League.

(b) Demosthenes delivered his three Olynthiac speeches—but while Athens deliberated, Philip acted.

(c) Athens was prevented from sending full support to Olynthus as Philip had persuaded cities of Euboea to revolt and secede from Athens.

(d) Olynthus was razed to the ground and the inhabitants dispersed as slaves in Macedonia.

7 *The Peace of Philocrates, 346*
(a) Reasons for Athenian overtures of peace.

(b) Ten envoys included Aeschines, Philocrates and Demosthenes.

(c) Philip received them at Pella.

(d) The peace terms recognised the status quo.

(e) Philip's reservation about Phocis.

(f) The Athenian assembly ratified the treaty, but there was a delay of several months before Philip took the oath.

(g) Before the Athenian envoys reached home, Philip marched through Thermopylae to attack Phocis.

8 *The destruction of Phocis*
(a) Athens refused Philip's invitation to join him in settling the Sacred War.

(b) Towns of Phocis were destroyed; an annual fine was to be paid for the funds embezzled from Delphi.

(c) Macedonia was granted the seat vacated by Phocis on the Amphictyonic Council

(d) Philip presided over the Pythian Festival at Delphi.

(e) Philip valued his reception by the Greeks.

Demosthenes — a Roman copy. The original, which stood in the agora, has been lost

Part C

Demosthenes of Athens

1 Read Plutarch's life of Demosthenes, noting his character and his involvement in and contribution to Athenian political life.

The following are some quotes from Plutarch to help you build up a picture of this great fourth-century orator.

(a) *Character*: 'Demosthenes was sharp and even forceful in avenging any wrongs done to him.'[1]

(b) *Background*: 'Demosthenes' father died when he was seven and left him a considerable inheritance . . . but he was disgracefully treated by his guardians, who appropriated part of his patrimony to their own uses . . . .'[2]

(c) *The beginning of his career as an orator*: '. . . Demosthenes was obliged to make his first appearance in the courts in the effort to recover his property; thereafter he developed such skill and power in pleading and later in public debate, . . . he outstripped all his rivals among the orators in the public assembly.'[3]

He 'created the impression that he was not really an eloquent speaker, but that the skill and the power of his oratory had been acquired by hard work.'[4]

(d) *His venture into politics*: 'It was after the outbreak of the Phocian war (356–346 B.C.) that he first began to take an active part in affairs: we know this partly from his own statements and partly from the speeches he made against Philip.'[5]

(e) *His policy*: '. . . once he had found a noble cause to engage his political activity, that is the defence of the Greeks against Philip, he fought for it with admirable spirit.'[6]

'. . . he allowed no act of Philip's to pass uncriticised, and seized upon every occasion to incite and inflame the Athenians against him.'[7]

2 Read some of Demosthenes' orations, particularly his Philippics. (Refer to *Greek Political Oratory*.)

(a) *The first Philippic, 351*
This is one of his most practical speeches. In it he informed the Athenians that Philip was casting a net about them and that his ambition would never be satisfied. He urged the Athenian people to awake from their apathy and fight. It was a time to end futile diplomacy and a time to enlist citizen troops to supplement the mercenaries, to vote supplies, and to keep a small naval force permanently in the northern Aegean.

(b) *The second Philippic, 346*
This was an abusive attack on Philip as 'the common enemy of Greece' who was bent on the destruction of Athens. Yet Philip, in order to preserve peace, had offered to submit the question of the Thracian cities to arbitration. Nevertheless, Demosthenes and the war party refused the overture.

(c) *The third Philippic, 341*
This speech was a call to all Greece to declare war on Philip, whose peaceful pretensions were not supported by his actions.

Demosthenes points out 'that the peace he speaks of is a peace which you are to observe towards Philip while he does not observe it towards you'. In fact, he declares that Philip is openly at war with Athens and has been so 'from the very day when he annihilated the Phocians' and that 'there is no degree of insolence he does not commit' against the Greeks.

He reprimands the Athenians and the Greeks for allowing Philip to grow so powerful, and complains that 'so deep have the lines been dug which sever city from city' that the Greeks cannot unite and form any combination for mutual support or friendship. He stresses that they must send help to the Chersonese and Byzantium immediately and make immediate preparations for war, 'for though all but ourselves give way and become slaves we at least must contend for freedom'.

While Demosthenes advocated his anti-Macedonian policy Isocrates, an essayist and teacher, wrote a letter to Philip urging him to lead a free and united Greece against Persia. Years before, he had urged the Greeks to accept joint leadership of Athens and Sparta against the Persians. He firmly believed that the Greeks could not unite by themselves and that the days of the small city-states, with their petty quarrels, were over. According to Isocrates, Philip was the only man who could impose unity on Greece, as he had the power, the ability to organise and the money. However, Isocrates was an idealist who believed that it was not Philip's aim to dominate Greece by force and that Greece could be unified by persuasion.

Exercise for discussion
Having considered Demosthenes' attitude to Philip and Isocrates' belief in the future of Greece, discuss the following questions.
1 Was Demosthenes' policy justified in the light of the situation in Athens, the people's attitude, the past failures of the Greeks and the breakdown of the city-state?
2 Was Demosthenes a man of narrow vision or a defender of liberty and autonomy at all costs?

Part D

Thessaly and Thracian Chersonese
1 In the years 346–342, Philip was busy organising Thessaly and expanding eastward towards the western shore of the Black Sea. Explain why this caused grave concern in Athens.
2 The peace of Philocrates, which was really a period of undeclared war, was openly broken by Athens in the Thracian Chersonese. Explain why.
3 Byzantium and Perinthus in the Propontis were nominal allies of Macedon, but they declined to help in the Chersonese. Philip besieged them, but failed; this was his most serious setback since his accession. Why did he fail in the Propontis region?

The second Sacred War (339) and the Battle of Chaeronea (338)
1 Another amphictyonic quarrel gave Philip his second opportunity to enter Greece and settle the differences there. Give details of the events leading to Philip's intervention.
2 Philip used this call for help as a means to carry out his own plans and he fortified the town of Elatea in Phocis. What were his plans?
3 A crisis faced Athens in 338 and Demosthenes then revealed his practical statesmanship and efficiency.
   Comment on this, with particular reference to Demosthenes' attempts to persuade Thebes, the traditional enemy of Athens, to join them in an alliance.
4 Philip made no serious military effort until late in 338, but when he struck it was with characteristic swiftness and certainty of aim. Briefly describe the Battle of Chaeronea (338).
5 Philip's treatment of his two opponents, Athens and Thebes, differed greatly. Account for this.

Lion of Chaeronea

The first and second congresses of Corinth (338–337)

1 Philip summoned a congress of Greek states to meet at Corinth; Sparta alone refused to attend.

What was the purpose of this congress? What were the main features of this Panhellenic League in terms of (a) military arrangements, (b) autonomy, (c) Philip's position within it, (d) the relationship between the Greek states?

2 In 337 a second congress was called, and at it Philip put forward his military plans. What were these plans and how far were they implemented?

3 'Philip created unity of the Greek states, and internal harmony.' To what extent is this statement true?

His death and an evaluation of his work

In 336 Philip was assassinated by one of his own officers, at his daughter's wedding. His reign began and ended in violence.

Philip II has not received due credit in history for two reasons:

1 His arch opponent was Demosthenes, one of the greatest orators in antiquity, and most of our knowledge is drawn from prejudiced sources.

2 He was overshadowed by the genius and achievements of his son, Alexander. Theopompus of Chios, a fourth-century historian, wrote of Alexander that 'never did Europe produce so great a man'.

Evaluate his achievements.
- He united Macedonia.
- He had most of Greece under his control, but envisaged a partnership between the Greeks and the Macedonians.
- He organised a powerful national army.
- He made Macedonia financially secure.
- He planned and put into operation a united Greek effort against Persia.

Evaluate his methods.
Consider to what extent he used
- diplomacy;
- force and threat of force;
- bribery;
- promises, later broken;
- opportunism;
- pro-Macedonian political parties.

Evaluate his treatment of the Greeks, including
- brutality towards Olynthus;
- leniency towards Athens after Chaeronea;
- harshness towards Thebes after Chaeronea;
- no change in Greek governments after the congress of Corinth;

- an attempt to bring an end to the disruptive and disastrous factional conflicts within Greek cities;
- imposition of unity from without.

Evaluate the following statements:

- 'Among the world's political and military geniuses there have been few greater. The vast meaning of Alexander in the history of civilisation is an index to the greatness of his father.'[8]
- 'Philip was the organiser who generally precedes the conqueror and grows the laurels for his successor to wear.'[9]
- Philip has been called by both ancient and modern writers 'A foreign despot who wrought the destruction of Greek liberty'.[10]

Essay topics

1 To what extent did Philip solve the internal problems of his state?

2 What methods were used by Philip of Macedon to extend his control within Greece? How successful was he?

Further reading

Primary sources

Greek Political Oratory (Demosthenes, Isocrates).
The Public Orations of Demosthenes, trans. A. W. Pickard.
Plutarch. *The Age of Alexander (Demosthenes).*

Secondary sources

Bury J. B. & Meiggs, R. *A History of Greece.*
Hammond, N. G. L. *A History of Greece to 322 B.C.*
Hogarth, D. G. *Philip and Alexander of Macedon.*
Kagan, D. *Problems in Ancient History*, vol 1.
Laistner, M. W. L. *A History of the Greek World 479–323 B.C.*

Alexander the Great

Sources

THE MATERIAL written about Alexander during his lifetime and immediately after his death has been lost except for fragments, of which there are approximately 400, from thirty writers.

Lost sources

The original account of Alexander's expedition into Asia was written by Callisthenes, the nephew of Aristotle, who accompanied Alexander. It was his job to keep an official record of the expedition, as well as to send frequent accounts to the Greek cities. He would obviously have used those reports to create a favourable impression of Alexander to the Greeks. However, when Callisthenes fell out with Alexander and was subsequently executed, it is possible that an anti-Macedonian bias became apparent in the works of many notable writers of the time.

Callisthenes' account

Some of Alexander's generals recorded, soon after his death, their personal recollections of him and his actions. Ptolemy, who established himself in Egypt, left a favourable impression, and much of this is included in the works of Arrian. Aristobulus was another contemporary of Alexander who served under him during his expedition.

Ptolemy's account

Existing sources

The five surviving sources for knowledge of Alexander — written between three and five centuries after his death — are Diodorus, Quintus Curtius, Plutarch, Justin and Arrian.

Arrian

Arrian's *Campaigns of Alexander* is the most complete and reliable account, as he names his sources, two of which were contemporaries of Alexander. Arrian says that in his opinion the most reliable writers on the subject were Ptolemy and Aristobulus, not only because they accompanied Alexander but, in the case of Ptolemy, since he was a king himself it would have been more disgraceful for him to lie than for anyone else. Moreover, since both wrote after Alexander died, they had nothing to lose or to gain from writing other than what happened.

Plutarch

Plutarch's account of Alexander is generally favourable, although some of it verges on the romantic. He refers to a large number of sources, one of whom was Callisthenes, the 'official' historian of Alexander.

Justin's work is regarded as unreliable and Curtius is probably suspect; Diodorus contains valuable material, but his dates are confused and his geography is inaccurate.

Because much of the evidence is contradictory, there have been many interpretations of Alexander. It is difficult to tell which sources have been altered, embellished or invented.

Many interpretations of Alexander

Modern historians, such as Tarn, Badian, Burn, Wilcken, Robinson and Welles, have shown how controversial Alexander was by presenting a range of interpretations of his personality and achievements. C. B. Welles expresses the problem thus: 'There have been many Alexanders. No account of him is altogether wrong'.[1] He speaks of the reasonable, mythical, humanitarian, brutal and terrifying Alexander, and of Alexander the dreamer.

Even the most outstanding scholars do not always agree on aspects of Alexander's personality, aims and policy.

Features of Alexander's inheritance, personality and education

Legacy of Philip

When Alexander came to the throne at the age of twenty, he inherited a strong and powerful state, a trained and experienced army with excellent generals, overlordship of the Greek world and the expedition against Persia already set in motion.

Similarities to Philip

He had many personality traits in common with his father, such as quickness in decision making, intellectual perception, personal courage and leadership. He revealed his ability as a warrior at sixteen years of age. When Philip was fighting the Byzantines, Alexander had been left as his father's lieutenant in Macedonia and rather than sit idle he reduced the rebellious Maedi, captured their city, drove out the inhabitants and

Arrian's view of Alexander's personality and abilities.

'Great personal beauty'

'Invincible powers of endurance'

'Brave and adventurous'

'Keen intellect'

'Strict in the observance of his religious duties'

'Noble was his power of inspiring men and filling them with confidence'

'His word and his bond were inviolable'

'Temperate in the pleasures of the body'

'Happy in his deductions from observed facts'

'In military dispositions he was always masterly'

'Uncanny instinct for the right course in a difficult situation'

'His ability to seize the moment for a swift blow was beyond praise'

'Took risks with the utmost boldness'

'Hungry for fame'

'Passion for glory'

'He poured out his money without stint for the benefit of his friends'

Arrian admits that he found fault with some of the things Alexander did ('in the passion of the moment he sometimes erred'), but he was not ashamed 'to express ungrudging admiration' for the man himself. (Refer to Arrian, VII: 28–30.)

The illustration is of a marble head of Alexander, from Pergamum

settled a colony of Greeks there, naming it Alexandropolis. He also led the victorious cavalry charge at Chaeronea when he was only eighteen. Throughout his life he exposed himself to considerable risk, and always shared the dangers with his Macedonian troops.

Features inherited from Olympias

From his mother, Olympias, he inherited a vivid, romantic imagination, a passionate nature and a strong will for power. From an early age he was taught to regard himself as set apart from other men and to believe that he had a special relationship with the gods. Plutarch describes in detail the mystery, dreams, oracles and omens associated with his birth.

Queen Olympias

His preoccupation with the Heroic Age

In his childhood and throughout his life he found inspiration in the Heroic Age, revering both Heracles and Achilles. He became absorbed in winning renown and glory for himself by performing noble deeds and surpassing the feats of the gods and the mythical heroes. Alexander was concerned when Philip captured a city or won a great victory because he was afraid that there would be nothing great or spectacular for him to show the world. 'He cared nothing for pleasure or wealth but only for deeds of valour and glory'.[2] His visit to Troy in 334 immediately after crossing the Hellespont was to sacrifice to Athena and pay homage to the Greek heroes of the Trojan War, particularly to Achilles. One reason for his controversial visit to the oracle of Ammon in the Libyan desert in 332 was, according to Arrian, that Perseus and Heracles had consulted it and he wanted to find out if he would equal them in fame.

The influence of Aristotle

Alexander became a pupil of Aristotle, the most celebrated philosopher of his time, when Philip decided that his strong-willed son needed guidance and control. It was from Aristotle that he received his principles of ethics and politics. Tarn suggests that 'Aristotle had presumably taught him that man's highest good lay in right activity of the soul and Alexander had modified this for himself into strenuous energy of soul and body both'.[3] Other characteristics of Alexander that fitted into the Aristotelian 'great-souled man' were his generosity, a deep affection and concern for his intimate friends, and consideration for women.

His energy and endurance were an inspiration to his men; despite the greatest obstacles or difficulties, Alexander kept going and, by sharing the miseries of his troops, made them better able to endure. Arrian records an incident during the agonising crossing of the Gedrosian Desert when everyone, including Alexander, was tormented by thirst. Alexander refused water himself because there was not enough for everyone; he poured it into the desert, but 'the water wasted by Alexander was as good as a drink for every man in the army'.[4]

His ability to endure hardship

To troops and friends his generosity was unbounded. Before crossing to Asia he lavishly assigned to his companions almost all he possessed in Macedonia; he kept very little of the treasure captured from the Persians for himself; he paid off his men's debts, and rewarded them for their service. 'Alexander was by nature exceptionally generous and became even more so as his wealth increased. His gifts were always bestowed with grace and courtesy . . .'.[5]

His generosity

Examples of his affection and consideration for his friends are recounted by Plutarch and his chivalrous treatment of the women and children of Darius' family, captured after Issus, earned him Darius' gratitude even as he died. '. . . the gods will repay him for his courtesy towards my mother and my wife and my children.'[6]

His affection for friends

Alexander was a lover of all kinds of learning and reading, and had the insatiable curiosity and persistence of a scientist and explorer. But on the other hand, there was a less attractive side to him and as the stress and hardship involved in his conquests—and opposition to him—increased, this became more apparent.

His curiosity

He was supposedly a heavy drinker, as were many Macedonians (including his own father), and despite his great self-discipline he found it difficult to control his violent temper under the influence of drink and was sometimes shaken by passionate outbursts. However, Arrian says that 'his drinking bouts were prolonged not for their own sake—for he was never in fact a heavy drinker—but simply because he enjoyed the companionship of his friends'.[7] Plutarch agrees with this and says that the impression that he was a heavy drinker arose because he liked to have long conversations with his friends, and lingered over his drink. Despite these comments, it must be admitted that the burning of Persepolis and the death of Cleitus did occur while he and others were drinking heavily.

A heavy drinker

When faced with treachery or opposition, he was ruthless. Sometimes his savage cruelty went beyond what was necessary and he showed a streak of vindictiveness. His cruelty to Bessus is vividly described by Plutarch, and his butchery at Massaga was regarded as 'a blot on his career as a soldier'.[8] However, he was a Macedonian king, and as an absolute ruler he could tolerate no opposition to his politics or his person. Opposition could be seen only as conspiracy and revolt. It had to be crushed before it destroyed him, and he therefore had to be more ruthless than his

Ruthless and savage at times

enemies — for example, concerning the supposed conspiracy involving Philotas. His father's example — of crushing all claimants to the throne, and a violent death — was not unusual. Very few Macedonian kings died a natural death.

An enigma

Alexander was an enigma. His intellect was Greek, his temperament was Macedonian and his religious faith sprang from both Greek and Macedonian sources.[9] According to C. B. Welles his nature was dual, but in gigantic proportions:

> . . . on the one hand the radiant hero, charming as a friend to his intimates, as a leader to his army, as the father figure to the enlisted man; on the other hand he was the well-known, terrifying, menacing, angry, gloomy king'.[10]

Problems faced by Alexander, 336–335

His succession

Alexander had to deal first with the matter of his succession, a problem not unusual in Macedonia. Attalus, the father of Philip's second wife Cleopatra, was sponsoring his daughter's infant son as a claimant to the throne. Since Alexander had not been on good terms with his father and the Macedonian nobles had to vote on the succession, Alexander's position was precarious. Attalus was murdered on the orders of Alexander, and Cleopatra and her son were killed at the request of Alexander's mother, Olympias.

Ratification of his position in Greece

General unrest in Greece on his father's death was suppressed when Alexander made a lightning march through central Greece, forcing the Greeks to recognise him and acknowledge his succession to his father's position in the Amphictyonic League. As well, he was elected commander-in-chief of the League of Corinth, and ratified his father's plans against the Persians.

Campaigns against adjacent tribes

Problems nearer home required a swift and decisive campaign. The restless tribes of Thrace and Illyria were subdued in a skilful exhibition of his military prowess, which revealed the quality of his Macedonian soldiers and cavalry.

Revolt of the Greeks

Destruction of Thebes

Demosthenes stirred up trouble in Athens, the Thebans killed their Macedonian garrison, and rumours of Alexander's death led to a general revolt of the Greeks. Alexander appeared before the walls of Thebes and took the city, which was sacked and razed to the ground. His soldiers killed 6000 Thebans, and 30 000 were sold into slavery. Only a few priests, the family of the poet Pindar, and a few others who had connections with Macedonia escaped harsh punishment. Alexander hoped that such a severe example might terrify the rest of Greece into obedience. His savagery here went beyond what was necessary to gain that obedience and Plutarch says that he later often repented his severity and felt such remorse that it made him more lenient to others in the future. He believed that some of his later actions and problems were due to the anger of Dionysus, the protector of Thebes.

Alexander at first demanded that Demosthenes be handed over to him, but later relented. He was lenient towards the Athenians and forgave them all their past offences. Arrian says that he does not find it remarkable that Alexander made a few mistakes—either from impetuosity or from anger—since he was young, but he was certain that Alexander, of all the monarchs of old, was the only one who had the nobility of heart to be sorry for his mistakes'.[11] Alexander was now master of Greece.

Attitude to Athens

Expedition against the Persian Empire

What was Alexander's goal when he crossed into Asia at the head of an army?

His aims

Was it simply a Panhellenic war of revenge against the Persian Empire? It was not a truly Panhellenic affair, since the Greeks provided only a small infantry (7000) and cavalry (600) force, 5000 Greek mercenaries and a small naval force of 160 ships. The latter were soon dismissed.

Revenge against Persia?

Those who maintain that he intended only the conquest of Asia Minor cite the following facts: that he left the bulk of his army at home with Antipater to deal with insurrections among the Greeks, that he took only 30 000 infantry and 5000 cavalry, and that he had only 70 talents of ready cash and thirty days' provisions.

Limited to Asia Minor?

If he aimed at conquering Darius' empire, why did he not stop when Darius was killed and his capital taken? Tarn suggests that since India was once part of the empire of Darius I, then it was necessary to invade it to complete the conquest of that empire.

The conquest of Darius' Empire?

Did he aim at world conquest? Although Tarn says that there is no reason to suppose this was the case, Arrian states that

World conquest?

> his plans, whatever they were, had no lack of grandeur or ambition: he would never have remained idle in the enjoyment of any of his conquests... On the contrary he would have continued to seek beyond them for unknown lands, as it was ever his nature, if he had no rival, to strive to better his own best'.[12]

Was conquest his only goal? As a true pupil of Aristotle he could never have envisaged a campaign of conquest exclusively. He would have seen it also as an expedition for exploration, scientific research, expansion of Hellenic culture and the performance of noble deeds beyond mere military actions. From the beginning he took with him poets, historians, scientists, philosophers, surveyors, mapmakers and geographers.

More than mere conquest?

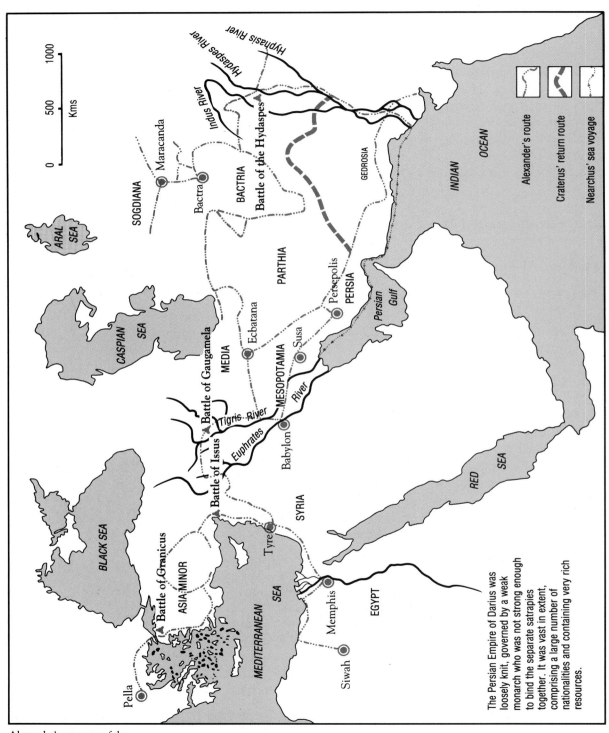

Alexander's route

Craterus' return route

Nearchus' sea voyage

The Persian Empire of Darius was loosely knit, governed by a weak monarch who was not strong enough to bind the separate satrapies together. It was vast in extent, comprising a large number of nationalities and containing very rich resources.

Alexander's conquest of the
Persian Empire, 334–323

The conquest of Asia Minor

The Battle of the Granicus River, 334

Refer to Plutarch, *Alexander*, 16; Arrian, I:13–15.

'Alexander was obliged to fight at the very gates of Asia, if he was to enter and conquer it.'[13]

The Persians waited on the far side of the Granicus, while the army of Alexander crossed the deep and swiftly flowing river through a hail of spears and climbed a steep, wet and treacherous slope before engaging them in battle.

First victory at Granicus

It was predominantly 'a cavalry battle with, as it were, infantry tactics: horse against horse, man against man, locked together...'.[14] Once the Persian centre failed to hold, owing to the swift Macedonian cavalry attack, the Persian wings folded. The experience of the Macedonians, the weight of their attack and the superiority of their arms won the day.

Alexander, leading the way across the river at the head of the right wing, was saved from death by Cleitus, who severed the enemy arm raised above Alexander's head.

Alexander saved from death

Greek mercenaries who had taken little part in the battle were surrounded by Alexander's men and butchered, except for approximately 2000 who were taken as prisoners and used for hard labour.

Bronze statue of Alexander astride Bucephalus

Results of the battle

1 Greek prisoners were sent in chains to Macedonia.
2 Spoils were sent to the Greeks.
3 A Macedonian governor was appointed as satrap.
4 Sardis surrendered and the Lydians had restored to them their ancient freedom and customs.

Asia Minor subdued and organised

5 Ephesus and the Ionian cities welcomed Alexander as a liberator—democracies were established.
6 Miletus held out, but was taken with the help of the Greek fleet.
7 Alexander disbanded his fleet due to (a) lack of funds to maintain it, (b) its being no match for the Persian navy, (c) his fear of the possible disloyalty of the Greeks and (d) 'A fleet was no longer of any use to him: by seizing the coastal towns he could reduce the Persian navy to impotence, for they would then have no port on the Asian coast which they could use, and no source of replacement for their crews.'[15]
8 Halicarnassus in Caria, defended by the brilliant general Memnon and protected by the Persian fleet, fell to Alexander's siege engines. The satrapy was given to a loyal Carian Princess, Ada.

Way open to Syria

9 Alexander advanced into Cilicia and seized the mountain passes into Syria.

The conquest of Syria

The Battle of Issus, 333

Read Plutarch, *Alexander*, 20; Arrian II:7–8.

'Fortune certainly presented Alexander with the ideal terrain for the battle . . .'.[16]

Darius, with his enormous army, had left his camp on the plains and was caught by Alexander in a defile between the mountains and the sea, divided by the Pinarus River. The site favoured Alexander's smaller numbers.

Huge Persian army defeated — difficult victory

Alexander, leading the right wing of the cavalry, outflanked the enemy left, but the Macedonian centre was having some trouble with the hard-fighting Greek mercenaries in the Persian centre. Alexander delivered a flank attack, cutting them to pieces. Alexander's left wing fought desperately until Darius fled, followed by his Persian cavalry. Issus was not an easy victory for Alexander.

Results of the battle

Darius' family captured

1 Darius' headquarters were taken; his mother, wife and three children were captured but were shown great sympathy by Alexander. Darius' treasure was sent to Damascus.

The Battle of Issus;
(a) Alexander, (b) Darius
III (From a mosaic found at
Pompeii)

2 A letter from Darius requesting the release of his family was met by a demand from Alexander that Darius appear in person and address Alexander as 'King of All Asia'.

3 Alexander did not immediately pursue Darius, as he needed to secure the Syrian coast and Egypt.

4 Byblus and Sidon yielded, but Tyre held out for seven months.

Darius' offer refused

5 Darius sent another letter offering Alexander all of his empire west of the Euphrates, and his daughter's hand in marriage. Alexander refused.

The siege of Tyre and Gaza, 332

Long and difficult siege in Phoenicia

Refer to Plutarch, *Alexander*, 24; Arrian, II:17–25.

Tyre was one of the strongest fortresses in the ancient world. Alexander 'besieged Tyre for seven months, constructing moles and siege artillery on the landward side, and blockading it with 200 triremes by sea'.[17] In the autumn of the same year he laid siege to Gaza.

Results of the siege

1 Eight thousand people in Tyre were killed and 30 000 sold into slavery.

2 The city was spared and recolonised.

3 Gaza met the same fate.

The entry into Egypt, 332–331

Egypt taken without force

Refer to Plutarch, *Alexander*, 26–7; Arrian, III:1–6.

In 332 Mazaces, the Persian governor of Egypt, hearing the report of the Battle of Issus and Darius' flight to safety, was induced 'to receive Alexander with a show of friendship and to offer no obstacle to his free entry into Egypt and its cities.'[18]

As a result:

1 Alexander was installed in Egypt as pharaoh.

2 He established there the greatest of his Alexandrias.

3 He journeyed to Cyrene.

4 He visited the oracle of Ammon at Siwah.

5 Egypt was organised by him—the potential strength of the country impressed him and 'he judged it to be unsafe to put it all into the hands of one man'.[19]

6 Alexander returned to Syria and then advanced to Mesopotamia, since it was now safe to pursue Darius.

The conquest of Persia

The Battle of Gaugamela, 331

Read Plutarch, *Alexander*, 24; Arrian, III:8–16.
  Gaugamela, on the left bank of the Tigris, was

> level and open, all places where a broken surface might obstruct the movement
> of cavalry having been worked on some time previously by the Persian troops,
> so that all of it was now good going for both chariots and cavalry.[20]

Darius had a larger and better-organised army than at Issus and was *Final defeat of Darius*
accompanied by 200 scythe-bearing chariots and a few elephants. Because
of his smaller numbers Alexander organised a reserve formation, with
orders to face about in case of an encircling movement. Also, Darius'
chariots were of no real use since Alexander's phalanx was trained to open
lanes to allow them through. Alexander's cavalry on the left made the
usual charge, and the Persian centre collapsed under the thrust of the
Macedonians. Darius fled once again. Parmenio, in trouble, was saved by *Darius flees to safety*
the Thessalian cavalry.

Results of the battle

1 Darius fled to Media.
2 Babylon and Susa welcomed Alexander without resistance and he *Babylonia and Persia*
   received incalculable treasures. *taken*
3 At Persepolis he first took his seat on the royal throne under the golden
   canopy. The palace at Persepolis was burnt down on the order of
   Alexander.
4 After Persia was organised, Alexander set off in pursuit of Darius.
   Ecbatana submitted.
5 Darius was killed in Bactria by his own satrap, Bessus, and his followers. *Darius' death*
   Bessus assumed power.
6 Alexander buried Darius with all royal honours in the ancestral tombs
   at Persepolis.
7 Alexander was proclaimed 'King of Kings'.

The conquest of the north-east provinces (Bactria and Sogdiana) 330–328

As the successor of Darius, Alexander had to take possession of the far-
eastern provinces and to punish Bessus for Darius' murder.
  The years in Bactria and Sogdiana tested Alexander's initiative. He *Bactria, Sogdiana*
crossed the Hindu-Kush and the Oxus and Jaxartes Rivers, established the *subdued*

northernmost limit of his empire at Alexandria Eschate, captured Bessus, faced the skilful general Spitamenes, Satrap of Sogdiana, devised means to lay siege to mountain strongholds, and faced the Scythian nomads.

Invasion of India

The Battle of the Hydaspes River, 326

Read Plutarch, *Alexander*, 60; Arrian V:8–18.

Alexander in India

Between the Indus and Hydaspes Rivers many Indian princes (for example, Taxiles) welcomed him and became his allies, but at the Hydaspes he was met by a formidable army led by King Porus, who also had a large squadron of elephants.

Battle with Porus

Alexander had to cross the swollen river, but it could not be done directly because the elephants would have caused the horses to go mad with terror. Alexander cunningly created many false alarms until Porus was lulled into a sense of security. Under cover of darkness Alexander led a selected force, on hay-filled floats, across the river several miles upstream. Porus, taken by surprise, sent his son to intercept him with 2000 mounted troops and 120 chariots, but they were defeated and Porus had to make the decision as to whether he should advance to meet Alexander or await the crossing of the remainder of the army. The ensuing battle was the hardest ever fought by the Macedonians and revealed the bold originality and brilliance of Alexander. Porus faced the king, but was attacked from the rear by the rest of Alexander's army; the Indian losses were enormous.

A rare medallion showing Alexander, astride Bucephalus, battling Porus, the Indian king, on his elephant

314

Results of the battle

1 Porus was treated with respect and Alexander restored his sovereignty over his subjects, adding more territory to Porus' kingdom.
2 Alexander established a city on either side of the Hydaspes—Bucephala, in honour of his horse, and Nicaea ('Victory').
3 The rest of the Punjab was conquered easily, as far as the Hyphasis River.
4 Alexander's ambition to move further east was brought to an end by his army's refusal to go beyond the Hyphasis.
5 Alexander moved down the Indus to its mouth, fought a strenuous campaign against the Malli (325), but was close to death from injuries.

New cities on Hydaspes

Macedonians refuse to go further

The return to Babylon

One third of Alexander's army, under Craterus, took the direct route to the head of the Persian Gulf, while Alexander directed his admiral, Nearchus, to sail with a fleet (built on the Indus River) around the coast. His instructions were to make careful observations with the object of opening up a sea route for commerce between India and the Euphrates. Alexander himself took 30 000 men and began a terrible march through the waterless Gedrosian Desert, where he lost approximately half of his troops. Eventually the army and navy were reunited; Alexander returned to Persepolis and later to Babylon.

Sea route charted

Gedrosian Desert crossing

Alexander — military genius

There is no controversy about Alexander's military genius and Burn says 'No soldier in history is more indisputedly "great" than Alexander'.[21] He started, of course, with the advantage of Philip's army and he did have a number of reverses, such as the destruction of Pharnuches' force by Spitamenes and the march through the Gedrosian Desert. His genius, however, is apparent in every aspect of warfare and in every military undertaking between those of the Granicus and Hydaspes Rivers.

There are two aspects of his brilliance:
- tactical insight and strategic planning;
- leadership of his men.

Brilliant tactician and leader of men

Tactical insight and strategic planning

He was able to modify and adapt his tactics to suit each opponent and he handled the unknown enemy as well as he handled the Greek or Persian infantry.

Varied deployment of troops

He varied the disposition of his troops—for example, Granicus was essentially a cavalry contest; he overcame the danger of encirclement by a larger army at Gaugamela; he used his infantry against Porus because the cavalry could not face the elephants, and at his first meeting with the Scythian nomads in the desert, he countered their tactics and defeated them.

He made the phalanx mobile, able to manoeuvre to open its ranks and to charge at the double.

Overcame all obstacles

He was able to devise means to overcome every obstacle. His siege operations against Tyre and those against Aornus were totally different, and he was able to find the right method of fighting the guerilla tactics of his opponents in central Asia.

Flexible in his approach

He won by making rapid marches; by taking his enemy by surprise and forcing them to change their plans; by applying overwhelming force at the crucial point; by deception; by never putting anything off; by using the principle of 'march divided, fight united' and by campaigning at all seasons.

His lines of communication were carefully guarded, so that any reinforcements were always able to reach the main army.

Leadership of his men

Use of psychology

His ability to lead his men was due to his personal magnetism, to the fact that he shared all their dangers with them and to his use of the psychology of victory.

He knew how to keep his men's affections, and when to relax discipline. By using amusements such as athletic and musical contests at their halting places, he kept up his men's morale and also encouraged them with rewards of money. Although their morale broke at the Hyphasis River, he had maintained it intact during eight difficult years.

City building

Purpose of his 'Alexandrias'

One of the biggest problems faced by Alexander was the need to unite the diverse peoples and cultures within his empire in order to prevent it falling apart. Tarn believes that Alexander saw that the only way to really create a unifying force was to promote the fusion of Europe with Asia on the basis of Greek culture; one way to achieve this was through the founding of many cities, particularly in the East. Although he was supposed to have founded seventy cities, the existence of only twenty-five can be substantiated.

Features of the cities

- Most were east of the Tigris River.
- Many of them derived their names from his — 'Alexandria'.
- Most were new settlements, but some were built on the sites of existing native villages and towns.
- Some were flourishing, populous cities, while others were military colonies.
- Choice of site varied according to the main purpose as seen by Alexander.

Most located in the East

Alexandria Rhacotis, in Egypt, was designed specifically to be a great centre of trade and in the third century became the greatest centre of commerce, Greek science and literature in the Mediterranean.

Alexandria in Egypt

> When he saw what wonderful natural advantages the place possessed — for it was a strip of land resembling a broad isthmus, which stretched between the sea and a great lagoon, with a spacious harbour at the end of it . . . he ordered the plan of the city to be designed so that it would conform to this site.[22]

Alexandria Eschate (the 'furtherest' or 'ultimate'):

'Furthest' Alexandria

> It was his intention to found a city on the Tanais (Jaxartes R.) and to name it after himself. The site, he considered, was a good one; a settlement there would be likely to increase in size and importance, and would also serve both as an excellent base for a possible future invasion of Scythia and as a defensive position against raiding tribes from across the river.[23]

As well as Alexandria Eschate (Khojent), the cities of Alexandria Areion (Herat) and Alexandria Arachosia (Kandahar) were located on the main caravan routes, and retain their importance today.

The cities were intended by Alexander also to be part of a vast scheme of colonisation, which differed from the earlier Greek colonial movement of the eighth and seventh centuries in that it involved settlers from many different cities. It was hoped that Greeks (mercenaries, traders, craftsmen), Macedonians and natives would coexist and intermarry, and that Greek culture would spread outwards from these centres. These cities differed from the Greek poleis of mainland Greece and Asia Minor in that they were not fully autonomous, but were under the control of a governor appointed by Alexander. Institutions and laws were based on the Greek model and applied to Greeks and non-Greeks alike.

Colonisation

Not fully autonomous

Alexander may have intended this arrangement to be only temporary, to be replaced in time by full autonomy.

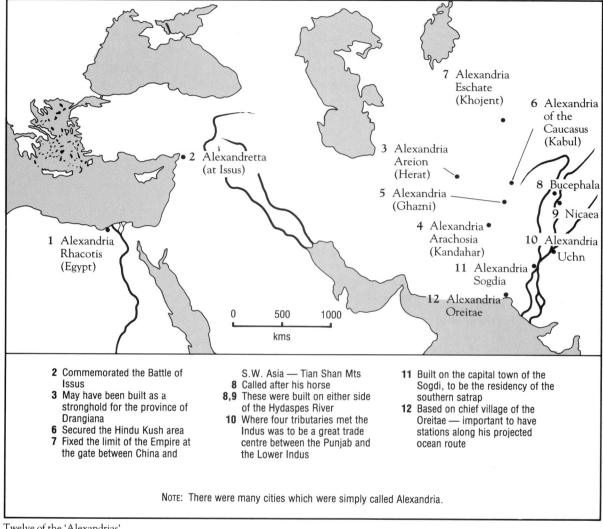

Twelve of the 'Alexandrias'

Map labels:

7 Alexandria Eschate (Khojent)
6 Alexandria of the Caucasus (Kabul)
3 Alexandria Areion (Herat)
2 Alexandretta (at Issus)
5 Alexandria (Ghazni)
8 Bucephala
9 Nicaea
4 Alexandria Arachosia (Kandahar)
10 Alexandria Uchn
1 Alexandria Rhacotis (Egypt)
11 Alexandria Sogdia
12 Alexandria Oreitae

0 500 1000
kms

2 Commemorated the Battle of Issus
3 May have been built as a stronghold for the province of Drangiana
6 Secured the Hindu Kush area
7 Fixed the limit of the Empire at the gate between China and S.W. Asia — Tian Shan Mts
8 Called after his horse
8,9 These were built on either side of the Hydaspes River
10 Where four tributaries met the Indus was to be a great trade centre between the Punjab and the Lower Indus
11 Built on the capital town of the Sogdi, to be the residency of the southern satrap
12 Based on chief village of the Oreitae — important to have stations along his projected ocean route

NOTE: There were many cities which were simply called Alexandria.

Alexander as a statesman

His work unfinished

It is difficult to judge Alexander as a statesman, since his work was just beginning when he died. His views had been changing and developing, and it is unlikely that he would have left the political arrangements as they were.

Judgment of men often mistaken

He was often mistaken in his judgment of men and when he returned from India he found 'a great many irregularities on the part of government officials, acts of violence against individuals and robbing of temples and

318

PHOENICIA

Apart from Tyre, Phoenician cities continued to be ruled by native princes who owed allegiance to Alexander. The high priests still governed Judaea according to the law.

Financial superintendents were responsible to Harpalus, the royal treasurer at Babylon. The taxation districts were separate from the satrapies and larger. Harpalus' position was superior to that of any satrap.

BABYLON

First Persian satrap (Mazaeus) was appointed, but without military command. (Military power and finances were in Macedonian hands.) This was the basis for all future appointments.

PROBLEMS FACED BY ALEXANDER IN ADMINISTRATION

Separation of civil, military and financial authority

Respect for institutions of conquered peoples

system of government

The great diversity of race, language, religion, customs and level of development

Racial tolerance and religious freedom

The need to avoid any rigid

The vast extent of the empire and geographic obstacles to communication

Using established forms where possible

Suppression of piracy, brigandage and civil war

Choosing competent and trustworthy administrators and governors

Right of every subject to appeal to Alexander

Finding a way of coordinating this heterogeneous empire

Encouragement of trade by reform of coinage

Including other nationals in governing classes

ASIA MINOR

Satraps were primarily Macedonian generals with troops.
There were separate financial superintendents. Alexander kept coinage in his own hands.

Innovations in coinage — Alexander introduced a uniform silver currency on the Attic standard, although he allowed the older currency to circulate and did not force it on Babylon or Phoenicia.

EGYPT

Alexander retained the native officials, appointed two native governors, for upper and lower Egypt. Financial superintendent was Cleomenes — used native tax collectors. The army of occupation was under three Macedonian commanders.

Aspects of Alexander's administration

tombs'.[24] Cleomenes, the financial superintendent and later governor of Egypt, was corrupt. He had a bad criminal record in Egypt, extorting large amounts of treasures from the priests and temples. The grain merchants of Egypt were adversely affected by his monopoly of the export of corn and this also contributed to the famine in Greece between 330 and 326. Harpalus, the royal treasurer at Babylon, embezzled funds, and of the eighteen Iranian satraps appointed by Alexander as part of his policy of joint rule, ten had to be removed for incompetence or executed either for treason or the murder of their subjects. Several raised their own private armies.

Did not alter inefficient satrapy system

Alexander has been criticised for not immediately overhauling the administration—particularly the satrapy system—when he returned from India. However, he was still preoccupied with exploration and conquest, so he simply punished or threatened the offenders and appointed new satraps.

The satrapy system had already been seen to be highly inefficient prior to Alexander's conquests and he may have intended to replace it with some other form of administration—perhaps smaller, more manageable units.

Separation of civil and military powers

His separation of financial, civil and military powers showed political wisdom, while his reform of the coinage contributed to trade and economic prosperity throughout the empire and involved Athens as a trading partner instead of a competitor.

His ideal not realised

The statesmanlike ideal of an empire characterised by racial equality and intermarriage, and based on Hellenic culture, unfortunately did not succeed as he planned it. However, he opened up the East to Greek enterprise and his successors followed his economic policy of city building and encouraging Greek travellers, traders and craftsmen to seek their fortunes in the new cities of the East.

Unfortunately, 'Alexander died with the real task yet before him'.[25]

Alexander and his Macedonians

From devotion to resentment

The relationship of the Macedonian nobles and soldiers with Alexander varied from total loyalty and devotion on the one hand to resentment and open opposition on the other.

When he crossed the Hellespont at the age of twenty-two he was supported by a group of powerful nobles, whose loyalty was never in doubt. They had already enthusiastically embraced the Persian campaign under Philip, which they saw as their war. Towards the end of his life, he held a banquet at Opis as a reconciliation between himself and his Macedonians. What had occurred in the ten years between these events to increase the tension between him and his men?

Consider the following views:

E. Badian, in an article called 'Alexander the Great and the Loneliness of Power', expressed the view that Alexander was determined to seek independence and security from the powerful nobles who surrounded him and held most of the commands. When his leadership, courage and success won him the enthusiastic support of the army, he gradually used all opportunities to undermine the nobles, particularly the family of Parmenio.

Conflict with nobles inevitable

When Alexander realised that his Macedonians would not go on forever but wanted to settle down and enjoy the spoils of victory, he knew he would have to get the support of his new subjects and attempt to conciliate the Persian aristocracy. Tension and conflict between Alexander and his nobles became inevitable, whether due to personal antagonism or political opposition.

He realised that he could not count on the absolute submission of the present generation of nobles and soldiers, and so he aimed at a new ruling class of mixed blood, which would be free from national allegiance and tradition.

Aimed at a new ruling class

Ulrich Wilcken, in *Alexander the Great*, argues that as Alexander advanced through Asia his view of the empire and his position in relation to the conquered peoples changed. After Gaugamela, the idea took shape that there was a possibility of breaking down the old barriers between East and West. The idea may have developed out of the political necessity of enrolling Persians in the army, owing to the lack of Macedonians, and from the knowledge that the best guarantee for the security and permanence of his Asiatic Empire was for Macedonians and Persians to share the rule. However, Alexander did not practise Asiatic absolution towards his Macedonians, and in his plan for joint rule the command was always reserved for Macedonians. Unfortunately, they generally took a hostile attitude to Alexander's attempts to build a bridge between Persians and Macedonians. The Macedonians saw themselves as the victors and looked with contempt on the defeated barbarians, although many had no objection to taking the women as wives.

Breaking down of barriers resented

Macedonian hostility to barbarians

Particular incidents that affected his relationship with his Macedonians

The following incidents tend to reveal the negative side of Alexander's relationship with his Macedonians, but it should be remembered that despite the many things which throughout the campaign he had done to hurt their feelings, they were still his captains, generals and governors of provinces and he had suffered alongside them for ten years, sharing their

Always promoted his troops' interests

321

labours and distress, paying their debts, marrying as they married, giving them noble burials, rewards and the bulk of the treasures captured. Despite the few occasions when he had to put their loyalty to the test and despite their refusal to go beyond the Hyphasis River in India, they still followed him to the end.

The adoption of Persian dress

Some features adopted

About 330, after Alexander's advance into Parthia, he began to adopt Persian dress, although the statements concerning this are contradictory. Arrian says that he emulated the extravagance and splendour of the barbaric kings and assumed the 'Median dress in place of what Macedonians have worn from time immemorial'.[26] On the other hand, Plutarch is adamant that he did not adopt the entire costume of a Persian king, that he refused to wear the trousers, sleeved vest or tiara and that he adopted a style that was a modest and stately compromise.

Behaved according to Persian or Macedonian customs

At first he wore it only when as King of Asia he was in the presence of the barbarians, or with his closest friends. In the same way, he punished Persians such as Bessus according to Persian law and when he sat in judgment on his oriental subjects, he sat on a golden throne in a magnificent audience tent. His Macedonians, however, were judged and sentenced according to Macedonian law, before the assembly of the Macedonian army — as in the case of Philotas — and when he despatched documents to Antipater in Macedonia, he used the royal seal of Macedonia, not the seal of the King of Asia.

Means of conciliating subjects

Although Alexander may have acquired a taste for oriental luxury, it is generally agreed that his adoption of Persian dress was a means of conciliating his new subjects — particularly the Persian aristocracy, since they were the administrators of the empire and he would have need of their services. Arrian says it was 'a matter of policy: by it he hoped to bring the Eastern nations to feel that they had a king who was not wholly a foreigner'.[27] Similarly, Plutarch believed that if Alexander shared the local habits and customs, it would be 'a great step towards softening men's hearts'.[28]

Objections of Macedonian nobility

It displeased many of his Macedonians, especially the family of Parmenio, who according to Badian were the most vocal objectors to it. However, the majority 'admired his other virtues so much that they considered they ought to make concessions to him in some matters which either gave him pleasure or increased his prestige'.[29]

The execution of Philotas and Parmenio

Parmenio was Alexander's chief of staff and in charge of the whole infantry. He had been loyal to Philip and had supported Alexander's claim to the succession. His son Philotas, older than Alexander, was the commander of the famous Companion cavalry. Other members of

Parmenio's family dominated the high commands.

Plutarch maintains that Philotas came under suspicion when it was reported by his mistress that he often boasted, when drunk, *Suspicions against Philotas*

> that all the greatest achievements in the campaign had been the work of his father and himself. Then he would speak of Alexander as a mere boy who owed his title of ruler to their efforts.[30]

Alexander ordered the girl to continue reporting any of Philotas' boastful or angry criticisms.

Despite Philotas' indiscretions, Alexander kept silent, perhaps because of Parmenio's loyal support. However, he must have known that the father and son would be a formidable opposition if they ever decided to lead a revolt against his authority.

Philotas had been approached by a Macedonian soldier named Cebalinus who, knowing of a conspiracy against Alexander, demanded that Philotas take him and his brother to the king with information that was urgent. Philotas twice failed to arrange the interview with Alexander, after which the brothers became suspicious of Philotas' motives. Because of his previous knowledge of Philotas' drunken criticisms, Alexander was more inclined to listen to those who suggested that a common soldier like Dimnus (the supposed instigator of the plot) would not have undertaken such a plan on his own initiative and that someone of much greater power must be involved. *Evidence of conspiracy*

Philotas' failure to notify Alexander

Philotas was arrested and brought to trial before the Macedonians. It is doubtful that he was implicated in the conspiracy, but Arrian, on the evidence of Ptolemy, says that Philotas was convicted when

> the persons who had reported the affair came forward, with various irrefutable proofs of his own guilt and that of his fellow-conspirators, of which the most damning was that he admitted knowledge of a plot against Alexander but had said nothing about it in spite of the fact that he was in the habit of visiting Alexander's tent twice a day.[31]

He was probably only guilty of failing to arrange an interview. He was executed, and a secret message was sent to Cleander, Parmenio's second-in-command in Media, to put the old general to death also.

Why was it necessary to execute Parmenio, who had given long and loyal service to Philip and Alexander? According to Robinson, Macedonian law dictated that the relatives of a man convicted of treason must also be put to death, so the 'execution of Parmenio was judicial'.[32] Alexander could of course easily have persuaded the army to take different action, since Parmenio had great influence and prestige not only with the Macedonians, but with the mercenary soldiers as well. It was exactly that influence that worried Alexander, since on the death of Philotas, Parmenio could have led a general revolt against him. *Justification of deaths of Philotas and Parmenio*

Purge of Parmenio's family and supporters

A number of Parmenio's supporters and relatives were brought to trial; some escaped, some were acquitted and some executed. Parmenio's son-in-law Alexander of Lyncestis, who was of royal blood, was put to death as a possible pretender to the throne.

Bitterness against Alexander

These events left a legacy of bitterness and, says Plutarch, 'made Alexander dreaded by his friends, above all by Antipater'[33] in Macedonia. Because of the importance of the Companion Cavalry and its closeness to Alexander, it was divided between Cleitus and Hephaestion so that not even a personal friend should control alone such a formidable body.

Attempts at assimilation of Persian and Macedonian

At some point before he reached Sogdiana, Alexander had occasion to put the loyalty of his Macedonian troops to the test. He felt anxious that they might refuse to follow him any further in his campaign. Although he regained their loyalty and they pleaded to be allowed to follow him wherever he went, he implemented a policy to ensure adequate troops in the future and to reconcile Asiatic and Macedonian traditions as well. He

Training of Persian youth

selected 30 000 Persian boys and ordered that they be taught Greek and the use of Macedonian weapons and tactics, in the belief that a policy of assimiliation would contribute to the security of his empire while he was far away, because it would be based on goodwill rather than on force.

Marriage to Roxane

It was about this time that he married Roxane, a Bactrian, as a further indication of his policy of reconciliation. Some of his friends supported him in this policy, but others disapproved. Hephaestion, Alexander's closest friend, joined him in his changed habits, while Craterus, Alexander's ablest young officer since the death of Philotas, clung to Macedonian customs. Alexander used Hephaestion in his dealings with the Persians, and Craterus liaised with the Greeks and Macedonians.

The murder of Cleitus

Cleitus, the leader of one of the Companion divisions and the man who had saved Alexander's life at the Battle of the Granicus River, was killed by Alexander in a drunken brawl at Maracanda in Sogdiana in 328.

Cleitus' growing resentment

Cleitus for some time had been resentful of Alexander's adoption of Eastern manners and of the excessive flattery of his courtiers, but accounts differ as to the exact cause of his unseemly behaviour to the king at this time. The whole company was very drunk, including Alexander.

Varying accounts of the argument

One account describes those who sought the king's approval by indulging in sycophantic expressions, comparing his deeds with those of Heracles. Others went on to declare Philip's achievements as commonplace compared with those of Alexander. Plutarch maintains that the argument began over a song which made fun of a Macedonian blunder.

Whatever the cause, Cleitus, very drunk and by nature hot-tempered, began to insult Alexander. He reminded Alexander that he had saved his life and that the great successes won over the Persians were not achieved by Alexander alone, but were the work of the whole Macedonian army. It was Macedonian blood which had made Alexander so great that he could now disown his own father and claim to be the son of Ammon.

When Alexander accused him of stirring up trouble with the Macedonians, Cleitus suggested that Alexander should spend all his time with the barbarians, who would prostrate themselves before his white Persian tunic, and not bother with free men who spoke their minds. Alexander, hurt and furious by these words, ran him through with a spear, despite the attempts of all there to stop the argument.

The whole affair 'was a misfortune rather than a deliberate act',[34] but it did reveal the bitterness towards Alexander and the continuing tension felt by some of his closest associates.

Cleitus' death accidental

Horrified by what he had done, Alexander took to his bed for three days, without food or drink. He made no attempt to justify his crime. Both Arrian and Plutarch mention that the sophist Anaxarchus, in order to comfort Alexander, suggested that Zeus had Justice and Law seated by his side to show that whatever was done by a ruler was lawful and just. Although these words consoled him, they were also to make him more autocratic and proud in his dealings with the Macedonians. It is believed that a resolution was later passed convicting Cleitus posthumously of treason, thus making Alexander's action legitimate.

Alexander's reaction

His actions legitimised

Alexander may have now felt free to implement other eastern customs; it is at this time he attempted to introduce prostration among the Macedonians and Greeks.

Prostration (proskynesis)

To the Persians, *proskynesis* (prostration) was a social not a religious gesture. It was performed by all Persians to their king as a mark of their deepest reverence. Since the Persians did not regard their king as a god, it did not signify worship. To the Greeks and Macedonians, however, prostration was only performed before a god.

Persian and Greek view of prostration

Alexander attempted to introduce this eastern custom to his Macedonians and Greeks, although he must have known it was dangerous to involve the Greeks. It was obviously a political move to introduce a common court ceremonial to show the equal position of the Persians with the Macedonians. If he adopted some other procedure for everyone, the Persians would not regard him as their real king. He tried it out with his close associates at a dinner and while the Macedonians offered no actual opposition, their displeasure and anger were obvious — especially the older Macedonians, who disliked all aspects of Alexander's orientalism.

Prostration a political, but dangerous move

Arrian says: 'There were plenty of people moreover, who, to flatter him, submitted to this servile behaviour: Anaxarchus the sophist was one of the worst'.[35]

Callisthenes' refusal

However, among the first Greeks called on to perform this act was Callisthenes, the philosopher and grandnephew of Aristotle. He was a man of great eloquence and had attracted the admiration of both the younger and older generations of Macedonians. He refused to perform *proskynesis*, and was 'the only man to express in public the resentment which all the oldest and best of the Macedonians felt in private'.[36] Although he stressed that Alexander was fit for any honour a man could earn, Callisthenes urged him not to forget the difference between honouring a man and worshipping a god.

Alexander backed down

Although Alexander was greatly annoyed at Callisthenes' speech, he told the Macedonians to forget the matter and said that they would not be called on to prostrate themselves in the future. Plutarch says that 'by persuading the king not to insist on this tribute he [Callisthenes] delivered the Greeks from a great disgrace and Alexander from an even greater one'.[37] Yet it was to Alexander's credit that he did not insist on its performance, although it was a setback to his policy.

The tie between Alexander and Callisthenes was broken and the king now regarded him as the head of an opposition.

The conspiracy of the pages

Relationship between Alexander and Callisthenes damaged

Alexander was now inclined to listen to those who spread stories of Callisthenes' conceit, and because of the latter's influence with the young men it was easy to implicate him in the conspiracy which a group of pages instigated.

The adolescent sons of the Macedonian nobles were trained as the personal attendants of the king, looking after his person, guarding him when he was asleep and accompanying him when out riding or hunting. One of these pages, Hermolaus, had been whipped by Alexander in front of the others for killing a boar before Alexander could strike it himself. Hermolaus was determined to exact a revenge for his brutal insult and, with the support of five others, planned to murder Alexander while he was asleep. The plot was foiled and Alexander informed.

Pages' plan to murder Alexander
No proof of Callisthenes' involvement

There was no proof that Callisthenes had anything to do with the conspiracy, and in fact even under the stress of torture the boys confessed that the plot was entirely their own. Curtius believed that Hermolaus, at his trial, declared that Alexander's inhuman arrogance could no longer be endured. However, Alexander was prepared to believe the worst about Callisthenes.

Callisthenes' death

The boys were stoned to death, but the fate of Callisthenes has been variously reported. As a Greek, he should have been tried by the members of the League of Corinth and it is believed by some sources that Alexander held him in prison until this could occur. Ptolemy says he was hanged, while Aristobolus claims that he accompanied the army in chains for seven months, until his health deteriorated so much that he died.

The mutiny of the troops at the Hyphasis River in India

After weeks of innumerable hardships, monsoon rains and the most difficult battle yet fought (against King Porus), the Macedonians were determined not to go beyond the Hyphasis River. Arrian says that the sight of Alexander undertaking 'an endless succession of dangerous and exhausting enterprises was beginning to depress them'.[38] They had lost their enthusiasm, and grumbled amongst themselves until Alexander addressed them, urging them on. He described what they had achieved to date and warned them that while there remained unconquered peoples to the east and north, there was the possibility of losing some of those marginal areas so courageously won. He invited comment, but soon discovered the limit of what he could expect from them.

Troops refuse to go further east

Coenus spoke for them all, explaining how the men were yearning for home where they could live in peace and enjoy the treasures that Alexander had enabled them to win. He emphasised that a successful man should know when to stop.

Alexander unable to change their minds

Alexander reacted angrily, declared that he would continue with or without them and retired to his tent, hoping they would change their minds, but they were determined not to be manipulated and they resented Alexander's outburst.

When Alexander took the omens for a crossing of the river, they proved unfavourable and he decided to withdraw. It was the only defeat he had ever suffered.[39]

Unfavourable omens

As the army fought its way down the Indus River to the sea, Alexander took many risks while leading his men into the attack. On one occasion he was so severely wounded that the men believed he had died. 'Recovering from the first shock of grief, the men were plunged into helpless despair.'[40] When he appeared before them, they responded with shouts of joy, tears and blessings.

Purges of inefficient and corrupt officials

Prior to his march into India Alexander had put to death several top officials, such as Menander (one of the Companions), because he had refused to stay at his garrison post. 'By this time he [Alexander] was already feared by his men for his relentless severity in punishing any dereliction of duty.'[41]

After the disastrous march through the Gedrosian Desert with its terrible toll of death and suffering, Alexander carried out a purge of all those top government officials and army officers guilty of maladministration, plunder of temples, acts of violence and incitement to revolt. Cleander was one of the first officers to be executed, and the purge went on for months. During this time Harpalus, the royal treasurer, fled to the west with the embezzled funds from the treasury. He was accompanied by

Severity towards corrupt officials

a force of mercenaries and sought asylum in Athens.

Alexander was just as severe on corrupt and inefficient Persians.

The marriage festival at Susa

Purpose of mass marriage at Susa

On his return to Susa in 324, Alexander put into operation an idea which he had been formulating more and more in the preceding few years. In order to have a dominant group to administer and safeguard his empire (the Macedonians alone were insufficient), he encouraged the inter-marriage of Persians and Macedonians.

Alexander's marriage to Darius' daughter

In a sumptuous Persian-style wedding ceremony, Alexander and ninety of his Macedonians took as wives women from the noblest Persian families. To confirm his position as King of Asia, Alexander married Darius' eldest daughter, Stateira (sometimes called Barsine). He also registered and rewarded those 10 000 Macedonian soldiers who had previously taken Asiatic wives.

Attitude of Macedonians

Although many felt honoured to share a wedding ceremony with their king, the Macedonians resented the foreign form of the ceremony. The fact that many of the soldiers and officers left behind their Persian wives and children when they returned home is often cited as an example of Alexander's failure, but it could very well have been his idea, as Tarn suggests, that these marriages were intended to produce children who would remain to grow up and become loyal soldiers and administrators, having lived all their life in the camp.

Changes in the army

Persian units in the army

The 30 000 young Persians who had been trained on Macedonian lines were paraded before him at Susa, and these *epigoni* (inheritors) were incorporated as a separate unit into the army.

> It is said that their coming caused much bad feeling among the Macedonians, who felt it was an indication of his many efforts to lessen his dependence for the future upon his countrymen.[42]

Foreign troops in cavalry

Alexander had reorganised his army after his return from India, and Arrian twice mentions the Macedonians' resentment at the inclusion of foreign troops in the units of the Companions. Wilcken suggests that Alexander had previously followed a system of separate but parallel formations in the cavalry, but that he later introduced Persians and Iranians into the crack Macedonian cavalry regiments. He also enrolled a number of distinguished Persians and Iranians into the Guard (*agema*).

Macedonians' anger and suspicions

The anger of the Macedonians against Alexander — because they believed that he no longer cared for his own people — gained strength. To placate them, he promised to pay off all the debts they had incurred throughout the campaign if each man entered his name and the amount of the debt on a schedule being prepared. However, many of them believed that this was Alexander's way of learning which men were unable to make do on their army pay. Their suspicion and lack of confidence hurt and angered him, since he believed that a king should only speak the truth to his subjects. He removed the necessity of registering their names, and paid off their debts in good faith.

The mutiny and reconciliation at Opis

At Opis (on the Tigris River) Alexander, hoping to gratify his men, announced that all the sick and disabled and those unfit for service because of age were to be discharged, with very generous gratuities, and sent home.

Believing that Alexander already undervalued their services, they felt he was deliberately humiliating them and in their resentment called on him to send all his Macedonians home as useless, while he went on to conquer the world with 'his corps of young ballet soldiers'.[43]

Resentment regarding discharges

Furious at their reaction, Alexander prepared to make do with oriental troops; he began recruiting Persians for a new royal squadron and appointing Persian officers to high commands.

The Macedonians finally came to their senses and begged to be forgiven for their jealousy, anger and ingratitude. Alexander eventually responded to their claims of repentance, pardoned them and, in order to regain their loyalty for any future campaign, called them all *syngeneis* (kinsmen), making even the common soldier equal to the noblest Persian. He held a great banquet of reconciliation and then, once he had courted the Macedonians, did as he had always planned — that is, dismissed those no longer fit for service.

Repentance and re-conciliation banquet

The banquet, at which according to Arrian 9000 people were present, was to mark the end of the mutiny and since the mutiny was due to the jealousy of the Macedonians at Alexander's treatment of the Persians, a prayer for harmony and partnership in rule was made. This prayer simply aimed at a reconciliation between Alexander and his Macedonians and between the Macedonians and the Persians.

Prayer for harmony and partnership

Sir William Tarn uses a few words from the Opis prayer to formulate a theory that Alexander was praying for the unity of all mankind and universal brotherhood, but both Badian and Wilcken have effectively criticised this view.

Alexander's death

In 323 Alexander contracted swamp fever in Babylon and for eleven days lay close to death. Nothing could keep his men away from him, and as they filed past him 'he struggled to raise his head, and in his eyes there was a look of recognition for each individual as he passed'.[44] They were

Grief at Alexander's death

filled with grief and bewilderment at the thought of losing the one person who through the strength of his will had guided them for more than twelve years. To them he was *Alexandros Aniketos*—'invincible Alexander'.

Alexander and the Greeks

Relationship with the Greeks

Macedonian hegemony unpopular

According to Tarn, the most important people in Alexander's world were the Greeks. His relations with the Greeks of the mainland were determined by his position as Hegemon of the League of Corinth, a position he had inherited from his father. Whatever Philip's intention was for the League—be it to unite a state traditionally disunited and warring or as an instrument of Macedonian control—it was obvious that the Macedonian hegemony over Greece was not popular and had to be maintained by Macedonian garrisons, pro-Macedonian governments and the constant vigilance of Antipater, who was left in charge. Alexander did not discount the possibility of a Persian-instigated Greek uprising. While Antipater was widely disliked, it was Alexander whom many of them hated. In general, however, their attitude was one of caution, of avoiding provocative actions while Alexander was alive and winning victories in Asia. Of course, the Spartans had not joined the League of Corinth in 338 and had refused to join again in 336; therefore, they were not bound by its resolutions, and within a few years of Alexander's departure for Asia they were stirring up trouble in Greece.

Greeks avoided provocation

In Athens there were sharp differences of opinion, with a vocal and hostile minority led by Hyperides. Demosthenes at this stage kept in the background. The majority, led by Lycurgus, who was influential for about twelve years, avoided causing any provocation to Antipater or Alexander. Alexander, after his success at Granicus 'anxious to give the other Greek states a share in the victory',[45] sent the Athenians, in particular, 300 full suits of Persian armour, and on the rest of the spoils had the following inscription engraved: 'Alexander the son of Philip and the Greeks (except for the Lacedaemonians) dedicate these spoils taken from the Persians who dwell in Asia'.[46] This was obviously a piece of useful propaganda, since the Greeks played only a small part in the victory.

Alexander's attempts to placate Greeks

The Greek mercenaries fighting for Persia who were captured at Granicus were sent in chains to hard labour in Macedonia for 'contravening the League of Corinth by fighting in a foreign army against their own countrymen'.[47] Throughout his campaign in the East Alexander continued his hard line against Greek mercenaries in foreign employ, regarding them as criminals.

The Greek city-states of Asia Minor were brought over to the side of Alexander either voluntarily or by force, and in most cases he overthrew the ruling cliques and established democracies. The evidence suggests that the island-states were enrolled in the League of Corinth and were liable for contribution. Traitors, such as the oligarchs of Chios, were tried before the Council of the League. However, the Greek cities of the Asiatic mainland were treated as Alexander's free allies.

Position of Greeks of Asia Minor

Spartan revolt

Prior to the Battle of Issus in 333, King Agis IV of Sparta communicated with Persia to form an anti-Macedonian coalition. He travelled to Siphnos, to raise money for the war and to ask that as many ships and men as possible should be sent to him in the Peloponnese. Although the defeat of Darius at Issus was a setback for him, Agis remained in the area, continuing his preparations and managing to raise a considerable amount of money to build up a mercenary force. Although efforts to enlist Athens' support failed, Agis appealed to the Greeks to unite in defence of their freedom. He had some initial success, defeating a Macedonian force in the Peloponnese, and then marched against pro-Macedonian Megalopolis. Antipater, with League troops raised in Thessaly and central Greece to augment his own Macedonians, marched into Arcadia and inflicted a crushing defeat on the Greeks. With the death of Agis in battle, the opposition to Macedon collapsed. Sparta's punishment was decided by the League of Corinth, but an appeal by Sparta to Alexander resulted in the punishment of only the ringleaders of the revolt, and the imposition of a fine to be paid to Megalopolis.

Spartan opposition to Macedon defeated

The Harpalus affair

Some years later, the war party in Athens gained the upper hand and Demosthenes was again influential in the affairs of the city. This may have been due to a belief that Alexander, absent for so long in the East, would never return to the West. An incident which strained relations between Alexander and the Athenians — and led to the banishment of Demosthenes — involved Harpalus, Alexander's treasurer. He had embezzled a large sum from the royal treasury and fled from Babylon to Athens in 324, accompanied by a small mercenary force. Fearing Alexander, who at times frightened even his best friends, he appeared at Piraeus, but was refused admittance.

Flight of Harpalus to Athens

He returned later, pleading with the Athenians to receive and protect him as a suppliant, which they did, only to be put into a difficult situation

Demosthenes accused of corruption

when Alexander's admiral in the Aegean was sent to demand Harpalus' extradition. The Athenians, rather than hand over the suppliant, put him in prison and deposited the stolen funds in the Parthenon, in trust for Alexander. When it was discovered that some of the money was missing, an investigation was carried out in the belief that some of the leading orators had been bribed by Harpalus to adopt an anti-Macedonian stance. According to Plutarch, Harpalus had the ability to judge a man's greed and he saw this greed in the eyes of Demosthenes. Demosthenes was found guilty, with several others, and withdrew to Aegina. Harpalus, who had presumably escaped from prison and sought safety in Laconia, was assassinated by one of his own officers.

Decree to restore exiles

Demand for restoration of exiles

Before the affair of Harpalus was concluded, the Greeks received a communication from Alexander, via his envoy Nicanor, concerning the restoration of Greek exiles. In 324, the decree restoring exiles to their cities was read before those assembled at the Olympic Festival.

> King Alexander, to the Banditties of the Grecian cities: We were not the cause of your banishment, but we will be (the cause) of the return of you all into your own country, excepting such as are banished for outrageous crimes; of which things we have written to Antipater, requiring him to proceed by force against all such as shall oppose your restoration.[48]

Alexander felt it necessary to issue such a decree because most mercenaries were exiles and many were wishing to return home or were disbanded. The large number of exiles and mercenaries was symptomatic of the violent political strife in the Greek states. It was a statesmanlike act on the part of Alexander, since the mercenaries were becoming a focus of discontent both inside and outside Greece.

Opposition by Athens

Diodorus says that many people approved of the restoration of the exiles, but the Athenians and Aetolians objected to it. The Aetolians opposed the decree because they had recently expelled the inhabitants of Oeniadae and occupied the city, and to comply with the decree would mean their own evacuation from the city. The Athenians some twenty-five years previously had expelled the Samians and established Athenian cleruchs in the island. Both the Aetolians and Athenians thought of resisting, but because 'they were not at present able to cope with Alexander, they judged it more advisable to sit still and watch until they found a convenient opportunity'.[49]

Alexander's deification

Like other aspects of Alexander's career, the question of his deification has created controversy among modern historians. Although there is much literary and epigraphic material concerning the restoration of the exiles, there is virtually nothing about his request for deification (*apotheosis*). Arrian does not refer to it and Plutarch is silent about it in his *Alexander*, while Diodorus and Curtius, who both mention the exiles' decree, do not refer to it either. Arrian, however, says that in 323 delegations from Greece visited Alexander in Babylon to offer him golden crowns, but it is thought that this was related to the recall of the exiles.

Controversy over request for deification

If there was a request issued from Susa in 324 that he should be recognised as a god, it was directed solely to the Greeks of the Corinthian League, not to the Macedonians or any other people in his empire.

Except in Egypt, the idea of a ruler as divine was unknown in the East at this stage, but it was acceptable to the Greeks, who were always ready to grant divine honours to a mortal who in the eyes of his contemporaries had performed superhuman tasks, or to benefactors or other notables. Heracles, by his deeds, was placed among the Olympians and Lysander was worshipped as a god, with altars and prayers, by the oligarchs of Samos; Philip, Alexander's father, was paid divine honours by his supporters in Ephesus, where a statue of him was set up in the Temple of Artemis. Aristotle, in his *Politics*, said that if there was a man who was incomparably superior to other men in his ability and political capacity, then he was 'as a god among men'. Certainly, Alexander's achievements entitled him on his return from India to be accepted as a god, if any man were to be so honoured. There was no sharp distinction in the eyes of the Greeks between gods and men.

Greek view of divine honours

Added to this was the knowledge that seven years before he had been greeted by the priest of Zeus Ammon at Siwah as the son of a god. We shall never know what questions Alexander asked the oracle or what answers he received, although he said that he had 'received (or so he said) the answer which his heart desired'.[50] Although Plutarch says that 'Alexander did not allow himself to become vain or foolishly conceited because of his belief in his divinity',[51] his continued successes must have increased the feeling that he was in some way descended from Zeus Ammon.

Alexander's view of his own divinity

Tarn believes that Alexander's request for deification 'was a limited political measure for a purely political purpose and nothing else'.[52] According to him, by ordering the restoration of the exiles Alexander was overstepping his constitutional rights as Hegemon of the League, and to overcome his interference in their internal affairs he needed a higher status, such as that of a god. Many historians dispute this view. One

A purely political motive?

reason put forward by Wilcken as to why the Greeks agreed to his request for deification without too much objection was that they separated the political and religious spheres, and divinity had no influence on the practice of political life. They made a clear distinction between the worship of a god and obedience to an earthly leader. Wilcken's view is that the request for deification was due to an inner, religious experience and not to a purely political motive, although he does recognise that it would have greatly enhanced Alexander's prestige.

Balsdon, in his *Divinity of Alexander the Great*, suggests that the request for deification did not come from Alexander but from supporters in the Greek cities, who, now that he was on his way west again, would do anything to ingratiate themselves with him and compromise their opponents.

A religious belief?

A silver tetradrachm from Egypt shows Alexander the Great wearing the elephant scalp and the ram's horns of Zeus Ammon

Towards an estimate of Alexander

Consider carefully all the following views.

Arrian

'It is my belief that there was in those days no nation, no city, no single individual beyond the reach of Alexander's name; never in all the world was there another like him . . . .'[53]

Tarn

'Alexander was fortunate in his death. His fame could hardly have increased but it might perhaps have diminished.'[54]

Tarn also believes that Alexander — whatever else he may have been — was one of the supreme fertilising forces in history. He lifted the civilised world out of one groove and set it in another. He began a new epoch; nothing could again be as it had been.

Welles

'Alexander was his own greatest accomplishment.'

'He destroyed the Persian Empire and opened up the East to Greek rule and settlement; and neither Greeks nor Orientals were ever the same again.'[55]

Hogarth

'Alexander did more than any single man to break down the proud division of the world into few Greeks and myriad barbarians . . . [and] to make one part of the world known to the other.'[56]

Burn

'He wrote his name across the Near and Middle East for two hundred years and yet his work was ephemeral in that the Empire which he left even in the strong hands of the early Seleucids, was dying on its feet from the first generation.'[57]

Essay topics

1 How did Alexander organise his empire? Why did it split up so soon after his death?

2 How did Alexander attempt to unify the various peoples and cultures within his empire? How successful was he?

Further reading

Primary sources

Arrian. *The Campaigns of Alexander.*
Plutarch. *The Age of Alexander.*

Secondary sources

Burn, A. R. *Alexander the Great and the Hellenistic Empire.*
Bury, J. B. & Meiggs, R. *A History of Greece.*
Ehrenberg, V. 'Alexander and the Greeks'.
Hammond, N. G. L. *A History of Greece to 322 B. C.*
Hogarth, D. G. *Philip and Alexander of Macedon.*
Robinson, C. A. 'Alexander and Parmenio'.
Tarn, W. W. 'Alexander the Great', in Cambridge Ancient History, vol. 6.
Welles, C. B. 'Alexander's Historical Achievement'.
Wilcken, Ulrich. *Alexander the Great.*

Notes to the text

Full details of all works mentioned below appear in the Bibliography, page 345.

Chapter 1: Introduction

1. Parke, *Greek Oracles*.
2. Bowra, *Greek Lyric Poetry*.
3. Ibid.
4. Ibid.

Chapter 2: Greek colonial expansion, 800–500 B.C.

1. Strabo, VI: 2.4 in Finley, *Early Greece*, p. 94.
2. Finley, *Early Greece*, p. 94.
3. Hesiod, pp. 376–8, 695–7.
4. Herodotus, II: 150–5, 178–82.
5. Hammond, p. 113.
6. Ibid.
7. Thucydides, I: 38.

Chapter 3: Greek tyrants of the seventh and sixth centuries B.C.

1. Herodotus, III: 39.
2. Thucydides, I: 13.
3. Herodotus, I: 24.
4. Ibid., III: 39.
5. Ibid., II: 182.
6. Ibid., V: 92.
7. Ibid., III: 122.

Chapter 4: Sparta

1. Plutarch, *Lycurgus*, p. 40.
2. Michel, p. 20.

3. Andrewes, *The Greek Tyrants*, p. 77.
4. Ibid., p. 76.
5. Plutarch, *Lycurgus*, p. 46.
6. *Elegy and Iambus*.
7. Ibid.
8. Plutarch, *Lycurgus*, p. 50.
9. Xenophon, *The Constitution of the Lacedaemonians*, 2.
10. Ibid.
11. Ibid., 3.
12. Ibid., 4.
13. Plutarch, *Lycurgus*, p. 67.
14. Herodotus, VII: 209.
15. Plutarch, *Lycurgus*, p. 65.
16. Ibid., pp. 55–6.
17. Aristophanes, *Lysistrata*, p. 183.
18. Herodotus, V: 75.
19. Ibid., VI: 57.
20. Ibid.
21. Plutarch, *Lycurgus*, p. 46.
22. Ibid., p. 70.
23. Ibid., p. 72.

Chapter 5: The development of Athens in the sixth century

1. Thucydides, I: 3.
2. Plutarch, *Solon*.
3. Andrewes, *The Greek Tyrants*, p. 78.
4. Plutarch, *Solon*, 13.
5. Aristotle, *Athenian Constitution*, 2.
6. Plutarch, *Solon*, 13.
7. Aristotle, *Athenian Constitution*, 5.
8. Ibid.

9. Aristotle, *Athenian Constitution*, 5.
10. Plutarch, *Solon*, 14.
11. Ibid., 16.
12. Aristotle, *Athenian Constitution*, 12.1
13. Ibid., 9.1.
14. Plutarch, *Solon*, 25.
15. Aristotle, *Athenian Constitution*, 13.1–2.
16. Plutarch, *Solon*, 29.
17. Herodotus, I: 59.
18. Ibid.
19. Aristotle, *Athenian Constitution*, 15.1.
20. Ibid., 15.2.
21. Ibid., 16.2.
22. Ehrenberg, *From Solon to Socrates*, p. 79.
23. Aristotle, *Athenian Constitution*, 17.3.
24. Ibid., 18.1.
25. Ibid., 19.1.
26. Thucydides, VI: 59.
27. Plutarch, *Pericles*, 3.
28. Finley, *The Ancient Greeks*, p. 76.
29. Aristotle, *Athenian Constitution*, 20.1
30. Aristophanes, *Lysistrata*, pp. 190–1.
31. Aristotle, *Athenian Constitution*, 20.4.
32. Ibid., 21.2.
33. Ibid., 22.2.
34. Ibid., 22.1.
35. Ibid., 22.3.
36. Herodotus, V: 81.

Chapter 6: The conflicts between the Greeks and the Persians

1. Herodotus, I: 1.
2. Ibid., VII: 152.
3. Ibid., V: 52.
4. Ibid., VIII: 97.
5. Ibid., V: 105.
6. Ibid., 33.
7. Ibid., 93.
8. Ibid., 98.
9. Ibid.
10. Ibid., 105.
11. Ibid., VI: 11.
12. Ibid., 15.

13. Ibid., 46.
14. Burn, *Persia and the Greeks*, p. 263.
15. Ibid., pp. 240, 362.
16. Ibid., p. 253.
17. Plutarch, *Themistocles*, 3.
18. Herodotus, VII: 23.
19. Ibid.
20. Ibid.
21. Ibid., 18–23.
22. Ibid., 7–30.
23. Thucydides, I: 138.
24. Plutarch, *Themistocles*, 3.
25. Ibid., 5.
26. Ibid., 19.
27. Ibid., 3.
28. Plutarch, *Aristides*, 3.
29. Herodotus, VII: 143.
30. *Troezen Inscription*, lines 44–5.
31. Herodotus, VIII: 1.
32. Ibid., VII: 143.
33. Ibid., 140–3.
34. Aeschylus, p. 133.
35. Herodotus, VIII: 74.
36. Aeschylus, p. 133.
37. Thucydides, I: 73.
38. Herodotus, VIII: 123.
39. Ibid., IX: 61.
40. Ibid., VIII: 129.
41. Ibid., IX: 105.
42. Ibid., 121.
43. Pausanias, V: 23, 1–2.
44. Herodotus, IX: 81.
45. Thucydides, I: 132–3.
46. Herodotus, VIII: 2.
47. Ibid.
48. Ibid., 46.

Chapter 7: The rise to power of Athens, 478–445 B.C.

1. Plutarch, *Cimon*, 6.
2. Thucydides, I: 95.
3. Ibid., 75.
4. Plutarch, *Aristides*, 23.

5. Thucydides, I: 96.
6. Plutarch, *Aristides*, 24.
7. Aristotle, *Athenian Constitution*, 23.5.
8. Plutarch, *Cimon*, 5.
9. Ibid.
10. Ibid., 6.
11. Ibid., 15.
12. Ibid., 16.
13. Thucydides, I: 97
14. Plutarch, *Cimon*, 12.
15. Ibid., 13.
16. Thucydides, I: 92.
17. Ibid., 90.
18. Plutarch, *Themistocles*, 20.
19. Ibid., *Pericles*, 7.
20. Thucydides, I: 102.
21. Ibid., 75.
22. Ibid., 99.
23. Ibid.
24. Ibid., 75.
25. *Athenian Tribute Lists*, vol. II, A1.
26. Ibid., D10.
27. Ibid.
28. Ibid., D15.
29. Ibid., D10.
30. Plutarch, *Pericles*, 11.
31. Ibid., 19.
32. Ibid., 23.
33. Ibid., 12.
34. *Athenian Tribute Lists*, vol. II, D17.
35. Thucydides, I: 76.
36. Ibid., II: 63.

Chapter 8: Periclean Athens

1. Thucydides, II: 41.
2. *The Constitution of the Athenians.*
3. Ibid.
4. Thucydides, III: 37.
5. Ibid., 38.
6. Ibid., V: 68.
7. Ibid., VI: 31.
8. Lysias, 21, 24–4.
9. Aristotle, *Athenian Constitution*, 49.4.

10. Ibid., 49.1.
11. Thucydides, II: 46.
12. Euripides, lines 642–51.
13. Xenophon, *Economicus*, 7, 35–7.
14. Lycias, 1, 6–17.

Chapter 9: The Peloponnesian War, 431–404 B.C.

1. Thucydides, V: 26.
2. Ibid., I: 1.
3. Ibid., 22.
4. Ibid.
5. Ibid., 23.
6. Ibid., 55.
7. Plutarch, *Pericles*, 30.
8. Thucydides, I: 67.
9. Ibid., 68.
10. Ibid., 71.
11. Ibid., 79.
12. Ibid., 86.
13. Ibid., II: 7.
14. Plutarch, *Pericles*, 29.
15. Bury, *The Ancient Greek Historians*, p. 101.
16. Thucydides, II: 17.
17. Ibid., 21.
18. Plutarch, *Pericles*, 33.
19. Thucydides, II: 22.
20. Plutarch, *Pericles*, 34.
21. Thucydides, II: 50.
22. Plutarch, *Pericles*, 34.
23. Ibid., 39.
24. Aristophanes, *Knights*, p. 41.
25. Aristotle, *Athenian Constitution*, 28.3.
26. Plutarch, *Nicias*, 8.
27. Thucydides, III: 13.
28. Thucydides, III: 36.
29. Ibid., 68.
30. Ibid., 81.
31. Ibid., IV: 41.
32. Ibid., 27.
33. Ibid., 28.
34. Ibid., 40.
35. Bury & Meiggs, p. 279.

36. Thucydides, IV: 81.
37. Ibid., 84.
38. Ibid., 108.
39. Ibid., 80.
40. Ibid., 117.
41. Ibid., V: 16.
42. Plutarch, *Nicias*, 9.
43. Aristotle, *Athenian Constitution*, 28.3.
44. Plutarch, *Nicias*, 7.
45. Ibid., 4.
46. Thucydides, V: 16.
47. Plutarch, *Nicias*, 6.
48. Ibid., 9.
49. Thucydides, V: 26.
50. Ibid., 84–116.
51. Ibid., 89.
52. Ibid., 93.
53. Plutarch, *Alcibiades*, 16.
54. Ibid., 2
55. Ibid.
56. Ibid., 23.
57. Ibid., 26.
58. Thucydides, VII: 87.
59. Plutarch, *Alcibiades*, 17.
60. Thucydides, VI: 11.
61. Ibid., 24.
62. Ibid., 13.
63. Ibid., 28.
64. Ibid., 31.
65. Plutarch, *Alcibiades*, 21.
66. Ibid.
67. Plutarch, *Nicias*, 16.
68. Thucydides, VI: 92.
69. Ibid., VII: 27.
70. Ibid., 21.
71. Ibid., 43–4.
72. Ibid., 48.
73. Ibid., 70–1.
74. Ibid., 75.
75. Ibid., 86.
76. Ibid., 87.
77. Plutarch, *Alcibiades*, 23.
78. Ibid., 25.
79. Ibid.
80. Thucydides, VIII: 56.
81. Ibid., 96.
82. Ibid., 97.
83. Plutarch, *Lysander*, 10.
84. Ibid., 7.
85. Thucydides, II: 65.
86. Ibid., I: 23.
87. Plutarch, *Lysander*, 17.
88. Ibid., 24.

Chapter 10: Spartan and Theban leadership of Greece

1. Plutarch, *Lysander*, 13.
2. Ibid., 23.
3. Plutarch, *Agesilaus*, 15.
4. Ibid.
5. Ibid.
6. Isocrates, *Panegyric*, 115–22.
7. Fragmentary inscription, in Botsford.
8. Xenophon, *Hellenica*, VII: 5.
9. Thucydides, VI: 92.
10. Plutarch, *Lysander*, 19.
11. Xenophon, *Hellenica*, V: 1.25.

Chapter 11: The rise of Macedon under Philip II, 359–336 B.C.

1. Plutarch, *Demosthenes*, 12.
2. Ibid., 4.
3. Ibid., 6.
4. Ibid., 8.
5. Ibid., 12.
6. Ibid.
7. Ibid., 16.
8. Plutarch, *Alexander*, 59.
9. Stobart.
10. Laistner, p. 263.

Chapter 12: Alexander the Great

1. Welles, 'Review', p. 9.
2. Plutarch, *Alexander*, 5.
3. Tarn, p. 423.
4. Arrian, VI: 26.
5. Plutarch, *Alexander*, 39.
6. Ibid., 43.

7. Arrian, VII: 30.
8. Plutarch, *Alexander*, 59.
9. Hammond, p. 641.
10. Welles, 'Review', p. 9.
11. Arrian, VII: 29.
12. Ibid., 2.
13. Plutarch, *Alexander*, 16.
14. Arrian, I: 15.
15. Ibid., 20.
16. Plutarch, *Alexander*, 20.
17. Ibid., 24.
18. Arrian, III: 1.
19. Ibid., 6.
20. Ibid., 9.
21. Burn, *Alexander the Great*, p. 274.
22. Plutarch, *Alexander*, 26.
23. Arrian, IV: 1.
24. Ibid., VII: 4.
25. Tarn, p. 423.
26. Arrian, IV: 8.
27. Ibid., VII: 30.
28. Plutarch, *Alexander*, 45.
29. Ibid.
30. Ibid., 48.
31. Arrian, III: 26.
32. Robinson, p. 16.

33. Plutarch, *Alexander*, 49.
34. Ibid., 50.
35. Arrian, IV: 9–10.
36. Plutarch, *Alexander*, 54.
37. Ibid.
38. Arrian, V: 25.
39. Ibid., 29.
40. Ibid., VI: 13.
41. Plutarch, *Alexander*, 57.
42. Arrian, VII: 6.
43. Plutarch, *Alexander*, 57.
44. Arrian, VII: 26.
45. Plutarch, *Alexander*, 16.
46. Arrian, I: 17.
47. Ibid.
48. Diodorus, 18.8.
49. Ibid.
50. Arrian, III: 4.
51. Plutarch, *Alexander*, 28.
52. Tarn, p. 419.
53. Arrian, VII: 30.
54. Tarn, pp. 121, 144.
55. Welles, 'Review', p. 9.
56. Hogarth, p. 277.
57. Burn, *Alexander the Great*, p. 274.

Glossary

acropolis	'high town' — a high, rocky outcrop
agema	royal guard in the army of Alexander
agoge	Spartan training and discipline
agora	market place, meeting place
anarchia	situation in which no archons were elected
apoikia	settlement far from home
archegates	divine leader of a colony
archon	Athenian magistrate
aristoi	'best men'
autarkeia	self-sufficiency
axones	wooden tablets inscribed with laws of Solon
basileus	king (archon basileus: king-archon)
bibasis	exercise performed by Spartan girls
boule	council
bouleuterion	council house
caddichus	container used in recording votes
choregoi	rich citizens who provided and financed choruses for festivals
cleruchy	settlement of Athenian citizens overseas
demarchos	leader of a deme
deme	territorial unit, such as a village
demiourgoi	craftsmen
demokratia	government by the people
demos	common people
dikasteria	courts
diolkos	stone-paved way
ecclesia	assembly
eirens	Spartan boys in their nineteenth year
eisphora	special wartime tax
ephebe	military cadet (Athens)
ephor	'overseer' — chief magistrate (Sparta)
epigoni	'inheritors' — Persian soldiers trained as the Macedonians
episkopoi	commissioners sent by Athens to set up 'puppet' governments
eponymous archon	chief magistrate of Athens
eunomia	reign of good order

eupatridae	nobles
georgoi	small farmers
gerontes	members of the gerousia
gerousia	Spartan council of elders
harmosts	military governors
hegemon	leader
hektemoroi	small farmers — 'sixth parters'
hellenodikai	judges
hellenotamiae	treasurers of the Greeks
heliaea	people's court
helot	state-owned serf (Sparta)
herm	stone column, with sculpted head
hetairai	female companions
hippeis	men able to equip themselves for the cavalry — second of Solon's census-classes
historia	research or inquiry
hoplite	heavy-armed Greek infantryman
horoi	stone pillars indicating obligation to creditors
hubris	extreme pride or arrogance
hypaspists	shield-bearers in Alexander's infantry
inferior	Spartan not entitled to citizenship
isonomia	equality of rights among citizens
isopoliteia	agreement by which citizens of one city could be given citizenship in another
klepsydra	water-clock
kleroi	allotments of land
krypteia	secret police in Sparta
liturgies	public duties imposed on wealthy citizens
neodamodes	freed helots (Sparta)
oikistes	founder of a colony
oligarchy	government by the few
ostrakon	piece of broken pottery inscribed with the name of a person to be ostracised
paidonomos	public guardian — supervisor of education (Sparta)
peltasts	mobile, light-armed troops
pentacosiomedimni	'men of 500 bushels' — richest of Solon's census classes
pentacontaetia	fifty-year period
penteconter	fifty-oared ship
perioeci	'dwellers around' — section of society, with particular reference to Sparta
phidition	a public meal or mess (Sparta)
phoros	contribution of money
phratriae	brotherhoods
phylae	tribes
polemarch	military commander

polis	Greek city-state
probouleuma	motions placed before the assembly
proboleutic	preparing and deliberating on bills in council
probuli	board of ten commissioners (Athens)
proskynesis	prostration
prostatai	officers in charge of a port
proxenia	guest friendship between individuals and between city-states
prytaneis	presidents (Athens)
psephismata	decrees passed by the people
pythioi	men appointed to consult the Oracle at Delphi
satrapy	Persian province ruled by a governor (satrap)
seisachtheia	'shaking off of burdens'
Spartiate	another word for Spartan
spondaphores	heralds
strategos	general
symbola	agreement on legal aid to be given to a citizen of one place in the territory of another
syngeneis	kinsmen—applied by Alexander to his Macedonian troops
synoecism	amalgamation of towns into one unit
syssition	a public meal or mess (Sparta)
theoroi	sacred envoys, in contact with an oracle
thetes	free labourers
tholos	building on the Acropolis which housed the prytaneis
timocracy	government by the wealthy
triaconter	thirty-oared boat
trierarch	rich citizen responsible for outfitting and maintaining a ship in the Athenian navy
trittys	regional divisions created by Cleisthenes
tyrannos	ruler with no hereditary right to power
zeugitae	those who produced 200 bushels a year, or the equivalent—third of Solon's census classes

Bibliography

Primary sources

Aeschylus. *The Persians*. Penguin Classics, Harmondsworth, 1986.

Aristophanes. *Ecclesiazusae*. Penguin Classics, Harmondsworth, 1965.

_____ . *The Knights*. Penguin Classics, Harmondsworth, 1984.

_____ . *Lysistrata*. Penguin Classics, Harmondsworth, 1973.

_____ . *The Wasps*. Penguin Classics, Harmondsworth, 1965.

Aristotle. *The Athenian Constitution*, trans. P. J. Rhodes. Penguin Classics, Harmondsworth, 1984.

_____ . *The Politics*, trans. T. A. Sinclair. Penguin Classics, Harmondsworth, 1985.

Arrian. *The Campaigns of Alexander*. Penguin Classics, Harmondsworth, 1971.

Athenian Tribute Lists, vol. 2, ed. B. D. Merritt, H. T. Wade-Gery & M. F. McGregor. American School of Classical Studies at Athens, Princeton, NJ, 1939–53.

Diodorus Siculus. *Universal History*. Loeb Classical Library. Heinemann, London, 1933–67.

Euripides. *Women of Troy*. Penguin Classics, Harmondsworth, 1979.

Greek Historical Inscriptions, ed. R. Meiggs & N. Lewis. Oxford University Press, Oxford, 1969.

Greek Political Oratory (Demosthenes, Isocrates). Penguin, Harmondsworth, 1986.

Herodotus. *The Histories*, trans. A. de Sélincourt. Penguin, Harmondsworth, 1972.

Hesiod. *Works and Days*, trans. H. G. Evelyn-White. Loeb Classical Library. Harvard University Press, Cambridge, Mass., 1936. (Also Penguin Classics, 1985.)

Isocrates. *Panegyric*, vol. 1, trans. G. Norlin. Loeb Classical Library. Harvard University Press, Cambridge, Mass., 1928.

Lysias. Trans. N. R. E. Fisher, in *Classical Studies for Schools*, Study Materials no. 4, Classics Department, Otago University, NZ, 1980.

The Old Oligarch (Pseudo-Xenophon). *The Constitution of the Athenians*, trans. N. Lewis in *The Fifth Century B.C.* Toronto University Press, 1971.

Pausanias. *A Description of Greece*, trans. W. H. S. Jones & H. A. Ormerod. Loeb Classical Library. Heinemann, London, 1965–69.

The Public Orations of Demosthenes, trans. A. W. Pickard. Cambridge University Press, 1912.

Plutarch. *The Age of Alexander (Agesilaus, Alexander, Demosthenes, Pelopidas)*, trans. Ian Scott-Kilvert. Penguin, Harmondsworth, 1973.

——— . The *Lives of the Noble Greeks (Lycurgus)*, ed. Edmund Fuller. 5th edn. Laurel Classics. Dell, NY, 1966.

——— . *The Rise and Fall of Athens (Alcibiades, Aristides, Cimon, Lysander, Nicias, Pericles, Solon, Themistocles)*. Penguin Classics, Harmondsworth, 1973.

Strabo. *Geography*, text and trans. in H. G. Jones, *The Geography of Strabo*. Loeb Classical Library. Harvard University Press, Cambridge, Mass., 1917–33.

Thucydides. *History of the Peloponnesian War*, trans. Rex Warner. Penguin Classics, Harmondsworth, 1972.

Tyrtaeus. *Elegy and Iambus*, vol. 1, ed. J. M. Edmunds. Loeb Classical Library. Harvard University Press, 1931.

The Troezen Inscription, trans. M. A. Jameson, from 'Waiting for the Barbarian' in *Greece and Rome*, second series, 8. Clarendon Press, Oxford, 1961.

Xenophon. *The Constitution of the Lacedaemonians*, trans. H. G. Dakyns, in W. McDermott & W. Caldwell, *Readings in the History of the Ancient World*, 2nd edn. Holt, Rinehart & Winston, NY, 1970.

——— . *Economicus*, interpretation by Leo Strauss. Cornell University Press, Ithaca, 1970.

——— . *Hellenica (A History of My Times)*, trans. Rex Warner. Penguin Classics, Harmondsworth, 1966.

Secondary sources

Adcock, F. E. *Thucydides and His History*. Cambridge University Press, Cambridge, 1963.

Andrewes, Antony. *Greek Society*. Penguin, Harmondsworth, 1986.

——— . *The Greek Tyrants*. Hutchinson University Library, London, 1974.

The Athenian Citizen. American School of Classical Studies at Athens, Princeton, NJ, 1960.

Badian, E. 'Alexander the Great and the Unity of Mankind'. *Historia*, 7.

Barrow, R. *Athenian Democracy*. Macmillan Education, London, 1959.

Barrow, Robin. *Greek and Roman Education*. Macmillan Education, London, 1976.

_____ . *Sparta*. Allen & Unwin, London, 1975.

Boardman, John. *The Greeks Overseas*. Thames & Hudson, London, 1980.

Botsford, G. W. *A Source Book of Ancient History*. Macmillan, London, 1934.

Bowra, C. M. *Greek Lyric Poetry from Alcman to Simonides*. 2nd edn. Clarendon Press, Oxford, 1961.

_____ . *Periclean Athens*. Weidenfeld & Nicolson, London, 1971.

Burn, A. R. *Alexander the Great and the Hellenistic Empire*. English Universities Press, London, 1959.

_____ . *The Lyric Age of Greece*. Arnold/St Martin's Press, NY, 1960.

_____ . *Pericles and Athens*. English Universities Press, London, 1956.

_____ . *Persia and the Greeks — the Defence of the West, 546–478 B.C.* Edward Arnold, London, 1962.

Bury, J. B. *The Ancient Greek Historians*. Dover Publications, NY, 1958.

Bury, J. B. & Meiggs, R. *A History of Greece*. 4th edn. Macmillan Press, London, 1975.

Cambridge Ancient History, vols 5 & 6. Cambridge University Press, 1964.

De Ste Croix, G. E. M. *The Origins of the Peloponnesian War*. Duckworth, London, 1972.

Ehrenberg, V. 'Alexander and the Greeks', in *Ancient Society and Institutions*, Blackwell, Oxford, 1978.

_____ . *From Solon to Socrates*. Methuen, London, 1968.

Eliot, C. W. J. *Coastal Demes of Attica*. Toronto University Press, 1962.

Ellis, J. R. & Milns, R. D. *The Spectre of Philip*. Sydney University Press, 1983.

Finley, M. I. *The Ancient Greeks*. Penguin, Harmondsworth, 1963.

_____ . *Early Greece — the Bronze and Archaic Ages*. Chatto & Windus, London, 1977.

Forrest, W. G. *The Emergence of Greek Democracy*. Weidenfeld & Nicolson, London, 1972.

French, A. *The Athenian Half-century*. Sydney University Press, 1984.

Graham, A. J. *Colony and Mother City in Ancient Greece*. Barnes & Noble, NY, 1971.

Hamilton, J. R. *Alexander the Great*. Hutchinson University Library, London, 1973.

Hammond, N. G. L. *A History of Greece to 322 B.C.* Clarendon Press, Oxford, 1967.

Hignett, C. *A History of the Athenian Constitution*. Oxford University Press, Oxford, 1952.

Hill, G. F., Meiggs, R. & Andrewes, A. *Sources for Greek History from the Persian to the Peloponnesian War*. Clarendon Press, Oxford, 1966.

Hogarth, D. G. *Philip and Alexander of Macedon*. Murray, London, 1897.

Horsley, G. H. R. *Some Aspects of the Athenian Empire*. History Teachers' Association of NSW, Rozelle, n.d.

Jones, A. H. M. *Athenian Democracy*. Blackwell, Oxford, 1960.

Kagan, D. *The Archidamian War*. Cornell University Press, Ithaca, 1974.

_____ . *The Outbreak of the Peloponnesian War*. Cornell University Press, Ithaca, 1969.

_____ . *Problems in Ancient History*, vol. 1. Macmillan, London, 1966.

Kitto, H. D. F. *The Greeks*. Penguin, Harmondsworth, 1967.

Laistner, M. W. L. *A History of the Greek World, 479–323 B.C.* 3rd edn. Methuen, London, 1962.

Lewis, N. *The Fifth Century B.C.* Toronto University Press, 1971.

McDermott, W. & Caldwell, W. *Readings in the History of the Ancient World*. 2nd edn. Holt, Rinehart & Winston, NY, 1970.

Meiggs, R. *The Athenian Empire*. Oxford University Press, Oxford, 1972.

Michel, H. *Sparta*. Cambridge University Press, Cambridge, 1964.

Muir's Atlas of Ancient and Classical History. 6th edn. George Philip & Son, London, 1973.

Parke, H. W. *Greek Oracles*. Hutchinson, London, 1967.

Robinson, C. A. 'Alexander and Parmenio', in *The Impact of Alexander the Great*, ed. Eugene N. Borza. European Problems Studies. Dryden Press, NY, 1974.

Stobart, J. C. *The Glory That Was Greece*. Sidgwick & Jackson, London, 1984.

Tarn, W. W. 'Alexander the Great', in *Cambridge Ancient History*, vol. 6. Cambridge University Press, Cambridge, 1964.

Tod, M. N. *A Selection of Greek Historical Inscriptions*. Clarendon Press, Oxford, 1933.

Trevor, A. A. *The Ancient Near East and Greece*, vol. 1 of *History of Ancient Civilization*. Harcourt, Brace & World, San Diego, 1936.

Ure, P. N. *The Origin of Tyranny*. Cambridge University Press/Macmillan, 1922.

Welles, C. B. 'Alexander's Historical Achievement', *Greece and Rome*, 12.2, 1965.

_____ . 'Review of F. Schachermeyer's *Alexander der Grosse Ingenium und Macht*', in *The Impact of Alexander the Great*, ed. Eugene N. Borza. European Problems Studies, Dryden Press, NY, 1974.

Wilcken, Ulrich. *Alexander the Great*. Chatto & Windus, London, 1932.

Acknowledgements

Passages quoted in the text are from the following publications:
Aeschylus, *The Persians*, Penguin Classics, Harmondsworth, 1986; Andrewes, Antony, *The Greek Tyrants*, Hutchinson University Library, London, 1974; Aristophanes, *Knights*, Penguin Classics, Harmondsworth, 1984; Aristophanes, *Lysistrata*, Penguin Classics, Harmondsworth, 1973; Aristotle, *The Athenian Constitution*, trans P J Rhodes, Penguin Classics, Harmondsworth, 1984; Arrian, *The Campaigns of Alexander*, Penguin Classics, Harmondsworth, 1971; *Athenian Tribute Lists*, Vol II, ed B D Merritt, H T Wade-Gery and M F McGregor, American School of Classical Studies at Athens, Princeton, New Jersey, 1939–53; Botsford, G W, *A Source Book of Ancient History*, Macmillan, London, 1934; Burn, A R, *Alexander the Great and the Hellenistic Empire*, English Universities Press, London, 1959; Burn, A R, *Persia and the Greeks*, Edward Arnold, London, 1962; Bury, J B, *The Ancient Greek Historians*, Dover Publications, New York, 1958; Bury, J B and Meiggs, R, *A History of Greece*, 4th edition, Macmillan Press, London, 1975; Bowra, C M (ed), *Greek Lyric Poetry from Alcman to Simonides*, 2nd edition, Clarendon Press, Oxford, 1961; Diodorus Siculus, *Universal History*, Loeb Classical Library, Heinemann, London, 1933–67; Ehrenberg, V, *From Solon to Socrates*, Methuen, London, 1968; Euripides, *Women of Troy*, Penguin Classics, Harmondsworth, 1979; Finley, M I, *The Ancient Greeks*, Penguin, Harmondsworth, 1963; Finley, M I, *Early Greece — The Bronze and Archaic Ages*, Chatto and Windus, London, 1977; Hammond, N G L, *A History of Greece to 322 B C*, Clarendon Press, Oxford, 1967; Herodotus, The Histories, trans A de Sélincourt, Penguin, Harmondsworth, 1972; Hesiod, *Works and Days*, trans H G Evelyn-White, Loeb Classical Library, Harvard University Press, Cambridge, Mass, 1936; Hogarth, D G, *Philip and Alexander of Macedon*, Murray, London, 1897; Isocrates, *Panegyric*, Vol I, trans G Norlin, Loeb Classical Library, Harvard University Press, Cambridge, Mass, 1928; Laistner, M W L, *A History of the Greek World 479–323 BC*, 3rd edition, Methuen, London, 1962; Lysias, trans N R E Fisher, in *Classical Studies for Schools*, Study Materials No 4, Classics

Department, Otago University, New Zealand, 1980; Michel, H, *Sparta*, Cambridge University Press, Cambridge, 1964; The Old Oligarch, *The Constitution of the Athenians*, trans N Lewis in *The Fifth Century BC*, Toronto University Press, 1971; Parke, H W, *Greek Oracles*, Hutchinson, London, 1967; Pausanias, *A Description of Greece*, trans W H S Jones and H A Ormerod, Loeb Classical Library, Heinemann, London, 1965–69; Plutarch, *The Age of Alexander*, trans Ian Scott-Kilvert, Penguin, Harmondsworth, 1973; Plutarch, *The Lives of the Noble Greeks (Lycurgus)*, ed Edmund Fuller, 5th edition, Laurel Classics, Dell, New York, 1966; Plutarch, *The Rise and Fall of Athens*, Penguin Classics, Harmondsworth, 1973; Robinson, C A, 'Alexander and Parmenio' in *The Impact of Alexander the Great*, ed Eugene N Borza, European Problems Studies, Dryden Press, New York, 1974; Stobart, J C, *The Glory that was Greece*, Sidgwick & Jackson, London, 1984; Tarn, W W, 'Alexander the Great', in *Cambridge Ancient History*, Vol 6, Cambridge University Press, Cambridge, 1964; Thucydides, *History of the Peloponnesian War*, trans Rex Warner, Penguin Classics, Harmondsworth, 1972; Trevor, A A, *The Ancient Near East and Greece*, Vol I of *History of Ancient Civilisation*, Harcourt, Brace & World, San Diego, 1936; *The Troezen Inscription*, trans M A Jameson from 'Waiting for the Barbarian' in *Greece and Rome*, second series, 8, Clarendon Press, Oxford, 1961; Tyrtaeus, *Elegy and Iambus*, Vol I, ed J M Edmunds, Loeb Classical Library, Harvard University Press, 1931; Welles, 'Review of F Schachermeyer's *Alexander der Grosse Ingenlum und Macht*, in *The Impact of Alexander the Great*, ed Eugene N Borza, European Problems Studies, Dryden Press, New York, 1974; Xenophon, *The Constitution of the Lacedaemonians*, trans H G Dakyns, in W McDermott and W Caldwell, *Readings in the History of the Ancient World*, 2nd edition, Holt, Rinehart & Winston, New York, 1970; Xenophon, *Economicus*, interpretation by Leo Strauss, Cornell University Press, Ithaca, 1970; Xenophon, *Hellenica (A History of My Times)*, trans Rex Warner, Penguin Classics, Harmondsworth, 1966.

The publisher's thanks are due to the following for permission to reproduce copyright photographs on the following pages:
Acropolis Museum: 134, 143; *Antikenmuseum Berlin, Staatliche Museen Preussischer Kulturbesitz:* 68; *Bibliothèque Nationale:* xix, 32 (vase), 304; *The British Museum:* 17 (halteres), 18 (runners), 47 (pottery), 60, 188, 200 (Lapith, horse), 233, 261, 314; *Istanbul Archaeological Museum:* 303; *Kunsthistorisches Museum, Vienna:* Front cover; *The Metropolitan Museum of Art, New York:* 19, 35 (krater), 110, 214 (stele); *Ministry of Culture, Athens:* 14, 15 (charioteer), 27 (plaque), 35 (amphora); *Musée du Louvre:* 65, 68 (hoplites), 88, 200 (frieze), 232; *Museo Nazionale di Ravenna:* 129

(herm); *Museum of Fine Arts, Boston:* 38 (oinochoe), 46; *National Museum, Florence:* 27 (triaconter); *Olympia Archaeological Museum:* 127 (helmet); *Staatliche Antikensammlungen und Glyptothek, Munich:* 18 (wrestlers), 35 (oinochoe); *Vatican Museum:* 85, 93 (amphora), 296; *Wadsworth Atheneum:* 58

Every effort has been made to trace and acknowledge copyright, but in some instances this has not been possible.

Index

Note: Page numbers of illustrations are given in italics. Maps and diagrams are indicated by (m) or (d) respectively following the page number.